An Archaeological Study of the Red House, Port of Spain, Trinidad and Tobago

An Archaeological Study of the

RED HOUSE

Port of Spain, Trinidad and Tobago

EDITED BY **BASIL A. REID**

The University of the West Indies Press
Jamaica • Barbados • Trinidad and Tobago

The University of the West Indies Press
7A Gibraltar Hall Road, Mona
Kingston 7, Jamaica
www.uwipress.com

ISBN: 978-976-640-672-1 (print)
978-976-640-673-8 (Kindle)
978-976-640-674-5 (ePub)

Cover photograph: The Red House. Courtesy of the Office of the Parliament
of the Republic of Trinidad and Tobago.
Cover and book design by Robert Harris
Set in Minion Pro 10.5/14.2 x 27

The University of the West Indies Press has no responsibility for the persistence or
accuracy of URLs for external or third-party Internet websites referred to in this
publication and does not guarantee that any content on such websites is, or will remain,
accurate or appropriate.

Printed in the United States of America.

Contents

Acknowledgements

I WISH TO THANK ALL OF THE AUTHORS of the various chapters for their seminal contributions. It was indeed a pleasure working with them. Their chapters, many of which are based on groundbreaking research, will significantly enhance our understanding of the archaeology of Trinidad and Tobago and the wider Caribbean.

This edited volume was a direct result of the first phase of the Red House Restoration Archaeological Project which spanned from 1 July 2013 to 31 January 2015. I am grateful to all those who contributed to this project in myriad ways. I am especially thankful to the Office of the Parliament of the Republic of Trinidad and Tobago for both administratively spearheading and funding the project. In this regard, I single out for special commendation the former Speaker of the House, the Honourable Mark Wade; the Clerk of the Office of the Parliament, Jacqui Sampson-Meiguel; and the project administrator of the Red House Restoration Committee, Neil Jaggassar. I also wish to thank the following former and current members of staff of the Office of the Parliament for assisting with the project: Sarah Khan, Kenan Gangadeen, Karim Mohammed, Avinash Ragoonanan and Stephen Williams.

I place on record my gratitude to the following for their scholarly and professional input to the Red House Restoration Archaeological Project: Lovell Francis, Mike Rutherford, Brent Wilson, Michael Sutherland, John Krigbaum, George D. Kamenov, Georgia L. Fox, Corinne L. Hofman, Bert Neyt, Dolores Piperno, Mary Malainey, Timothy Figol, D. Andrew Merriwether, Michel Shamoon-Pour, Lars Fehren-Schmitz, John J. Schultz, Patrisha L. Meyers, Neal H. Lopinot, Gifford J. Waters, R. Grant Gilmore III, Amit Seeram, Sarah Hosein, Michaela Pierre, Surendra Arjoon and Cecil Hodge. It should be noted that most of these persons contributed chapters to the volume.

I salute the following field assistants for their dedication and hard work, without which the project would not have been possible: Camelia Ali, Abrahim Anoop, Samuel Anoop, Shondell Anthony, Nigel Baptiste, Sarah Bharath, Sacha Blake, Naveen Boccara, Isaac Browne, Eon Brumigin, Brent Cameron, Mark DeSilva, Marlon Maxwell, Nathaniel Dinzey, Natoya Eastman, Kendell Etienne, Lanya Fanovich, Samuel Foster, Christopher George, Mark Grant, Keith Guevara, Karen Harper, Leston Hernandez, Damien Ibrahim, Jaysi Johnson, Shonette

Joseph, Caleb Lewis, Mikhail Lovell, Maria Mahase, Adrian Maraj, Aaron
Maxwell, Maurice Metiver, Nafisah Mohammed, Aaron Mohammed, Ashley
Noel, Kelvin O'Neil, Keron Ramkissoon, Nigel Samlalsingh, Nyron Samlalsingh,
Ronshetta Traweil and Andre Wells. I also thank the following finds processors
for their seminal contributions: Kevin Ali, Jason Antoine, Jeromy Antoine,
Kristianne Bhagan, Dion Carrington, Emmanuel Dabreo, Louise Dover, Shad
Gobinsingh, Marcus Hamilton, Jennifer Jemmott, Kerry-Ann Khell, Stephanie
Logie, Andrew Maurice, Jeavon O'Neil, Stephon Richardson, Michael Rodriguez,
Lancelot Samuel, Krystal Singh, Shawntelle-Ann Syriac-Lynch and Wayne
Talbot. The following archaeological illustrators should also be commended
for their valuable contributions: Karina Ramnath, Joel Reyes, Dominic Koo,
Kevin Ali and Verne DuBois.

I hereby thank the following employees of Amcoweld Limited, who ably
supported the work of the field assistants: Chris Agard, Junior Alfred, Zaheer
Ali, Clayroy "Biggie" Anthony, Glenturner Bridgelal, Eon Browne, Damion
Bullard, Steve Cooper, Shareef Geetam, Kerron Jackson, Kumar Maharaj, Ashook
Roopnarine and Davindra Sanichara. The field assistants were supervised by
Sade Grant and Samuel Reyes while both the finds processors and archaeological
illustrators were supervised by Zara Ali and Makini Emmanuel. I thank these
site managers for their stellar contributions. I am grateful to Atiba DeSouza and
Maxwell Thomas of UDeCOTT as well as the management team of Amcoweld
Limited for providing logistical support during the Red House Restoration
Archaeological Project. I also wish to thank Binta Trotter, the structural engineer assigned to the project, for providing technical advice to the archaeological
crew during excavations.

I gratefully acknowledge the assistance of Christopher Thomas of campus IT
services at the University of the West Indies, St Augustine. Thomas converted
multiple image files, all of which are used in this volume. I am grateful to both
Judith Marchan and Marlon Green of the National Trust of Trinidad and Tobago
for furnishing me with information on historical and archaeological sites that
are currently gazetted and protected under the National Trust Act of Trinidad
and Tobago. John Krigbaum – one of the volume's contributors – assisted with
the editorial tweaking of the glossary of terms. I hereby thank Krigbaum for his
generous contribution. I also am grateful to Renee Nelson, my former research
assistant at the University of the West Indies, St Augustine, for typing various
documents, portions of which were used in this publication. Also, thanks to
Nelson for collating the notes on contributors. Thanks to Arti Ramsaroop, my
current teaching assistant at the University of the West Indies, St Augustine,
for collating the abstracts for the volume. Simone Mejias, in the Department of
History of the University of the West Indies, St Augustine, printed a hard copy
of the manuscript. This exercise was useful as it enabled us to identify images

with questionable resolution quality before a soft copy of the finalized manuscript was sent to the University of the West Indies Press. I hereby thank Mejias for her kind assistance. I appreciate the generous assistance given by Lorraine Nero and Maude-Marie Sisnette of the West Indiana and Special Collections Division of the Alma Jordan Library of the University of the West Indies, St Augustine, who facilitated the scanning of several maps used in chapters 8 and 9. Bridget Brereton, professor emerita in the Department of History at the University of the West Indies, St Augustine, referred me to several primary and secondary historical sources on social life in nineteenth-century Port of Spain. I wish to thank Brereton for her support. I am grateful to Neal H. Lopinot of the Center of Archaeological Research of Missouri State University for editorially reviewing and improving chapter 9 of the volume. Thanks to the University of the West Indies at St Augustine for facilitating my involvement in the project by granting me leave of absence for almost eighteen months. Joseph Powell, general manager of the University of the West Indies Press, is hereby thanked for actively encouraging this edited volume from beginning to end. Shivaun Hearne of the University of the West Indies Press provided well-needed guidance in improving the resolution quality of several images used in the publication. I thank her for her kind assistance in this matter. Last but certainly not least, I am very grateful to my beloved wife, Joan, and our son, Gavin, for their patience, encouragement and unswerving moral support during the project and during the editing and collating of this book.

BASIL A. REID

INTRODUCTION

An Archaeological Study of the Red House

BASIL A. REID

THIS VOLUME, *AN ARCHAEOLOGICAL STUDY OF THE RED HOUSE, PORT OF SPAIN, TRINIDAD AND TOBAGO,* is based on a collection of eleven research papers that developed out of the Red House Restoration Archaeological Project. In March–April 2013, archaeological discoveries were made in the basement of the Red House during inspection works by Amcoweld (a Trinidadian firm contracted by the Urban Development Corporation of Trinidad and Tobago [UDeCOTT]).[1] Shortly thereafter, the Office of the Parliament of the Republic of Trinidad and Tobago hired Basil A. Reid and his archaeological crew to undertake a detailed study of the site from 1 July 2013 to 31 January 2015. In order to extract as much information as possible from the site, a comprehensive research agenda was devised for the project, involving both local and international scholars.

Radiocarbon dating was the primary dating method used to establish time-lines for the pre-colonial Red House site. Over one hundred samples of human, non-human mammalian, mollusc and charcoal materials, together with one pottery sherd containing carbon, were sent overseas for carbon 14 dating. Radiocarbon dates range from 125 to 1395 CE, suggesting that the pre-colonial Red House site was a relatively large native settlement that was continuously inhabited for over twelve hundred years (Reid 2015, 123).

Based on the pre-colonial pottery found at the site, it appears that Red House pre-colonial natives were Saladoid and post-Saladoid peoples. Although preceding Archaic Age groups (namely the Ortorioid and the Casimiroid) practised some level of plant manipulation, the Saladoid were the first fully horticultural native people to have colonized the Caribbean.[2] Upon entering the Caribbean around 500 BCE,[3] the Saladoid quickly settled all of the islands of the region from Trinidad and Tobago in the south to as far as Puerto Rico in the north (Keegan 1992; Reid 2009; Wilson 2007). The timeline of Saladoid colonization in Trinidad should have ended in 600 CE and in the northern Lesser Antilles around 800/900 CE (Hofman and Reid 2014). However, the presence of Saladoid-type pottery well into the fourteenth century – a period generally considered to be post-Saladoid – suggests that there was a local, resident native population at the Red House site for over twelve hundred years. The original Saladoid settlers simply reproduced themselves, establishing a relatively large village community in this area until the late fourteenth century.

Historical research revealed that the native village at the Red House site was located west of the original St Ann's River and might have fronted the Gulf of Paria during pre-colonial times (chapter 8, this volume). In 1787, during the Spanish colonial period, the course of the original St Ann's River was diverted by Governor Don José Maria Chacón so that it ran to the east of the city, along the foot of the Laventille Hills. In pre-colonial times, the shoreline of the Gulf of Paria was much closer to the site than it is today. Land reclamation in Port of Spain during the Spanish and British colonial periods – which occurred long after the native village at the Red House site had been abandoned – has since created some distance between this native village site and the Gulf of Paria (chapter 8, this volume).

Featured in this book are a miscellany of significant findings relating to the biological profiles, DNA, diet and subsistence, mobility and ceramic technology of the Red House pre-colonial natives. Additionally, the volume provides a discourse on pre-colonial and colonial-period artefacts and biofacts; the role of the site's pre-colonial inhabitants as dynamic, self-reflexive history-makers together with the colonial archaeology and history of the Red House from earliest times to 1907. Also included are two papers on heritage management. The first paper explores archaeological and values-based heritage management while the second focuses on the creation of a GIS archaeological information system (AIS) that was developed specifically for the project.

THE HISTORY AND SIGNIFICANCE OF THE RED HOUSE

Built in 1907, the Red House has been the seat of Trinidad and Tobago's parliament for over one hundred years (figure I.1). This structure is the second to be built on the site; the foundation stone for the first was laid by then-governor of Trinidad Sir Henry McLeod on 15 February 1844. In 1897, as Trinidad was preparing to celebrate the Diamond Jubilee of Queen Victoria, the buildings were given a coat of red paint, and the public promptly referred to them thereafter as the Red House. This direct ancestor of the present Red House was destroyed by fire during the water riots on 23 March 1903, which saw sixteen people killed and more than forty people injured. Construction of the current Red House commenced the following year on the same site and was opened to the public on 4 February 1907 by the governor, Sir H.M. Jackson. The architectural design of the Red House is Beaux-Arts style.

The Red House remains most of the enduring and imposing historic build-

Figure I.1.
The Red House
in Port of Spain,
Trinidad and
Tobago. Courtesy
of the Office of the
Parliament of the
Republic of Trinidad
and Tobago.

ings in Port of Spain, Trinidad and Tobago, and recent events have helped to further solidify it in the historical consciousness of the citizenry of Trinidad and Tobago. In July 1990, for example, the Red House was the site of the Jamaat al Muslimeen coup attempt, during which the prime minister and other members of the government were held hostage for six days and twenty-four people were killed. Prior to 2000/2001, the Red House was utilized by members of public for civil marriage ceremonies as well as for the registration of births, deaths and land titles. Generations of schoolchildren in Trinidad and Tobago grew up hearing about the importance of the Red House from their parents, teachers and other caregivers. Due to the recent discovery of several Amerindian human burials, the First Peoples of the twin island republic revere the Red House as a sacred site.

The Red House is therefore iconic and is an integral part of the city's historical landscape. Located in the heart of Port of Spain (figures I.2 and I.3) in the county of St George (UTM coordinates: E-662617.70/ N-1177841.92 [Zone 20P; Naparima 1972]), the second and current Red House is bounded by Abercromby Street to the east, Hart Street to the south, Knox Street to the north and St Vincent Street to the west (see figures I.4 and I.5). The responsibility UDeCOTT has been given in restoring the Red House includes retrofitting the interiors for adaptive reuse by Trinidad and Tobago's parliament.

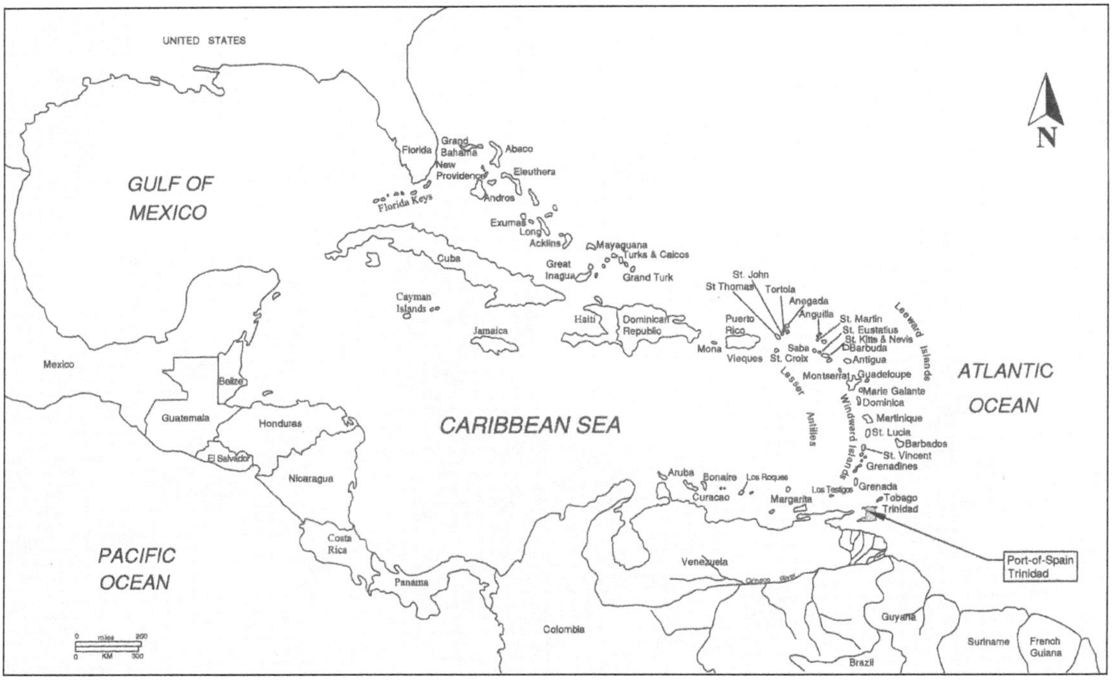

Figure I.2.
Map of the
Caribbean and
circum-Carib-
bean, showing the
location of Port of
Spain, Trinidad and
Tobago. Drawn by
Cecil Hodge.

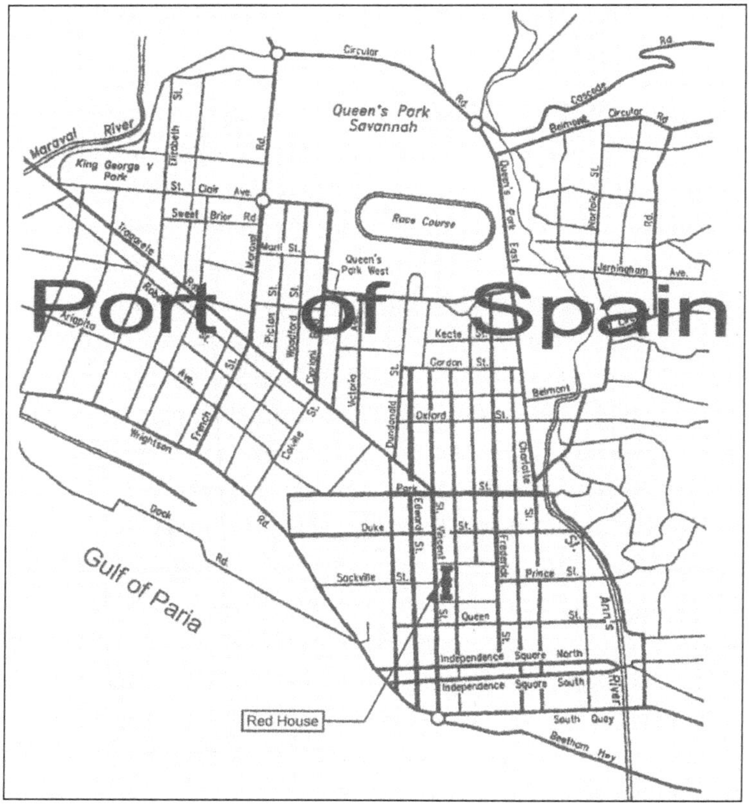

Figure I.3.
Map of Port of
Spain, Trinidad and
Tobago, showing the
location of the Red
House. Drawn by
Cecil Hodge.

Figure I.4.
Map of commercial
Port of Spain sur-
rounding the Red
House. Map created
by Google Earth Pro,
courtesy of Patrisha
Meyers.

RESEARCH METHODOLOGY

Site Disturbance

Once excavation began in earnest, the archaeology crew quickly realized that the Red House site was heavily disturbed. In several archaeological strata, pre-colonial finds (mostly pottery), biofacts and human biological remains were found commingled with European material culture; this commingling was directly related to repeated cycles of construction and backfilling since the construction of the original Red House buildings in 1843–44. In archaeological research, site disturbance does not automatically relegate a site to an insignificant status. Other important archaeological sites, also disturbed, have also been found throughout the Caribbean, for example, Lavoutte in north St Lucia near St Castries (Hoogland and Hofman 2013), Grand Bay in Carriacou (Fitzpatrick et al. 2009) and St John in southwestern Trinidad (Reid 2014, 325). Sites that are partially disturbed or overlaid with debris from modern activities can present useful research opportunities if they contain organic and inorganic remains that can be subjected to a battery of scientific tests. Interestingly enough, although the Red House site was heavily disturbed, we were able to identify a pre-colonial layer (or cultural horizon) throughout much of the site at a depth ranging from 1.2 metres to 1.5 metres from topsoil. This layer can be described as either dark brown or dark gray sandy loam, consisting mainly of molluscs and pre-colonial pottery, occasioned by the presence of human burials, non-human faunal material, stone artefacts and charcoal.

Excavation

During March/April 2013, Amcoweld workers, based on UDeCOTT's instructions, dug inspection units where the existing depths of the Red House basement foundation were unknown, and in areas considered critical for structural analysis. As a consequence, the first activity undertaken by the archaeology crew as of 1 July 2013 was the continued excavation of these inspection units to sterile levels in order to recover both artefacts and biological remains. Sterile levels for the following units: CEP #9, CEP #5, CEP #4, BM #5, CEP #3, BM #4, CEP #8, CEP #13, CEP #1, CEP #2, CEP# 10 and CEP #17 and so on ranged from a low of 1.09 metres to a high of 2.8 metres from concrete basement (table I.1). The Red House's basement, with an area of 4,403.25 square metres, was subdivided by the archaeology crew into three sections: A, B and C (see figure I.5). Areas were subdivided into smaller areas in order to make the process of excavation and data recording much more manageable. Crawl spaces and rooms were subdivided sometimes equally, numerically and according to specific locations – for example, southeast crawl space, subdivision 1; section B, southeast rotunda, Air Handler Plant Room, subdivision 3; section B, room G26, northwest rotunda, subdivision 2.

Initially, rooms and crawl spaces were excavated to sterile levels, but due to concerns of the negative impacts such depths could have on the structural integrity of the Red House building, field assistants were eventually advised by Binta Trotter, the structural engineer assigned to the project, to excavate to a maximum of depth of 1.5 metres and even less. Seven units (measuring 2 metres × 2 metres) were excavated on the periphery of the Red House (figure I.5). It was originally assumed that there might have been considerably less site disturbance on the periphery. The excavation of BAR#1 to BAR#7 was therefore designed to compare the level of site disturbance in these external units with archaeological deposits in the Red House basement. A similar commingling of pre-colonial and colonial artefacts and biofacts characterized BAR#1 to BAR#7, signalling that site disturbance at the Red House extended beyond the building and was in fact characteristic of the entire site (Reid 2015, 20).

Excavation, whether done solely by members of the archaeology crew or by Amcoweld workers, was based on a layered approach. Each inspection unit or room was excavated according to natural levels; with each natural level differ-

Table I.1. Average Sterile Depths of Areas/Inspection Units in the Red House

Section	Areas/ Inspection Units	Sterile Depth from Concrete (m)	Sterile Depth from Topsoil (m)	Sterile Depth from Floor Boards (m)
Section A				
North Parliament Chamber	1. CEP #4	1.88	1.64	–
	2. CEP #5	1.09	0.99	1.65
	3. BM #5	2.54	2.20	–
North Link	4. CEP #3	2.26		–
	5. CEP #7	–	1.97	2.14
	6. CEP #14	2.18	1.75	–
	7. CEP #15	3.05	2.80	–
	8. CEP #18	1.74	1.56	–
	9. M #4	1.75	1.42	–
Section B				
Rotunda	10. CEP #1	2.80	2.18	–
	11. CEP #2	3.25		–
	12. CEP #8	3.08		–
	13. CEP #13	2.89	2.00	–
	14. CEP #16	2.13	1.96	–
Section C				
South Link	15. BM #1	2.54	1.73	–
South Parliament Chamber	16. CEP #10	2.90	2.75	–
	17. CEP #17	–	1.75	–
Periphery				
Periphery	18. CEP #9	–	1.26	–

entiated by soil colour, texture and components. Natural soil levels are single events or actions that leave discrete, detectable traces in the archaeological sequence of stratigraphy. They can represent deposits such as the backfill of a builder's trench (also called "construction trench"). On-site data recording included a mix of plans, sketches, stratigraphic profiles, and field notes, as well as photographs (taken with scales and directional arrows). Standing sieves (measuring 6 mm) were the primary data recovery tools used on site.

Finds Processing and Post-Excavation Analyses

During sieving, finds of similar types (molluscs, lithics, glass etc.) were placed in labelled recloseable plastic bags of varying sizes (gallon, quart and snack). Either at the completion of excavation of an archaeological stratum or at the end of the workday, these bags were taken to the Finds Processing Unit. Paper labels with contextual information were also placed inside the bags, with two

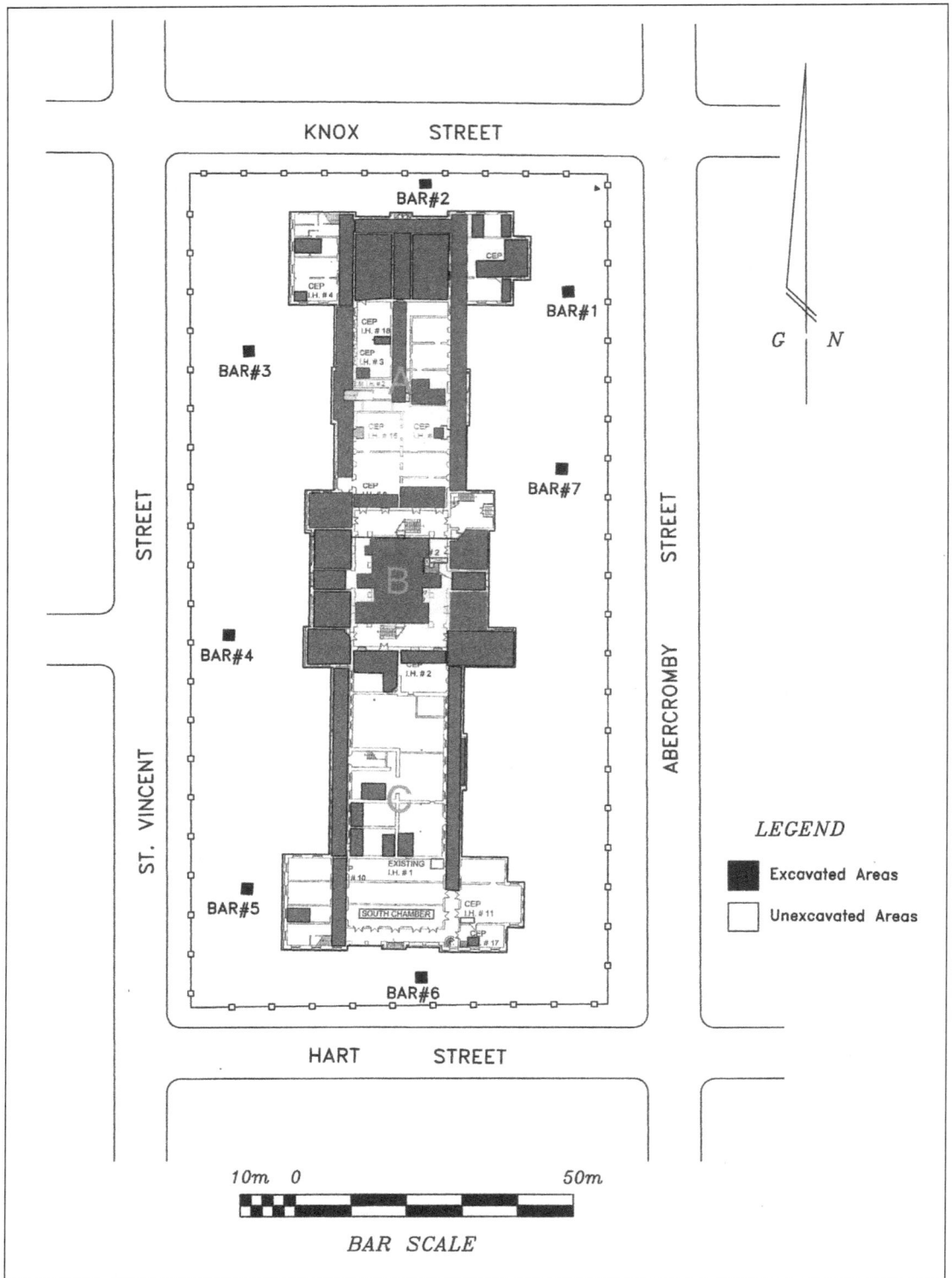

Figure I.5. Plan of the Red House site showing the excavated vis-à-vis the unexcavated areas. Drawn by Cecil Hodge.

labels being placed in each bag with bone and one label per bag for all other types of material. Excavation would be temporarily halted whenever human skeletal remains were found, thereby facilitating the detailed drawing and photographing of human skeletal discoveries. Excavation would resume after the burials were meticulously removed from the site and taken to the Finds Processing Unit. All recovered finds were placed in labelled plastic bags and subsequently carried to that unit, located in close proximity to the Red House building, where they would be sorted, washed (if necessary), catalogued, drawn (if necessary) and subjected to a variety of first-aid conservation treatments (if necessary).

Archaeological finds were cleaned and catalogued in the order in which they were excavated. The cleaning of the artefacts and biofacts involved washing with tap water (with the aid of toothbrushes) before they were left on trays to air-dry. Metals, due to their corrosive properties were dry-brushed, not washed. Charcoal, which was bagged separately from the other finds, was not cleaned in any way; it was exclusively air-dried. Pre-colonial and colonial ceramics, molluscs, glass and faunal remains were washed using tap water only; no detergents were used. Once dried, the finds were sorted per type, per soil level and per excavation unit.

For ceramics and glass, the pieces were separated according to specific features of each vessel (e.g., rim, body, base, handle). Artefactual groups that promised to provide specific cultural information about the site, such as pre-colonial *adornos* and seals on glass bottles, were bagged separately. Colonial ceramics were divided according to ware types. Faunal remains were bagged based on the type of bones that were present, such as long bones, vertebrae, jaws/teeth and cranial fragments. Molluscs were divided into whole valves or fragments according to species, provided that they were identifiable. Cleaned artefacts and biofacts were then catalogued on the basis of forms specific to each type of find (for example, pre-colonial ceramics, buttons, molluscs and so on).

Research and Scientific Analyses

Primarily because of the heavy disturbance, it was decided at the outset that a variety of scientific techniques would be necessary to extract as much information as possible from the large body of organic and inorganic remains recovered during excavation. Collectively known as archaeometry (Hofman 2014, 53–54), these scientific techniques include, but are not necessarily restricted to, radiocarbon dating, stable carbon, nitrogen, lead, oxygen and strontium isotope analyses, lipid residue analysis, starch grain and phytolith analyses, mitochondrial DNA analysis and pottery fabric analysis. Archaeometric techniques can be used for a variety of purposes, such as:

1. Determining the ages of sites and artefacts
2. Identifying the cultural affiliations of groups of people

3. Tracing patterns of human migration
4. Providing insights into the dietary profiles and food acquisition strategies of past societies
5. Establishing the source areas and reconstructing the manufacturing processes of raw materials

In addition to archaeometry, the project benefited from bioarchaeological studies, non-human faunal and lithic (stone) analyses, ethnohistory and ethnography. Previous research of other pre-colonial and colonial sites found elsewhere in the Caribbean and beyond was used to inform our interpretations of several archaeological findings (Reid 2015). Interpreting colonial finds was aided considerably by the rich array of documentary/archival sources on both the Red House and Port of Spain.

During the project, select samples of human bone and dog bone were sent to Beta Analytic (Miami, Florida) for radiocarbon dating; genetic analysis was undertaken by Michel Shamoon-Pour and D. Andrew Merriwether of Binghamton University in New York and Lars Fehren-Schmitz of the University of California, Santa Cruz; and isotopic analysis was conducted by John Krigbaum and George Kamenov of the University of Florida in Gainesville. Selected grindstone artefacts for starch grain and phytolith analyses were sent to Dolores Piperno of the Smithsonian Tropical Research Institute in Panama. Additionally, a sample of pre-colonial ceramics for lipid analyses were shipped to Mary Malainey at Brandon University in Manitoba, Canada, and a sample of pre-colonial ceramics for petrographic and chemical analyses were dispatched to Corinne Hofman of Leiden University in the Netherlands. Lithics were identified by Brent Wilson of the University of the West Indies at St Augustine (Trinidad and Tobago), and faunal remains were identified by Kristianne Bhagan (one of the finds processors), generously assisted by Mike Rutherford of the University of the West Indies, St Augustine. Helping to guide the research efforts of finds processors engaged in the cataloguing of various colonial finds were Georgia Fox of California State University, Chico; Neal Lopinot of Missouri State University in Springfield, Missouri; Grant Gilmore III of Charleston College in South Carolina; and Gifford Watters of the Florida Museum of Natural History, University of Florida, Gainesville.

A key archaeological methodology at the Red House site was the creation of a GIS archaeological information system (AIS). This was specifically designed to manage, visualize, interrogate and analyse spatial and temporal data generated during the project. In September 2013 Michael Sutherland of the Department of Geomatics Engineering and Land Management at the University of the West Indies, St Augustine, along with his team, developed a three-dimensional spatial database for the project. The 3D database was constructed using a GIS, specifically ESRI ArcGIS 10.1. Selected staff members of the Red House Restoration

Archaeological Project were trained to use ArcGIS 10.1 by Sutherland and his team.

The foregoing discussion captures the major steps involved in excavating, documenting and researching the site. Papers in this volume are the result of the collective efforts of scores of individuals who worked collaboratively, over an extended period of time, to help make the Red House Restoration Archaeological Project a major success. The following chapter descriptions provide summaries of the major, salient points raised in each of the book's eleven chapters.

CHAPTER DESCRIPTIONS

The volume is divided into three parts. Part 1 focuses on the pre-colonial period, part 2 on the colonial period and part 3 on heritage management.

Part 1: The Pre-colonial Period

Comprised of seven chapters, part 1 focuses on the lifeways of the pre-colonial people who inhabited the Red House site from 125 to 1395 CE. Co-authored by Basil A. Reid, Brent Wilson, Zara Ali, Louise Dover, Sade Grant and Samuel Reyes, chapter 1, entitled "The Pre-colonial History-Makers of the Red House Site", presents the Red House pre-colonial indigenes as dynamic, self-reflexive history-makers. The discussion primarily revolves around their burials, ceramics and stone tools. Although archaeology is the major data source in this paper, ethnography and ethnohistory are used on occasion to help interpret some of the archaeological findings. Chapter 1 is premised on a revisionist definition of history which embraces not only written records but all human actions, including those recorded orally and reflected in the archaeological record. This undercuts the conventional view that history in Trinidad and Tobago and the Caribbean began with written records that were ushered into the region with the arrival of the first Europeans.

Chapter 2, co-authored by Michel Shamoon-Pour, Lars Fehren-Schmitz, D. Andrew Merriwether and Basil A. Reid, represents the first mtDNA study of pre-colonial human remains in Trinidad and Tobago, and should therefore be considered as highly significant for the twin island republic and the wider Caribbean. Entitled "Mitochondrial DNA Analysis of Pre-contact Human Remains from the Red House Site", the paper summarizes the results of the paleogenetic investigation of human skeletal remains found at the Red House site. The remains of six individuals – predating phase 1 of the project – were sent to the Department of Anthropology at Binghamton University for genetic testing, while the remains of thirty-one individuals recovered during phase 1 of the project were sent to the University of California, Santa Cruz, Paleogenomics

Lab. Mitochondrial SNPs and partial sequences were identified for twenty individuals, making definitive haplogroup assignment possible in seventeen cases, all belonging to Amerindian lineages of haplogroups C1 (10), A (4), D1 (2), and B (1). Of the thirty-one sets of remains, twenty-four were dated to the tenth to fourteenth centuries CE, while the rest yielded timelines from the third to seventh centuries CE.

Chapter 3, entitled "Multi-Isotopic Analysis of the Red House Site Skeletal Remains: Inferring Paleodiet and Paleomobility from Recovered Bones and Teeth", by John Krigbaum, George D. Kamenov, Laura Van Voorhis and Basil A. Reid, presents isotopic data for recovered human remains (n = 38) and select fauna (n = 10) from the site. The study seeks to address issues of paleodiet and paleomobility in relation to the pre-colonial Red House sample. Light isotope ratios from bone collagen ($\delta^{13}C$, $\delta^{15}N$), bone apatite ($\delta^{13}C$), tooth enamel apatite ($\delta^{13}C$, $\delta^{18}O$) and heavy isotope ratios from tooth enamel ($^{20n}Pb/^{204}Pb$, $^{87}Sr/^{86}Sr$) are presented. Results support a mixed C_3 terrestrial- and marine-based diet, with significant $\delta^{13}C$ differences in all tissues analysed between the Saladoid (n = 9) and post-Saladoid (n = 22) human samples. A dietary shift from broad-spectrum terrestrial to increased marine with a mix of $C_3/CAM/C_4$ plant food resources is proposed; however, similar $\delta^{15}N$ values between the two support a maritime-based dietary focus. Data presented by Krigbaum et al. are compared to broadly contemporaneous circum-Caribbean sites to assess regional trends. Saladoid individuals show greater heterogeneity in $^{87}Sr/^{86}Sr$, but the observed ranges for $^{87}Sr/^{86}Sr$ and $^{20n}Pb/^{204}Pb$ in most tooth enamel samples are consistent with expected "local" variability on the geologically complex island of Trinidad. Although post-Saladoid sample size is small, for the observed sex differences the Pb ratios of the females seem to be "non-local" compared to the "local" Pb ratios of the males analysed. Krigbaum et al. conclude that this difference suggests a pattern of patrilocal residence among the post-Saladoid people of the Red House site.

In chapter 4, entitled "A Bioarchaeological Study of Human Skeletons from the Red House", John J. Schultz, Patrisha L. Meyers and J. Marla Toyne argue that Red House archaeological site burials do not reflect a natural attritional cemetery but more closely represent a cross-sectional sample of approximately twelve hundred years of life and death on the island of Trinidad. This bioarchaeological analysis of skeletal remains combines multiple indicators of demography, disease, trauma and cultural modification of the body to provide an overall interpretation of health, activity patterns and interpersonal violence. A minimum of sixty individuals were identified, including both males and females as well as juveniles. The variety of pathological conditions included dental disease, joint pathology, non-specific inflammatory lesions, antemortem fractures, and cultural modifications. According to Schultz et al., the significance of the Red House burials lies not in any of these individual conditions but in their contribution to the interpretation of pre-Columbian lifeways on the island of Trinidad and in the Lesser Antilles.

In chapter 5, entitled "Lipid Residue Analysis of Pre-colonial Ceramics from the Red House", Mary Malainey, Timothy Figol, Basil A. Reid, Makini Emmanuel and Andrew Maurice provide insight into the foodways of the pre-contact indigenous community at the Red House, based on the analysis of lipid residues on the walls of thirty-six pottery sherds. Derivatives of their total lipid extracts were analysed using gas chromatography (GC), high temperature GC (HT-GC) and high temperature gas chromatography with mass spectrometry (HT-GC/MS). Residue identifications were based on fatty acid decomposition patterns of experimental residues, lipid distribution patterns and the presence of biomarkers. Ten lipid residues were identified as medium fat content and low fat content plant residues. Another eight lipid residues had high levels of C18:0. Residues with high and moderate-high levels of C18:1 isomers also occurred. The fatty acid composition of two residues bordered medium and moderate-high fat content. Thirteen residues were characterized on the basis of lipid biomarkers and triacylglycerol distribution. Evidence of plant products were detected in two of these residues, and others represented plant and animal combinations with animal residues being dominant in one and plant residues being dominant in another. This study is the first of its kind for Trinidad and Tobago and therefore represents an important milestone in archaeological research in the twin island republic.

Co-authored by Zara Ali, Brent Wilson, Mike Rutherford, Lanya Fanovich, John Krigbaum and Laura Van Voorhis and entitled "Initial Interpretations of the Red House Faunal Assemblage", chapter 6 provides a brief overview of the entire faunal assemblage that has, to date, been recovered from the site. Given that the Red House site is a multi-component, multi-period site, the study is based on the following chronology: Saladoid (125–600 CE), post-Saladoid (600–1395 CE) and Colonial (1500–1950 CE). Presented in this chapter are the distribution, diversity and dominance of the molluscs; basic interpretations of species abundance based on NISP for the vertebrates; radiocarbon dating results where applicable coupled with isotopic data from the tooth enamel of select dogs (n = 9) and one prehistoric peccary. Additionally, the paper includes short remarks about choice artefacts made from shell and bone.

Chapter 7, entitled "Petrographic and Chemical Analyses of Pre-colonial Ceramics from the Red House Site" and co-authored by Patrick Degryse, Corinne L. Hofman, Basil A. Reid, Bert Neyt and Krystal Singh, discusses the results of petrographic and chemical analyses of sixteen ceramic samples from the Red House site. This chapter challenges the conventional pre-colonial model for Trinidad, which stipulates that the Saladoid, Arauquinoid and Mayoid pottery series are located in the Red House pre-colonial timeline of 125 to 1395 CE. The data were compared to clay samples collected on the island. During the study, five hypotheses were used as a central framework for interpreting the data. While the results of these analyses indicate that fifteen of the ceramic samples belong to the Saladoid (Palo Seco) complex, no evidence for either Guayabitoid or Mayoid ceramics was discerned. The fabric of most of the ceramic samples point to local clay sourcing. The study also suggests that the population of Trinidad was not completely replaced by the Arauquinoid newcomers and that the Red House was inhabited by a locally based community that produced pottery from local clays over an extended period.

Part 2: The Colonial Period

Part 2 is comprised of two papers: chapters 8 and 9. Authored by Lovell Francis and entitled "The Colonial History of Port of Spain and the Red House from the Late Fifteenth Century to 1907", chapter 8 traces the history of Port of Spain under the Spanish from the late fifteenth century and subsequently under the British after 1797. It discusses key milestones in both the founding and development of Port of Spain as well as the events leading to the building of the first and second Red House buildings. Much of the paper focuses on the social, economic and political contexts for life in colonial Port of Spain and the extent to which the emergence of Red House was influenced by these historical contingencies.

Chapter 9, entitled "An Archaeological Review of the Colonial Red House Site, 1844–1907" and co-authored by Makini Emmanuel, Georgia L. Fox and Gifford Waters, reviews the primary colonial finds recovered from the Red House, most of which chronologically relate to the nineteenth and twentieth centuries. These finds, according to Emmanuel et al., mirror the life and times of the Red House as a grandiose British colonial space; a work facility for a succession of British governors and their staff; a venue for meetings between governors and members of the legislative council, and the scene of social gatherings involving invited dignitaries and members of the local elite. Although Trinidad has had a diverse colonial past, very few archaeological studies of this period have been undertaken. This paper is therefore noteworthy, as it provides an archaeological synopsis of an era in Trinidad and Tobago's history which, over the years, has received insufficient scholarly attention. Moreover, the book chapter examines urban colonial archaeology in Trinidad and Tobago, and as such represents the first study of its kind in the twin island republic.

Part 3: Heritage Management

Both chapters 10 and 11 of part 3 round out the volume. Co-authored by Michael Sutherland, Amit Seeram, Sarah Hosein and Basil A. Reid, chapter 10, entitled "Developing a GIS Archaeological Information System for the Red House" is trained on the design and development of an AIS of the site, based on a GIS. In Sutherland et al.'s view, this AIS will not only facilitate easy access of information but will provide a digital database amenable to continuous updating as new information on the Red House comes to light. ArcGIS is the primary software utilized to store, manage, analyse and present spatio-temporal archaeological data, but data were also preliminarily processed in AutoCAD. The AIS generated by this project represents an important milestone in automated archaeological data capture in the twin island republic, given the national and international historical, archaeological and political significance of the Red House.

Chapter 11, co-authored by Basil A. Reid, Neil Jaggassar and Peter E. Siegel and entitled "The Red House Restoration Archaeological Project: An Example of Archaeological and Values-Based Heritage Management", discusses the holistic approach taken in managing what was arguably a landmark archaeological project in Trinidad and Tobago. The co-authors contend that the Red House Restoration Archaeological Project can be considered as a quintessential example of archaeological heritage management and values-based heritage management in Trinidad and Tobago and the Caribbean. Funded and administratively spearheaded by the Office of the Parliament of the Republic of Trinidad and Tobago and primarily staffed by faculty and students from the University of the West Indies at St Augustine, the project recovered some of the most significant archaeological finds in Trinidad and Tobago. The building itself, located in the heart of Port of Spain, was the seat of Trinidad and Tobago's parliament for over one hundred years and is therefore iconic, an integral part of the city's historical landscape. As earlier indicated, due to the discovery of several Amerindian human burials, the First Peoples of the twin island republic revere the Red House as a sacred site. This chapter explores the specific steps taken, at the outset of the project, to satisfy the often competing interests of its diverse stakeholders, namely, the government, the academic community, the First Peoples and the general public.

CONCLUSION

Based on a multidisciplinary approach, the volume showcases important, often groundbreaking archaeological scholarship, which should be of considerable interest to both academic and general audiences. The diverse collection of cultural materials recovered from the site, as well as the battery of techniques applied in the study of these materials, should generate much academic interest locally, regionally and internationally. Practitioners and scholars of Caribbean archaeology, bioarchaeology, anthropology, history, heritage studies, historic architecture and tourism should find something of value in these pages. The book will also be of considerable interest to the general public in the Caribbean and beyond, especially the people of Trinidad and Tobago.

NOTES

1. The Urban Development Corporation of Trinidad and Tobago is a limited liability company registered under the Companies Ordinance (ch. 13, no. 1) which was incorporated in 1994. While UDeCOTT has a reporting relationship to the Ministry of Housing and Urban Development, it is a private company which is wholly owned by the government and also reports to the Corporation Sole, the minister of finance. UDeCOTT's primary objective is to deliver projects that meet its clients' objectives using the highest-quality project management and development services. UDeCOTT is responsible, inter alia, for developing the urban renewal of the capital city, Port of Spain, into a business and financial centre.

2. The Saladoid subsisted on a combination of root crop horticulture (bitter cassava and sweet potatoes), hunting, fishing, and the gathering of edible animal and plant foods (Boomert 2014, 336).

3. The oldest Saladoid site found in Trinidad and Tobago is Lover's Retreat (in Tobago), which in 2004 yielded an early radiocarbon date of 770 to 380 BCE (Reid 2005). In all, two successive ceramic complexes are known from Trinidad: Cedros (200 BCE–1 CE) and Palo Seco (1–750 CE). Cedros pottery is characterized by small- to medium-sized bowls and jars that exhibit a variety of bichrome and polychrome painted, incised and modelled designs (Boomert 2014, 336–37).

REFERENCES

Boomert, A. 2014. Trinidad and Tobago. In Reid and Gilmore 2014, 335–38.

Fitzpatrick, S.M., M. Kappers, Q. Kaye, C.M. Giovas, M.J. LeFebvre, M. Hill-Harris, S. Burnett, J.A. Pavia, K. Marsaglia and J. Feathers. 2009. "Pre-Columbian Settlements on Carriacou, West Indies". *Journal of Field Archaeology* 34 (3): 247–66.

Hofman, C.L. 2014. "Archaeometry". In Reid and Gilmore 2014, 53–54.

Hofman, C.L., and B.A. Reid. 2014. "The Saladoid". In Reid and Gilmore 2014, 300–303.

Hoogland, L.P., and C.L. Hofman. 2013. "From Corpse Taphonomy to Mortuary Behavior in the Caribbean: A Case Study from the Lesser Antilles". In *The Oxford Handbook of Caribbean Archaeology*, edited by W.F. Keegan, C.L. Hofman and R. Rodriquez Ramos, 452–69. Oxford: Oxford University Press.

Keegan, W.F. 1992. *The People Who Discovered Columbus*. Gainesville: University Press of Florida.

Reid, B.A. 2005. *Archaeological Excavations of Lover's Retreat (TOB-69), Tobago, Phases 2&3), Final Report.* Conducted for Island Investment Limited (May).

———. 2009. *Myths and Realities of Caribbean History.* Tuscaloosa: University of Alabama Press.

———. 2014. "St John Site (Trinidad)". In Reid and Gilmore 2014, 325.

———. 2015. *Red Restoration Archaeology Report, Phase 1, for the Period July 1, 2013–January 31, 2015.* Port of Spain: Office of the Parliament of the Republic of Trinidad and Tobago.

Reid, B.A., and R.G. Gilmore III, eds. 2014. *Encyclopedia of Caribbean Archaeology.* Gainesville: University Press of Florida.

Wilson, S.M. 2007. *The Archaeology of the Caribbean.* Cambridge University Press.

PART 1

THE PRE-COLONIAL PERIOD

CHAPTER 1

The Pre-colonial History-Makers
of the Red House Site, 125–1395 CE

BASIL A. REID, BRENT WILSON, ZARA ALI, LOUISE DOVER,
SADE GRANT AND SAMUEL REYES

ON THE BASIS OF A SELECTION OF ARCHAEOLOGICAL data recovered from the Red House, this chapter presents the pre-colonial inhabitants of the site as dynamic, self-reflective history-makers. This represents a significant departure from what is conventional in Trinidad and Tobago and the rest of the Caribbean, where history is often seen as beginning with the advent of written records that were ushered into the region with the arrival of the first Europeans. Studying pre-colonial societies in the ethnographic present inaccurately portrays them as timeless primitives completely devoid of a history until the arrival of the early Europeans (Fagan 2002; Reid 2009).

In the archaeological literature, the pre-colonial peoples of the New World are routinely labelled as prehistoric, with "prehistoric" generally referring to the time before written history (Darvill 2002). However, the dichotomy of prehistory versus history is really a product of Western linear time conception and is therefore not entirely applicable to a study of native societies in the Caribbean (Reid 2009). Daniel (1962, 10) posited that if history was linked to the full sweep of human development on the earth, then how could there be a time before history? How could there be a prehistory? (Schmidt and Mrozowski 2013, 1.) Further, many of the rapidly transpiring historical processes thought to have been largely a product of modernity – interethnic interactions, migrations, religious movements, political collapses and reorganizations, wars and the like – also played out among non-Western societies in the premodern world (Gilmore and O'Donoughue 2015, 1; Bradley 2002, 3–5; Cobb 2005; Sassaman 2010, 1–5).

The archaeological evidence suggests that the Red House pre-colonial inhabitants were not static, timeless or ahistorical; rather, they were active individuals who modified and transformed their society in definite relationships to one another (Miller and Tilley 1984). They were dynamic culture brokers, *bricoleurs*, traders, social negotiators and history-makers capable of devising "complex strategies to solve their problems and meet their goals", a perspective described by Elizabeth Brumfiel (1992, 551–67) as "agent-centred". These issues will be fleshed out in this chapter, with much of the discussion coalescing around burials, ceramics and stone tools recovered from the Red House site.

REVISIONIST DEFINITIONS OF HISTORY

Traditional accounts have all too often portrayed prehistoric societies as "cold" (*sensu* Lévi-Strauss 1966) and virtually unchanging for centuries or millennia (Gilmore and O'Donoughue 2015, 1). However, since the 1980s and 1990s this Eurocentric concept of history has come under heavy academic scrutiny (Gell 1996; Gosden 1994; Schmidt 1997a; Schmidt and Patterson 1995; Wolf 1982). History is increasingly being defined as embracing all human actions, whether these were recorded orally or in writing or reflected exclusively in the archaeological record (Reid 2009; Sahlins 1987).

The tendency by scholars to present the concepts of history and time as one and the same is reflective of the increasingly prevalent reconceptualization of history. All human actions produce time (or history), and every human act constitutes an event or part of a succession of events (Gosden 1994). Westerners think of the passage of the human experience along a straight, if branching, highway of time that is durational and irreversible. For example, in linear time events that occurred on 12 December 1917 or 2 March 2001 can never be repeated and are therefore part of an irreversible time frame. Since the advent of the commoditized hourly clock system of European capitalism (Thompson 1967), Western linear time has been precisely measured and controlled through the use of watches, clocks and Greenwich Meridian time zones (Gosden 1994, 131–32).

The Amerindians of Trinidad and Tobago, whose past was largely undocumented and whose time conception was predominantly cyclical, are usually perceived as completely lacking in histories of their own, even though their past extended as far back as almost eight thousand years ago (Reid 2009). However, Hastrup (1992) correctly argued that the Western views of the past and of time are clearly different from those ancient or non-Western societies but are in no way superior to them. In many non-Western societies, time (or history) can be based both on seasons and on annual festivals coupled with the birth and death of important persons in communities. For instance, in the 1930s Evans-Pritchard observed that the time conception of the Nuer of Sudan in North Africa revolved around dates linked to their wet and dry seasons, group social activities (ecological time-reckoning) and Nuer relations to one another in respect to age and kinship ties (structural time-reckoning) (Evans-Pritchard 1939) (figure 1.1). For more contemporary groups, such as the Luo people of western Kenya, time, or history, is also cyclical, comprising a host of temporal measures

May	June	July	August	September	October	November	December	January	February	March	April

R A I N S D R O U G H T

R I V E R S R I S E R I V E R S F A L L

H O R T I C U L T U R E

Preparation of gardens for first millet sowing and for maize

Preparation of gardens for second millet sowing

BURNING OF THE BRUSH

F I S H I N G

BUILDING & REPAIRING

Harvest maize   Harvest first millet crop   Harvest second millet crop

H U N T I N G A N D
C O L L E C T I N G

SCARCITY OF FOOD

PLENTY OF FOOD

V I L L A G E S C A M P S

Older people return to village

Younger people return to village

Younger people in early camps   Everyone in main dry-season camps

Wedding, initiation, mortuary, and other ceremonies

Main season for raiding Dinka

involving life, generational and ritual cycles. The Bali calendar is to some extent not a scheme of time measurement but rather a component of a cyclical system of actions. Essentially, this system revolves around ritual observances (such as temple festivals, which occur sporadically throughout the year), personal actions dictated by the conjunction of personal days (birthdays, auspicious days, etc.) and days recognized as being good for particular activities, such as getting married, making a start on an important project, and so on (Gell 1996).

It is likely that pre-colonial peoples of the Caribbean, including the inhabitants of the Red House site, used techniques similar to those of the early Hawaiians of the Pacific (Sahlins 1987) and the Nuer people of Sudan of Africa (Evans-Pritchard 1939) to measure or reckon time. These included wet and dry seasons, social events, village ceremonial feastings, life passages (such as the initiation of boys to men and girls to women), as well as the deaths of individuals in their communities. Such events were probably transmitted orally through successive generations and became part of the collective memories or histories of these native societies.

Agency theory is key to ascribing historical consciousness and history-making capabilities to pre-colonial peoples. At the heart of agency theory is the basic agreement that people are not uniform automatons, merely reacting to changes in the external world, but, instead, that they "play a role in the formation of the social realities in which they participate" (Barfield 1997, 4). In other words, it acknowledges that people purposefully act and alter the external world through their actions (Dornan 2002, 304), even pre-colonials who lived deep in time.

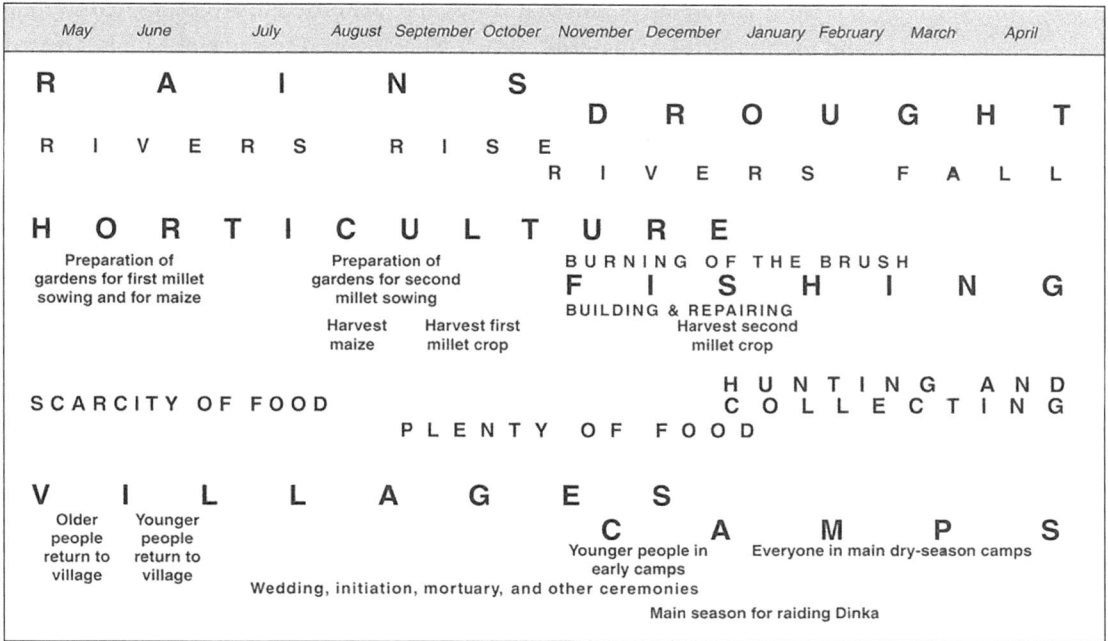

Figure 1.1.
Nuer time-reckoning system based on seasons and social activities. Reproduced from Evans-Pritchard, "Nuer Time-Reckoning".

It is through human action that landscapes are ordered, dwellings maintained and mobile forms of material culture (such as pottery and stone tools) created (Gosden 1994, 16).

However, human actions are not done in a vacuum but are usually guided by the cultural order or ideological structure of their respective societies. In contemporary Trinidad and Tobago, nationals invariably act with reference to their country's ideological structure that is predicated on its western form of government as well as its ethnic, religious and cultural plurality (Bissessar and La Guerre 2015). By the same token, the behaviours and dispositions of the Red House pre-colonials of Trinidad were usually guided by an ideological structure that was grounded on South American/Antillean native cosmology (Siegel 1996). Dornan (2002) argues that an agency-oriented archaeology helps us to better understand the interaction between the generally accepted cultural order or *structure* and the ever-fluid dynamics of human practice or *agency* (Sahlins 1981; italic emphasis is mine).

Given its centrality to the chapter, a brief discussion of South American/ Antillean cosmology is hereby presented.

SOUTH AMERICAN/ANTILLEAN COSMOLOGY

South American cosmology can be characterized as profoundly polytheistic and animistic. It revolves around a common belief in a vast number of spirits related to nature – the forest, the sky, rivers and mountains – as well as ghost spirits, referred to as "the shadows of the deceased". The South American cosmos is likened to a "cake" consisting principally of three layers – the sky world, the material world and the underworld – all of which are equally real. Positive spirits inhabit the sky world. Symbolized by the sun and the jaguar, the sky world has strong male associations and is characterized by the moon, murky waters and reptiles. In the middle is the world of material experience. Populated by Indians and animals (which in themselves are manifestations of both sky-world and underworld spirits), the material world usually has the village in its centre (Roe 1982).

As the primary repository of ritual knowledge, the shaman presides over and directs the numerous rituals and ceremonies performed in the village. He is the intermediary between the community and the spirit world (Roe 1997; Reid 2004). To enter either the sky or underworld, it is necessary for the shaman to attain an altered state of consciousness, which is achieved through ingesting one of the varieties of hallucinogenic agents naturally available in the tropical rain forests.

The *axis mundi* is an important feature of the sacred centre, a connector between the layers of the cosmos which supposedly provides an access route or vertical "bridge" for the shaman to travel through the universe in order to communicate with ancestor spirits (Reichel-Dolmatoff 1971). A cave, a rock shelter, a central plaza or a central house post may serve as the axis mundi. Notions of sacred and profane space are central to South American cosmology. Across Amazonia, a motley collection of attributes characterizes the sacred and profane realms of the cosmological landscape. While the sacred bears strong male associations and is generally related to andocentric activities, the profane, being female, centres around "traditional" female activities (Roe 1982; Reid 2004).

The South American/Antillean native cosmology represented an essential organizing principle for pre-colonial indigenous societies in the Caribbean. It was manifested in all aspects of life, including the structure and organization of the community (Siegel 1996). It would appear that the dichotomy between male and female, as well as the sacred and profane, was partly designed to justify and reinforce the sexual division of labour and, by extension, allegedly create a sense of balance and "cosmic" order in society (Roe 1982).

BURIALS

Perhaps, no single event in archaeology is more demonstrative of purposeful action and human intentionality than the disposal of the dead (Tarlow and Stutz 2013). Red House burials[1] are also reflective of South American/Antillean cosmology, which at its core is cyclical time expressed in birth, death, burial rites, interment, rebirth, renewal, propagation and ancestor veneration (Siegel 1996). The emplacement of a burial is a conscious act "in which the unthought habits meet with thought-out symbolic forms" (Gosden 1994, 18).

Burial Descriptions

The burial positions of several Red House skeletons varied: some were flexed, seated or fully extended. Sixteen crouched and seated and seven supine (or fully extended) burials were clearly identified (Reid 2015). Similar to Saladoid skeletons excavated in the Maisabel burial ground in Puerto Rico, the flexed fetal burial position at the Red House site may have symbolized death as a form of rebirth to a new status (Siegel 1996).

Among the mortuary findings at the Red House site were a skull in pot burial and three sets (probably bundles) of long bones (Reid 2015). The skull in pot burial, which was found at a depth of 1.2 metres from topsoil, holds special cultural significance (see figure 4.1 [in chapter 4, this volume]). Skull in pot burials were usually associated with ancestor veneration, generally accorded to such important persons in these early native societies as chiefs, tribal leaders or their offspring (Hoogland and Hofman 2013). This harkens to similar practices documented by the early colonial chroniclers, who mentioned that bones were kept in the houses as *cemíes* (Breton 1978 [1647]; Pané 1999), reflecting the importance accorded to these skeletal remains within the community of the living. Both the skull in pot and the three sets of long bones represent secondary burials (i.e., burials removed from their original context and redeposited elsewhere in the Red House basement). Secondary depositions consist of complete skeletons and bundles of long bones or crania.

The manipulation and removal of bones after decomposition, as well as the secondary deposition of skeletal parts or cremated remains may point to this recursive connection between the living and the dead (Hoogland and Hofman 2013). The presence of primary partially rearranged burials can be cited as yet another example of death manipulation by early native communities in the Caribbean. These burials were the result of one or more parts of the skeleton being removed and then redeposited either in the same grave or elsewhere. The human skeleton found in section B, subdivision 8, of the rotunda of the Red House site may be an example of a primary partially rearranged burial.

Many natives in the Caribbean buried their deceased wrapped in hammocks and bandages. At the Lavoutte site in St Lucia, for example, a cluster of three individuals were buried in elongated grave pits in a supine position, with tightly flexed legs (Hoogland and Hofman 2013), suggesting that the deceased were wrapped in hammocks or baskets in very small graves. This type of burial pattern is depicted in the anthropomorphic petroglyphs along the Caguitas River, Caguas Municipio, in Puerto Rico (Roe 1997, 156). A classic example of this type of burial at the Red House site is the human skeleton found in subdivision 1 of G43.

Given the heavy Red House site disturbance and the absence of postholes showing where native houses once stood, it is difficult to determine the contexts in which the deceased were originally buried. Despite this, based on archaeological research from elsewhere in the Caribbean (Reid and Gilmore 2014), it is likely that the sixty deceased individuals so far recovered from the Red House site were buried in a variety of places, such as (1) in-habitation spaces, specifically near the houses, next to posts, in postholes and under the house floors; (2) in middens; (3) in a central plaza. Items 1, 2 and 3 would suggest a pattern of residential burial based on social memory. In other words, people would rebuild their houses and bury their dead in the same location for many centuries or use former settlements as burial grounds (Morsink 2009; Van den Bel and Romon 2010; Hoogland and Hofman 2013). There is evidence of grave clusters at the Red House site, suggesting that a possible kinship relationship existed between the deceased and particular living households at the Red House site during pre-colonial times.

Age Grades

At the Red House site, sixty complete and incomplete human skeletons were unearthed. This number includes forty-seven adults and thirteen juveniles (Schultz and Meyers 2015). Adults include young, middle and older age classes. Juveniles represent one infant (0–1 year), eight young children (1–6 years), three older children (6–12) and one adolescent (12–20). Although it is not possible to determine ancestry for many individuals, morphological traits of the skulls are consistent with those of Amerindians (Schultz and Meyers 2015). Radiocarbon dates, based primarily on collagen (dietary protein) extracted from human skeletons, provide a chronology ranging from 125 to 1395 CE.

Clearly, the Red House burials represent multiple age grades that were interred over a period of more than 1,200 years. In other words, several generations were buried at the site. This holds much significance for understanding the role that the older or more mature members of the community might have played in both mentoring and orally transmitting time-honoured cultural traditions to their younger counterparts. Schmidt (2013) argues that ancestors were key history-makers in non-Western societies, as they often cajoled and gave guidance, evoking social memories and bringing the past into the present – a process described by Ray (1987, 68) as "presencing" the past.

Burial Goods

Various stone artefacts (millingstones and beads) as well as pottery were found in direct association with at least nine skeletons at the Red House site, suggesting that these items might have been interred as burial goods. Elizabeth Righter observed the same phenomenon of the ritual economy at the Tutu site on St Thomas: "Objects of ornamentation and magico-religious objects, such as greenstone inlays, are found in dispersed midden at Tutu (St Thomas [US Virgin Islands]), associated with early occupations houses. This disposal pattern suggests ceremonial or sacred 'ritual disposal'. These objects of spiritual and personal value most likely were offered during ritual feasting and disposal associated with human burial and ancestor worship" (Righter 2002, 350). The presence of burial goods and the burial positions both suggest that the deceased at the Red House site were interred in a timely, purposive manner, based on rites of passage, reflective of South American/Antillean cosmology.

Burials in Shell Middens

Based on anecdotal observations, over thirteen skeletal remains were interred in shell-bed middens at various localities throughout the Red House basement.

The shell beds primarily consist of mangrove oysters (*Crassostrea rhizophorae*). Luby and Gruber (1999) argue that important symbolic meanings were associated with the practice of interring human remains in shell beds. In their view, Amerindians would often bury their ancestors in these mollusc-rich environments to ensure a continuing supply of food for the deceased in the afterlife. It is clear that shell-bed middens are not just accumulations of refuse but are also socially constructed landscapes that serve as places for daily practices and rituals that are inextricably tied to social memory (Thompson 2010).

Based on a study of stratigraphic sequences, fifty-eight radiocarbon dates, human burials and funerary paraphernalia from a large shell mound on Santa Cruz Island in California, Gamble (2017) is of the view that the mound was a persistent place where early visitors had significant feasts, constructed dwellings, buried their dead and performed ceremonies where select groups of infants, children and adults were revered. A similar scenario might have existed at the Red House shell-bed midden. Most of the over one hundred radiocarbon dates – which yielded multiple timelines – were derived from human burials (Reid 2015). Additionally, as earlier mentioned bioarchaeological assessments of the site by Schultz and Meyers (2015) confirmed the presence of multiple age grades among the Red House burials. These findings, together with the discovery of burial goods, suggest that the Red House shell-bed midden might have been a place that was inhabited by successive generations of natives whose memories of the past were negotiated, interpreted, (re)interpreted and commemorated in rituals and public events, some associated with the deceased (Meskell 2007, 224).

CERAMICS

Time is not an abstract entity but a practical daily involvement with the [material] world (Gosden 1994, 1). Pottery making by the pre-colonial inhabitants of the Red House site can be considered as timed action, which uses the imprint of the past to create an anticipation of the future. Conceivably, Red House potters used South American cosmology as their frame of reference or "imprint of the past" to produce ceramics. There was, of course, the anticipation that these manufactured pots would subsequently be utilized for cooking, food preparation, serving and magico-religious purposes (Boomert 2000; Sajo 2014). These pottery-related activities probably took place in different locations and at different times from where the ceramics were originally manufactured. According to Gosden (1994, 16), "Every act contains within it implicit links to other acts separated in time and space. These future acts orientate and shape the present one and it is the flow of life as a whole which gives each act point and purpose."

As mentioned in the introduction, this volume, pre-colonial pottery found at the Red House appears to be distinctly Saladoid.[2] Named after the site of Saladero in Venezuela, the term "Saladoid" refers to a pottery series that was first identified along the Lower Orinoco (Hofman and Reid 2014) as well as the makers of this pottery series.[3] Saladoid ceramics found at the Red House are usually characterized by red paint, black paint, white-on-red (WOR) paint, black and polychrome paint, zone-incised cross hatchings (ZIC), broad-lined incisions, and D-shaped handles. In addition, sixty-nine *adornos* were recovered from the site. While most of the Saladoid potsherds found at site are undecorated, the presence of decorated and complex modelled sherds provide the diagnostic evidence attesting to their Saladoid cultural origin.[4]

Bricolage

The Red House potters applied a variety of paints to ceramic pots. They were also actively engaged in clay sourcing and the firing of an assortment of ceramic pots. These actions were all purposeful and tantamount to history making. However, their role as *bricoleurs* was perhaps the most significant, as it reflected the extent to which they were able to appropriate technological and ritual knowledge (Schmidt 1996, 1997b). As part of the dynamic interplay between ritual and technology, *bricolage* specifically refers to the process of fabrication in which the *bricoleur* assembles an object – be it ritual or myth – from the elements that exist in the cultural repertoire available to the fabricator (*bricoleur*) (Lévi-Strauss 1966). While the shamans, the chief repositories of ritual knowledge in Saladoid society, were predominantly men, it is likely that women made the ceramic vessels and the *adornos* that were part of these vessels. Ethnographic case studies from both Central and South America (Arnold 1988) point to the predominance of female potters, Arnold asserting that in tropical areas where men are actively engaged in significant responsibilities in the dry season, the division of labour is so structured that pottery making is largely a female activity. It is therefore reasonable to assume that the Saladoid potters at the Red House site were predominantly women. With respect to the sixty burials recovered from the Red House site, while it was not possible to accurately assess biological sex for nineteen adult individuals, thirteen individuals (21.67%) were assessed as female and sixteen individuals as male (26.67%), including the one adolescent (Schultz and Meyers 2015). It is therefore apparent that women were among the pre-colonial residents of the Red House site.

Technological know-how is an important hallmark of bricolage (Schmidt 1996). Saladoid *bricoleurs* had esoteric knowledge of clay properties, mineral and botanical inclusions, vessel forming, firing and complex modelling and complex-modelled incisions. Complex modelling required skilful manipulation of the clay to create *adornos* with eyes depicted by punctuations, punctuated pellets, short gashes or slits. In addition, *adornos* were modelled with protruding foreheads, "topknots" – that is, distinctive, round pom-pom–like tops and semi-circular and pointed headdresses. The creation of anthropomorphic, zoomorphic and anthropozoomorphic images by Saladoid *bricoleurs* also necessitated the careful application of ritual knowledge from the cultural repertoire available to the fabricator (Reid 2004).

Roget (1997, 101) posits that "in its vision of the world, each culture selects from among the infinite themes offered by its natural environment". Clearly, therefore, informed and often calculated decisions were made by Saladoid potters about the selection of specific animal species and human images for *adornos* (Reid 2004). Not only was this demonstrative of human intentionality, it also underscored the recursive relationship between the sacred and the profane. Women represent the profane in South American/Antillean cosmology, yet in all likelihood Saladoid female *bricoleurs* were important culture brokers in utilizing both ritual and technological knowledge to produce ceramic vessels and associated effigies. The dynamic interplay between the sacred and the profane was further reflected in the manner in which these vessels might have been used.

Ritual Uses of Adornos

Adornos were usually affixed to and modelled as part of Saladoid ceramic vessels (figure 1.2), resulting in ornate vessels that were invariably trotted out during ceremonial feastings. The variety of Saladoid pottery forms, coupled with the quality of manufacture and intricate ornamentation, suggest that its ceremonial component was principally designed for the public display of food and other goods as an expression of status, rank or kinship affiliation. Such displays could have been part of ceremonies involving competitive demonstrations or wealth accompanied by gift giving or even property destruction (Boomert 2013).

The ornamented fine ware might have been used primarily for the serving of food during ceremonial feasts, held for the extensive following of local head-men, "great men", who due to personal qualities were able to dominate in war and exchange, attracting large followings through gift giving. Feasts of this kind would have been held on the occasion of initiation rituals, marriages and burials of high-ranking persons (Morsink 2009).

In all probability, these zoomorphic and anthropozoomorphic Saladoid ceramic art pieces functioned similarly to *cemíes* (or *zemíes*). *Cemíes* are traditionally defined as sacred objects representing dieties in a wide range of forms with alleged cosmological power (Sajo and Siegel 2014, 355) that helped humans to maintain the proper cosmic balance between the corporeal and the spiritual. It is likely that the Saladoid at the Red House native village used these ceramic art pieces as *cemíes* that provided purported ubiquitous links between the natural and the spiritual worlds.

Figure 1.2.
A selection of
Saladoid (Palo Seco)
adornos.

By representing a variety of faunas on vessels, the Saladoid and post-Saladoid Red House inhabitants, through their shamans, paid homage to such deities, thus "placating" them and by extension reputedly creating peace and cosmic harmony within their societies. Such harmony was considered essential for the proper functioning of all aspects of social and economic life, such as childbirth, hunting, fishing, warfare and trade (Reid 2004). In short, the utilization of these vessels in a variety of sacred and profane contexts, ranging from shamanic rituals to village festivals or communal feasts among warriors and/or traders, can perhaps be interpreted as attempts to secure supernatural approval for the daily ebb and flow of village life. The propitiation and manipulation of these supposed omnipresent, powerful but ambivalent spirits ostensibly made social life possible (Reid 2004).

STONE TOOLS

Throughout the archaeological record, in all areas of the world, the most frequent evidence of past human activity that we have are stone tools (Kooyman 2001). In many cases, suitable raw material was not locally available, and people had to acquire it from more distant locations. By studying details of composition for the lithic types used, we can uniquely characterize each local source of material and so trace where exotic lithic material came from (Kooyman 2001). This can in turn provide insight into past patterns of trade and contact (Kooyman 2001) and elite exchange (Reid and Curet 2014).

There is no such thing as an isolated act. Every action we perform is contained within a network of actions stretching across time and space. For instance, the simple act of acquiring, grinding and knapping stones has implicit within it the purposes for which the finished tools will be used (Gosden 1994). These purposes exist in the future and may involve activities that will be carried out in another location (Gosden 1994), for example, lapidary trade (Reid 2014), hunting, gardening and food preparation (Rouse 1992).

In 2013 and 2014, Brent Wilson, professor of palaeontology, stratigraphy and sedimentology at the University of the West Indies, St Augustine, examined the various lithics recovered from the site. According to Wilson (2013, 2014 and 2015, pers. comm.), the metasandstone and phyllite, which comprise 29% and 32.5% of all artefacts, respectively, are of local origin. The few chert items may have been made with local material, such as that found at Chert Hill in the Central Range (Trinidad). Wilson identified two items made from dacite (an acid igneous rock most likely found in the Lesser Antilles).

There are no records of garnet gneiss, on which the metamorphic rocks tend to be of lower grade (chloritic schist and phyllite) in Trinidad; therefore, the three fragments of garnet gneiss found were in all likelihood imported from elsewhere. Suitable rocks might be found in the Cordillera de la Costa Belt, Venezuela. Serpentinite – a grey-green, low-temperature metamorphic rock composed of one or more serpentine group minerals – is a semi-precious exotic stone, and presence of examples at the site clearly suggests that lapidary artisans in either highland Venezuela or Margarita expended much of their time and expertise producing such items for export to the pre-colonial natives of the Red House site in Trinidad. However, some speculation can be made regarding provenance. Serpentinite artefacts have been found in pre-Hispanic sites in the high Venezuelan Andes, although serpentinites do not crop out there. A northern South American origin, including the island of Margarita (about 400 kilometres west of Trinidad) is suggested for serpentine (Brent Wilson 2013, 2014 and 2015, pers. comm.).

Three metasandstone grindstones from the site were sent to Dolores Piperno (senior scientist of the Smithsonian Tropical Research Institute in Panama) for both starch grain and phytolith analyses. While the starch grain analysis was uninformative as only a single unidentifiable starch grain was recovered, phytolith analysis of sediments removed from the stones revealed the presence of maize (*Zea mays*) cob and palm (Palmae) (Piperno 2014, pers. comm.). It appears that both cultivars were ground on locally available grindstones for dietary purposes. At the Red House site, local stones were frequently used as expedient tools for grinding plant materials, hunting and scraping the hides of animals; however, the non-local lithics were often worn as pendants. Importantly, non-local stones reflected trade contacts and elite exchange (Reid and Curet

2014) between the pre-colonials of the Red House site and their counterparts in South America and the Lesser Antilles.

The Saladoid who inhabited much of the eastern and southern Caribbean actively participated in lapidary trade. Excavations at Blanchisseuse in northern Trinidad in March 2007, for example, unearthed a stone derived from a fine-grained, acidic, extrusive igneous volcanic rock that was probably from the Lesser Antilles (Reid 2009). In the northern Lesser Antilles, information from excavated beads in Trants, Montserrat, strongly suggests that Trants was a prehistoric lithic bead-manufacturing centre that specialized in carnelian beads (Murphy et al. 2000). The study of these trade contacts, through lithic sources (including those relating to the Red House site), provides important insights into ancient social relations, past patterns of mobility and group territory size (Kooyman 2001). It also showcases the history-making capabilities of pre-colonial natives through their inventiveness, creativity and purposeful actions.

DISCUSSION AND CONCLUSIONS

One of the strengths of archaeology as a discipline resides in its unique time depth, and indeed time is essential to archaeology as it constitutes part of the reason for its existence (Shanks and Tilley 1987, 32–41). Archaeological time – which is westernized, linear and progressive – has become the overarching framework for understanding the chronology of early indigenous communities in the Caribbean (Reid 2009, 6–7) and beyond (Bradley 1991; Clark 1992). Primarily reflected in radiocarbon dating, seriation and stratigraphy, archaeological time has been the principal benchmark used by Caribbean scholars to chronologically order early pre-colonials into groups such as the Ortoiroid, Saladoid, Barrancoid, Troumassan Troumassoid, Suazan Troumassoid, Ostionoid, Taino, Guanahatabey and Island-Carib (Keegan and Hofman 2017; Reid and Gilmore 2014; Rouse 1992; Wilson 2007). However, while archaeological time has facilitated this rough classification, it provides limited insight into how these various communities might have conceptualized and managed their own time or histories. This approach has been described by Fabian (1983) as a denial of coevalness, a denial that archaeologists effect through the labelling of pre-colonial histories of the Other as primitive, prehistoric or mythological. On the basis of a selection of archaeological finds from the Red House, this chapter argues that the history of non-Western communities can be more holistically constructed through the use of ethnography, indigenous knowledge, ethnohistory and archaeological data (Fagan 2002, 21–22; Reid 2004; Schmidt and Mrozowski 2013), producing more realistic, often complex histories of pre-colonial and even contemporary indigenous groups, especially those operating without written calendars

(Bohannan 1953; Dietler and Herbich 1993; Evans-Pritchard 1939; Hantman 2013; Reid 2009; Rizvi 2013; Schmidt 1996).

There is always the temptation, however, to view only major developments in pre-colonial societies as historical by nature (see Gillespie 2007; Harding 2005), despite the fact that all events (including those that are considered mundane) are part of the historical narrative. Hendon (2010, 25) is of the view that routine practices, while not always consciously planned or deliberate, are nevertheless the result of intentional subjects making decisions about how to best use their time and complete certain tasks. Making a ceramic vessel or pounding maize on a millingstone might have been considered routine by the Red House pre-colonials, inasmuch as driving a car to and from work or shopping for groceries at the supermarket are considered routine by contemporary people. However, all human actions – whether they are significant or routine, conducted in deep in time or carried out very recently – are fundamentally historical by nature. As Gillespie (2007, 847) points out, "It is not a good trade-off to give [pre-colonial] people back their history only to take away their agency except in rare moments of a [transformative] historical event." This view is supported by Gilmore and O'Donoughue (2015, 6), who correctly assert that "continuities in practice, especially over long periods of time, deserve the same level of consideration and analysis as practical ruptures".

History embraces all human actions, whether these were recorded orally or in writing or reflected exclusively in the archaeological record (Reid 2009). By being more attentive to time perceptions of the Other, researchers, when using archaeological time, will be able to recover meanings from the archaeological record that have all too often been ignored. The foregoing discussion brings into sharp perspective the fact that the Red House Saladoid and post-Saladoid natives were dynamic, self-reflexive and active human agents who modified their society in definite relationships to one another (Miller and Tilley 1984). Rather than being passive, timeless indigenes, the Red House pre-colonials created their own histories through dynamic social relations and a multiplicity of practical actions that are often reflected in the archaeological record (Gosden 1994; Reid 2009; Wolf 1982).

NOTES

1. Images of the Red House burials can be reviewed in the following: B.A. Reid, *Red House Restoration Archaeology Project Report, Phase 1, for the Period July 1, 2013–January 31, 2015*. This book can be accessed via UWILinc of the University of the West Indies: http://uwin-primo.hosted.exlibrisgroup.com /primo_library/libweb/action/search.do;jsessionid=55CE252FBBBB582D

9C9959AEBB40C122?fn=search&ct=search&initialSearch=true&mode
=Basic&tab=everything_tab&indx=1&dum=true&srt=rank&vid=STA&frbg=&t
b=t&vl%28freeText0%29=red+house+restoration+report%3B+basil+reid&scp
.scps=scope%3A%28%22OPE%22%29%2Cscope%3A%28STA%29%2
Cscope%3A%28MON%29%2Cscope%3A%28%22CAV%22%29%2Cprimo_central
_multiple_fe. Also, National Library and Information Systems Authority (Trinidad
and Tobago), the University of Trinidad and Tobago library and the National Library
of Jamaica: http://nlj.worldcat.org/title/red-house-restoration-archaeology-project
-office-of-the-parliament-of-the-republic-of-trinidad-and-tobago-final-report-phase
-1-for-the-period-july-1-2013-january-31-2015/oclc/950021149&referer=brief_results.

2. The timeline of Saladoid colonization in Trinidad should have ended in 600 CE
    and in the northern Lesser Antilles around 800/900 CE. However, the presence of
    Saladoid-type pottery well into the fourteenth century – a period generally consid-
    ered to be post-Saladoid – suggests that there was a local, resident native population
    at the Red House site for over twelve hundred years. The original Saladoid settlers
    simply reproduced themselves, establishing a relatively large village community
    in this area until the late fourteenth century.

3. Although preceding Archaic Age groups in the Caribbean (both the Ortoiroid and
    Casimiroid) practised some level of plant manipulation, the Saladoid were the first
    fully horticultural native people to have colonized the Caribbean. Upon entering
    the Caribbean around 500 BCE, the Saladoid quickly settled all of the islands of the
    region from Trinidad and Tobago in the south to as far as Puerto Rico in the north
    (Reid 2009).

4. While the Red House pre-colonial ceramics are distinctly Saladoid, certain defin-
    ing characteristics of the assemblage suggest that they can properly be defined as
    Saladoid (Palo Seco). Palo Seco pottery is a local adaptation of the Saladoid pottery
    series with several of its traits (especially after 350 CE), resulting from trade/interac-
    tion between the Saladoid of Trinidad and the Barrancoid of South America (Sajo
    2014). The typical characteristics of Palo Seco pottery are moderately thick, coarse
    and soft, grit-tempered pottery, geometric lugs and modelled, incised *adornos*,
    few of which show concave backs (Boomert 2000). The radiocarbon dates of the
    Palo Seco assemblage range from the time of Christ to 650 CE. Palo Seco pottery
    vessels come in a variety of shapes and sizes. The common forms are bowls with a
    wide range of rims, from thick to elaborate compound rims. Other vessel shapes
    include asymmetrical, bottle-like vessels, spouted vessels, almost pear-shaped jars,
    and double-spouted jars. Decoratively, Palo Seco pottery show painted, incised,
    punctuated and modelled motifs. Painted decoration is defined especially by white-
    on-red painting, sometimes combined with black-painted designs and black painted
    lines separating white- and red-painted areas. The gradual adoption of Barrancoid
    ceramic modes by the Palo Seco potters of Trinidad reflects the growing interac-
    tion between the Saladoid communities of the island and Los Barrancos (Classic
    Barrancas) complex, which had been developing on the Lower Orinoco since the
    first centuries of our era (Boomert 2013).

REFERENCES

Arnold, D.E. 1988. *Ceramic Theory and Cultural Process*. Cambridge: Cambridge University Press.

Barfield, T., ed. 1987. *The Dictionary of Anthropology*. Oxford: Oxford University Press.

Bissessar, A., and J.G. La Guerre. 2015. *Trinidad and Tobago and Guyana: Race and Politics in Two Plural Societies*. Lanham, MD: Lexington Books.

Bohannan, P. 1953. Concepts of Time among the Tiv of Nigeria. *Southwestern Journal of Anthropology* 9, no. 3 (Autumn): 251–62.

Boomert, A. 2000. *Trinidad, Tobago and the Lower Orinoco Interaction Sphere: An Archaeological/Ethnohistorical Study*. Alkmaar, the Netherlands: Cairi.

———. 2013. Gateway to the mainland. In *The Oxford Handbook of Caribbean Archaeology*, edited by W.F. Keegan, C. Hofman and R. Rodriguez Ramos, 141–54. Oxford: Oxford University Press.

Bradley, R. 1991. "Ritual, Time and History". *World Archaeology* 23:209–19.

———. 2002. *The Past in Prehistoric Societies*. London: Routledge.

Breton, R. 1978 [1647]. *Relations de l'ile de la Guadeloupe*. Vol. 1. Basee-Terre, St Kitts: Société d'histoire de la Guadeloupe.

Brumfiel, E.M. 1992. "Distinguished Lecture in Archaeology: Breaking and Entering the Ecosystem-Gender, Class, and Faction Steal the Show". *American Anthropologist* 94:551–65.

Cobb, C.R. 2005. "Archaeology and the 'Savage Slot': Displacement and Emplacement in the PreModern World". *American Anthropologist* 107 (4): 563–74.

Clark, G. 1992. *Space, Time and Man: A Prehistorian's View*. Cambridge: Cambridge University Press.

Daniel, G. 1962. *The Idea of Prehistory*. Baltimore: Penguin Books.

Darvill, T. 2002. *The Concise Oxford Dictionary of Archaeology*. Oxford: Oxford University Press.

Dietler, M., and I. Herbich. 1993. "Living on Luo Time: Reckoning Sequence, Duration, History and Biography in a Rural African Society". *World Archaeology* 25, no. 2 (*Conceptions of Time and Ancient Society*): 248–60.

Dornan, J.L. 2002. "Agency and Archaeology: Past, Present and Future Directions". *Journal of Archaeological Method and Theory* 9, no. 4 (December): 303–29.

Evans-Pritchard, E. 1939. "Nuer Time-reckoning". *Africa: Journal of the International African Institute* 12:189–216.

Fagan, B. 2002. *World Prehistory: A Brief Introduction*. 5th ed. Englewood, NJ: Prentice-Hall.

Fabian, J. 1983. *Time and the Other: How Anthropology Makes Its Object*. New York: Columbia University Press.

Gamble, L.H. 2017. "Feasting, Ritual Practices, Social Memory, and Persistent Places: New Interpretations of Shell Mounds in Southern California". *American Antiquity* 82 (3): 427–51.

Gell, A. 1996. *The Anthropology of Time*. Oxford: Berg.

Gillespie, S.D. 2007. Comment on "Eventful Archaeology: The Place of Space in Structural Transformation" by R. Beck, D. Bolender, J. Brown and T. Earle. *Current Anthropology* 48:846–47.

Gilmore, Z.I., and J.M. O'Donoughue, eds. 2015. *The Archaeology of Events: Cultural Change and Continuity in the Pre-Columbian Southeast.* Tuscaloosa: University of Alabama Press.

Gosden, C. 1994. *Social Being and Time.* Blackwell.

Hantman, J.L. 2013. "Sites in History, History in Sites: Archaeology, Historical Anthropology, and Indigenous Knowledge in the Chesapeake". In Schmidt and Mrozowski 2013, 201–19. Oxford: Oxford University Press.

Harding, J. 2005. "Rethinking the Great Divide: Long-Term Structural History and the Temporality of Events. *Norwegian Archaeological Review* 38:88–101.

Hastrup, K. 1992. *Other Histories.* London: Routledge.

Hendon, J.A. 2010. *Houses in a Landscape: Memory and Everyday Life in Mesoamerica.* Durham, NC: Duke University Press.

Hofman, C.L., and B.A. Reid. 2014. "The Saladoid". In Reid and Gilmore 2014, 300–3.

Hoogland, L.P., and C.L. Hofman. 2013. "From Corpse Taphonomy to Mortuary Behavior in the Caribbean: A Case Study from the Lesser Antilles". In *The Oxford Handbook of Caribbean Archaeology*, edited by W.F. Keegan, C. Hofman and R. Rodriguez Ramos. Oxford: Oxford University Press, 452–69.

Keegan, W.F., and C.L. Hofman. 2017. *The Caribbean Before Columbus.* Oxford: Oxford University Press.

Kooyman, B.P. 2001. Understanding Stone Tools and Archaeological Sites. Albuquerque: University of New Mexico Press.

Lévi-Strauss, C. 1966. *The Savage Mind.* Chicago: University of Chicago Press.

Luby, E.M., and M.F. Gruber. 1999. "The Dead Must be Fed: Symbolic Meanings of the Shellmounds of the San Francisco Bay Area". In *Cambridge Archaeological Journal* 9 (1): 95–108.

Meskell, L. 2007. "Back to the Future: From the Past in the Present to the Past in the Past". In *Negotiating the Past in the Past*, edited by Norman Yoffee, 215–26. Tucson: University of Arizona Press.

Miller, D., and C. Tilley. 1984. *Ideology, Power and Prehistory.* Cambridge: Cambridge University Press.

Morsink, J. 2009. "A 'Maison'-Perspective on Social Practices and Development in the Pre-Columbian Caribbean". Paper presented at the 23rd International Congress for Caribbean Archaeology, Antigua.

Murphy, A.R., D.J. Hozjan, C.N. de Mille and A.A. Levinson. 2000. "Pre-Columbian Gems and Ornamental Materials from Antigua, West Indies". *Gems and Gemology* 36 (3): 234–45.

Pané, F.R. 1999. *An Account of the Antiquities of the Indians.* Durham, NC: Duke University Press.

Ray, K.W. 1987. "Material Metaphor, Social Interaction and Historical Reconstructions: Exploring Patterns of Association and Symbolism in the Igbo-Ukwu Corpus". In *The Archaeology of Contextual Meanings,* edited by I. Hodder, 66–78. Cambridge: Cambridge University Press.

Reichel-Dolmatoff, G. 1971. *Amazonian Cosmos: The Sexual and Religious Symbolism of the Turkano Indians.* Chicago: University of Chicago Press.

Reid, B.A. 2004. "Reconstructing the Saladoid Religion in Trinidad and Tobago". *Journal of Caribbean History* 38, 2 (2004): 243–78.

———. 2009. *Myths and Realities of Caribbean History.* Tuscaloosa: University of Alabama Press.

———. 2014. "Lapidary Trade". In Reid and Gilmore 2014, 218.

———. 2015. *Red House Restoration Archaeology Report, Phase 1, for the Period July 1, 2013–January 31, 2015.* Port of Spain: Office of the Parliament of the Republic of Trinidad and Tobago.

Reid, B.A., and L.A. Curet. 2014. "Elite Exchange in the Caribbean". In Reid and Gilmore 2014, 140–41.

Reid, B.A., and R.G. Gilmore III, eds. 2014. *Encyclopedia of Caribbean Archaeology.* Gainesville: University Press of Florida.

Righter, E. 2002. *The Tutu Archaeological Village Site: A Multi-disciplinary Case Study in Human Adaptation (Interpreting the Remains of the Past).* London: Routledge.

Rizvi, U.A. 2013. "Creating Prehistory and Protohistory: Constructing Otherness and Politics of Contemporary Indigenous Populations in India". In Schmidt and Mrozowski 2013, 141–57.

Roe, P.G. 1982. *The Cosmic Zygote: Cosmology in the Amazon Basin.* Rutgers University Press: New Brunswick.

———. 1997. "Just Wasting Away: Taíno Shamanism and Concepts of Fertility". In *Taíno Pre-Columbian Art and Culture from the Caribbean,* edited by F. Bercht, E. Brodsky, J.A. Farmer and D. Taylor. New York: Monacelli, 124–57.

Roget, P. 1997. "The Taino Vision: A Study in the Exchange of Misunderstanding". In *The Indigenous People of the Caribbean,* edited by Samuel M. Wilson. Gainesville: University Press.

Sahlins, M. 1981. *Historical Metaphors and Mythical Realities: Structure in the Early History of the Sandwich Islands Kingdom.* Special Publication No. 1, Association for the Study of Anthropology in Oceania. Ann Arbor: University of Michigan Press.

———. 1987. *Islands of History.* Chicago: University of Chicago Press.of Florida: 100–8.

———. 1992. *The Tainos: Rise and Decline of the People Who Greeted Columbus.* New Haven, CT: Yale University Press.

Sajo, A. 2014. "Palo Seco (Trinidad)". In Reid and Gilmore 2014, 273–74.

Sajo, A., and P.E. Siegel. 2014. "Zemíes (Cemíes)". In Reid and Gilmore 2014, 355.

Sassaman, K.E. 2010. "Getting from the Late Archaic to Early Woodland in Three Middle Valleys (Those Being the Savannah, St Johns, and Tennessee)". In *Trend, Tradition and Turmoil: What Happened to the Southeastern Archaic? Proceedings of the Third Caldwell Conference, St Catherines Island, Georgia, May 9–11, 2008,* edited by David Hurst Thomas and Matthew C. Sanger, 229–35. Anthropological Papers of the American Museum of Natural History 93, New York.

Schmidt, P.R. 1996. "Rhythmed Time and Its Archaeological Implications". In *Aspects of African Archaeology: Papers of the 10th PanAfrican Association for Prehistory and Related Studies,* edited by G. Pwiti and R. Soper, 654–59. Harare: University of Zimbabwe Publications.

———. 1997a. "Archaeological Views on a History of Landscape Change in East Africa". *Journal of African History* 38:393–421.

————. 1997b. *Iron Technology in East Africa: Symbolism, Science, and Archaeology*. Bloomington: Indiana University Press.

————. 2013. "Historical Archaeology, Colonial Entanglements, and Recupertaing: 'Timeless' Histories through Structuralism". In Schmidt and Mrozowski 2013, 92–116.

Schmidt, P.R., and S.A. Mrozowski, eds. 2013. *The Death of Prehistory*. Oxford: Oxford University Press.

Schmidt, P.R., and T.C. Patterson, eds. 1995. *Making Alternative Histories: The Practice of Archaeology and History in Non-Western Settings*. Santa Fe: School of American Research Press.

Schultz, J.J., and P.L. Meyers. 2015. *Analysis of Human Skeletons Recovered during the Red House Archaeology Project*. Prepared for Basil Reid, lead archaeologist, Red House Restoration Archaeological Excavation Team Office of the Parliament of the Republic of Trinidad and Tobago, G-7 Tower D, Port of Spain International Waterfront Centre, 1A Wrightson Road, Port of Spain, Trinidad and Tobago.

Siegel, P.E. 1996. "Ideology and Culture Change in Puerto Rico: A View from the Community". *Journal of Field Archaeology*, 23:313–33.

Shanks, M., and C. Tilley. 1987. "Abstract and Substantial Time". In *Archaeological Reviews from Cambridge* 6:32–41.

Tarlow, S., and L.N. Stutz, eds. 2013. *The Oxford Handbook of the Archaeology of Death and Burial*. Oxford Handbooks. Oxford: Oxford University Press.

Thompson, E.P. 1967. "Time, Work-Discipline, and Industrial Capitalism". *Past and Present*, no. 38 (December): 56–97.

Thompson, V.D. 2010. "The Rhythms of Space-Time and the Making of Monuments and Places during the Archaic". In *Trend, Tradition, and Turmoil: What Happened to the Southeastern Archaic*, edited by David Hurst Thomas and Matthew C. Sangar, 217–27. New York: American Museum of Natural History.

Van del Bel, M., and T. Romon. 2010. "A Troumassoid Site at Trois-Rivières, Guadeloupe FWI: Funerary Practices and House Patterns at La Pointe de Grande Anse". *Journal of Caribbean Archaeology* 9:1–17.

Wilson, S.M. 2007. *Archaeology of the Caribbean*. Cambridge: Cambridge University Press.

Wolf, E. 1982. *Europe and the People without History*. Berkeley: University of California Press.

CHAPTER 2

Mitochondrial DNA Analysis of Pre-contact Human Remains from the Red House Site

MICHEL SHAMOON-POUR, LARS FEHREN-SCHMITZ,
D. ANDREW MERRIWETHER AND BASIL A REID

THE GROWING BODY OF RESEARCH ON THE GENETICS of populations from around
the globe provides a unique insight into the demographic events by which
humans populated the earth. In order to make inferences about the modes and
routes of past migrations, molecular anthropologists utilize the genetic data
obtained from present-day as well as ancient populations. The genetic study of
past populations is possible through the analysis of ancient DNA (aDNA) – the
genetic material extracted from the human remains. Due to the better preservation of DNA in skeletal remains, bones and teeth are the most likely sources of
aDNA. That said, any type of biological material is a potential source of aDNA.
When human aDNA is available, we are able to investigate the relationship
between ancient societies and modern populations, and to establish the inter-
relatedness of individuals within the archaeological contexts, as well as their
genetic traits. The non-human aDNA can also inform anthropological study:
plant and animal aDNA can reveal the complicated histories of domestication,
and aDNA from pathogens can help understanding the spread of infectious
diseases among ancient societies.

Here we present for the first time the results of our study of human remains
discovered during the excavation at Port of Spain's Red House site. Genetic analysis was performed at the University of California Santa Cruz and Binghamton
University. Mitochondrial single nucleotide polymorphisms (SNPs) and partial
sequences were identified for twenty pre-colonial individuals, making definitive
haplogroup assignment possible in seventeen cases. All individuals belonged
to Amerindian lineages of mitochondrial haplogroups C1 (10), A (4), D1 (2)
and B (1). Overall, the makeup of lineages observed in the Red House sample
resembles that of the present-day Trinidadian First Peoples as well as the pre-
colonial populations of the Caribbean. Our results also confirm the presence of
lineages in pre-contact Trinidad which are closely related to lineages reported

from contemporary populations of South America. This chapter presents the first genetic study of pre-colonial human remains in Trinidad and Tobago and should therefore be considered as highly significant for the archaeological study of the twin island republic as well as the wider Caribbean.

BACKGROUND INFORMATION

The period 1 July 2013 to 31 January 2015 is considered to be phase 1 of the Red House Restoration Archaeological Project. However, during the period March to May 2013, there were limited archaeological activities at the Red House that were spearheaded by the late Peter Harris. Following the discovery of human skeletal remains during this preliminary phase, bone fragments and teeth belonging to six individuals were submitted for genetic analysis to Dr D. Andrew Merriwether's Ancient DNA Laboratories in the Anthropology Department of Binghamton University, Binghamton, New York. These samples – comprised of molars and premolars (from CEP 9, CEP 13, CEP 4, BM 5), skull fragments (from CEP 5) and fragments of (most probably) humerus (from CEP 3) – were tested by Dr Michel Shamoon-Pour. During phase 1 of the Red House Restoration Archaeological Project, forty-seven samples of bone (skull fragments, diaphysis fragments) and teeth from thirty-one individuals were dispatched to the University of California Santa Cruz (UCSC) Paleogenomics Lab, where they were genetically tested by Dr Lars Fehren-Schmitz.

Radiocarbon dating of approximately forty samples from the Red House site indicate that the human remains recovered from the site all belonged to individuals who lived during the pre-colonial or pre-contact era, with the time-line ranging from 125 to 1395 CE (Reid 2015). Of the thirty-one sets of remains, twenty-four were dated at the tenth to fourteenth centuries CE, while the rest yielded timelines from the third to seventh centuries CE.

Additionally, sixty complete and incomplete human skeletons were unearthed from the Red House basement. This number includes forty-seven adults and thirteen juveniles (Schultz and Meyers 2015). Adults include young, middle and older age classes. Juveniles represent one infant (<1 year), eight young children (1–6 years), three older children (6–12 years) and one adolescent (12–20 years) (see chapter 9, this volume). As indicated in both the introduction and chapter 1 of this volume, the makers of the pre-colonial pottery found at the Red House site appear to be Saladoid and post-Saladoid peoples.

METHODOLOGY

Upon arrival, samples from the Red House site sent to the UCSC Paleogenomics Lab were prepared for ancient DNA extraction following standardized protocols to minimize the risk of DNA contaminations as described by Fehren-Schmitz et al. (2010). In the case of bone fragments, small pieces were cut out using a dentist hand-tool with a diamond-tip saw blade. All samples were immersed in bleach for several minutes, then rinsed with purified, DNA-free water and dried by exposing both sides to ultraviolet (UV) light. The cleaned samples were then pulverized using a ball mill, and the bone powders were stored at −20° C. Bone and tooth powder inputs for each extraction weighed 0.1 gram. Extraction of DNA followed protocols described by Fehren-Schmitz et al. (2014). For each sample, at least two independent sets of extractions were performed.

Similarly, samples submitted to Binghamton University were handled according to standard protocols of D. Andrew Merriwether's ancient DNA laboratories in order to minimize DNA contamination. Samples were handled only inside the ancient DNA extraction laboratory, where positive air pressure inhibits the flow of the air from outside. The entire lab surfaces are regularly decontaminated with bleach and exposure to the UV light. The specimens were first cleaned and decontaminated by rinsing in DNA-free deionized water, followed by immersion in bleach for three minutes, further rinsing with water and finally exposing specimens to UV for ten minutes each side. After decontamination, specimens of about 0.1 gram of tooth or bone powder were drilled from each individual set of remains. DNA extraction was performed according to a revised version of Yang et al.'s (1998) protocol. This protocol includes decalcification of powder by spinning in 2 ml EDTA (0.5 M) in room temperature for ninety-six hours, followed by centrifuging at 700 rpm for one minute and then incubating in a solution of 1.5 ml dH_2O and 0.5 ml ProteinaseK (20 mg/ml) at 30 rpm at 55° C for two days. Two ml of each sample were then transferred to a filtered centrifugal tube and centrifuged at 5,100 rpm for thirty minutes. Samples were washed by 750 μl PB buffer and then transferred to a filtered Qiagen column. After centrifuging at 12,800 xg for one minute, samples were washed with 750 μl PE buffer and subsequently centrifuged once again at 12,800 for one minute. The columns were then transferred into a 2 ml screw-cap tube and samples dissolved in 100 μl of TE buffer. Extraction controls were used to detect possible contamination. For each specimen, the entire process of decontaminating, drilling and extraction was carried out at least twice.

At the UCSC Paleogenomics Lab, the preservation of mitochondrial DNA (mtDNA) extracted from samples was first tested by amplifying a 156 bp fragment of the mtDNA Hypervariable Region 1 (HVR1). This small fragment comprises many SNPs used to determine Amerindian mtDNA haplogroups. Also, in order to get the complete sequence of the HVR1 region, polymerase chain reaction (PCR) tests were conducted using a set of primers that target three overlapping fragments encompassing positions 16024 to 16425. The details of PCR setup, including the primers sequences and conditions, as well as other downstream applications, are described by Fehren-Schmitz et al. (2010). Amplification success was tested by running amplicons on 2.5% agarose gels. Analysis of the sequence data was performed with Big Dye Terminator chemistry on an ABI Prism 310 Genetic Analyzer (Applied Biosystems, Foster City, CA).

To further determine the mtDNA haplogroups, a multiplex amplification system was employed that types twenty-six mtDNA coding region SNPs in parallel (Coutinho et al. 2014). The advantage of applying this methodology in our study of ancient samples is that it utilizes DNA fragments that are several times smaller than fragments targeted in the previously mentioned PCR-sequencing methods. Due to the highly fragmented character of ancient DNA, there is a low probability that fragment sizes above 100bp are preserved in the ancient specimen, leading to higher success rate of this method relative to sequencing of HVR1 fragments. Fragment length analysis for the SNPs followed, and this employed single base extension (SBE) PCR and capillary electrophoresis. Also, to genotype the Y-chromosomal haplogroups of male individuals, a similar multiplex SBE approach was taken. Targeting nine Y-chromosomal SNPs, this assay made the identification of most Amerindian Q and C haplogroups possible. Protocols, primers and experimental conditions are described by Fehren-Schmitz et al. (2011). If initial amplifications proved to be successful, the PCR was replicated at least three times, generating four independent PCR results for each fragment amplified. This procedure was performed for each of the two extracts generated from each sample.

DNA extracted from seven sets of samples in D. Andrew Merriwether's lab in Binghamton University was tested to amplify a 409bp long sequence that encompassed the HVR1 region of mtDNA. This was made possible by amplifying four overlapping fragments targeted by primers shown in table 2.1. PCR reactions were set at the volume of 25 μl as following: 3 μl extract, 1 U platinum *Taq* (Invitrogen Ltd; www.invitrogen.com), 2.5 μl PCR buffer, 1.5 μl MgSO$_4$ (25 mM), 0.5 μl dNTP and 0.25 μl of each primer (20 μM). Negative and positive controls were used in all PCR runs. Further PCR tests used the same protocol, except higher volumes of template (6 μl, 10 μl) or dilutions of extract (1/10, 1/20 and 1/60) were used to overcome the lack of success in DNA amplification. Primary PCR tests using 3, 6 and 10 μl of templates did not produce positive results. Following an inhibition test proving the presence of moderate to strong inhibition in all extractions, a series of PCR tests using serial dilutions of extracts were performed, yielding positive results for at least one primer set for all specimens. In all tests, negative controls failed to amplify. Sequencing was performed on an ABI 3730xl DNA Analyzer (Applied Biosystems, Foster City, CA). Haplogrep2 (Weissensteiner et al. 2016) was used to assign sequences to haplogroups according to PhyloTree Build 17 (van Oven and Kayser 2009).

Table 2.1. Primers and Conditions Used for Amplification of HVR1 Region

Primer	Sequence (5'–3')	Annealing Temp
16021F	CTGTTCTTTCATGGGGAAGC	55 C°
16156R	CTACAGGTGGTCAAGTATTTAT	
16106F	GCCAGCCACCATGAATATTGT	58 C°
16251R	GGAGTTGCAGTTGATGTGTGAT	
16190F	CCATGCTTACAAGCAAGT	53 C°
16355R	GGGATTTGACTGTAATGTGCT	
16327F	CGTACATAGCACATTACAGT	51 C°
16429R	GCGGGATATTGATTTCACGG	

RESULTS

The UCSC Paleogenomics Lab

The mtDNA haplogroup was successfully determined for fifteen out of thirty-one individuals whose remains were studied (table 2.2). All these individuals belonged to later periods and were dated to the eleventh to fourteenth century CE. Also, Y-chromosomal SNPs were successfully typed for two of these individuals. Given that age of samples adversely affect the preservation of DNA, it is not surprising that successful retrieval of genetic data was mostly limited to samples from the latest periods. The lack of amplification success for 55% of samples can directly be correlated with the poor state of preservation of the specimen. In general, poor DNA preservation in the Caribbean is expected due to the tropical environment (Burger et al. 1999, Lalueza-Fox et al. 2001, 2003).

Of the successfully analysed samples, a majority (66.6%) belong to Haplogoup C, comprised of 26.6% C1b (four individuals) and 40% C1d (six individuals). Haplogroups A2 and D1 were each found in 13.3% of the sample (two individuals), and one individual was assigned to haplogroup B2 (6.6%). In comparison with previous studies, a majority of these haplogroups, specifically A2, C1b and D1, have been identified as the main mtDNA lineages of pre-Columbian Taíno and Ciboney populations (Lalueza-Fox et al. 2001, 2003). The other haplogroups found among the Red House individuals, C1d and B2, are known to be present in very low frequencies in modern populations of the Antilles but are prevalent among populations of central and northern Venezuela (Gõmez-Carballa et al. 2012; Lee and Merriwether 2015). The A2, C1b and D haplotypes observed in the Red House sample most likely reflects a continuous gene flow from mainland

Table 2.2. Haplogroup Assignment of Fifteen Red House Individuals Studied at the UCSC Paleogenomics Lab

Unit	Section	Lab Sample No	mtDNA Haplogroup
Section A, CEP 7	CEP7	RH9	C1b
Section A, G38, Sd 2	G38	RH20	D1
Section A, G43, Sd 1	G43	RH14	A2
Crawl Space NE, Sd (1)	NE_CS	RH5	B2
Crawl Space NE, Sd (2)	NE_CS	RH1	C1d1
Section A, North Parliament Chamber, Sd2	NPC	RH13	C1b
Section A, NPC, Sd (1)	NPC	RH7	C1d1
Section A, NPC, Sd (2)	NPC	RH6	C1d1
Section A, North Parliament Chamber, Sd7	NPC	RH10	C1d1c1
Crawl Space NW, Sd (2)	NW_CS	RH2	C1d1
Section B, Rotunda Fountain Area, Sd 7	RFA	RH11	A2
Section B, Rotunda Fountain Area, Sd 8	RFA	RH24	C1b
Section B, Rotunda Fountain Area, Sd 5	RFA	RH25	C1b
Section B, Rotunda Fountain Area, Sd 7	RFA	RH8	C1d1c1
Section B, Rotunda Fountain Area, Sd 8	RFA	RH21	D1

South America into the Lesser Antilles during the later pre-contact periods, as was suggested by Lalueza-Fox et al. (2003) and Moreno-Estrada et al. (2013).

Furthermore, the Y-chromosome SNP typing of two individuals from the Red House site verified that they belonged to the Amerindian Y haplogroup Q1a3a (also referred to as Q-M3). This haplogroup is most prevalent in South and Central American populations (Bisso-Machado et al. 2012). Overall, these results confirm an Amerindian origin of both maternal and paternal lineages for these individuals.

Binghamton University

Sequencing of HVR1 region led to the identification of partial sequences for five of seven individuals whose remains were studied. Table 2.3 summarizes these results.

While the short length of reproduced sequences made definitive assignment of haplogroups difficult, sequences for two individuals can be definitely assigned to mtDNA haplogroup A. More specifically, sequence for one individual (CEP 5) matches only two lineages of haplogroup A as defined in the latest version of Phylotree (van Oven and Kayser 2009): A2ai, previously reported in Mexican Americans (Kumar et al. 2011; Diroma et al. 2014), and A2ac, which has been found among Cayapa of Ecuador (Tamm et al. 2007) and among Columbians from Medellin (Diroma et al. 2014).

In case of CEP 9, a rather rare combination of four SNPs can be identified as haplogroup C1b10, which has previously been reported from Mexico (Kumar et al. 2011). It should be noted that C1b10 is the only possible match based on the assumption of an Amerindian American ancestry. From a global perspective, this partial mtDNA sequence is also a match for F1 haplogroup, a subclade restricted to South Asia.

The HVR1 partial sequence of the CEP 4 individual presents an interesting challenge in that none of the three SNPs found in this haplotype (16073A, 16094d, 16394T) have been previously described in association with any particular haplogroup. In fact, these mutations have rarely been reported before. An extensive research in previous studies led to discovery of two individuals reported with mutation 16073A and two others with mutation 16394T. Samples with 16073A included a haplogroup B4 individual from China (Gan et al. 2008) and a B5

Table 2.3. mtDNA Mutations and Predicted Haplogroups for Samples Studied at Binghamton University

Specimen	Sequence Range(s)	Mutations (based on rCRS)	mtDNA Haplogroup	Other Possible Haplogroups
CEP5	16192–16317	16213A, 16223T, 16290T	A2ai or A2ac	None
CEP13	16106–16156, 16273–16355	16290T, 16319A	A	None
CEP9	16021–16252	16129A, 16162G, 16172C, 16218T	C1b101*	F1a1
CEP4	16021–16156, 16381–16429	16073A, 16094d, 16394T	?	None of these SNPs have been defined in Phylotree
CEP3	16024–16251	16126C, 16224C	?	Numerous Hgs (due to small size of sequence)

*C1b10 is the only possible match under the assumption that this sample is indeed Native American.

individual from the Philippines (Delfin et al. 2014). 16394T was detected in one individual belonging to haplogroup B2 from Brazil (Prieto et al. 2011) as well as a haplogroup D mitogenome with inconsistent mutations (Behar et al. 2007) of unknown origin. The third mutation, 16094d, has been listed in Behar et al.'s (2012) as a deletion previously identified in mtDNA, but we were not able to identify any sample with this mutation in previous studies.

DISCUSSION

All Amerindian mtDNA lineages belong to subclades of only five haplogroups: A, B, C, D and X (Schurr 2004). While some lineages of these haplogroups are exclusive to certain regions, the rest are present in different frequencies in populations across North, Central, and South America. Previous mtDNA studies have provided evidence for continuity of indigenous maternal lineages in the Caribbean. Our current knowledge of the mtDNA diversity in the present-day Caribbean is mainly informed by studies from three large islands of the Greater Antilles (Cuba, Hispaniola, Puerto Rico), as well as two Lesser Antilles islands of Trinidad and St Vincent (Benn Torres et al. 2015; Feliciano Velez, 2007; Marcheco-Teruel et al. 2014; Martinez-Cruzado et al, 2005; Mendizabal et al. 2008; Moreno-Estrada et al. 2013; Vilar et al. 2014). Overall, the results of the Caribbean population genetic studies point to differences between Greater and Lesser Antillean populations as well as variation between and within the islands in each region. The results of these studies hint at multiple migratory events and several expansions from South America into the Caribbean, as well as possibility of Mesoamerican contribution to the peopling of the Greater Antilles. So far, only a few aDNA studies have investigated the genetics of the pre-contact Caribbean populations (Lalueza-Fox et al. 2001, 2003; Mendisco et al. 2015; Nieves-Colón 2014). The analysis of mtDNA recovered from the skeletal remains found at Taíno sites in the Dominican Republic and Ciboney sites in Cuba has revealed strong affinity between these ancient populations and modern South American populations (Lalueza-Fox et al. 2001, 2003). Similar to linguistics and archaeological evidence, these findings inform the hypotheses on the colonization of the Caribbean islands from South America.

Focusing on the Lesser Antilles, it has been shown that 58% of individuals from the Santa Rosa First Peoples Community in Trinidad and 37% of the Garifuna of St Vincent represent indigenous mtDNA lineages (Benn Torres et al. 2015). All these individuals belonged to lineages from either A2 or C1 haplogroup. While A2 is especially common in Trinidad (71% of indigenous lineages, 42% of total), C1 is the more common haplogroup in St Vincent (56% of indigenous lineages, 21% of total). The only aDNA study of the Lesser Antilles prior to our study (Mendisco et al. 2015) identified mtDNA lineages for thirteen Late Ceramic

Age Guadeloupeans as belonging to A2 (5), C1 (5), and D1 (3) haplogroups. With A2 and C1 being the most common haplogroups in both ancient and contemporary Lesser Antilles, the previous findings signal at a continuous presence of these lineages before and after European contact. Our findings provide further evidence of the genetic make-up of the pre-colonial Lesser Antilles and the continuity of certain subclades in this region. In comparison, the Red House individuals belong to haplogroups C1 (10), A (4), D1 (2) and B (1). Overall, the make-up of lineages observed in the Red House sample resembles that of the ancient Guadeloupeans, and suggest continuity of some lineages in Trinidad.

Genetic analysis performed in the Paelogenomic Labs and Binghamton University proves Amerindian ancestry of all mtDNA lineages identified for human remains excavated from the Red House site. Our results also confirm the presence of lineages that are closely related to lineages reported from contemporary populations of northern South America. This discovery points to a gene flow between South America and Trinidad. This correlates well with archaeological findings that link the Red House site to Saladoid and post-Saladoid cultures, which are believed to have originated in South America (Hofman and Reid 2014; Reid 2015; Rouse 1992).

Our study also reveals the presence of lineages previously described as Mexican. It should be noted that these are rare lineages, which to date have been reported only in a few individuals from Mexico. These Mexican lineages may also be present in other populations in Central and South Americas and the Caribbean but are yet to be identified as such. Regarding the novel haplotype (16073A, 16094d, 16394T) identified for the CEP 4 individual: this individual may be representative of a mtDNA lineage (probably from haplogroup B or D) of native inhabitants of Trinidad and Tobago that have either been lost or have yet to be found in modern populations. This is not surprising, considering that results of previous studies hint at mass extinction of pre-contact mtDNA lineages across South America (Llamas et al. 2016).

Any proper interpretation of aDNA studies requires a clear understanding of the limitations of what the data can and cannot tell us. Perhaps the most important point when interpreting human aDNA results is the fact that individuals' genetic identities often predate their cultural, linguistic, religious and ethnic identities.[1] Moreover, haplotypic data such as mtDNA sequences and haplogroup-defining SNPs are relatively small with low resolution, and as such are not representative of the complete genetic diversity of individuals. Consequently, it is not uncommon for individuals from populations separated by ethnicity, nationality and language to have identical mtDNA or Y-chromosome haplotypes.[2]

CONCLUSION

While results of this study are in agreement with the archaeological context of the Red House samples, definitive assignment of mtDNA lineage for some samples requires a higher data resolution. We are planning to undertake further analysis of the Red House samples by sequencing complete mitochondrial genomes, as well as genome-wide SNP typing. The increased mtDNA resolution will allow for better understanding of the relationship between the lineages identified in the Red House individuals and other ancient and contemporary populations. The genome-wide data will allow us to address a broader range of questions and hypotheses including the population dynamic events such as population admixture, and to identify diachronic changes in the population structure of the pre-contact populations of Trinidad between the third and fourteenth centuries. Once accomplished, the results of these studies will be communicated through publications and presentations to experts in the field, and also to the people of Caribbean descent, particularly Trinidadians and Tobagonians.

NOTES

1. Specifically in regard with mtDNA, the accumulation of full mitogenome data from across the globe in the past decade has made possible more precise estimation of the ages of mtDNA lineages. Highly consistent across the studies and methodologies, the age estimate for most major subclades is in tens of thousands of years (Behar et al. 2012).

2. In fact, it is rarely the case that a haplotype is limited to geopolitical or linguistic boundaries.

REFERENCES

Behar, D.M., S. Rosset, J. Blue-Smith, O. Balanovsky, S. Tzur, D. Comas, R.J. Mitchell, L. Quintana-Murci, C. Tyler-Smith, R.S. Wells and Genographic Consortium. 2007. "The Genographic Project Public Participation Mitochondrial DNA Database". *PLOS Genetics* 3:e104.

Behar, D.M., M. van Oven, S. Rosset, M. Metspalu, E.L. Loogväli, N.M. Silva, T. Kivisild, A. Torroni and R. Villems. 2012. "A 'Copernican' Reassessment of the Human Mitochondrial DNA Tree from Its Root". *American Journal of Human Genetics* 90:675–84.

Benn Torres, J., M.G. Vilar, G.A. Torres, J.B. Gaieski, R. Bharath Hernandez, Z.E. Browne, M. Stevenson, W. Walters, T.G. Schurr and Genographic Consortium. 2015. "Genetic Diversity in the Lesser Antilles and Its Implications for the Settlement of the Caribbean Basin". *PLOS ONE* 10 (10): e0139192.

Bisso-Machado, R., M.C. Bortolini and F.M. Salzano. 2012. "Uniparental Genetic Markers in South Amerindians". *Genetics and Molecular Biology* 35:365–87.

Burger, J., S. Hummel, B. Hermann and W. Henke. 1999. "DNA Preservation: A Microsatellite-DNA Study on Ancient Skeletal Remains". *Electrophoresis* 20:1722–28.

Coutinho, A., G. Valverde, L. Fehren-Schmitz, A. Cooper, M.I. Barreto Romero, I. Flores Espinoza, B. Llamas and W. Haak. 2014. "AmericaPlex26: A Snapshot Multiplex System for Genotyping the Main Human Mitochondrial Founder Lineages of the Americas". *PLOS ONE* 9.

Delfin, F., A. Min-Shan Ko, M. Li, E.D. Gunnarsdóttir, K.A. Tabbada, J.M. Salvador, G.C. Calacal, M.S. Sagum, F.A. Datar, S.G. Padilla, M.C. De Ungria and M. Stoneking. 2014. "Complete mtDNA Genomes of Filipino Ethnolinguistic Groups: A Melting Pot of Recent and Ancient Lineages in the Asia-Pacific Region". *European Journal of Human Genetics* 22 (2): 228–37.

Diroma, M.A., C. Calabrese, D. Simone, M. Santorsola, F.M. Calabrese, G. Gasparre and M. Attimonelli. 2014. "Extraction and Annotation of Human Mitochondrial Genomes from 1,000 Genomes Whole Exome Sequencing Data". *BMC Genomics* 15, Suppl. 3: S2.

Fehren-Schmitz, L., W. Haak, B. Mächtle, F. Masch, B. Llamas, E. Tomasto Cagigao, V. Sossna, K. Schittek, J. Isla Cuadrado, B. Eitel and M. Reindel. 2014. "Climate Change Underlies Global Demographic, Genetic, and Cultural Transitions in Pre-Columbian Southern Peru". *Proceedings of the National Academy of Sciences USA* 111:9443–48.

Fehren-Schmitz, L., M. Reindel, E. Tomasto-Cagigao, S. Hummel and B. Herrmann. 2010. "Pre-Columbian Population Dynamics in Coastal Southern Peru: A Diachronic Investigation of Mtdna Patterns in the Palpa Region by Ancient DNA Analysis". *American Journal of Physical Anthropology* 141:208–21.

Fehren-Schmitz, L., O. Warnberg, M. Reindel, V. Seidenberg, E. Tomasto-Cagigao, J. Isla-Cuadrado, S. Hummel and B. Herrmann. 2011. "Diachronic Investigations of Mitochondrial and Y-Chromosomal Genetic Markers in Pre-Columbian Andean Highlanders from South Peru". *Annals of Human Genetics* 75:266–83.

Feliciano Velez, A. 2007. "Genetic Prints of Amerindian Female Migrations through the Caribbean Revealed by Control Sequences from Dominican Haplogroup A Mitochondrial DNAs". MS thesis, University of Puerto Rico, Mayaguez.

Gan, R.J., S.L. Pan, L.F. Mustavich, Z.D. Qin, X.Y. Cai, J. Qian, C.W. Liu, J.H. Peng, S.L. Li, J.S. Xu, L. Jin, H. Li and Genographic Consortium. 2008. "Pinghua Population as an Exception of Han Chinese's Coherent Genetic Structure". *Journal of Human Genetics* 53 (4): 303–13.

Gómez-Carballa, A., A. Ignacio-Veiga, V. Úlvarez-Iglesias, A. Pastoriza-Mourelle, Y. Ruíz, L. Pineda, Ú. Carracedo and A. Salas. 2012. "A Melting Pot of Multicontinental mtDNA Lineages in Admixed Venezuelans". *American Journal of Physical Anthropology* 147:78–87.

Hofman, C.L., and B.A. Reid. 2014. "The Saladoid". In *Encyclopedia of Caribbean Archaeology*, edited by B.A. Reid and R.G. Gilmore III, 300–303. Gainesville: University Press of Florida.

Kumar, S., C. Bellis, M. Zlojutro, P.E. Melton, J. Blangero and J.E. Curran. 2011. "Large Scale Mitochondrial Sequencing in Mexican Americans Suggests a Reappraisal of Native American Origins". *BMC Evolutionary Biology* 11:293.

Llamas, B., L. Fehren-Schmitz, G. Valverde, J. Soubrier, S. Mallick, N. Rohland, S. Nordenfelt, C. Valdiosera, S.M. Richards, A. Rohlach, M.I. Barreto-Romero, I. Flores-Espinoza, E. Tomasto-Cagigao, L. Watson-Jimenez, K. Makowski, I. Santiago-Leboreiro-Reyna, J. Mansilla-Lory, J.A. Ballivian-Torrez, M.A. Rivera, R.L. Burger, M. Constanza-Ceruti, J. Reinhard, R.S. Wells, G. Politis, C.M. Santoro, V.G. Standen, C. Smith, D. Reich, S.Y.W. Ho, A. Cooper and W. Haak. 2016. "Ancient Mitochondrial DNA Provides High-Resolution Timescale of the Peopling of the Americas". *Science Advances* 2:e1501385.

Lalueza-Fox, C., F.L. Calderón, F. Calafell, B. Morera and J. Bertranpetit. 2001. "MtDNA from Extinct Tainos and the Peopling of the Caribbean". *Annals of Human Genetics* 65:137–51.

Lalueza-Fox, C., M.T.P. Gilbert, A.J. Martínez-Fuentes, F. Calafell and J. Bertranpetit. 2003. "Mitochondrial DNA from Pre-Columbian Ciboneys from Cuba and the Prehistoric Colonization of the Caribbean". *American Journal of Physical Anthropology* 121:97–108.

Lee, E.S., and D.A. Merriwether. 2015. "Identification of Whole Mitochondrial Genomes from Venezuela and Implications on Regional Phylogenies in South America". *Human Biology* 1 (87): 29–38.

Marcheco-Teruel, B., E.J. Parra, E. Fuentes-Smith, A. Salas, H.N. Buttenschøn, D. Demontis, M. Torres-Español, L.C. Marín-Padrón, E.J. Gómez-Cabezas and V. Álvarez-Iglesias. 2014. "Cuba: Exploring the History of Admixture and the Genetic Basis of Pigmentation Using Autosomal and Uniparental Markers". *PLOS Genetics* 10 (7): e1004488.

Martinez-Cruzado, J.C., G. Toro-Labrador, J. Viera-Vera, M.Y. Rivera-Vega, J. Startek, M. Latorre-Esteves, A. Roman-Colon, R. Rivera-Torres, I.Y. Navarro-Millán, E. Gómez-Sánchez and H.Y. Caro-González. 2005. "Reconstructing the Population History of Puerto Rico by Means of mtDNA Phylogeographic Analysis". *American Journal of Physical Anthropology* 128 (1): 131–55.

Mendisco, F., M.H. Pemonge, E. Leblay, T. Romon, G. Richard, P. Courtaud and M.F. Deguilloux. 2015. "Where Are the Caribs? Ancient DNA from Ceramic Period Human Remains in the Lesser Antilles". *Philosophical Transactions of the Royal Society B* 370 (1660): 20130388.

Mendizabal, I., K. Sandoval, G. Berniell-Lee, F. Calafell, A. Salas, A. Martinez-Fuentes and D. Comas. 2008. "Genetic Origin, Admixture, and Asymmetry in Maternal and Paternal Human Lineages in Cuba". *BMC Evolutionary Biology* 8 (1): 213.

Moreno-Estrada, A., S. Gravel, F. Zakharia, J.L. McCauley, J.K. Byrnes, C.R. Gignoux, P.A. Ortiz-Tello, R.J. Martinez, D.J. Hedges, R.W. Morris, C. Eng, K. Sandoval, S. Acevedo-Acevedo, P.J. Norman, Z. Layrisse, P. Parham, J.C. Martinez-Cruzado, E.G. Burchard, M.L. Cuccaro, E.R. Martin and C.D. Bustamante. 2013. "Reconstructing the Population Genetic History of the Caribbean". *PLOS Genetics* 9 (11): e1003925.

Nieves-Colón, M.A. 2014. "Ancient DNA Analysis of Human Skeletal Remains from Pre-Columbian Puerto Rico". *American Journal of Physical Anthropology* 153:196.

Prieto L., B. Zimmermann, A. Goios, A. Rodriguez-Monge, G.G. Paneto, C. Alves, A. Alonso, C. Fridman, S. Cardoso, G. Lima, M.J. Anjos, M.R. Whittle, M. Montesino, R.M. Cicarelli, A.M. Rocha, C. Albarrán, M.M. de Pancorbo, M.F. Pinheiro, M. Carvalho, D.R. Sumita and W. Parson. 2011. "The GHEP-EMPOP Collaboration on mtDNA Population Data: A New Resource for Forensic Casework". *Forensic Science International: Genetics* 5 (2): 146–51.

Reid, B.A. 2015. *Red House Restoration Archaeology Report, Phase 1, for the Period July 1, 2013–January 31, 2015.* Port of Spain: Office of the Parliament of the Republic of Trinidad and Tobago.

Rouse, I. 1992. *The Tainos: Rise and Decline of the People Who Greeted Columbus.* New Haven, CT: Yale University Press.

Schultz, J.J., and P.L. Meyers. 2015. "Analysis of Human Skeletons Recovered during the Red House Archaeology Project". Prepared for Basil Reid, lead archaeologist, Red House Restoration Archaeological Excavation Team Office of the Parliament of the Republic of Trinidad and Tobago, G-7 Tower D, Port of Spain International Waterfront Centre, 1A Wrightson Road, Port of Spain, Trinidad and Tobago.

Schurr T.G. 2004. "The Peopling of the New World: Perspectives from Molecular Anthropology". *Annual Review of Anthropology* 33:551–83.

Tamm, E., T. Kivisild, M. Reidla, M. Metspalu, D.G. Smith, C.J. Mulligan, C.M. Bravi, O. Rickards, C. Martinez-Labarga, E.K. Khusnutdinova, S.A. Fedorova, M.V. Golubenko, V.A. Stepanov, M.A. Gubina, S.I. Zhadanov, L.P. Ossipova, L. Damba, M.I. Voevoda, J.E. Dipierri, R. Villems and R.S. Malhi. 2007. "Beringian Standstill and Spread of Native American Founders". *PLOS ONE* 2 (9): e829.

van Oven, M., and M. Kayser. 2009. "Updated Comprehensive Phylogenetic Tree of Global Human Mitochondrial DNA Variation". *Human Mutation* 30 (2): E386–94. http://www.phylotree.org.

Vilar, M.G., C. Melendez, A.B. Sanders, A. Walia, J.B. Gaieski, A.C. Owings and T.G. Schurr. 2014. "Genetic Diversity in Puerto Rico and Its Implications for the Peopling of the Island and the West Indies". *American Journal of Physical Anthropology* 155 (3): 352–68.

Weissensteiner, H., D. Pacher, A. Kloss-Brandstätter, L. Forer, G. Specht, H.J. Bandelt, F. Kronenberg, A. Salas and S. Schönherr. 2016. "HaploGrep 2: Mitochondrial Haplogroup Classification in the Era of High-Throughput Sequencing". *Nucleic Acids Research* 44 (W1): W58–63.

Yang, D.Y., B. Eng, J.S. Waye, J.C. Dudar and D.R. Saunders. 1998. "Improved DNA Extraction from Ancient Bones Using Silica-Based Spin Columns". *American Journal of Physical Anthropology* 105:539–43.

CHAPTER 3

Multi-Isotopic Analysis of the Red House Site Skeletal Remains

Inferring Paleodiet and Paleomobility from Recovered Bones and Teeth

JOHN KRIGBAUM, GEORGE D. KAMENOV,
LAURA VAN VOORHIS AND BASIL A. REID

ISOTOPIC ANALYSIS PROVIDES A VALUABLE TOOL OFTEN ADOPTED by archaeological research programs that aim to integrate traditional and more "modern" approaches to explore human diversity and complexity in the past. In the Caribbean, stable isotope paleodietary research has focused mainly on issues of diet and ecology (e.g., Keegan and DeNiro 1988; Krigbaum et al. 2013; Laffoon and de Vos 2011; Laffoon et al. 2016a; Norr 2002; Pestle 2010a, 2010b; Stokes 1998). Refined techniques and data on radiogenic strontium (Sr) ratios have been recently generated to address broader-scale questions of circum-Caribbean human and faunal paleomobility (e.g., Laffoon and Hoogland 2012; Laffoon et al. 2013a, 2013b). These data from bone and tooth enamel samples provide independent, individual assessment to interpret mobility and prehistoric social networks. As a result, these isotopic data may shed light on key social aspects of human behavior that would normally not be recovered or interpreted based on materials in the archaeological record.

Here we present a multi-isotopic analysis of a sample of human remains and select fauna recovered from the Red House site in Port of Spain, Trinidad (figure 3.1). Our goals are to address intrasite variation of buried individuals and to situate this important prehistoric sample in broader regional context. Specifically, we integrate light stable isotope ratios of carbon and nitrogen from bone collagen ($\delta^{13}C_{co}$ and $\delta^{15}N_{co}$) with light isotope ratios from bone/tooth enamel apatite ($\delta^{13}C_{ap}$ and $\delta^{18}O_{ap}$), coupling these predominantly dietary data with radiogenic strontium ($^{87}Sr/^{86}Sr$) and lead ($^{20n}Pb/^{204}Pb$) ratios from tooth enamel that serve as proxies of geographical origin (e.g., Bentley 2013). Data presented are comprehensive and include the first published Pb ratios from Trinidad in addition

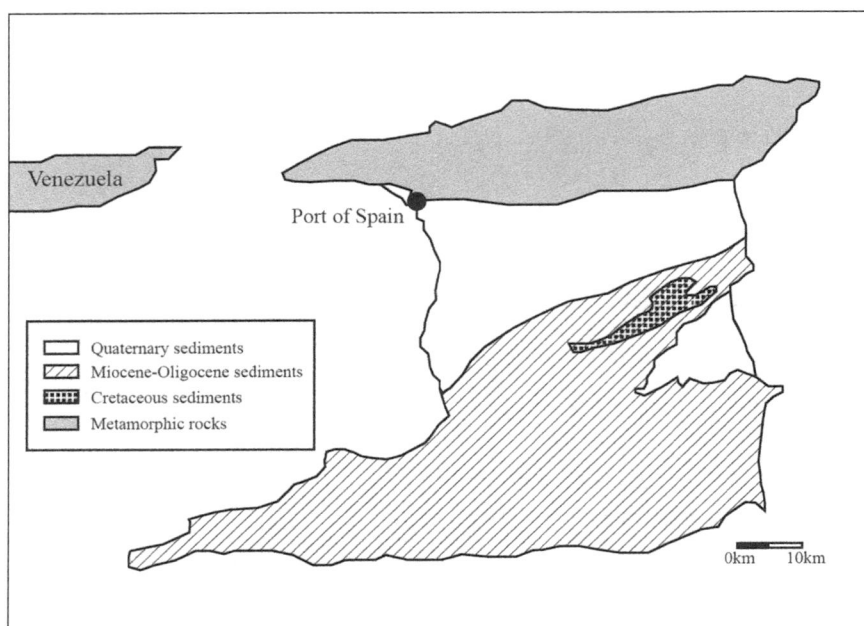

Figure 3.1.
Geological map of
Trinidad.

to a large suite of isotopic data for the Red House site diachronic Saladoid and post-Saladoid contexts.

Recent work by Giovas et al. (2016), Laffoon et al. (2012) and Pestle et al. (2013) demonstrates the inherent complexities in conducting this research. Isotopic data are unique and informative; however, they are also a direct reflection of the diverse ecological and geological backgrounds of the Caribbean. As a result, there are limitations to using isotopic proxies due to issues of equifinality, where similar isotopic results may occur in quite different contexts and/or "origins" across the Greater and Lesser Antilles (e.g., Laffoon et al. 2013a). The development of regional baselines for Sr ratios gleaned from local biota (Bataille et al. 2012; Laffoon et al. 2012) is a critical step toward improving knowledge about isotope variation in the region, but also important are more regionally based, site- and island-specific studies (e.g., Giovas et al. 2016; Laffoon et al. 2016b; Pestle et al. 2013) that highlight the key issues and conundrums in reconstructing human paleodiet and paleomobility. Limitations notwithstanding, the power of combining multi-isotopic analysis with bioarchaeological and zooarchaeological data from solid archaeological contexts offers fresh perspectives on the pre-colonial past of the Red House site.

BACKGROUND INFORMATION

Excavations from 2013 to 2014 yielded sixty human burials and associated remains of human activity in the basement of the Red House (Reid 2015). Focused efforts to date reported in this volume demonstrate the scale and importance of this prehistoric assemblage. Indeed, most of the human remains at the site were radiocarbon dated. While sixty burials were recovered, this isotopic study is based on thirty-eight individuals to address issues of dietary ecology and potential mobility/migration (table 3.1). Of this sample, thirty-one were directly radiocarbon dated (Reid 2015), and these individuals provide the unique opportunity to explore Saladoid (n = 9) and post-Saladoid (n = 22) changes in paleodiet and paleomobility. Before exploring diachronic aspects of diet for the Red House Site assemblage, we will discuss regional variability in prehistoric diet, citing key paleodietary studies (e.g., Healy et al. 2013; Krigbaum et al. 2013; Laffoon et al. 2013a, 2016a; Norr 2002; Pestle 2010a, 2010b; Stokes 1998, 2005) in the eastern circum-Caribbean, including the Lesser Antilles and the easternmost island of the Greater Antilles (i.e., Puerto Rico).

Table 3.1. Red House Human Skeletal Remains Sampled for Isotope Analysis

Burial Number	Level (m)	Cultural Period[1]	Sex[2]	Age[3]	Bone/Teeth Analysed[4]	BCL #[5]
A-CEP4-1	N/A				humerus/rib	2858
A-CEP7-1	1.31	Post-Saladoid	M	SA	rib , 1-M3	2865
A-CEP7-2	N/A				rib	2859
A-CSNE-1-2	1.36–1.54	Post-Saladoid	M	YA	rib, 2-M2s, 1-M3	2801, 2802, 2866
A-CSNE-1-3	1.29–1.45	Post-Saladoid	I	MA-OA	rib/long bone, 1-M1	2863, 2867
A-CSNE-2-1	1.30–1.49	Post-Saladoid	I	MA	rib/long bone, 1-I, 1-C, 1-M2, 1-M3	2799, 2800, 2862, 2868a, 2868b
A-CSNW-2-1	1.14–1.34		F	YA	rib, 2-M2s, 1-M3	2797, 2798, 2869
A-CSNW-4-1	1.30–1.55	Saladoid	I	OA	cranial, 1-M2	2870
A-CSNW-4-2	1.36–1.55	Saladoid	M	OA	rib, 1-M	2892
A-G38-2-1a	1.30–1.49	Post-Saladoid	F	MA-OA	rib, 1-I	2893
A-G38-2-SIP	1.20–1.32	Post-Saladoid	I	OC	long bone, 1-M1	2864
A-G43-1-1	1.05	Post-Saladoid	M	YA	rib	2890
A-G43-1-2a	1.28	Post-Saladoid	M	YA	rib, 1-M1	2871
A-G43-1-3a	1.33	Saladoid	M	MA	rib, 1-I1	2894
A-G43-2-1	1.08	Saladoid	M	MA-OA	rib, 1-PM3	2872
A-G43-2-2	0.37	Post-Saladoid	I	YC	rib	2873
A-G56-1-1	1.21–1.23	Saladoid	M	A	rib	2883

Table 3.1 continues

Table 3.1. Red House Human Skeletal Remains Sampled for Isotope Analysis (*continued*)

Burial Number	Level (m)	Cultural Period[1]	Sex[2]	Age[3]	Bone/Teeth Analysed[4]	BCL #[5]
A-G56-1-2	1.32	Saladoid	PF	A	rib	2884
A-G56-2-1	0.81–0.90	Post-Saladoid	I	A	rib	2885
A-G57-C-1	0.45–0.48		I	YC	long bone, 1-M1	2898
A-G57-C-2	0.47–0.61		PM	MA-OA	cranial, 1-M2	2899
A-G61-2-1	0.35		PM	YA-MA	long bone, 1-M3	2886
A-NPC-1-1	0.30–0.44	Post-Saladoid	PF	OA	long bone	2874
A-NPC-1-3a	0.70–0.83	Saladoid	F	OA	long bone	2875
A-NPC-2-1	0.33–0.47	Post-Saladoid	PM	A	cranial	2876
A-NPC-2-2	0.34–0.61	Post-Saladoid			humerus/rib	2860, 2877
A-NPC-2-3	0.39–0.73	Post-Saladoid	F	MA-OA	femur/rib, 1-PM4	2861, 2878
A-NPC-2-4	0.41–0.63	Post-Saladoid	F	OA	long bone	2879
A-NPC-3-1	0.45–0.64	Post-Saladoid	I	A	long bone, 1-M3	2880
A-NPC-5-1	0.47–0.63	Post-Saladoid	PF	YA	metacarpal/metatarsal	2891
A-NPC-6-1	0.37	Saladoid	F	OA	long bone, 1-PM3	2881
A-NPC-7-1	1.2	Saladoid	M	MA-OA	long bone, 1-M2	2882
B-RFA-5-1	1.13	Post-Saladoid	I	A	rib	2887
B-RFA-5-2	1.5	Post-Saladoid	M	OA	rib, 1-PM3	2895
B-RFA-7-1	1.46–1.56	Post-Saladoid	F	OA	rib, 1-M3	2888
B-RFA-7-2a	1.46–1.56	Post-Saladoid	M	MA	rib, 1-PM	2896
B-RFA-8-1	1.34–1.57	Post-Saladoid	F	MA-OA	rib, 1-I	2897
B-RFA-8-2	1.45	Post-Saladoid	F	YA-MA	rib, 1-I2	2889

[1]Red House Restoration Archaeology Report (Reid 2015, 42–45, 52–54).
[2]I = indeterminate, M = male, PM = probable male, F = female, PF = probable female.
[3]YC = young child, OC = older child, SA = subadult, YA = young adult, MA = mature adult, OA = older adult.
[4]M1 = first molar, M2 = second molar, M3 = third molar, I = incisor, PM = premolar.
[5]Most individuals were assigned one University of Florida BCL number for each bone/tooth pair analysed.

PALEODIET AND PALEOMOBILITY IN THE CIRCUM-CARIBBEAN

Stable isotopes from bone and teeth provide important data for the individual sampled that complement other lines of evidence collected from archaeological sites, such as faunal remains (Katzenberg 2008). Isotopic methods are now well established, and given careful sample selection and screening, preserved bone/teeth may yield signals that are characteristic of past individual diet and potential origin. Stable isotopes of carbon ($\delta^{13}C_{co}$) and nitrogen ($\delta^{15}N_{co}$) from bone collagen, for example, represent dietary protein consumed, while carbon ($\delta^{13}C_{ap}$) from bone or tooth enamel ($\delta^{13}C_{en}$) apatite represents "total" diet consumed (Ambrose 1993). Bone samples tend to provide a long-term average dietary signal for the individual sampled, while particular teeth reflect a more discrete range of time during the period of enamel mineralization. For example, human incisors and the first molar (M1) reflect early childhood diet, which in large part may be reflective of mother's milk (prior to weaning), whereas premolars and the second molar (M2) reflect middle childhood and the third molar (M3) later childhood diet. The analysis of teeth and bone provides a comprehensive dataset that can address myriad questions about individual life history, in addition to providing valuable comparisons between sample populations at both local and regional scales.

Pestle (2013) provides a useful review of the pioneering stages of paleodiet research in the Caribbean, and Laffoon and colleagues (e.g., 2012, 2013a) have reviewed the history of paleomobility studies in the region, and have underscored the need to quantify bioavailable strontium in baseline reconstructions (e.g., Bataille et al. 2012; Laffoon et al. 2016b). These research projects demonstrate the broad complexity of isotopic systems and the conundrums of paleodiet reconstruction, principally because the isotopic composition of potential foodstuffs is so broad (Pestle 2013) and the preservation of organic food remains is often so poor in the archaeological record.

Pestle (2010b) and Stokes (1998, 2005) sample a number of Ceramic Age sites from Puerto Rico in the easternmost Greater Antilles, and the isotopic data generated support a diverse subsistence economy that couples both terrestrial and marine-based food resources, with potential C_4 carbohydrates evident in some sites/samples. Saladoid sites include Maisabel (Laffoon et al. 2013a; Stokes 1998, 2005), Punta Candelero, Tibes and Paso del Indio (Pestle 2010a). A number of studies have focused on diet and isotope ecology in the Eastern Taino region of the Leeward Islands, northern Lesser Antilles. Data from Tutu, St Thomas (Norr 2002), Anse à la Gourde, Guadeloupe (Laffoon and de Vos 2011; Laffoon and Hoogland 2012; Laffoon et al. 2013a) and Saba (Laffoon and Hoogland 2012; Laffoon et al. 2013a) support a predominantly maritime-based diet, with differential inputs of terrestrial food resources depending upon island size and proximity to larger land masses (Stokes 2005).

In the Windward Islands of the southern Lesser Antilles, Krigbaum et al. (2013) present paleodietary data from the Grenadines based on remains recovered from Grand Bay, Carriacou. Although this site is situated not too far north of Trinidad, the findings suggest that reef-based ecosystems and the harvesting of shellfish, in addition to mixed C_3-based terrestrial foods, were characteristic of a largely maritime-based diet. These data are quite distinct from St Lucia, where Laffoon et al. (2016a) published data from human remains recovered from the site of Lavoutte which provides an important contrast to the small island of Carriacou in the Grenadines, as well as to other Leeward Island and Greater Antilles sites discussed above.

Finally, at the southern edge of the Windward Islands in Trinidad, two separate studies have been published to date that include human isotopic data from individuals recovered from the site of Manzanilla on the northeastern part of the island (Healy et al. 2013; Laffoon et al. 2013b). Data reported suggest a C_3-based foraging pattern with moderate marine input (Healy et al. 2013), and a fair degree of variability in Sr ratios suggests diverse origins of several individuals interred at that site (Laffoon et al. 2013a). Although the sample size is low for both studies, the Manzanilla site provides an important contrast to the Red House site data presented below.

TRINIDAD IN GEOLOGICAL CONTEXT

Although Trinidad is often considered to be a socio-economic part of the Caribbean, geographically the island is part of the South American mainland. Trinidad also shares key geological features with Venezuela to the west. The Northern Range of Trinidad is an extension of the Paria Peninsula, Venezuela (Algar and Erikson 1995), which is characterized principally by metamorphic rocks (micaceous and carbonaceous schists, phyllites, quartzites), Mesozoic limestones and recent colluvial and alluvial deposits (figure 3.1; see chapter 7, this volume). The Caroni Plains to the south of the Northern Range are composed mainly of Quaternary alluvial deposits. South of the Caroni Plains, the island's geology is dominated by Miocene-Oligocene sediments with some Cretaceous sedimentary exposures (figure 3.1). The Cretaceous sediments include predominantly dark shales, silicified siltstones and claystones with rare quartzite and limestone outcrops. Similar Cretaceous sediments are found in Venezuela, which suggests broadly similar sedimentary conditions during the Cretaceous. The Tertiary sediments are composed mainly of shales and sandstones (Barr and Saunders 1968). The Paleogene deposits are overlain by younger sandstones and grey silty clays that are likely sourced from the older rocks exposed to the north and south in Trinidad.

This diverse geology should also be reflected in the heavy isotope proxies that can provide signatures of distinct geological regions and their relative age. Hodell et al. (2004), for example, develop a regional baseline data for the Yucatan peninsula and the Mayan lowlands. Their work shows a strong correlation of Sr ratios from bedrock geology to Sr ratios from associated plants and soils. Similarly, Sharpe et al.'s (2016) follow-up demonstrates a similar pattern of variation in Pb ratios, albeit independent of Sr ratios, across the Mayan region. This work, collectively, demonstrates the utility of multi-isotopic analysis to characterize geological areas to assess prehistoric issues of mobility.

TRINIDAD IN REGIONAL CONTEXT

Trinidad and Tobago are continental islands that originally formed as part of the mainland of South America, and from which they became detached due to the global rise in sea level in the late and post-Pleistocene. In prehistoric times they served as a link between the continent and the Caribbean archipelago that was crucial for human migration and the exchange and diffusion of cultures (Boomert 2000). Both islands formed part of an extensive Amerindian inter-action sphere, which also included the lower Orinoco Valley, the coastal zone of eastern Venezuela and the western littoral of the Guianas. These areas were interconnected during prehistoric and contact periods by an intricate system of sea channels, rivers, lagoons and estuaries (Boomert 2014).

The Ortoiroid

Migrating from northeastern South America, early Archaic populations settled in Trinidad around 6000 BCE and evidence includes eleven midden sites, five flint deposits and thirteen individual finds (Boomert 2000, 54). Most of the approximately twenty-nine Archaic sites identified to date are situated in the southern half of the island (Boomert 2000, 48–49). Culturally, all Archaic sites in Trinidad can be assigned to a single tradition, the Ortoiroid series. By 3000–1000 BCE, the southwestern portion of Tobago was colonized by Archaic settlers of the Milford complex who had originated in Trinidad. Using large dugouts, the Archaic migrants from the eastern littoral of Venezuela and Trinidad eventually reached the Leeward and Virgin Islands, where they may have encountered other Archaic colonists who came from the Greater Antilles. It is likely that the Warao of the Orinoco delta and Northwest Guyana are the present-day descendants of the Ortoiroid people. In fact, as recently as the mid-twentieth century, Warao groups from the Orinoco delta paid regular trading visits to Trinidad.

The Saladoid

As indicated in chapter 1, this volume, while most of the Saladoid potsherds found at the Red House site are undecorated, the presence of decorated and complex modelled sherds provides diagnostic evidence attesting to their Saladoid cultural origin. Around 500 BCE, settlers of the Saladoid series moved into Trinidad from eastern Venezuela. These pottery-making Amerindians, who had migrated to the Venezuelan coast from the lower Orinoco Valley, subsisted on a combi-nation of root crop horticulture (bitter cassava and sweet potatoes), hunting, fishing and the gathering of edible animal and plant foods (Petersen 1997). The Saladoid colonists were able to adapt very successfully to their local environment and interacted well with the last Archaic survivors of the Venezuelan coastal zone (of the Manicuaran subseries), from whom they learned about maritime technology and acquired the navigational skills required to reach the southern Windward Islands (Boomert 2014). In all, two successive Saladoid ceramic complexes are known from Trinidad: Cedros (200 BCE–1 CE) and Palo Seco (1–750 CE). Tobago has three Saladoid complexes: Courland (100 BCE–350 CE); Mount Irvine (100–350 CE); and Friendship (350–750 CE).

The Arauquinoid

Arauquinoid domination eventually stretched as far as the east Venezuelan littoral and Trinidad, where the Arauquinoid-influenced Barrancoid pottery led to the emergence of ceramics of the Bontour complex in 750/800 CE (Boomert 2014). The Arauquinoid series is called "Guayabitoid" in Trinidad and in the northeastern part of Venezuela mainly because only some of the traits of this series diffused to Trinidad during this period (Dorst 2000). Apparently, Arauquinoid ceramics had less ceremonial significance than the ceramics of the Saladoid-Barrancoid period, which suggests that the transition from Saladoid/ Barrancoid to Arauquinoid in Trinidad and elsewhere represented a genuine cultural break. This does not mean that the previous Saladoid-Barrancoid population of the island was completely replaced by the Arauquinoid newcomers. On the contrary, a steady cultural transition that primarily involved a locally based population seems to characterize Trinidad throughout the Ceramic Age. People lived in villages characterized by circular house structures surrounded by shell midden deposits in which they buried their dead, as was customary during the Saladoid/Barrancoid period.

The Mayoid

The Mayoid series was the final Amerindian ceramic tradition of Trinidad before European contact. It emerged in 1300 CE, about two centuries before

Columbus encountered the island on his third journey to the West Indies in 1498. Mayoid pottery may have been manufactured until the mid-eighteenth century. The exclusive use of *caraipe* (burnt tree bark) as a tempering material is one of its defining characteristics (Boomert 2014). The strong resemblance between Mayoid cooking jars and the "buck-pots" (pepper pots) of the Arawak (Lokono) in the Guianas suggests strong cultural affinities between the two groups. This connection is further bolstered by the rare occurrence of a typically Koriabo-Cayo necked vessel in Mayoid archaeological sites. Mayoid ceramics of Trinidad were apparently manufactured by both the Nepoio and Arawak people. While several socially complex multi-ethnic and multilingual native groups emerged during the Mayoid period in Trinidad, Tobago at this time was predominantly inhabited by Suazan Troumassoid and by Island-Carib populations after 1450 CE (Boomert 2014).

To further our temporal analysis based on recovered ceramics, sixteen pre-colonial pottery samples were sent to Professor Corinne L. Hofman at Leiden University in the Netherlands for fabric analysis. The primary objective of this exercise was to determine if any of the pre-colonial ceramics found at the Red House bore *cauxi*[1] or *caraipe*[2] temper – materials normally associated with later Guayabitoid (750/80–1300 CE) and Mayoid (1300–1800 CE) native groups. Radiocarbon dates indicate that the pre-colonial timeline of the Red House spanned from 125 to 1395 CE; however, the timeline of Saladoid colonization in Trinidad should have ended in 600 CE and around 800/900 CE in the northern Lesser Antilles. Given that the pre-colonial timeline of the Red House site spanned over a period of one thousand years – long after the Saladoid colonization should have ended – there was justification to verify if some of the pottery found at the site might have been the result of subsequent Guayabitoid and Mayoid colonization of the site. The ceramic analysis failed to provide evidence of either cauxi or caraipe in any of the sixteen pottery samples analysed for temper from the Red House site (Hofman, pers. comm. 2015; also see chapter 7, this volume).

With this important information, it seems the Saladoid population of Trinidad was not completely replaced by the Arauquinoid newcomers and that the Red House might have been inhabited by a locally based indigenous community that produced pottery from local clays for over an extended period (see chapter 7, this volume). This view is supported by Boomert, suggesting that "a steady cultural transition that primarily involved a locally based population characterized Trinidad throughout the Ceramic Age" (Boomert 2014, 338; Boomert et al. 2013; also chapter 7, this volume).

To discern dietary ecology and mobility patterns in prehistoric Trinidad, isotopic analysis was performed on samples of human bone (n = 38 individuals, n = 42 samples) and tooth enamel (n = 31 individuals, n = 38 samples). We also include select faunal teeth (n = 10) recovered from the Red House site excavations (Reid 2015) to augment the human results presented (but see chapter 6, this volume). Bone collagen, bone apatite and tooth enamel apatite from these samples were prepared in the Bone Chemistry Lab (BCL) at the University of Florida following basic procedures outlined in Ambrose (1993).

All bone and tooth samples were assigned a BCL number, and tooth and bone were initially cleaned by hand with toothbrushes and scalpels to remove any debris and/or impurities from the cortical surface or tooth crown. "Cleaned" bone samples were then placed in beakers with deionized distilled water (DDI-H_2O) for sonication and then air-dried. Ceramic mortars and pestles were then utilized on the cleaned bone fragments, and sampled bone powder was sieved into two fractions for bone collagen (0.25–0.5 mm) and bone apatite (0.25 mm) analysis.

For teeth, each tooth was sampled using a Brassler dental drill and a Dedeco NM slim separating disc to produce a wedge of tooth enamel ca. 100 mg. Adhering dentin along the interior portions of the wedge and any exogenous debris were removed using a dental drill and carbide bit. Once cleaned, the enamel chunk was split into a smaller sample (ca. 20–30 mg) and ground using an agate mortar and pestle. The larger sample (ca. 40–50 mg) was retained as a "bulk" sample chunk of tooth enamel (for Sr and Pb) and placed in a 1.5 mL microcentrifuge tube for subsequent column chemistry.

Bone collagen was prepared by the demineralization of ca. 0.5 g of ground bone (0.25–0.5 mm) in ca. 12–13 mL of 0.2 M hydrochloric acid (HCl) using 15 mL tubes for approximately twenty-four hours, and after centrifugation, the HCl was refreshed in each sample until the samples were completely demineralized; in this case, seven days. Demineralized samples were then rinsed to neutral pH with DDI-H_2O and followed by treatment with ca. 12 mL of 0.125 M sodium hydroxide (NaOH) for sixteen hours. Samples were then rinsed to neutral pH and transferred to a 20 mL scintillation vial with ca. 10 mL of 10^{-3} M HCl, then transferred to a 95°C oven for four to five hours. Samples were then spiked with 100 µl of 1 M HCl to completely dissolve the collagen and heated at 95°C for another four to five hours. Solubized samples were then transferred back to their respective 15 mL vial (cleaned), centrifuged, and the solution was then transferred to its 20 mL scintillation vial and reduced to ca. 2 mL at 65°C. Samples were then placed in the freezer and then lyophilized for ninety-six hours, weighed to determine collagen yield and prepared for mass spectrometry in the Stable Isotope Laboratory at the University of Florida. The collagen samples were then weighed and loaded into tin capsules for elemental analysis using a Carlo-Erba NA1500 CNS elemental analyser and subsequent isotope ratio analysis with a Delta V isotope ratio mass spectrometer (IRMS).

Bone apatite was prepared using the finer bone fraction (<0.25 mm), of which ca. 0.5 g was weighed and placed in a 15 mL centrifuge tube and ca. 12 to 13 mL of 50:50 bleach (~2.5%) or sodium hypochlorite (NaOHCl) was added. After twenty-four hours, the samples were refreshed, and then once fully oxidized (about forty-eight hours), the samples were rinsed to neutral pH and ca. 12–13 mL of 0.2 M acetic acid (CH_3COOH) was added for sixteen hours. Samples were then rinsed to neutral pH, decanted, placed in the freezer and then lyophilized for seventy-two hours. All pretreated bone apatite samples were then weighed and loaded into a Kiel carbonate prep device connected to a Finnegan MAT 252 IRMS. For tooth enamel samples, a similar procedure was adopted, but ca. 20 to 25 mg of tooth powder was weighed and placed in a 1.5 mL microcentrifuge tube, after which 50:50 bleach was added for about eight hours and rinsed to neutral. Then 0.2 M acetic acid was added for about eight hours, after which samples were rinsed to neutral, frozen and then lyophilized before being loaded into the Kiel for IRMS. All light-stable isotope ratios are expressed in standard delta notation, and carbon and oxygen isotope ratios are reported relative to VPDB, and nitrogen isotope ratios are reported relative to AIR.

For heavy isotope analysis of Sr and Pb ratios, requisite column chemistry was conducted in a "clean lab", where prepared tooth enamel chunks were dissolved in precleaned Teflon vials with 1 mL 8N nitric acid (HNO_3) on a 120°C hotplate for twenty-four hours under laminar flow. Following methods outlined in Valentine et al. (2008), ion chromatography was used to separate Pb and Sr from single aliquots, using Dowex 1X-8 and Sr-selective crown ether resin (Eichrom Technologies, Incorporated), respectively. Sr and Pb ratios were analysed separately using a Nu Plasma multi-collector inductively coupled plasma mass spectrometer (MC-ICP-MS), using time-resolved analysis (TRA) for Sr and the Tl-normalization technique for Pb (Kamenov et al. 2004). Sr ratios ($^{87}Sr/^{86}Sr$) are reported relative to the NBS 987 standard $^{87}Sr/^{86}Sr = 0.71024$ (±0.00003, 2σ) while Pb ratios ($^{20n}Pb/^{204}Pb$) are reported relative to the NBS 981 standard $^{206}Pb/^{204}Pb = 16.937$ (±0.004, 2σ), $^{207}Pb/^{204}Pb = 15.490$ (±0.003, 2σ) and $^{208}Pb/^{204}Pb = 36.695$ (±0.009, 2σ).

RESULTS

Paleodiet

Red House isotopic results for bone collagen and bone apatite samples are presented in tables 3.2 and 3.3 and figures 3.2 and 3.3. For all individuals analysed

Table 3.2. Red House Light Isotope Ratios for Human Bone Collagen and Bone Apatite

Burial Number[1]	BCL #	δ¹³C_ap (‰ vs VPDB)	δ¹⁸O_ap (‰ vs VPDB)	δ¹⁵N_co (‰ vs AIR)	δ¹³C_co (‰ vs VPDB)	wt %N	wt %C	C:N	δ¹³C_ap-co (‰ vs VPDB)
A-CEP4-1	2858	−8.9	−2.8	14.0	−13.7	14.23	39.17	3.2	4.8
A-CEP7-1	2865	−10.4	−3.9	13.8	−15.4	15.86	42.70	3.1	5.0
A-CEP7-2	2859	−10.6	−3.3	13.9	−15.3	15.61	41.86	3.1	4.7
A-CSNE-1-2	2866	9.0	−2.8	13.9	−14.7	14.95	40.26	3.1	5.7
A-CSNE-1-3	2863/2867	−9.3	−3.9	14.2	−14.0				4.8
A-CSNE-2-1	2862/2868	−9.6	−2.8	12.3	−14.5				4.9
A-CSNW-2-1	2869	−8.7	−3.1	13.4	−13.7	4.84	12.95	3.1	5.0
A-CSNW-4-1	2870	−10.9	−2.7	13.2	−17.6	11.19	30.68	3.2	6.6
A-CSNW-4-2	2892	−12.2	−2.7	13.4	−17.4	13.65	37.96	3.2	5.2
A-G38-2-1a	2893	−9.5	−3.0	13.7	−13.8	13.91	38.45	3.2	4.4
A-G38-2-SIP	2864	−10.3	−2.4	14.2	−14.3	15.41	41.44	3.1	4.0
A-G43-1-1	2890	−9.3	−2.8	14.3	−14.1	14.36	39.75	3.2	4.9
A-G43-1-2a	2871	−9.6	3.-2	15.0	−13.6	10.19	27.74	3.2	4.0
A-G43-1-3a	2894	−10.6	−2.5	14.4	−15.0	14.13	39.07	3.2	4.4
A-G43-2-1	2872	−10.0	−2.6	13.6	−16.3	9.83	26.82	3.2	6.3
A-G43-2-2	2873	−10.5	−2.8	16.4	−15.1	9.08	24.49	3.1	4.6
A-G56-1-1	2883	−11.2	−2.6	13.6	−15.8	14.62	40.50	3.2	4.6
A-G56-1-2	2884	10.3	−2.7	12.2	−16.8	14.04	39.14	3.3	6.4
A-G56-2-1	2885	−8.3	−3.1	12.3	−13.1	15.47	42.45	3.2	4.8
A-G57-C-1	2898	−8.7	−2.7	10.1	−15.8	1.38	5.05	4.3	
A-G57-C-2	2899	N/A	N/A	10.1	−16.6	2.65	8.63	3.8	
A-G61-2-1	2886	−7.0	−2.7	N/A	N/A	0.79	2.80	4.1	
A-NPC-1-1	2874	−8.1	−2.6	11.8	−12.9	7.99	21.42	3.1	4.8
A-NPC-1-3a	2875	−12.0	−2.7	11.9	−18.8	11.02	30.13	3.2	6.9

Table 3.2 continues

A-NPC-2-1	2876	-6.2	-3.1	13.3	-11.8	11.90	32.45	3.2	5.6
A-NPC-2-2	2860/2877	-8.3	-3.1	12.3	-13.5				5.3
A-NPC-2-3	2878	-9.2	-3.1	14.3	-14.8	14.17	39.42	3.2	5.7
A-NPC-2-4	2879	-7.3	-3.1	11.9	-14.4	10.68	29.29	3.2	7.2
A-NPC-3-1	2880	-7.0	-2.6	12.6	-12.4	13.53	37.57	3.2	5.4
A-NPC-5-1	2891	-9.2	-2.3	14.3	-14.3	15.53	42.97	3.2	5.1
A-NPC-6-1	2881	-10.1	-2.7	12.4	-15.7	14.80	41.15	3.2	5.6
A-NPC-7-1	2882	-10.4	-2.5	13.4	-16.2	11.27	31.23	3.2	5.8
B-RFA-5-1	2887	-9.9	-2.8	13.7	-15.4	15.10	41.43	3.2	5.5
B-RFA-5-2	2895	-9.7	-2.7	13.1	-15.8	14.65	40.57	3.2	6.0
B-RFA-7-1	2888	-8.1	-3.1	13.2	-11.9	14.67	40.85	3.2	3.7
B-RFA-7-2a	2896	-8.3	-2.8	12.9	-12.9	14.16	39.21	3.2	4.6
B-RFA-8-1	2897	-7.5	-3.1	12.7	-12.9	13.95	39.08	3.3	5.4
B-RFA-8-2	2889	-9.9	-3.1	12.0	-16.0	14.51	40.31	3.2	6.1
A-CSNE-1-3	2867	-9.2	-3.8	14.1	-14.0	13.55	35.68	3.1	4.8
A-CSNE-1-3	2863	-9.4	-3.9	14.3	-14.1	14.54	39.63	3.2	4.7
	2863/2867	-9.3	-3.9	14.2	-14.0				4.8
A-CSNE-2-1	2862	-9.5	-2.6	12.3	-14.8	15.35	41.39	3.1	5.3
A-CSNE-2-1	2868	-9.7	-3.0	12.2	-14.3	10.76	29.96	3.2	4.6
	2862/2868	-9.6	-2.8	12.3	-14.5				4.9
A-NPC-2-2	2860	-8.1	-2.9	12.2	-13.4	12.68	34.11	3.1	5.3
A-NPC-2-2	2877	-8.4	-3.2	12.5	-13.7	14.49	40.08	3.2	5.2
	2860/2877	-8.3	-3.1	12.3	-13.5				5.3
A-NPC-2-3	2861	-8.8	-3.1	*14.0*	-14.0	*3.48*	*9.42*	3.2	5.2
A-NPC-2-3	2878	-9.2	-3.1	14.3	-14.8	14.17	39.42	3.2	5.7

[1]Samples with results italicized are not used in subsequent analyses due to poor yields.

Table 3.3. Descriptive Statistics of Isotopic Data for Bone Collagen and Bone Apatite from Red House Humans

	Total Samples Analysed			Saladoid Sample			Post-Saladoid Sample		
	Total[2]	Males	Females	Total	Males	Females	Total	Males	Females
$\delta^{13}C_{ap}$									
N	35	12	12	9	5	3	23	7	8
Mean	−9.4	−9.7	−9.2	−10.9	−10.9	−10.8	−8.9	−8.9	−8.6
SD[1]	1.34	1.51	1.33	0.79	0.86	1.01	1.14	1.36	0.98
Range	−12.2 to −6.2	−12.2 to −6.2	−12.0 to −7.3	−12.2 to −10.0	−12.2 to −10.0	−12.0 to −10.1	−10.4 to −6.2	1−0.4 to −6.2	−9.9 to −7.3
$\delta^{18}O_{ap}$									
N	35	12	12	9	5	3	23	7	8
Mean	−2.9	−2.9	−2.9	−2.6	−2.6	−2.7	−3.0	−3.1	−2.9
SD	0.35	0.39	0.27	0.08	0.08	0.03	0.38	0.42	0.30
Range	−3.9 to −2.3	−3.9 to −2.5	−3.1 to −2.3	−2.7 to −2.5	−2.7 to −2.5	−2.7 to −2.7	−3.9 to −2.3	−3.9 to −2.7	−3.1 to −2.3
$\delta^{13}C_{co}$									
N	35	12	12	9	5	3	23	7	8
Mean	−14.7	−14.9	−14.7	−16.6	−16.1	−17.1	−14.0	−14.0	−13.9
SD	1.61	1.57	1.93	1.16	0.85	1.61	1.18	1.40	1.31
Range	−18.8 to −11.8	−17.4 to −11.8	−18.8 to −11.9	−18.8 to −15.0	−17.4 to −15.0	−18.8 to −15.7	−16.0 to −11.8	−15.8 to −11.8	−16.0 to −11.9
$\delta^{15}N_{co}$									
N	35	12	12	9	5	3	23	7	8
Mean	13.4	13.7	12.8	13.1	13.7	12.2	13.4	13.8	13.0
SD	1.00	0.60	0.94	0.80	0.40	0.24	1.13	0.74	1.05
Range	11.8 to 16.8	12.9 to 15.0	11.8 to 14.3	11.9 to 14.4	13.4 to 14.4	11.9 to 12.4	11.8 to 16.4	12.9 to 15.0	11.8 to 14.3
$\Delta^{13}C_{ap-co}$									
N	35	12	12	9	5	3	23	7	8
Mean	5.2	5.2	5.5	5.8	5.2	6.3	5.1	5.1	5.3
SD	0.82	0.71	1.01	0.88	0.78	0.66	0.78	0.71	1.06

[1]SD = standard deviation.

[2]Total does not include three individuals with low bone collagen yields and high C:N (italicized in table 3.2).

(n = 38), four were sampled twice (rib, long bone fragment). Three individuals had bone samples with low collagen yields and high atomic C:N outside of the acceptable range of 2.9 to 3.6 (DeNiro 1985; table 3.2).

Individuals with good bone collagen yields (n = 35) have average $\delta^{13}C_{co}$ (−14.7 ± 1.61‰) and $\delta^{15}N_{co}$ (13.4 ± 1.00‰) values that support a maritime-based protein diet. The bone apatite average $\delta^{13}C_{ap}$ (−9.4 ± 1.34‰) reflects "total diet" and supports this contention, while average $\Delta^{13}C_{ap-co}$ (5.3 ± 0.82‰) suggests intermediate ("monoisotopic") spacing between isotopically similar protein and energy components of the diet. Apatite-collagen spacing suggests an overall mixed diet with terrestrial C_3/CAM and marine protein-based foods coupled with terrestrial C_3 plants – a truly "mixed" diet.

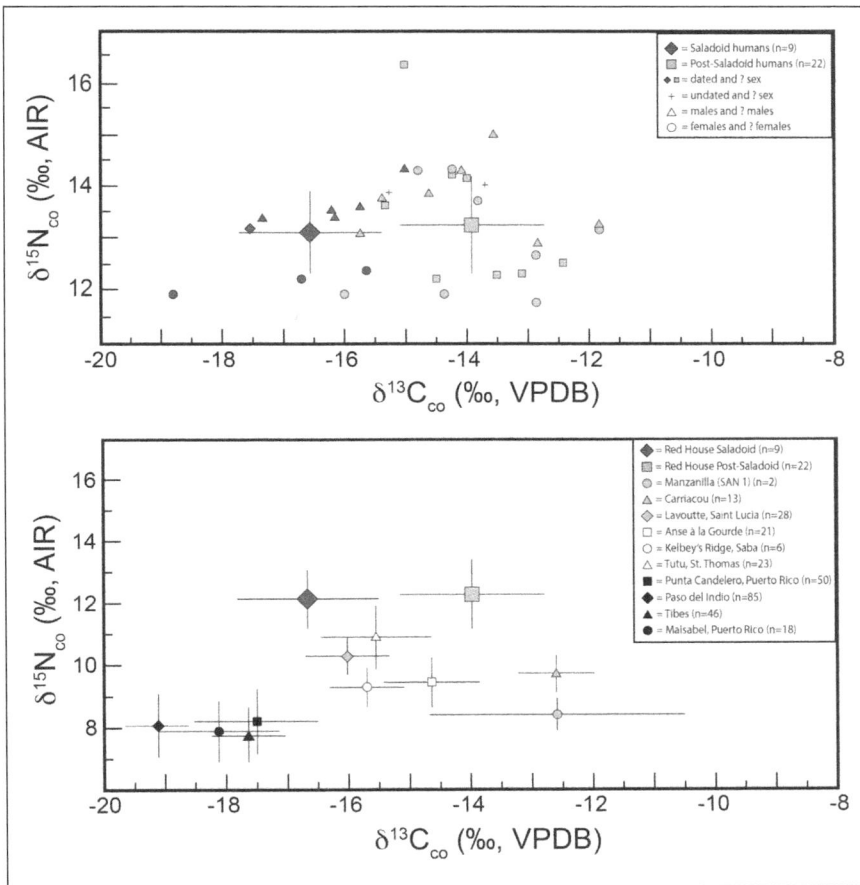

Figure 3.2. (*a*) Bivariate plot of Red House human bone collagen $\delta^{13}C$ and $\delta^{15}N$ values (mean ± 1σ). (*b*) Bivariate plot of Red House human mean bone collagen $\delta^{13}C$ and $\delta^{15}N$ values (± 1σ), compared to data from prehistoric sites in the Leeward Islands: Trinidad (Healy et al. 2013), Carriacou (Krigbaum et al. 2013), St Lucia (Laffoon et al. 2016a); the Windward Islands: Guadeloupe (Laffoon and Hoogland 2012; Stokes 1998), Saba (Laffoon and Hoogland 2012; Stokes 1998), St Thomas (Norr 2002) and Puerto Rico (Stokes 1998; Pestle 2010b).

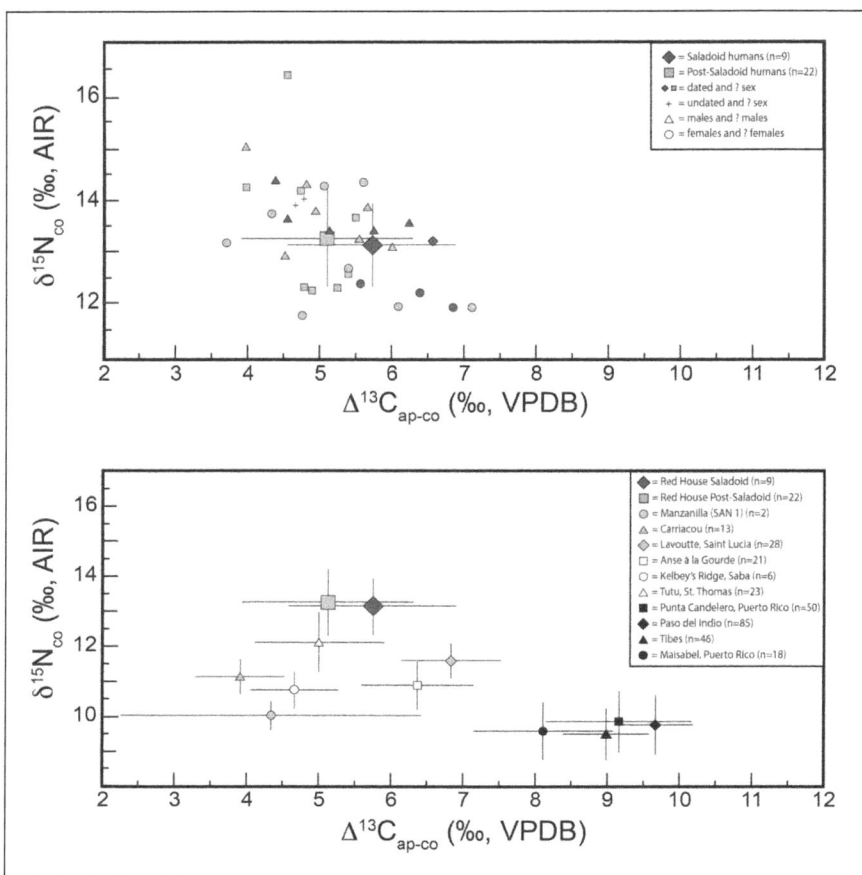

Figure 3.3. (*a*) Bivariate plot of Red House human bone apatite-collagen spacing ($\Delta^{13}C_{ap-co}$) and $\delta^{15}N$ values (mean ± 1σ). (*b*). Bivariate plot of Red House human mean $\Delta^{13}C_{ap-co}$ and $\delta^{15}N$ (± 1σ), compared to data from prehistoric sites in the Leeward Islands: Trinidad (Healy et al., 2013), Carriacou (Krigbaum et al., 2013), St Lucia (Laffoon et al. 2016a); the Windward Islands: Guadeloupe (Laffoon and Hoogland 2012; Stokes 1998), Saba (Laffoon and Hoogland 2012; Stokes 1998), St Thomas (Norr 2002), and on Puerto Rico (Stokes 1998; Pestle 2010b).

We examined the intrasite Red House data by cultural period. Using an unpaired two-tailed t-test (p < 0.0001), the Saladoid (n = 9) average $\delta^{13}C_{co}$ (−16.6 ± 1.16‰) is significantly different when compared to the post-Saladoid (n = 23) average $\delta^{13}C_{co}$ (−14.0 ± 1.40‰), with the latter being more ^{13}C-enriched. This significant trend (p = 0.005) is also apparent between the Saladoid $\delta^{13}C_{ap}$ (−10.9 ± 0.79‰) and post-Saladoid $\delta^{13}C_{ap}$ (−8.9 ± 1.14‰) bone apatite results. Interestingly, $\Delta^{13}C_{ap-co}$ is not significant (p = 0.078), and the Saladoid mean (5.8 ± 0.88‰) is higher than the post-Saladoid mean (5.1 ± 0.78), which suggests a slight ^{13}C-enrichment in the principle energy source in the Saladoid sample. Although observed mean $\Delta^{13}C_{ap-co}$ is not significant, these subtle diachronic shifts seem to suggest a slight shift in energy-based foods, which may well reflect changes in preferred dietary carbohydrate between the two periods.

An interesting pattern can be observed by examining in more detail the isotopic differences by sex. For the total sample identified to sex, including "possible" sex assessments, a significant difference ($p = 0.01$) for $\delta^{15}N_{co}$ is observed between males ($13.7 \pm 0.60‰$) and females ($12.8 \pm 0.94‰$). By cultural period, the difference is quite marked ($p < 0.001$), with Saladoid males ($13.7 \pm 0.40‰$) exhibiting higher $\delta^{15}N_{co}$ values than Saladoid females ($12.2 \pm 0.24‰$), albeit sample size is small in this earlier group.

With respect to Red House human ($n = 31$) and faunal tooth enamel ($n = 10$), all isotopic results are presented in tables 3.4 and 3.5 and figures 3.4–3.6 (see chapter 6, this volume, for discussion of faunal results). For carbon, all human teeth assayed regardless of developmental age (early, middle and late) have an average $\delta^{13}C_{en}$ ($-10.2 \pm 1.30‰$) consistent with a C_3-based maritime diet. Indeed, this average is offset from the bone apatite $\delta^{13}C_{ap}$ average by less than 1‰ (0.8‰). Such correspondence reinforces a "total diet" regime for carbon, using a 12.5‰ enrichment to estimate "average" $\delta^{13}C$ value of consumed foods, from $-22.7‰$ to $-21.9‰$, which is well within a "classic" marine ecosystem mixed with terrestrial C_3 plant and animal protein.

Because teeth that form during the "early" stages of development are influenced heavily by mother's milk, comparisons by cultural period and sex focus only on middle- and late-developing teeth, by individual. For the Saladoid sample ($n = 5$), average $\delta^{13}C_{en}$ ($-12.0 \pm 1.09‰$) is significantly different ($p < 0.0001$) from the post-Saladoid sample ($n = 12$) average $\delta^{13}C_{en}$ ($-9.7 \pm 0.97‰$). There is no significant difference ($p = 0.79$) between the post-Saladoid male ($n = 5$) and female ($n = 5$) sample, and no correlation can be made for the Saladoid population due to small sample size. Nonetheless, the $\delta^{13}C_{en}$ results confirm the observed pattern for $\delta^{13}C_{co}$ and $\delta^{13}C_{ap}$ and demonstrate significant dietary differences in "protein" and "total diet" between the Saladoid and post-Saladoid sample. Essentially, individuals identified as post-Saladoid have a diet that is more ^{13}C-enriched, although, interestingly, maritime dependence as gleaned from the $\delta^{15}N_{co}$ results is ostensibly unchanged between the two periods.

This pattern is supported by the subsample of prehistoric dog enamel assayed ($n = 9$), when the three "modern" Pb outliers are omitted (see below). Here, associated dog remains yield an average $\delta^{13}C_{en}$ of $-9.6 \pm 2.41‰$, and five of these dogs approach the $-10.2‰$ human average for the total Red House sample. Regionally, this pattern demonstrates a large maritime dietary component for all Caribbean samples, with the exception of the Greater Antilles human samples from Puerto Rico (figure 3.4B). The ^{15}N-enriched average values for humans observed for the Red House Site are absolutely higher in $\delta^{15}N$ than the samples from the Lesser Antilles (Leeward and Windward sites).

Table 3.4a. Red House Light Isotope and Heavy Isotope Ratios for Red House Human and Fauna Tooth Enamel Apatite Samples

Burial Number	Tooth[1]	Development[2]	BCL #	$\delta^{13}C_{en}$ (‰ vs VPDB)	$\delta^{18}O_{en}$ (‰ vs VPDB)	$^{87}Sr/^{86}Sr$	$^{208}Pb/^{204}Pb$	$^{207}Pb/^{204}Pb$	$^{206}Pb/^{204}Pb$
A-CEP7-1	M3	Late	2865	-9.7	-2.8	0.7106	39.407	15.777	19.587
A-CSNE-1-2	M2	Middle	2866	-10.4	-2.3	0.7099	39.245	15.779	19.437
A-CSNE-1-2	M2	Middle	2801	-10.8	-2.7	0.7099	39.425	15.782	19.594
A-CSNE-1-2	M3	Late	2802	-9.0	-2.6	0.7097	39.476	15.794	19.628
A-CSNE-1-3	M1	Early	2867	-8.4	-3.0	0.7103	39.317	15.772	19.395
A-CSNE-2-1	I	Early	2868a	-10.1	-2.3	0.7114	39.491	15.783	19.622
A-CSNE-2-1	C	Middle	2868b	-10.1	-1.6	0.7114	39.484	15.793	19.606
A-CSNE-2-1	M2	Middle	2799	-10.6	-2.6	0.7120	39.455	15.776	19.580
A-CSNE-2-1	M3	Late	2800	-9.5	-3.0	0.7119	39.539	15.791	19.712
A-CSNW-2-1	M2	Middle	2869	-10.6	-3.0	N/A	39.408	15.784	19.555
A-CSNW-2-1	M2	Middle	2797	-10.4	-3.3	0.7109	39.267	15.760	19.442
A-CSNW-2-1	M3	Late	2798	-10.5	-3.2	0.7112	39.530	15.797	19.733
A-CSNW-4-1	M2	Middle	2870	-13.3	-2.6	0.7134	39.552	15.791	19.623
A-CSNW-4-2	M2	Middle	2892	-12.9	-2.9	0.7130	39.413	15.771	19.484
A-G38-2-1a	I	Early	2893	-9.6	-2.1	0.7095	39.106	15.734	19.150
A-G38-2-SIP	M1	Early	2864	-11.0	-2.6	0.7098	38.999	15.732	19.130
A-G43-1-2a	M1	Early	2871	-11.0	-2.8	0.7104	39.345	15.773	19.459
A-G43-1-3a	I1	Early	2894	-10.9	-2.6	0.7104	39.227	15.742	19.257
A-G43-2-1	PM3	Middle	2872	-11.2	-2.5	0.7108	39.261	15.743	19.281
A-G57-C-1	M1	Early	2898	-9.7	-3.0	0.7102	39.369	15.768	19.441
A-G57-C-2	M2	Middle	2899	-10.2	-3.2	0.7112	39.374	15.775	19.486
A-G61-2-1	M3	Late	2886	-7.4	-3.3	0.7105	N/A	N/A	N/A
A-NPC-2-3	PM4	Middle	2878	-10.7	-2.8	0.7104	39.362	15.763	19.459
A-NPC-3-1	M3	Late	2880	-7.9	-1.7	0.7104	39.256	15.747	19.281

Table 3.4a continues

A-NPC-6-1	PM3	Middle	2881	-10.8	-2.6	0.7107	39.169	15.739	19.291
A-NPC-7-1	M2	Middle	2882	-11.8	-2.3	0.7105	39.116	15.741	19.291
B-RFA-5-2	PM3	Middle	2895	-10.1	-2.3	0.7101	39.398	15.773	19.555
B-RFA-7-1	M3	Late	2888	-8.9	-3.2	0.7100	39.295	15.753	19.350
B-RFA-7-2a	PM	Middle	2896	-8.4	-3.2	N/A	N/A	N/A	N/A
B-RFA-8-1	I	Early	2897	-11.3	-3.0	0.7100	39.301	15.745	19.297
B-RFA-8-2	I2	Early	2889	-9.6	-2.8	0.7099	39.308	15.759	19.391
A-CSNE-1-2	M2	Middle	2866	-10.4	-2.3	0.7099	39.245	15.779	19.437
A-CSNE-1-2	M2	Middle	2801	-10.8	-2.7	0.7099	39.425	15.782	19.594
A-CSNE-1-2	M3	Late	2802	-9.0	-2.6	0.7097	39.476	15.794	19.628
			Average (2866, 2801, 2802):	**-10.1**	**-2.5**	**0.7098**	**39.382**	**15.785**	**19.553**
A-CSNE-2-1	I	Early	2868a	-10.1	-2.3	0.7114	39.491	15.783	19.622
A-CSNE-2-1	C	Middle	2868b	-10.1	-1.6	0.7114	39.484	15.793	19.606
A-CSNE-2-1	M2	Middle	2799	-10.6	-2.6	0.7120	39.455	15.776	19.580
A-CSNE-2-1	M3	Late	2800	-9.5	-3.0	0.7119	39.539	15.791	19.712
			Average (2868b, 2799, 2800):	**-10.1**	**-2.4**	**0.7118**	**39.493**	**15.786**	**19.633**
A-CSNW-2-1	M2	Middle	2869	-10.6	-3.0	N/A	39.408	15.784	19.555
A-CSNW-2-1	M2	Middle	2797	-10.4	-3.3	0.7109	39.267	15.760	19.442
A-CSNW-2-1	M3	Late	2798	-10.5	-3.2	0.7112	39.530	15.797	19.733
			Average (2869, 2797, 2798):	**-10.5**	**-3.1**	**0.7111**	**39.402**	**15.780**	**19.577**

[1] I = incisor, C = canine, PM = premolar, M = molar (number corresponds to position in tooth row).

[2] I1, I2, M1 = early childhood; C, PM3, PM4, M2 = middle childhood; M3 = late childhood.

Table 3.4b. Red House Light Isotope and Heavy Isotope Ratios for Red House Human and Fauna Tooth Enamel Apatite Samples

Fauna Sampled

Taxon	Provenance	Tooth[1]	BCL #	$\delta^{13}C_{en}$ (‰ vs VPDB)	$\delta^{13}C_{cen}$ (‰ vs VPDB)	$^{87}Sr/^{86}Sr$	$^{208}Pb/^{204}Pb$	$^{207}Pb/^{204}Pb$	$^{206}Pb/^{204}Pb$
Tayassu tajacu	A-NPC-2	I2	3405	−13.9	−0.3	0.7132	39.306	15.764	19.395
Canis familiaris	A-NWCS-1	M1	3402	−10.8	−3.2	0.7101	39.091	15.733	19.167
Canis familiaris	B-R-G35-2	C	3403	−10.1	−1.9	0.7101	39.031	15.719	19.092
Canis familiaris	B-G26-NW Rotunda-2	C	3404	−10.1	−3.5	0.7101	39.258	15.751	19.297
Canis familiaris	Rotunda Fountain-5	M1	3406	−11.3	−3.0	0.7097	39.250	15.749	19.309
Canis familiaris	BM #1 Ext	PM4	3410	−10.6	−3.6	0.7107	38.701	15.668	18.742
Canis familiaris	BAR #5	PM4	3411	−4.8	−3.4	0.7101	40.146	16.378	19.146
Canis familiaris	A-NECS-5	PM4	3407	−8.2	−4.6	0.7089	36.875	15.512	17.103
Canis familiaris	A-NPC-NCS(East)-G57	C	3408	−8.2	−4.1	0.7092	37.484	15.552	17.662
Canis familiaris	A-NPC-6	PM4	3409	−8.4	−4.8	0.7088	37.402	15.548	17.555

2 N HCl Soil Leachate:

[1] I = incisor, C = canine, PM = premolar, M = molar (number corresponds to position in tooth row).

Table 3.5. Descriptive Statistics of Isotopic Data for Tooth Enamel Apatite from Red House Humans and Dogs

	Red House Total (Early, Middle, Late)[1]	Red House Total (Middle, Late)	Saladoid (Middle, Late)	Post-Saladoid (Middle, Late)	Prehistoric Dogs[3]
$\delta^{13}C_{en}$					
N	31	22	5	12	6
Mean	−10.2	−10.2	−12.0	−9.7	−9.6
SD[2]	1.30	1.43	1.09	0.97	2.41
Range	−13.3 to −7.4	−13.3 to −7.4	−13.3 to −10.8	−10.8 to −7.9	−11.3 to −4.8
$\delta^{18}O_{en}$					
N	31	22	5	12	6
Mean	−2.7	−2.7	−2.6	−2.6	−3.1
SD	0.43	0.47	0.21	0.51	0.67
Range	−3.3 to −1.6	−3.3 to −1.6	−2.9 to −2.3	−3.2 to −1.6	−3.6 to −1.92
$^{87}Sr/^{86}Sr$					
N	29	20	5	12	6
Mean	0.7107	0.7109	0.7117	0.7106	0.7101
SD	0.0009	0.0010	0.0014	0.0008	0.0003
Range	0.7095 to 0.7134	0.7097 to 0.7134	0.7105 to 0.7134	0.7097 to 0.71197	0.7097 to 0.7107
$^{208}Pb/^{204}Pb$					
N	29	20	5	11	6
Mean	39.341	39.371	39.302	39.395	39.246
SD	0.136	0.123	0.180	0.096	0.227
Range	38.999 to 39.552	39.116 to 39.552	39.116 to 39.552	39.245 to 39.539	38.701 to 40.146
$^{207}Pb/^{204}Pb$					
N	29	20	5	11	6
Mean	15.767	15.771	15.757	15.775	15.833
SD	0.020	0.019	0.023	0.016	0.034
Range	15.732 to 15.797	15.739 to 15.797	15.739 to 15.791	15.747 to 15.794	15.668 to 16.378
$^{206}Pb/^{204}Pb$					
N	29	20	5	11	6
Mean	19.452	19.499	19.394	19.526	19.125
SD	0.161	0.143	0.154	0.129	0.231
Range	19.130 to 19.733	19.281 to 19.733	19.281 to 19.623	19.281 to 19.712	18.742 to 19.309

[1]Tooth development: I1, I2, M1 = early childhood; C, PM3, PM4, M2 = middle childhood; M3 = late childhood (see table 3.4a).

[2]SD = standard deviation.

[3]Dog sample omits three "modern" outliers.

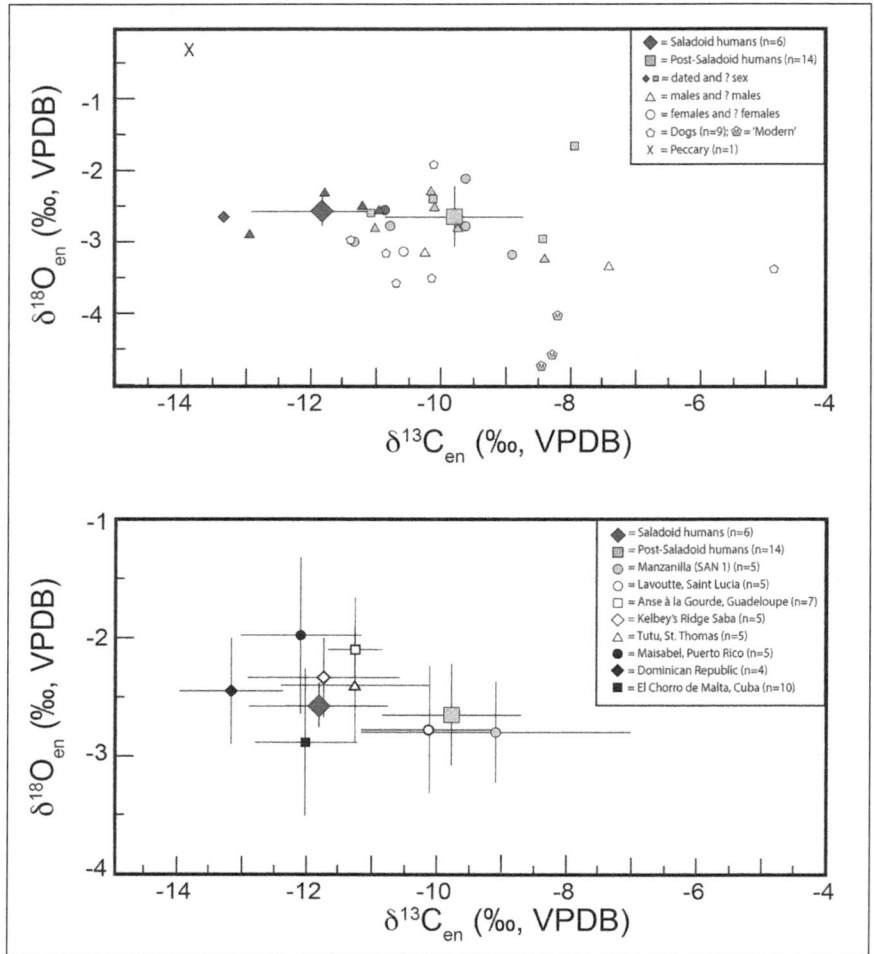

Figure 3.4. (*a*) Bivariate plot of Red House human and faunal tooth enamel apatite $\delta^{13}C$ and $\delta^{18}O$ values (mean ± 1σ). (*b*) Bivariate plot of Red House human mean tooth enamel apatite $\delta^{13}C$ and $\delta^{18}O$ values (mean ± 1σ) compared to data (Laffoon et al. 2013b) from prehistoric sites in the Leeward Islands (Trinidad and St Lucia); the Windward Islands (Guadeloupe, Saba, St Thomas); and the Greater Antilles (Puerto Rico, Dominican Republic, Cuba).

PALEOMOBILITY

Red House human and faunal tooth enamel were also assayed for oxygen light isotope ratios ($\delta^{18}O_{en}$) as well as strontium ($^{87}Sr/^{86}Sr$) and lead ($^{20n}Pb/^{204}Pb$) to assess human residential mobility and potential "non-local" outliers (see tables 3.4a, 3.4b and 3.5).

The light isotope complement to $\delta^{13}C_{en}$ is $\delta^{18}O_{en}$ and the Red House (n = 31) human mean (−2.7 ± 0.43‰) is close to the −2.6‰ human average shared by both Saladoid (n = 5) and post-Saladoid (n = 12) samples. As Laffoon et al. (2013a) report, however, there is minimal difference in $\delta^{18}O_{en}$ values in the

Lesser Antilles, and relying on too much averaging makes it difficult to discern clear patterns. There is a broad comparability between tooth enamel apatite and bone apatite, with average $\delta^{18}O_{en}$ of $-2.7 \pm 0.43‰$ and an offset with bone apatite $\delta^{18}O_{ap}$ of 0.2‰. One interesting aspect of these results is that the collared peccary (n = 1) is 2‰ more positive than the human results but it clearly comes from a deep-forested context where less evaporative regimes should be present. In this case, however, ^{18}O-enrichment indicates consumption of water from evaporative water bodies.

With respect to $^{87}Sr/^{86}Sr$ ratios (figure 3.5), the average Red House sample (n = 31) is 0.7107, which is slightly enriched to the modern seawater average of 0.7092. The human $^{87}Sr/^{86}Sr$ ratios range from 0.7095 to 0.7134 (table 3.5 and figures 3.5 and 3.6). The majority of the tooth enamel samples analysed fall within the local Sr range defined by Laffoon et al. (2012) based on an analysis of modern plants (n = 10) and archaeological snails (n = 6) from the island, with a $^{87}Sr/^{86}Sr$ average of 0.7095 ± 0.0009. With these constraints, four individuals and the peccary exhibit slightly higher $^{87}Sr/^{86}Sr$ than the posited Trinidad "local" range. However, the variation observed for $^{87}Sr/^{86}Sr$ across the entire sample and by cultural period (and by sex for the post-Saladoid sample) are not significantly different. Indeed, it is quite probable that, based on the local geology, there are regions in Trinidad with higher $^{87}Sr/^{86}Sr$ ratios than the defined local range (figure 3.5). In particular, this pattern should be evident for the Northern Range because it is composed mainly of metamorphic rocks (figure 3.1). Port of Spain is at the skirts of the Northern Range, so it is highly likely that humans living in this region exploited resources from the nearby highlands. Further sampling for bioavailable strontium variability on Trinidad would likely extend the local $^{87}Sr/^{86}Sr$ range to include more radiogenic (higher) $^{87}Sr/^{86}Sr$ ratios. This, in turn,

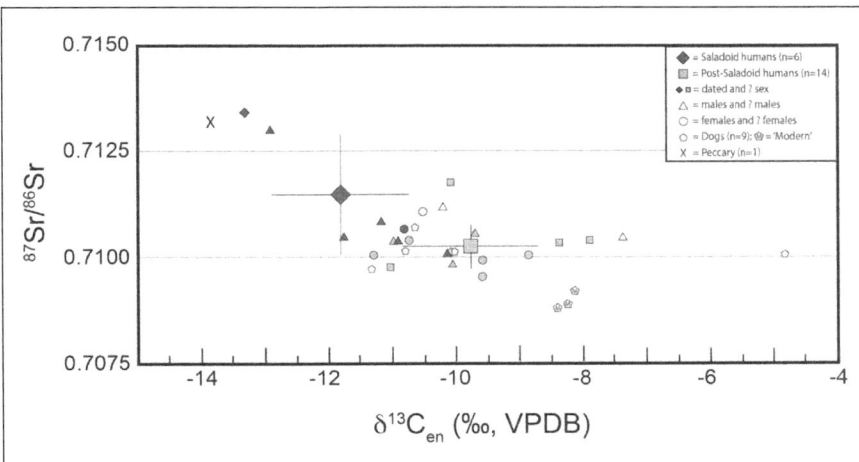

Figure 3.5. (*a*) Bivariate plot of Red House human and faunal tooth enamel apatite $\delta^{13}C$ and $^{87}Sr/^{86}Sr$ values (mean $\pm$ 1σ).

would support a "local" Trinidad origin for all humans sampled, as well as the peccary, included in this study. Regionally (figures 3.5 and 3.6b), this pattern is particularly evident in the fairly large overlap of lower Sr ratios and the elevated mean Sr ratios for the Trinidad samples.

Turning to Pb, there are no Pb isotope data for Trinidad rocks and soils other than one archaeological soil leachate (2 N HCl) analysed (table 3.4). The observed, relatively radiogenic and high Pb isotope ratios in the human samples are consistent with Pb derived from continental rocks. As mentioned above, the Northern Range is composed of South American metamorphic rocks. Furthermore, due to the proximity of Trinidad to South America, and the Orinoco in particular, the majority of the Tertiary sediments on the island were also derived from the continent. Previous work has demonstrated that the Pb isotopic signature observed in the Lesser Antilles is related to subducted sediments that also originated from the South American continent (Carpentier et al. 2008). Therefore, Trinidad and the Lesser Antilles will be expected to share similar Pb isotopic systematics. As a result, similar to the strontium situation discussed above, we are not able to distinguish "local" versus "non-local" origins in the Lesser Antilles, Trinidad or Venezuela based solely on Pb isotope ratios. This is most evident from the fact that the humans and the peccary sampled from Trinidad fall entirely in the Lesser Antilles Pb isotopic field.

The dogs are salient to interpreting the human results. They exhibit Pb ratios broadly similar to the humans, but several have much lower ratios, and there is one "outlier" with higher ratios (figure 3.6a). A similar trend towards lower Pb ratios has been reported in recent work by Giovas and colleagues (2016) on modern and archaeological small mammals from Carriacou in the Grenadines, Lesser Antilles. Detailed investigation in that study revealed that the Pb trend is due to the incorporation of modern anthropogenic Pb in the skeletal material of the small mammals. Therefore, the lower Pb ratios observed in three of the Trinidad dogs with $^{206}Pb/^{204}Pb$ ratios <19 may be deemed "modern", and likely these values are due to modern anthropogenic Pb exposure. These data suggest that these dog features may be intrusive and are likely not contemporary with the Saladoid or post-Saladoid humans sampled in this study.

All of the human Pb ratios plot in the Lesser Antilles field (figure 3.6a). Average $^{208}Pb/^{204}Pb$ (39.341), $^{207}Pb/^{204}Pb$ (15.767) and $^{206}Pb/^{204}Pb$ (19.452) for the total human sample (n = 29) are comparable to averages for middle- and late-developing teeth for both Saladoid (n = 5) and post-Saladoid (n = 11) individuals. Interestingly, however, there is a clear trend within the post-Saladoid sample by sex, albeit with a small sample size (figure 3.6a). This suggests that the females when compared to the males were born and grew up in different areas on the island.

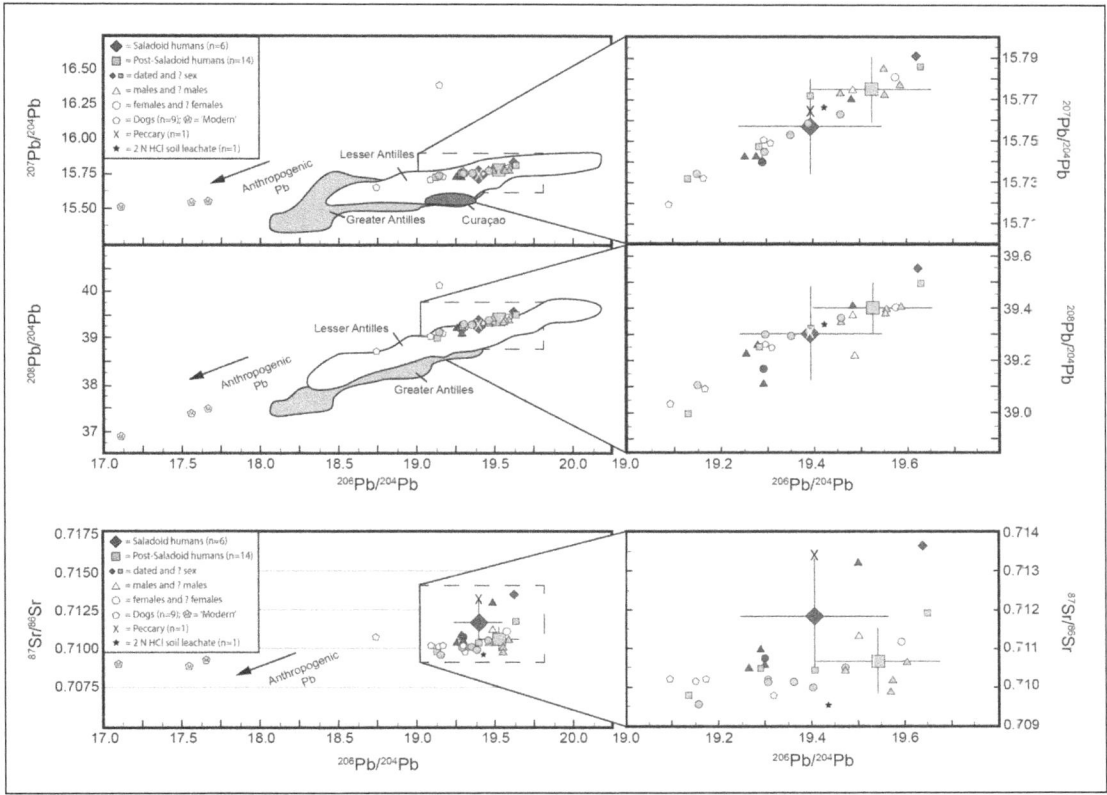

Figure 3.6. (*a*) Bivariate Pb ratio plots (^{206}Pb/^{204}Pb vs ^{207}Pb/^{204}Pb and ^{208}Pb/^{204}Pb) of Red House human and faunal tooth enamel with all data plotted (*on left*) and for "most" prehistoric Red House samples (*on right*). Anthropogenic Pb represents "modern" signal found in three dogs from Red House site. (*b*) Bivariate plot of ^{206}Pb/^{204}Pb and ^{87}Sr/^{86}Sr with all data plotted (*on left*) and for "most" prehistoric Red House samples (*on right*). Error bars represent 1σ and if absent fall within the space occupied by the symbol.

DISCUSSION AND CONCLUSIONS

Assessing patterns in the archaeological record is complicated by myriad factors, and this is clearly the case for some of the isotopic evidence presented above from the Red House site. There are clear patterns of subsistence change over time, and this is in line with observed patterns and diverse datasets from Trinidad and elsewhere. The Red House isotopic results provide a substantial corpus of data that may be compared to other contemporary Ceramic Age sites in the circum-Caribbean. From a dietary perspective, the data support a strong maritime protein component supplemented with terrestrial protein, carbohydrates and adaptations to rain forest resources (Petersen 1997). This broad spectrum diet is apparent isotopically in the diet of the Red House Saladoid people and is maintained to some degree. Indeed, the persistence of a maritime-based economy is apparent, as is a significant shift in dietary carbohydrates by post-Saladoid times.

At the Red House site, we are fortunate to have a well-dated and well-analysed burial assemblage (see chapter 4, this volume), and this contextual information can be assessed based on the isotopic variability presented in this chapter. In this instance, inferences regarding residential mobility can be made based on observed individual sex differences of Pb ratios. The inferred shift in residence patterns of post-Saladoid females based on Pb ratios mentioned above is a case in point (figure 3.6a). In this instance, for dated adults only, four post-Saladoid males and one post-Saladoid female are clustered around the $^{206}Pb/^{204}Pb$ post-Saladoid mean, while four post-Saladoid females fall outside of the 1σ range of error with lower $^{206}Pb/^{204}Pb$ values (<19.4), but are still well within the Lesser Antilles field. This pattern suggests residential mobility of females from their birthplace to the region encompassing the Red House site, where the four dated post-Saladoid males have higher $^{206}Pb/^{204}Pb$ values (>19.4). The pattern is discernible in figure 3.6b as well, however, here the $^{87}Sr/^{86}Sr$ ratios do not vary by sex. Interestingly, there is a clear shift between the Saladoid and post-Saladoid sample with respect to $^{87}Sr/^{86}Sr$, with the Saladoid sample exhibiting higher, more radiogenic values.

The overall post-Saladoid pattern observed from Pb ratios in particular suggests patrilocal residence during this period of prehistory on Trinidad. Patrilocal residence simply means that males (sons) may reside locally in their natal household (that of their father's), while "non-local" females may join their group through marriage. Similarly, "local" females (daughters) may leave their natal group and join "non-local" groups elsewhere. Other studies in other contexts have discussed similar patterns for patrilocal residence patterns, for example, in Neolithic Central Europe (Bentley 2013). In this instance, Sr ratio variance of females is greater than that of males, which, along with supporting archaeological evidence, suggests increased social diversity in southeastern Germany during the LBK (Linearbandkeramik). Bentley and colleagues have also identified potential matrilocal residence patterns in Southeast Asia, where at two famous sites in Thailand (Ban Chang and Khok Phanom Di), the opposite pattern is observed over time, namely, increased variance of males rather than females at each site, suggesting males rather than females moved into the region (Bentley et al. 2005).

The corpus of isotope work in the Caribbean is growing steadily, but often there is much information and bias present in the archaeological record that limits what can be assessed based on the evidence at hand. Strontium and lead ratios, for example, are two "heavy isotopes" that provide a unique view of individual life histories that are not possible through other means. The diachronic results from the Red House site presented above are in concert with existing notions of culture history in Trinidad during this dynamic time period. Further research with these isotopic proxies, as well as additional elements (e.g., sulphur), promise to shed further light on "local" scenarios that will allow new hypotheses to be raised and tested that address issues of paleodiet and paleomobility germane in the region.

ACKNOWLEDGEMENTS

A number of people have contributed to this study. First, we would like to thank all staff engaged in the Red House Site excavations for their careful work in the field and lab, and with sample selection to make this study possible. In particular, we acknowledge Zara Ali for her conscientious efforts. We would also like to thank Professor John Schultz and colleagues (University of Central Florida) for their thoughtful analysis of the assemblage of human remains and the age/sex assessments that contributed to this study. Dr Jason Curtis (University of Florida) conducted the light isotope mass spectrometry, and Dr Ashley Sharpe ably assisted with column chemistry and identified the collared peccary.

NOTES

1.   *Cauxi* are freshwater sponge spicules. Cauxi temper is usually associated with the Guayabitoid pottery series.
2.   *Caraipe* is the ash of the siliceous bark of a small tree, *Licania apetala*, which is locally known in the Amazon Valley and the Guianas as *coupepia*, *kwepi* (Kalina, Suriname) or *kauta* (Arawak, Guyana and Suriname). Caraipe is usually associated with the Mayoid pottery series.

REFERENCES

Algar, S., and J.P. Erikson. 1995. "Correlation of the Jurassic through Oligocene Stratigraphic Units". *International Geology Review* 37:313–34.

Ambrose, S.H. 1993. "Isotopic Analysis of Paleodiets: Methodological and Interpretive Considerations". In *Investigations of Ancient Human Tissue*, edited by M.K. Sandford, 59–130. Langhorne, PA: Gordon and Breach.

Barr, K.H., and J.B. Saunders. 1968. "An Outline of the Geology of Trinidad". *Transactions of the Fourth Caribbean Geological Conference*, 1–10.

Bataille, C.P., J. Laffoon and G.J. Bowen. 2012. "Mapping Multiple Source Effects on the Strontium Isotopic Signatures of Ecosystems from the Circum-Caribbean Region". *Ecosphere* 3:1–24.

Bentley, R.A. 2013. "Mobility and the Diversity of Early Neolithic Lives: Isotopic Evidence from Skeletons". *Journal of Anthropological Archaeology* 32:303–12.

Bentley, R.A., M. Pietrusewsky, M.T. Douglas and T.C. Atkinson. 2005. "Matrilocality during the Prehistoric Transition to Agriculture in Thailand?" *Antiquity* 79:865–81.

Boomert, A. 2000. *Trinidad, Tobago, and the Lower Orinoco Interaction Sphere: An Archaeological/Ethnohistorical Study*. Alkmaar, the Netherlands: Cairi.

———. 2014. "Trinidad and Tobago". In *Encyclopedia of Caribbean Archaeology*, edited by B.A. Reid and R.G. Gilmore III, 335–38. Gainesville: University Press of Florida.

Boomert, A., B. Faber–Morse and I. Rouse. 2013. *The Yale University Excavations in Trinidad of 1946 and 1953*. New Haven, CT: Yale University Press.

Carpentier, M., C. Chauvel and N. Mattielli. 2008. "Pb-Nd Constraints on Sedimentary Input into the Lesser Antilles Arc System". *Earth and Planetary Science Letters* 272:199–211.

DeNiro, M.J. 1985. "Postmortem Preservation and Alteration of *in vivo* Bone Collagen Isotope Ratios". *Nature* 317:806–9.

Dorst, M. 2000. "Manzanilla I: An Archaeological Survey of a Pre-Columbian Site in Trinidad". MA thesis, University of Leiden.

Giovas, C.M., G.D. Kamenov, S.M. Fitzpatrick and J. Krigbaum. 2016. "Sr and Pb Isotopic Investigation of Mammal Introductions: Pre-Columbian Zoogeographic Records from the Lesser Antilles, West Indies". *Journal of Archaeological Science* 69:39–53.

Healy, P.F., A. Keenleyside and M.C. Dorst. 2013. "Isotope Analysis and Radiocarbon Dating of Prehistoric Human Bone from the Manzanilla (SAN 1) Site, Trinidad". *Caribbean Connections* 3:30–45.

Hodell, D.A., R.L. Quinn, M. Brenner and G. Kamenov. 2004. "Spatial Variation of Strontium Isotopes (^{87}Sr/^{86}Sr) in the Maya Region: A Tool for Tracking Ancient Human Migration". *Journal of Archaeological Science* 31:585–601.

Kamenov, G.D., P.A. Mueller and M.R. Perfit. 2004. "Optimization of Mixed Pb-Tl Solutions for High Precision Isotopic Analyses by MC-ICP-MS". *Journal of Analytical Atomic Spectrometry* 19:1262–67.

Katzenberg, A.M. 2008. "Stable Isotope Analysis: A Tool for Studying Past Diet, Demography, and Life History". In *Biological Anthropology of the Human Skeleton*, 2nd ed., edited by M.A. Katzenberg and S.R. Saunders, 413–42. Hoboken, NJ: Wiley-Liss.

Keegan, W.F., and M.J. DeNiro. 1988. "Stable Carbon- and Nitrogen-Isotope Ratios of Bone Collagen Used to Study Coral-Reef and Terrestrial Components of Prehistoric Bahamian Diet". *American Antiquity* 53:320–36.

Krigbaum, J., S.M. Fitzpatrick and J. Bankaitis. 2013. "Human Paleodiet at Grand Bay, Carriacou, Lesser Antilles". *Journal of Island and Coastal Archaeology* 8:210–27.

Laffoon, J.E., G.R. Davies, M.L.P. Hoogland and C.L. Hofman. 2012. "Spatial Variation of Biologically Available Strontium Isotopes (^{87}Sr/^{86}Sr) in an Archipelagic Setting: A Case Study from the Caribbean". *Journal of Archaeological Science* 39:2371–84.

Laffoon, J.E., and B. de Vos. 2011. "Diverse Origins, Similar Diets: An Integrated Isotopic Perspective from Anse à la Gourde, Guadeloupe". In *Communities in Contact*, edited by C.L. Hofman and A. van Duijvenbode, 187–203. Leiden: Sidestone Press.

Laffoon, J.E., and M.L.P. Hoogland. 2012. "Migration and Mobility in the Circum-Caribbean: Integrating Archaeology and Isotopic Analysis". In *Population Dynamics in Prehistory and Early History: New Approaches Using Stable Isotopes and Genetics*, edited by E. Kaiser, J. Burger and W. Schier, 337–53. Boston: De Gruyter.

Laffoon, J.E., M.L.P. Hoogland, G.R. Davies and C.L. Hofman. 2016a. "Human Dietary Assessment in the Pre-colonial Lesser Antilles: New Stable Isotope Evidence from Lavoutte, St Lucia". *Journal of Archaeological Science: Reports* 5:168–80.

Laffoon, J.E., E. Plomp, G.R. Davies, M.L.P. Hoogland and C.L. Hofman. 2013a. "The Movement and Exchange of Dogs in the Prehistoric Caribbean: An Isotopic Investigation". *International Journal of Osteoarchaeology* 25:454–65.

Laffoon, J.E., T.F. Sonnemann, M.M. Antczak and A. Antczak. 2016b. "Sourcing Nonnative Mammal Remains from Dos Mosquises Island, Venezuela: New Multiple Isotope Evidence". *Archaeological and Anthropological Sciences* DOI 10.1007/s12520-016-0453-6.

Laffoon, J.E., R. Valcarcel Rojas and C.L. Hofman. 2013b. "Oxygen and Carbon Isotope Analysis of Human Dental Enamel from the Caribbean: Implications for Investigating Individual Origins". *Archaeometry* 55:742–65.

Norr, L. 2002. "Bone Isotopic Analysis and Prehistoric Diet at the Tutu Site". In *The Tutu Archaeological Village Site: A Multidisciplinary Case Study in Human Adaptation*, edited by E. Righter, 263–73. New York: Routledge.

Pestle, W.J. 2010a. "Bone Chemistry and Paleodiet at the Ceremonial Center of Tibes". In *Tibes: People, Power, and Ritual at the Center of the Cosmos*, edited by L.A. Curet and L.M. Stringer, 209–30. Tuscaloosa: University of Alabama Press.

———. 2010b. "Diet and Society in Prehistoric Puerto Rico: An Isotopic Approach". PhD dissertation, University of Illinois at Chicago.

———. 2013. "Stable Isotope Analysis of Paleodiet in the Caribbean". In *The Oxford Handbook of Caribbean Archaeology*, edited by W.F. Keegan, C.L. Hofman and R. Rodriguez Ramos, 407–17. New York: Oxford University Press.

Pestle, W.J., A. Simonetti and L.A. Curet. 2013. "^{87}Sr/^{86}Sr Variability in Puerto Rico: Geological Complexity and the Study of Mobility". *Journal of Archaeological Science* 40:2561–69.

Petersen, J.B. 1997. "Taino, Island Carib, and Prehistoric Amerindian Economies in the West Indies: Tropical Forest Adaptations to Island Environments". In *The Indigenous People of the Caribbean*, edited by S.M. Wilson, 118–30. Gainesville: University Press of Florida.

Reid, B.A. 2009. *Myths and Realities of Caribbean History*. Tuscaloosa: University of Alabama Press.

———. 2015. *Red House Restoration Archaeology Project Report, Phase 1, for the Period July 1, 2013–January 31, 2015*. Port of Spain: Office of the Parliament of the Republic of Trinidad and Tobago.

Sharpe, A.E., G.D. Kamenov, A. Gilli, D.A. Hodell, K.F. Emery, M. Brenner and J. Krigbaum. 2016. "Lead (Pb) Isotope Baselines for Ancient Human Migration and Trade in the Maya Region". *PLOS ONE* 11 (11): e0164871.

Stokes, A.V. 1998. "A Biogeographic Survey of Prehistoric Human Diet in the West Indies Using Stable Isotopes". PhD dissertation, University of Florida.

———. 2005. "Ceramic-Age Dietary Patterns in Puerto Rico: Stable Isotopes and Island Biogeography". In *Ancient Borinquen: Archaeology and Ethnohistory of Native Puerto Rico*, edited by P.E. Siegel, 185–201. Tuscaloosa: University of Alabama Press.

Valentine, B., G.D. Kamenov and J. Krigbaum. 2008. "Reconstructing Neolithic Groups in Sarawak, Malaysia". *Journal of Archaeological Science* 35:1463–73.

CHAPTER 4

A Bioarchaeological Study of the Human Skeletons from the Red House

JOHN J. SCHULTZ, PATRISHA L. MEYERS AND J. MARLA TOYNE

WHILE EXPANDING IN RECENT YEARS, BIOARCHAEOLOGICAL STUDIES OF skeletal remains and mortuary practices from the pre-Columbian Caribbean are still relatively limited and have traditionally focused on areas in the Greater Antilles such as Cuba, Jamaica, the Dominican Republic and Puerto Rico, with fewer populations studied in the Lesser Antilles (Crespo-Torres et al. 2013; Goodwin 1979; Sandford et al. 2002). Trinidad's location as the southernmost island in the Lesser Antilles created a natural gateway for early migration from South America through Trinidad and Tobago to the West Indies (Boomert 2000, 1–3). This geographic significance highlights the importance of the Red House skeletal sample, which provides a rare opportunity to analyse pre-Columbian remains while adding to the limited body of osteological knowledge available for the Lesser Antilles. The goals of this skeletal analysis included determining the minimum number of individuals (MNI), assessing the biological profile (sex estimation, age at death, ancestry assessment and stature estimation), evaluating antemortem conditions and identifying perimortem trauma.

Although the Red House archaeological site burials do not reflect a natural attritional cemetery (the gradual accumulation of burials from a single population living under similar cultural conditions or limited time period), they provide valuable clues, which contribute to a preliminary reconstruction of pre-Columbian lifeways (Margerison and Knüsel 2002). As such, this cross-sectional sample of approximately twelve hundred years of life and death on the island of Trinidad, represents a unique opportunity to explore life, health and disease experiences of the island's pre-Columbian inhabitants. A bioarchaeological approach was used to incorporate the skeletal analysis with the archaeological and cultural contexts from the Red House. Bioarchaeological investigations are cross-disciplinary collaborations that utilize multiple lines of evidence acquired from burials by many different disciplines, including physical anthropology, archaeology, genetics and chemistry (Larsen 2015). Agarwal and Glencross

(2011b, 1) describe "the duality of skeletal remains as both a biological and cultural entity [that] has formed the basis of bioarchaeological theoretical inquiry". This interpretive framework allows for the generation of inferences about certain cultural behaviors, which may include status, division of labour, social agency and interpersonal violence (Glencross 2011; Larsen 2015; Pearson and Buikstra 2006; Zuckerman and Armelagos 2011).

The Caribbean has not received the same level of attention to osteological analysis and documentation found in other parts of the world (Crespo-Torres et al. 2013; Goodwin 1979; Laffoon and de Vos 2011) and even fewer skeletal samples from the Lesser Antilles have been reported in the literature (Goodwin 1979, 477). Yet this insufficient documentation is not wholly due to a lack of skeletal remains or archaeological investigations. As Laffoon and de Vos (2011, 188) note, "although many burials have been found throughout this region, many if not most are generally in poor states of preservation. Cemeteries or burial areas containing large numbers of [well-preserved] burials or human skeletons are even more scarce". Further, both Sandford et al. (2002) and Laffoon and de Vos (2011) note that excavation of skeletal assemblages utilizing modern techniques and standards is rare in the Caribbean archipelago overall and even less prevalent in the Lesser Antilles. Following an assessment of skeletal remains recovered from St Croix in 1989, Doran (n.d., 14–15) pointed out that "very few New World island populations have been studied from an osteological standpoint". More recently, Sandford et al. (2002) asserts that their bioarchaeological analysis of the Tutu site on St Thomas, consisting of forty-two individuals, is one of the few studies to utilize contemporary techniques and perspective. This site therefore represents an excellent comparison sample for the Red House site based on its location in the Lesser Antilles, the pre-Columbian time period and the size of the skeletal sample. The bioarchaeological investigation of the Red House burials addresses the concerns of Sandford et al. (2002) and Lafoon and de Vos (2011) and offers a unique opportunity to generate detailed information regarding patterns of life for this island population.

POSTDEPOSITIONAL AND RECOVERY CONSIDERATIONS AT THE SITE

Postdepositional disturbances (the processes during and after burial that may result in significant moving, fragmentation or disarticulation of skeletal remains) posed a number of challenges for preservation of the human skeletal remains within the graves. First, there was a long and continued use of the site by Amerindians that more than likely led to extensive disturbance of graves at the site, particularly with new interments intruding into older interments. Moreover, the construction, reconstruction and renovation of the Red House building itself clearly cut into graves and displaced remains over time. Both processes led to commingled remains and the recovery of only partial burials. Limited skeletal preservation and incompleteness therefore impacts the overall interpretive power of these osteological analyses.

METHODS OF SKELETAL ANALYSIS

Evaluation of the Red House sample began with an assessment of each burial utilizing standard data collection procedures recommended by Buikstra and Ubelaker (1994). Once a complete skeletal analysis was performed, we produced individual reports, along the lines of "osteobiographies" (Saul 1978), including descriptions of the condition of remains, inventory and processing procedures, minimum number of individuals, sex and ancestry assessment, estimated age at death, estimated stature, antemortem conditions, perimortem trauma and postmortem modification.

Unfortunately, many of the skeletons were encased in the soil matrix and highly fragmented. Cleaning and reconstruction was necessary prior to skeletal analysis. In particular, we were interested in reconstructing crania for assessment of sex and ancestry and long bones for stature estimation. Inventories, gross analysis and photographic documentation of all materials allowed us to evaluate skeletal completeness and evidence of pathological conditions. Further details of the skeletal analysis can be found in Meyers (2016).

Minimum Number of Individuals (MNI)

When calculating MNI, duplication of skeletal elements was the first consideration (i.e., the same skeletal element from the same side). However, developmental age (juvenile or adult) and chronological age (young adult versus older adult), size of the bones, sex and robusticity, and when applicable, taphonomic criteria, were also considered when sorting commingled bones into individuals. Identifying human skeletal elements, particularly juvenile individuals that were commingled with faunal remains in numerous sections, increased the MNI. Finally, we considered the spatial relationships of *in situ* burials, such as horizontal and vertical distance to one another, as well as commingling of skeletal elements due to postdepostitional processes in the past.

Sex Estimation

When possible, sex was determined using morphological criteria of the skull, pelvis and morphological and metric criteria for the long bones (Byers 2011;

Ubelaker 1989). For more incomplete remains, sex was identified as probable male or probable female. Furthermore, indeterminate was used in cases of very limited and fragmented material when it was not possible to accurately estimate sex. The total number of females was calculated by adding probable female and female, while the total number of males was calculated by adding probable male and male. Juvenile sex was not estimated, as morphological characteristics do not develop until after puberty. As a result, sex was estimated only for adolescent skeletons (13–19 years of age).

Ancestry Assessment

Ancestry assessment was based on morphological criteria of the skull. In particular, traits of the face, dentition and cranial vault suture form represents the most accurate traits identified (Byers 2011; Ubelaker 1989). If these individuals represent a local Amerindian population, we would then expect them to display ancestral traits consistent with Asian populations such as shovel-shaped incisors (Ubelaker 1989).

Age at Death

Age at death was determined using a variety of skeletal standards and, whenever possible, multiple age indicators were used to provide the most accurate age estimate including the os coxa when present. For juveniles, the developing adult dentition standards by Ubelaker (1989) was used most often. Also, epiphyseal fusion of secondary ossification centres was considered (Baker et al. 2005; McKern and Stewart 1957; Schaefer 2008; Scheuer and Black 2000); and if complete long bones were present, they were measured to estimate age using standards by Maresh (1970) and Ubelaker (1989). Juvenile and adult age cohorts followed Baker et al. (2005) and Buikstra and Ubelaker (1994). When it was not possible to assign a specific adult age cohort, the individual was listed as adult.

Stature Estimation

Unfortunately, it was not possible to reconstruct the length of long bones for stature estimates for the majority of the individuals. The femur was preferred, but if it was not available, then the tibia or humerus was substituted. An estimated stature was then calculated for males and females. We used del Angel and Cisneros (2004), who modified regression equations by Genovés (1967), which is commonly used for archaeological Amerindian samples.

Pathological Conditions

All skeletal abnormalities were observed and recorded as to location and type of bone or dental modification. Where possible, we were able to classify dental pathology, degenerative joint changes, trauma and culturally induced skeletal modifications.

RESULTS AND DISCUSSION

Radiocarbon dates indicate that the remains span a time range between approximately 125 and 1395 CE, including both the Saladoid and post-Saladoid cultural periods (see introduction and chapter 1, this volume). For purposes of this skeletal analysis, the remains were aggregated into one skeletal sample. We estimate this collection represents a conservative MNI of sixty individuals. Table 4.1 provides a summary distribution of the sample including proportions of different age and sex categories.

Demographic Profile

The Red House skeletal sample represents forty-seven adults (78%) and thirteen juveniles (22%), including all age ranges and both sexes (table 4.1). However, it is interesting to note that there were substantially less juvenile remains recovered from the Red House site (22%) than from the Tutu site (48%). The largest juvenile age cohort at the Red House site was 2 to 6 years (69.2%), which encompasses the weaning period, a time of increased physiological stress (Lewis 2007). Assigning an age cohort to the forty-seven adults was difficult, as many aging characteristics were not preserved due to the fragmentary and incomplete nature of many skeletons. Out of forty-seven adult individuals, seventeen were assigned only as adult. Additionally, it was not possible to accurately estimate sex for twenty of the forty-seven adults, which are therefore listed as indeterminate. Overall, there are slightly fewer females than males (11:17).

While stature data could only be obtained for eight males and four females, these data reveal sexual dimorphism where the mean male stature is 8.26 centimetres taller than female mean stature. Overall, males average 160.12 centimetres (ranging from 157.67 to 161.22 centimetres), while females average 151.86 centimetres (ranging from 144.52 to 157.18 centimetres). This difference in mean stature between males and females is consistent with other Caribbean sites such as the Tutu Village site in St Thomas (average 158.2 centimetres for males compared to 149.3 centimetres for females) (Sandford et al. 2002).

Table 4.1. General Demographic Distribution for the Red House Skeletal Sample

Age in Years	N	Indeterminate Sex	# of Males	# of Females	Total Sample Frequency
NB (newborn)	0	0	–	–	0%
Infant (0–1)	1	1	–	–	2%
Young child (2–6)	9	9	–	–	15%
Older child (7–12)	2	2	–	–	3%
Adolescent (13–19)	1	0	1	0	2%
Young adult (20–34)	6	1	3	2	10%
Middle-aged adult (35–49)	14	2	7	5	23%
Older adult (50+)	10	4	2	4	17%
Subadult (age indeterminate)	0	0	0	0	0%
Adult (age indeterminate)	17	13	4	0	28%
Total sample	**60**	32	17	11	
Subsample Frequency		53.3%	28.3%	18.3%	

Pathological Conditions

Even though the demographic profile includes both males and females, as well as juvenile remains, we cannot treat this sample as a cohesive population. Without the refined chronology or assumptions of contemporaneity, it is difficult to apply a population based or quantitative osteological analysis (i.e., calculate prevalence or frequency of conditions). However, our more descriptive approach is valid for highlighting the major types and degree of expression of observable skeletal pathology present in this island-based sample (Pfeiffer 2003).

Multiple antemortem conditions were noted in both adults and juveniles, including dental pathology, osteoarthritic changes, indicators of infectious disease, culturally induced skeletal changes and trauma. Overall, thirty-five individuals exhibit some form of pathological bone condition (table 4.2). Of these 29% (ten) are female, 37% (thirteen) are male and 34% (twelve) are of indeterminate sex. Although it was not possible to narrow the age ranges for numerous adults, certain observations about bone disease could still be inferred. It has been suggested that multiple indicators of skeletal stress and disease provide the most comprehensive overview of group health (Cohen et al. 1994; Goodman 1993; Goodman and Martin 2002). However, as Temple and Goodman (2014) have recently pointed out, the use of the term "health" can be problematic, as levels of health can be difficult to define. That being said, at least five adult individuals ranging from middle-aged to older adult exhibited four or more antemortem conditions. Young adults exhibit the least number of pathological conditions, consistent with the fact that "as we age, our exposure to disease and trauma increases" (Buzon 2016, 63).

Table 4.2. An Overview of Antemortem Conditions Observed in the Red House Skeletal Sample

Burial #	Sex[1]	Age[2]	Non-Specific Stress / Infectious Disease[3]				Degenerative Joint Disease[4]			Dental Pathology[5]				Other[6]		
			CO	PH	PO	OM	OA	SO	SN	AC	AM	DA	LEH	ACM	BLA	FX
Adult Burials																
A-NPC-5-1	?F	YA					✓				✓					
B-RFA-8-2	F	YA-MA					✓	✓			✓					
A-G38-2-1a	F	MA-OA	✓				✓			✓	✓	✓				
A-G38-2-1b	F	MA-OA			✓						✓					✓
B-RFA-8-1	F	MA-OA			✓		✓	✓			✓					
A-NPC-2-3	F	MA-OA			✓		✓				✓		✓	✓		
A-NPC-1-3a	F	OA					✓				✓					
A-NPC-2-4	F	OA					✓				✓					
A-NPC-6-1	F	OA			✓						✓				✓	
B-RFA-7-1	F	OA					✓				✓					✓
A-NPC-2-1	?M	A					✓				✓					
A-G61-2-1	?M	YA-MA									✓					
A-G57-C-2	?M	MA-OA						✓				✓				
A-CSNE-1-2	M	YA	✓	✓			✓		✓							
A-G43-1-2a	M	YA							✓							
B-RFA-7-2a	M	MA		✓												
A-G43-1-3a	M	MA					✓				✓	✓		✓	✓	
A-CSNE-2-1	M	MA		✓			✓				✓	✓		Poss.		
A-G43-2-1	M	MA-OA									✓	✓		✓		✓
A-NPC-7-1	M	MA-OA														✓
A-CSNW-4-2	M	OA					✓	✓			✓	✓		Poss.	✓	✓
B-RFA-5-2	M	OA	✓	✓							✓	✓				
A-G56-1-2	Ind	A					✓									✓
A-NPC-2-2	Ind	A					✓									
A-NPC-3-1	Ind	A									✓					
B-G44-2-1	Ind	A														
B-RFA-5-1	Ind	A			✓											
B-RFA-5-LB	Ind	A			✓											
A-CSNE-1-3	Ind	MA-OA					✓	✓								
A-CSNW-4-1	Ind	OA									✓					
A-CSNW-4-3	Ind	OA									✓					
A-CSNW-4-4	Ind	OA									✓					✓
A-NPC-1-1	Ind	OA									✓					
Juvenile Burials																
A-CEP7-1	M	15–18 yrs												✓		
A-G43-1-4b	n/a	4–6 yrs			✓											
A-G38-2-SIP	n/a	6–8 yrs	✓	✓								✓				

Note: Individuals without pathological conditions are not listed.

[1]Sex: F = female, ?F = probable female, M = male, ?M = probable male, In = indeterminate.

[2]Age: YA = young adult, MA = middle-aged adult, OA = older adult, A = adult.

[3]Non-specific stress: CO = cribra orbitalia, PH = porotic hyperostosis. Infectious disease: PO = periostitis. OM = osteomyelitis.

[4]Degenerative joint disease: OA = osteoarthritis, SO = spinal ostephytosis, SN = Schmorl's nodes.

[5]Dental pathology: AC = poss apical cyst, AM = antemortem tooth loss, DA = dental abcess, LEH = linear enamel. Hypoplasia.

[6]Other: ACM = artificial cranial modification, BLA = bilateral asymmetry, FX = fractures.

As expected for pre-Columbian populations, many individuals exhibit advanced dental wear and dental calculus, as well as a variety of dental pathologies including enamel defects, periodontal disease, antemortem tooth loss, abscesses and caries. A total of 397 individual adult teeth were available for analysis. Of these, twelve adults exhibit a total of 26 obvious carious lesions. Since tooth decay is caused by bacterial fermentation and can be accelerated by the consumption of a carbohydrate (sugar and starch) rich diet, this may suggest a common agriculturally based diet for those individuals (Hillson 2008; Larsen 2015; Turner 1979). At least twenty-two individuals exhibit antemortem tooth loss, and two individuals exhibit periapical abscesses. Unsurprisingly, antemortem tooth loss increased with age and was the pathological condition most frequently noted. While anterior teeth were only recovered with eleven adult individuals and two juvenile individuals, only one adult and one juvenile exhibit signs of linear enamel hypoplasias (LEHs), or stress-related disruptions of decreased enamel thickness when the tooth crown is developing (Hillson 2002). Since LEHs of anterior teeth are quite ubiquitous among pre-Columbian populations, it is interesting to only observe a few individuals with these dental non-specific indicators of childhood stress. It is possible that fewer defects reflect a less stressful period of growth and development. However, considering the limited number of anterior dentitions available for analysis, it is not possible to support this conclusion.

Arthritis is also a commonly observed pathological condition in this sample. Several adult individuals exhibit joint osteoarthritis and vertebral osteophytosis. Osteoarthritis is generally a non-inflammatory arthritis of the synovial (highly moveable limb) joints that results in a progressive deterioration of joint and bone and cartilage and can be associated with activities or advanced age (Burt et al. 2013; Rogers and Waldron 1995). Spinal osteophytosis is identified as lipping, which occurs on the margins of the vertebral bodies due to issues with the annulus fibrosus (the outer section of the fibrocartilaginous intervertebral disks) (Burt et al. 2013; Rogers and Waldron 1995). Schmorl's nodes, which are scooped depressions of the vertebral bodes due to a vertical disk herniation (Burt et al. 2013; Rogers and Waldron 1995), are present in two adult individuals. Although six individuals exhibit spinal osteophytosis (ranging from mild to severe), it is not possible to determine the prevalence of spinal osteophytosis within the sample due to the fragmentary nature of the remains.

Fifteen individuals exhibit synovial joint osteoarthritis, including one individual (A-NPC-2-4) with eburnation (advanced bone polishing) of the right patella (knee) and the superior and inferior articular surfaces of the first and second cervical vertebrae. Almost all cases of osteoarthritis were observed in middle-aged or older adults. According to Larsen (2015), examining osteoarthritis can provide a general sense of activity for past populations, but it may be difficult to determine specific activities. Unfortunately, since it is not possible to determine the prevalence of osteoarthritis within the Red House sample due to the fragmentary nature of the remains, it is difficult to infer particular activities based on patterns of osteoarthritis.

Other pathological conditions included inflammatory bone lesions such as periostitis and osteomyelitis. These inflammatory responses may reflect a variety of infectious diseases, including bacterial infection and infection following traumatic injury, or they may be non-specific (Larsen 2015). However, since many other conditions leave no trace on the skeleton, we may be underestimating the prevalence or impact of these disease stressors (Waldron 2009; Wood et al. 1992). In this sample fifty-five femora were available for analysis and two femora, or 3.64% of the sample, exhibit periostitis. Forty-seven tibiae were available for analysis and eight tibiae, or 17.02% of the sample, exhibit periostitis and one tibia, or 2.13% of the sample, exhibit osteomyelitis. Forty-one fibulae were available for analysis and three fibulae, or 7.32% of the sample, exhibit periostitis. Fifty-seven humeri were available for analysis and one humerus, or 1.75% of the sample, exhibits osteomyelitis.

The incidents of inflammatory lesions in the Red House sample is fairly low when compared to the Tutu site, in which nearly all individuals exhibited such lesions (Sandford et al. 2002), including over 50% of bones affected on the parietals, patellae and tibiae. While the highest incident of inflammatory lesions for postcranial bones at the Red House sample was the tibiae (17.0%), the tibiae represented only the third highest percentage (54.8%) of affected bones at the Tutu site (Sandford et al. 2002). However, in the Tutu sample most of these lesions are consistent with possible chronic treponemal disease, and those at the Red House may represent non-specific periosteal reactions.

Common cranial vault pathology frequently associated with metabolic or dietary stresses include cribra orbitalia (lesions on the orbital roof) and porotic hyperostosis (lesions primarily affecting parietal bones) (Ortner 2003). While many of the crania were fragmentary, it is still possible to identify examples of cribra orbitalia and porotic hyperostosis. In this sample, there are two adult individuals with orbital roof lesions and three adult individuals with porous hypertrophic lesions. Similarly, cribra orbitalia and porotic hyperostosis are also identified in both adult and juvenile remains at the Tutu site. These lesions in this sample suggest they may have suffered from non-specific dietary or pathological stresses, potentially iron deficiency anemia (Walker et al. 2009; Larsen 2015; Lewis 2007).

One individual exhibiting a suite of pathological conditions related to stress during growth and development is an older child (A-G38-2-SIP), unfortunately represented by less than 25% of the skeleton (figure 4.1). However, even though the skeleton was fragmentary and poorly preserved, many pathological conditions

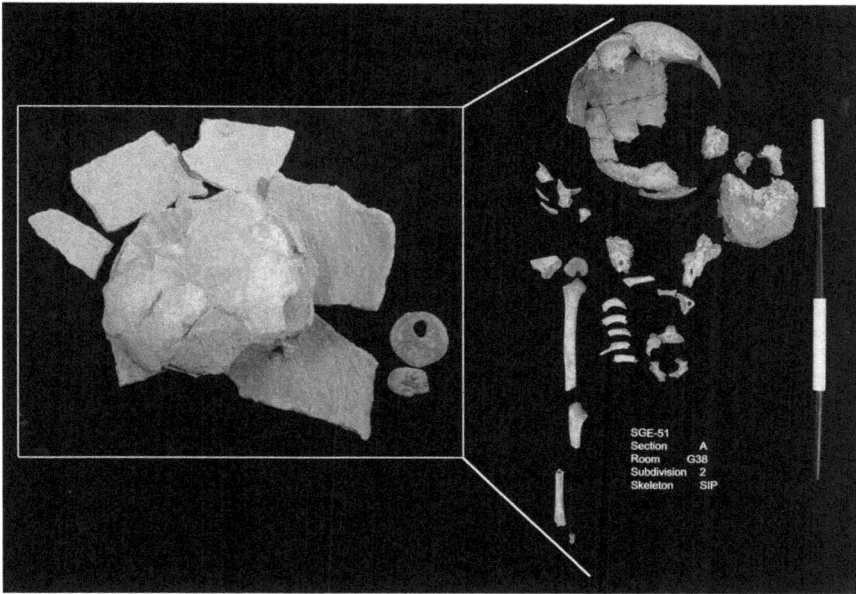

Figure 4.1.
Overall image of an older child (A-G38-2-SIP), including the burial bowl and associated grave goods (call out box), prior to processing and after reconstruction.

were observable, including an LEH to the permanent upper right central incisor, cribra orbitalia and porotic hyperostosis, as well as a large occlusal carious lesion to the lower left deciduous first molar. This individual was interred in a shallow bowl with significant grave goods and was the only burial of this kind recovered from the Red House site.

Cultural Modification

In addition to evaluating evidence of pathological conditions, identifying indicators of cultural behaviors can also provide important contributions to biocultural patterns in the skeleton. Within the Red House sample, there are several notable cultural indicators, including dental wear, artificial cranial modification and bilateral asymmetry.

One female individual (B-RFA-8-1) exhibits a pronounced groove on the occlusal surface of the right maxillary central incisor similar to examples from other pre-Columbian skeletal samples where teeth were used as tools (Mickleburgh 2007; Molnar 2011). This type of grooving more than likely represents an activity in which some type of cord was being pulled through the teeth. For example, although outside of the Caribbean, Lorkiewicz (2011) identified side-to-side grooves to both the maxillary and mandibular incisors and canine teeth of female individuals as consistent with pulling string for yarn production or weaving through their teeth.

Five individuals exhibit a unique form of flat wear on the anterior lingual surface of their maxillary incisors consistent with lingual surface attrition of the maxillary anterior teeth (known as "LSAMAT"). In their study of a skeletal population from the Corondó site in Brazil, Turner and Machado (1983) identified this pattern of dental wear as a cultural modification caused by using the anterior teeth as tools. Mickleburgh (2007) similarly reports multiple incidents of LSAMAT from the Anse à la Gourde site on Guadeloupe Island as does Larsen et al. (2002) for the Tutu Village site on St Thomas.

In addition to behaviors that inadvertently leave traces in skeletal remains, some practices such as artificial cranial modification may be intended to signal important social identities (Tiesler 2014). Of nineteen cranial vaults complete enough for observation, there are four examples and two possible examples of artificial cranial modification, including both sexes. Other possible examples were confounded by postdepositional fragmentation. Variation in cranial modification forms reflects tabular, tabular erect and oblique modification forms, which may suggest examples of intentional and unintentional modification (Buikstra and Ubelaker 1994).

While the specific objectives or meanings behind the intentional practice of artificial cranial modification vary greatly and are often regionally specific, certain cultural inferences are common (Torres-Rouff and Yablonsky 2005). The practice of visible body modification creates a tangible link between biology and culture. Tiesler (2014, 23) points out that artificial cranial modification is a marker of identity performed by parents on their children, "as it can only take place while the baby's skull is malleable". In general, the fontanelles of the cranial vault close and the bones of the calvarium harden and begin to fuse by the third year of life (Scheuer and Black 2000; Tiesler 2014), thereby limiting the period of time in which the greatest level of modification can be achieved. Viewed against the backdrop of developmental stages, this practice may also take its place along a continuum of "universal manifestations" reflected in a variety of rites of passage related to cultural and group identities (Tiesler 2014, 24). Artificial cranial modification has been noted in the Caribbean, and according to Sandford et al. (2002), fronto-occipital flattening is the most frequent type identified in the Greater Antilles and the Bahamas. Interestingly, artificial cranial modification was not found at the Tutu site, but it is quite common among contemporaneous mainland Central and South American groups and may suggest intraregional contact or migration to the island of different cultural groups.

Along with artificial cranial modification, other forms of skeletal remodelling can also offer information regarding cultural behaviors. Three individuals exhibit bilateral asymmetry recognized by expanded cortical thickness and enlarged muscle attachments sites of the long bones of the upper limb, especially of the humeri. The right humeri of three individuals are asymmetrically larger, but only one (A-CSNW-4-2) (figure 4.2) could be assessed for increased robusticity of the forearm; the other two are incomplete). Jurmain (1999) notes that mechanical

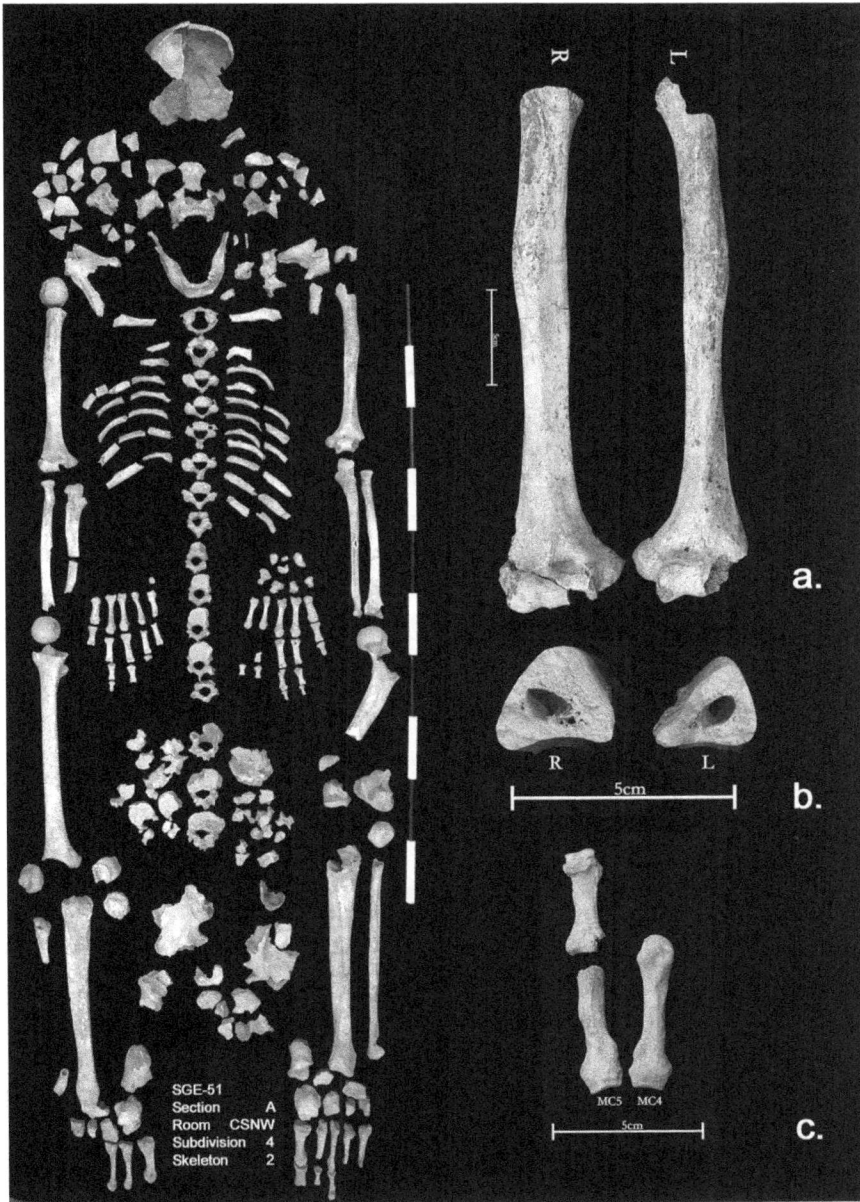

Figure 4.2.
Overall image
of an older male
(A-CSNW-4-2)
exhibiting bilateral
asymmetry of the
humeri (*a*) and
ulnae (*b*), as well as
a healed transverse
shaft fracture to the
right fifth metacar-
pal (*c*).

factors influence the shape, density and remodelling properties of bone, and Kennedy (1989, 155–56) points out that musculoskeletal markers represent a form of boney response to activity stress. Furthermore, Larsen (2015) proposes that asymmetry of the long bones, and the humerus in particular, has both a genetic and functional component. However, the functional component can be used in interpretation of past populations' activities, while here it may suggest a life of physical labour preferentially using the right arm. While a myriad of activities could be proposed that are linked to archaeological indicators of lifestyle, we may be better able to define major daily activities using these tantalizing clues preserved in the skeletons as more skeletal samples are examined from this area of the world.

Trauma

Overall, few antemortem (healed) traumatic injuries were identified in both males and females. With the exception of one individual who could only be aged as an adult, all cases are found in middle-aged and older adults. Three individuals exhibit healed transverse fractures of metacarpal shafts (figure 4.2). Fractures to the metacarpals can be the result of blows to the hands and can also occur when striking an object with a closed fist (often referred to as "boxer's fracture"). In addition, one probable female individual exhibits healed fractured ribs, even though ribs are poorly preserved overall. There are two instances of fractured long bones, including a healed displaced mid-shaft fracture to the

Figure 4.3.
Middle-older age male (A-NPC7-1), exhibiting a healed depressed fracture above the left orbit consistent with ante-mortem blunt force trauma.

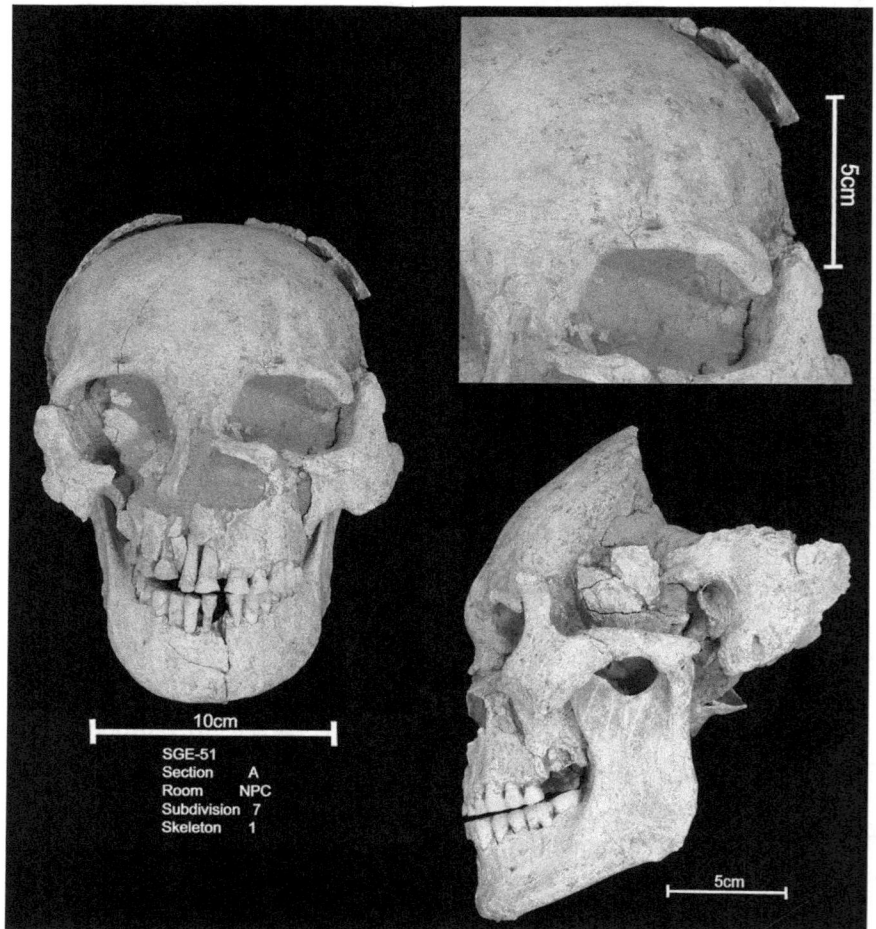

right humerus of an older probable male and a healed Colles's fracture with dorsal displacement to the distal left radius of a middle-aged or older male. While almost all of the observed fractures are consistent with direct trauma, they are likely to be accidental in nature.

On the other hand, of particular interest is a healed depressed fracture above the left orbit of an older male individual (A-NPC-7-1), which is consistent with blunt force trauma (figure 4.3). The location of this injury is more consistent with non-lethal interpersonal violence. Interestingly, while low levels of trauma were noted at the Tutu site, the authors believe there was no evidence for regular interpersonal violence (Sandford et al. 2002).

Perimortem Trauma

We only identified one individual, an adolescent male (A-CEP7-1), who exhibits a possible traumatic lesion consistent with perimortem interpersonal trauma, occurring at or around the time of death (figure 4.4). A depressed impact site (approximately 25 × 30 millimetres wide) with radiating fractures is consistent with blunt force trauma located on the anterolateral aspect of the left parietal. While significant, this single case does not necessarily indicate a consistent level of interpersonal violence in the community.

When interpreting the possibility of interpersonal violence in the Red House sample, both antemortem and perimortem trauma must be considered. Evidence of interpersonal violence noted in both the antemortem and perimortem periods within this sample indicates some level of social conflict. Harrod et al. (2012, 64) point out that "in intra-group conflict, non-lethal violence is similar to lethal violence in that the desired outcome of confrontation is to gain status or resources through the submission of the other individual(s)". While these skeletal traumatic lesions may represent intra or inter-group or island violence, without tighter chronological or more specific archaeological indicators, currently these examples do not allow for inferences about the experience of social violence.

SUMMARY AND CONCLUSION

This investigation makes a major contribution to the limited research identified by Sandford et al. (2002) and Laffoon and DeVos (2011), who pointed out that few excavations of skeletal assemblages utilizing modern techniques and standards have been undertaken in the Caribbean archipelago, and even fewer such investigations have been completed in the Lesser Antilles. While this sample does not represent a chronologically uniform population and is fragmentary in nature, the information gleaned about the individuals from the Red House site provides a wealth of information. For example, through osteological analyses

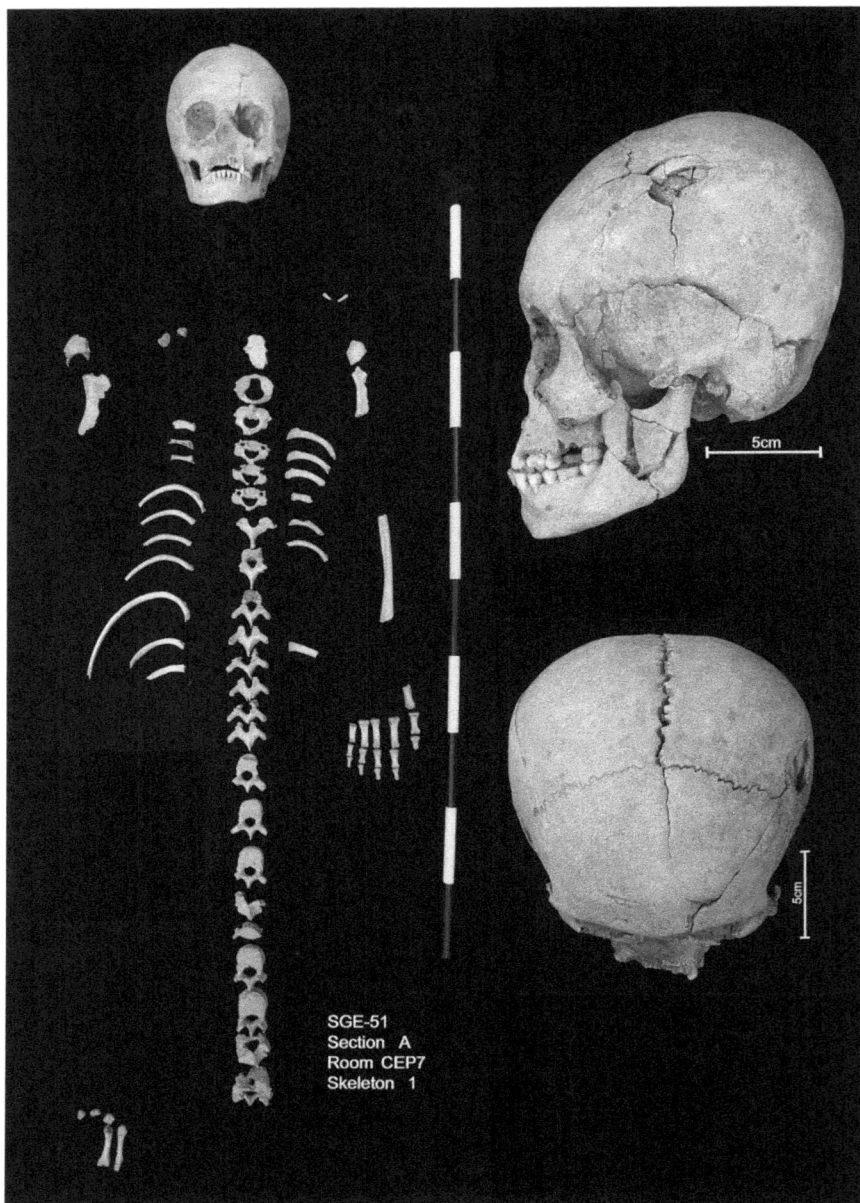

Figure 4.4.
Adolescent male (A-CEP7-1) exhibiting a depressed fracture to the left parietal consistent with perimortem blunt force trauma.

a minimum number of sixty individuals, representing males, females, adults and juveniles were identified.

Additionally, pathological conditions are consistent with other sites in the Lesser Antilles, such as the Tutu site, including cribra orbitalia, porotic hyperostosis, infectious bone disease, degenerative joint disease and dental pathologies. The presence and degree of expression of these bone diseases allows us to infer health and disease experiences regardless of the sample limitations (Pfeiffer 2003). However, when comparing the Red House sample to the Tutu sample

(Sandford et al. 2002), the overall number of individuals and bones affected with pathological conditions is notably less for the Red House sample. Although this may indicate that individuals living at the Red House site experienced less physiological stress during both growth and development and during later adulthood, the fragmentary nature of the sample may have resulted in an under-representation of pathological conditions. Indicators of cultural activity such as bilateral asymmetry of the upper limb bones, artificial cranial modification and dental wear indicative of the use of teeth as tools were also noted in the Red House sample, suggesting complex social identities and activity lifestyles. This valuable sample and initial analysis lays the foundation for future interpretations of pre-colonial life on Trinidad and other island populations in the Caribbean.

ACKNOWLEDGEMENTS

We wish to thank the Office of the Parliament of the Republic of Trinidad and Tobago for funding this research and Professor Basil Reid for inviting us to participate in this project. Also, we wish to acknowledge the gracious assistance that we received from numerous members of the Red House archaeological team while conducting our on-site research and after returning to UCF to complete the skeletal analysis.

REFERENCES

Agarwal, S.C., and B.A. Glencross, eds. 2011a. *Social Bioarchaeology*. Malden, CA: Wiley-Blackwell.

———. 2011b. "Building a Social Bioarchaeology". In Agarwal and Glenncross 2011a, 1–12.

Baker, B.J., T.L. Dupras and M.W. Tocheri. 2005. *The Osteology of Infants and Children*. College Station: Texas A&M Press.

Boomert, A. 2000. *Trinidad, Tobago and the Lower Orinoco Interaction Sphere: An Archaeological/Ethnohistorical Study*. Alkmaar, the Netherlands: Cairi.

Buikstra, J.E., and D.H. Ubelaker. 1994. *Standards for Data Collection from Human Skeletal Remains*. Fayetteville: Arkansas Archaeological Survey.

Buzon, M.R. 2016. "The Bioarchaeological Approach to Paleopathology". In *A Companion to Paleopathology*, edited by A.L. Grauer, 58–75. West Sussex, UK: Wiley-Blackwell.

Burt, N.M., D. Semple, K. Waterhouse and N.C. Lovell. 2013. *Identification and Interpretation of Joint Disease in Paleopathology and Forensic Anthropology*. Springfield, Illinois: Charles C. Thomas.

Byers, S.N. 2011. *Introduction to Forensic Anthropology*. 4th ed. New York: Allyn and Bacon.

Cohen, M.N., J.W. Wood and G.R. Milner 1994. "The Osteological Paradox Reconsidered". *Current Anthropology* 35 (5): 629–37.

Crespo-Torres, E.F., H.L. Mickleburgh and R.V. Rojas. 2013. "The Study of Pre-Columbian Human Remains in the Caribbean Archipelago: From Descriptive Osteology to a Bioarchaeological Approach". In *The Oxford Handbook of Caribbean Archaeology*, edited by W.F Keegan, C.L. Hofman and R. Rodriguez Ramos, 346–431. Oxford: Oxford University Press.

del Angel, A., and H.B. Cisneros. 2004. "Technical Note: Modification of Regression Equations Used to Estimate Stature in Mesoamerican Skeletal Remains". *American Journal of Physical Anthropology* 125:264–65.

Doran, G.H. N.d. "Osteological Analysis of the Human Skeletal Remains from the Aklis Site, St Croix, Virgin Islands". Report on file with Southeast Archaeological Center, National Park Service.

Genovés, S. 1967. "Proportionality of the Long Bones and Their Relation to Stature Among Mesoamericans". *American Journal of Physical Anthropology* 26:67–78.

Glencross, B.A. 2011. Skeletal Injury Across the Life Course: Towards Understanding Social Agency". In Agarwal and Glencross 2011a, 390–409.

Goodman, A.H. 1993. "On the Interpretation of Health from Skeletal Remains". *Current Anthropology* 34:281–88.

Goodman, A.H., and D.L. Martin. 2002. "Reconstructing Health Profiles from Skeletal Remains". In *The Backbone of History: Health and Nutrition in the Western Hemisphere*, edited by R.H. Steckel and J.C. Rose, 11–60. Cambridge: Cambridge University Press.

Goodwin, R.C. 1979. "The History and Development of Osteology in the Caribbean Area". *Revista Review Inter Americana* 8 (3): 463–94.

Harrod R.P., P. Liénard and D.L. Martin. 2012. "Deciphering Violence in Past Societies: Ethnography and the Interpretation of Archaeological Populations". In *The Bioarchaeology of Violence*, edited by D.L. Martin, R.P. Harrod and V.R. Pérez, 63–82. Gainesville: University Press of Florida.

Hillson, S. 2002. *Dental Anthropology*. Cambridge: Cambridge University Press.

———. 2008. "The Current State of Dental Decay". In *Techniques and Application in Dental Anthropology*, edited by J.D. Irish and G.C. Nelson 111–35. Cambridge: Cambridge University Press.

Jurmain, R.D. 1999. *Stories from the Skeleton: Behavioral Reconstruction in Human Osteology*. New York: Gordon and Breach.

Kennedy, K.A.R. 1989. "Skeletal Markers of Occupational Stress". In *Reconstruction of Life from the Skeleton*, edited by M.Y. Iscan and K.A.R. Kennedy, 129–60. New York: Allen R. Liss.

Larsen, C.S. 2015. *Bioarchaeology: Interpreting Behavior from the Human Skeletal*. Cambridge: Cambridge University Press.

Larsen, C.S., M.F. Teaford and M.K. Sandford. 2002. "The Tutu Teeth: Assessing Prehistoric Health and Lifeway from St Thomas". In *The Tutu Archaelogical Village Site: A Multidisciplinary Case Study in Human Adaptation*, edited by E. Righter, 230–49. New York: Routledge.

Laffoon, J.E., and B.R. de Vos. 2011. "Diverse Origins, Similar Diets: An Integrated Isotopic Perspective from Anse à la Gourde, Guadeloupe". In *Communities in Contact: Essays in Archaeology, Ethnohistory and Ethnography of the Amerindian Circum-Caribbean*, edited by C.L. Hofman and A. van Duijvenbode, 187–204. Leiden: Sidestone Press.

Lewis, M.E. 2007. *The Bioarcheology of Children: Perspectives from Biological and Forensic Anthropology*. Cambridge: Cambridge University Press.

Lorkiewicz, W. 2011. "Nonalimentary Tooth Use in the Neolithic Population of the Lengyel

Culture in Central Poland (4600–4000 BC). *American Journal of Physical Anthropology* 144:538–51.

Maresh, M.M. 1970. "Measurements from Roentgenograms". In *Human Growth and Development*, edited by R.W. McCammon, 157–200. Springfield, IL: Charles C. Thomas.

Margerison, B.J., and C.J. Knüsel. 2002. "Paleodemographic Comparison of a Catastrophic and an Attritional Death Assemblage". *American Journal of Physical Anthropology* 119:134–43.

McKern, T.W., and T.D. Stewart. 1957. "Skeletal Age Changes in Young American Males". *Quartermaster Research and Development Command (Tech Rept. EP)* 45:1–37.

Meyers, P.L. 2016. "Bioarchaeological Investigations of the Red House Archaeological Site, Port of Spain, Trinidad: A Pre-Columbian Mid-Late Ceramic Age Caribbean Population". MA thesis, University of Central Florida.

Mickleburgh, H.L. 2007. *Teeth Tell Tales: Dental Wear as Evidence for Cultural Practices at Anse à la Gourde and Tutu*. Leiden: Sidestone Press.

Molnar, P. 2011. "Extramasticatory Dental Wear Reflecting Habitual Behavior and Health in Past Populations". *Clinical Oral Investigations* 15:681–89.

Ortner, D.J. 2003. *Identification of Pathological Conditions in Human Skeletal Remains*. Oxford: Academic Press.

Pearson, O.M., and J.E. Buikstra. 2006. "Behavior and the Bones". In *Bioarchaeology: The Contextual Analysis of Human Remains*, edited by J.E. Buikstra and L.A. Beck, 207–66. New York: Academic Press Elsevier.

Pfeiffer, S. 2003. "The Health of the Moatfield People as Reflected in Paleopathological Features". In *Bones of the Ancestors: The Archaeology and Osteobiography of the Moatfield Site*, edited by R.F. Williamson and S. Pfeiffer, 205–22. Toronto: Canadian Museum of Civilization.

Rogers, J., and T. Waldron. 1995. *A Field Guide to Joint Disease in Archaeology*. New York: John Wiley.

Sandford, M.K., G. Bogdan and G.E. Kissling. 2002. "Biological Adaptation in the Prehistoric Caribbean: Osteology and Bioarchaeology of the Tutu Site". In *The Tutu Archaeological Village Site: A Multidisciplinary Case Study in Human Adaptation*, edited by E. Righter, 209–29. London: Routledge.

Saul, F.P. 1978. "Osteobiography: Life History Recorded in Bone". In *The Measures of Man*, edited by E. Giles and J. Fridlander, 372–82. Cambridge: Peabody Museum Press.

Schaefer, M.C. 2008. "A Summary of Epiphyseal Union Timings in Bosnian Males". *American Journal of Physical Anthropology* 18 (5): 536–45.

Scheuer, L., and S. Black. 2000. *Developmental Juvenile Osteology*. New York: Academic Press Elsevier.

Temple, D.H., and A.H. Goodman. 2014. "Bioarchaeology Has a 'Health' Problem: Conceptualizing 'Stress' and 'Health' in Bioarchaeological Research". *American Journal of Physical Anthropology* 155 (2): 1–6.

Tiesler, V. 2014. *The Bioarchaeology of Artificial Cranial Modifications: New Approaches to Head Shaping and Its Meanings in Pre-Columbian Mesoamerica and Beyond*. New York: Springer.

Torres-Rouff, C., and L.T. Yablonsky. 2005. "Cranial Vault Modification as a Cultural

Artifact: A Comparison of the Eurasian Steppes and the Andes". *HOMO-Journal of Comparative Human Biology* 56 (1): 1–16.

Turner, C.G., II. 1979. "Dental Anthropological Indications of Agriculture among the Jomon People of Central Japan". *American Journal of Physical Anthropology* 51:619–36.

Turner, C.G., and L.M.C. Machado 1983. "A New Dental Wear Pattern and Evidence for High Carbohydrate Consumption in a Brazilian Archaic Skeletal Population". *American Journal of Physical Anthropology* 61 (1): 125–30.

Ubelaker, D.H. 1989. *Human Skeletal Remains: Excavation, Analysis, Interpretation*, 2nd ed. Washington, DC: Taraxacum.

Waldron, T. 2009. *Paleopathology.* Cambridge: Cambridge University Press.

Walker, P.L., R.R. Bathurst, R. Richman, T. Gjerdrum and V.A. Andrusko. 2009. "The Causes of Porotic Hyperostosis and Cribra Orbitalia: A Reappraisal of the Iron-Deficiency-Anemia Hypothesis". *American Journal of Physical Anthropology* 139:109–25.

Wood, J.W., G.R. Milner, H.C. Harpending, K.M. Weiss, M.N. Cohen, L.E. Eisenberg, D.L. Hutchinson, R. Jankauskas, G. Cesneys, A. Katzenberg, J.R. Lukacs, J.W. McGrath, E.A. Roth, D.H. Ubelaker and R.G. Wilkinson. 1992. "The Osteological Paradox: Problems of Inferring Prehistoric Health from Skeletal Samples". *Current Anthropology* 33 (4): 343–70.

Zuckerman, M.K., and G.J. Armelagos. 2011. "The Origins of Biocultural Dimensions in Bioarchaeology". In Agarwal and Glencross 2011a, 15–34.

CHAPTER 5

Lipid Residue Analysis of Pre-colonial Ceramics from the Red House

MARY MALAINEY, TIMOTHY FIGOL, BASIL A. REID,
MAKINI EMMANUEL AND ANDREW MAURICE

IN 2014 THIRTY-SIX PRE-COLONIAL POTTERY SHERDS FROM THE site were submitted for lipid residue analysis to Professor Mary Malainey at Brandon University, Manitoba (Canada). This exercise was designed to reconstruct the former vessel contents of pre-contact indigenous pottery from the Red House and, from this, infer the foodways of the pre-colonial inhabitants of the site.

Excavations within the Amerindian cultural horizon recovered a range of faunal materials. These included remains from eight species of animals: *Mazama americana trinitatis* (red brocket deer), *Tayassu tajacu* (collared peccary) (figure 5.1), *Cuniculus paca* (lappe), *Dasypus novemcinctus* (nine-banded armadillo/ tatu), *Dasyprocta leporina* (red-rumped agouti), *Didelphis marsupialis insularis* (common opossum/manicou) (figure 5.2) and *Iguana iguana* (green iguana), as well as members of the *Chondrichthyes* (shark) class, *Ariidae* (catfish) (figure 5.3) and *Dasyatidae* (stingray) families (figure 5.4). In addition, over twenty-four types of mollusc gastropods and bivalves were retrieved from the site, with the mangrove oyster (*Crassostrea rhizophorae*) (figure 5.5), lucines (*Codakia* sp.) (figure 5.6) and Caribbean crown conch (*Melongena melongena*) (figure 5.7) accounting for 95% of all the molluscs that have to date been catalogued (Reid 2015). Mangrove oysters, which constitute the majority of shell discoveries at the Red House, are found predominantly in the form of shell middens. Apparently they were collected from nearby mangroves and brought to the site, where the soft tissues therein were consumed (Reid 2015).

Lipid residue analysis suggests a close correlation between pre-colonial pottery use and the preparation of a miscellany of animal and plant foods. It is likely that several of the items described in the previous paragraph were prepared, cooked and/or consumed in the ceramic vessels, represented by the thirty-six pre-colonial pottery samples. Derivatives of their total lipid extracts were analysed using gas chromatography (GC), high temperature GC (HT-GC)

Figure 5.1.
Collared peccary
(*Tayassu tajacu*).
Courtesy of Mike
Rutherford,
Department of Life
Sciences, University
of the West Indies,
St Augustine.

Figure 5.2.
Manicou (*Didelphis
marsupialis insu-
laris*). Courtesy of
Mike Rutherford,
Department of Life
Sciences, University
of the West Indies,
St Augustine.

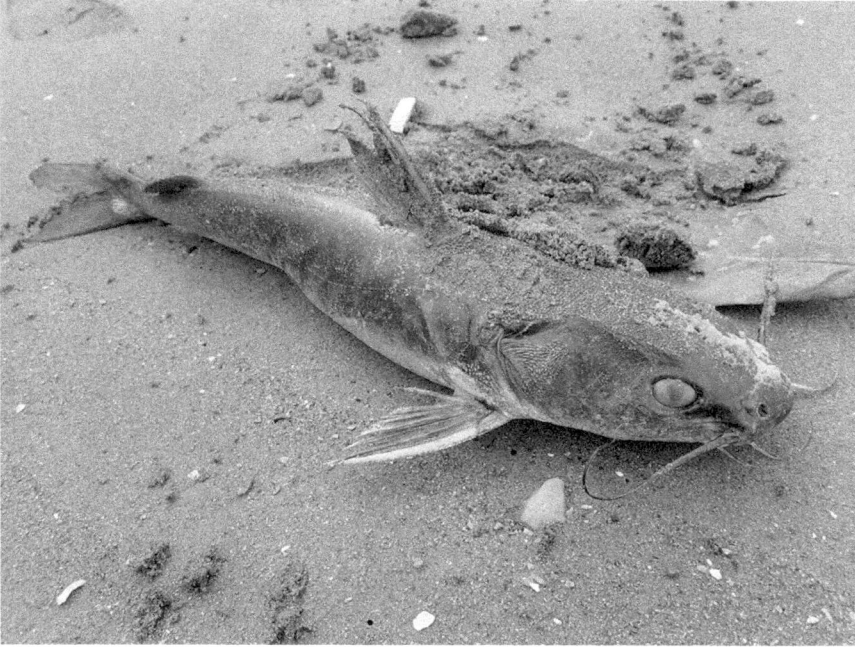

Figure 5.3.
Catfish (*Ariidae*).
Courtesy of Amy
Deacon, Department
of Life Sciences,
University of the
West Indies,
St Augustine.

Figure 5.4.
Stingray
(*Dasyatidae*).
Courtesy of Mike
Rutherford,
Department of Life
Sciences, University
of the West Indies,
St Augustine.

Figure 5.5.
Mangrove oyster
(*Crassostrea rhizo-
phorae*) from the
Red House site.
Courtesy of Zara Ali
and the Office of the
Parliament of the
Republic of Trinidad
and Tobago.

Figure 5.6.
Lucine (*Codakia* sp.).
Courtesy of Zara Ali
and the Office of the
Parliament of the
Republic of Trinidad
and Tobago.

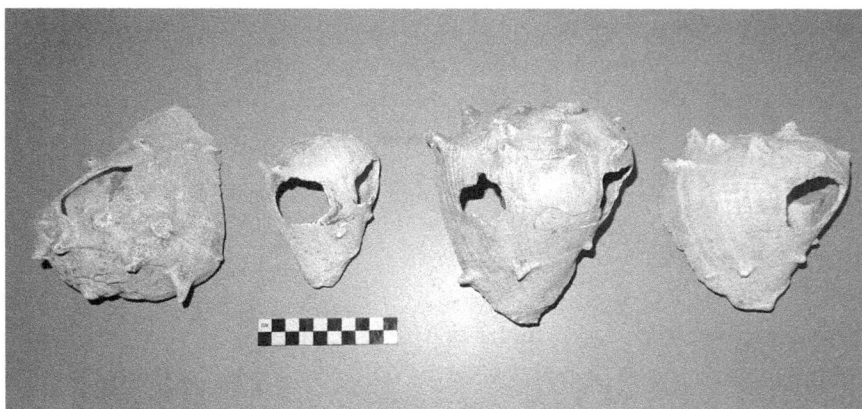

Figure 5.7.
Caribbean crown
conch (*Melongena
melongena*).
Courtesy of Zara Ali
and the Office of the
Parliament of the
Republic of Trinidad
and Tobago.

and high temperature gas chromatography with mass spectrometry (HT-GC/ MS). Residue identifications were based on fatty acid decomposition patterns of experimental residues, lipid distribution patterns and the presence of bio-markers. Ten lipid residues were identified as medium fat content and low fat content plant residues, and eight lipid residues had high levels of $C18:0$. Residues with high and moderate-high levels of $C18:1$ isomers also occurred. The fatty acid compositions of two residues bordered medium and moderate-high fat content. Thirteen residues were characterized on the basis of lipid biomarkers and triacylglycerol distribution, and in two of these residues evidence of plant products were detected. The others represented plant and animal combinations; animal residues were dominant in one and plant residues were dominant in another. Phytolith analysis of sediments removed from the grindstones, for instance, revealed the presence of maize cob phytoliths, suggesting that maize was ground with the implements (Piperno 2014); a palm phytolith, recovered from one of the grindstones, also suggests the use of palms (Piperno 2014).

LIPID RESIDUE ANALYSIS AND RED HOUSE
SITE PRE-COLONIAL POTTERY

Lipids are a broad category of compounds that are insoluble in water; those of archaeological interest include fatty acids, triacylglycerols, sterols, waxes and terpenes (Malainey et al. 2010). Rottländer (1990) noted that lipid analysis is suitable for the study of vessel contents because they are present in virtually all human food, they have a relatively high stability with increased temperature (up to 400°C) and their decomposition from cooking temperatures, compared to carbohydrates and proteins, is minimal.

The Saladoid inhabitants and their descendants probably used their ceramic vessels for storage, food preparation, cooking and serving. Vessels such as hammock-shaped bowls might have been used in both ceremonial and domestic contexts (Boomert 2000; Sajo 2014). Red House postsherds found in situ with human skeletal remains were selected to undergo lipid residue analysis. Sherds weighing no less than 10 grams from several different parts of the site were submitted for analysis. All specimens were unwashed and handled with gloved hands.

METHODOLOGY

Descriptions of the pottery samples analysed are presented in table 5.1. Possible contaminants were removed by grinding off exterior surfaces of each sample with a Dremel® tool fitted with a silicon carbide bit. Immediately thereafter, it was crushed with a hammer mortar and pestle and the powder transferred to an Erlenmeyer flask. Lipids were extracted using a variation of the method developed by Folch et al. (1957). The powdered sample was mixed with a 2:1 mixture, by volume, of chloroform and methanol (2 × 25 mL) using ultra-sonication (2 × 10 min). Solids were removed by filtering the solvent mixture into a separatory funnel, and the lipid/solvent filtrate was washed with 13.3 mL of ultrapure water. Once separation into two phases was complete, the lower chloroform-lipid phase was transferred to a round-bottomed flask and the chloroform removed by rotary evaporation. Any remaining water was removed by evaporation with 2-propanol (1.5 mL); 1.5 mL of chloroform-methanol (2:1, v/v) was used to transfer the dry total lipid extract to a screw-top glass vial with a Teflon-lined cap. The resulting total lipid extract was flushed with nitrogen and stored in a −20°C freezer.

Preparation of FAMES

A 400 μL (or 200 μL for residue 14TRN 29) aliquot of the total lipid extract solution was placed in a screw-top test tube and dried in a heating block under nitrogen. Fatty acid methyl esters (FAMES) were prepared by treating the dry lipid with 3 mL of 0.5 N anhydrous hydrochloric acid in methanol (68°C; 60 min). Fatty acids that occur in the sample as di- or triglycerides are detached from the glycerol molecule and converted to methyl esters. After cooling to room temperature, 2.0 mL of ultrapure water was added. FAMES were recovered with petroleum ether (2 × 1.5 mL) and transferred to a vial. The solvent was removed by heat under a gentle stream of nitrogen; the FAMES were dissolved in 75 μL (or 200 μL for residue 14TRN 29) of iso-octane then transferred to a GC vial with a conical glass insert.

Table 5.1. List of Pottery Samples from the Red House

Lab Number	Sample Code	Context Information	Level from Topsoil (m)	Description	Sample Mass (g)
14TRN 1	G43Sd2PS1108	Section A, G43, Subdivision Two (2)	1.08	Rim sherd	13.108
14TRN 2	G43Sd2PS2108[1]	Section A, G43, Subdivision Two (2)	1.08	Body sherd	14.535
14TRN 3	G43Sd1PS1133	Section A, G43, Subdivision One (1)	1.33	Base sherd	12.623
14TRN 4	G43Sd1PS2133	Section A, G43, Subdivision One (1)	1.33	Base sherd	12.078
14TRN 5	G43Sd1PS1128	Section A, G43, Subdivision One (1)	1.28	Basal sherd	14.369
14TRN 6	G43Sd1PS2128	Section A, G43, Subdivision One (1)	1.28	Body sherd	13.164
14TRN 7	G38Sd2PS1130	Section A, G38, Subdivision Two (2)	1.3–1.5	Body sherd	14.803
14TRN 8	G38Sd2PS2130	Section A, G38, Subdivision Two (2)	1.3–1.5	Base sherd	12.199
14TRN 9	G38Sd1PS1120	Section A, G38, Subdivision One (1)	1.2–1.32	Body sherd	10.669
14TRN 10	G38Sd1PS2120	Section A, G38, Subdivision One (1)	1.2–1.32	Body sherd	13.468
14TRN 11	NPCG56Sd1PS1121	Section A, North Parliament Chamber, G56, Subdivision One (1)	1.21	Base sherd	15 672
14TRN 12	NPCG56Sd1PS2121	Section A, North Parliament Chamber, G56, Subdivision (1)	1.21	Body sherd	13.190
14TRN 13	NPCSd2PS1041	Section A, North Parliament Chamber, Subdivision Two (2)	0.41–0.63	Body sherd	12.628
14TRN 14	NPCSd2PS2041	Section A, North Parliament Chamber, Subdivision Two (2)	0.41–0.63	Rim sherd	12.095
14TRN 15	NPCSd2PS1039	Section A, North Parliament Chamber, Subdivision Two (2)	0.39	Rim sherd	13.784
14TRN 16	NPCSd2PS2039	Section A, North Parliament Chamber, Subdivision Two (2)	0.39	Body sherd	14.379
14TRN 17	NPCSd2PS1034	Section A, North Parliament Chamber, Subdivision Two (2)	0.34	Body sherd	12.788
14TRN 18	NPCSd2PS2034	Section A, North Parliament Chamber, Subdivision Two (2)	0.34	Body sherd	12.887
14TRN 19	RFASd5PS1150	Section B, Rotunda, Fountain Area, Subdivision (5)	Soil–1.5	Base sherd	13.172

Table 5.1 continues

Table 5.1. List of Pottery Samples from the Red House (*continued*)

Lab Number	Sample Code	Context Information	Level from Topsoil (m)	Description	Sample Mass (g)
14TRN 20	RFASd5PS2150	Section B, Rotunda, Fountain Area, Subdivision (5)	Soil–1.5	Rim sherd	13.115
14TRN 21	RFASd7PS1146A	Section B, Rotunda, Fountain Area, Subdivision (7)	1.46–1.56	Rim sherd	9.975
14TRN 22	RFASd7PS2146A	Section B, Rotunda, Fountain Area, Subdivision (7)	1.46–1.56	Body sherd	10.678
14TRN 23	RFASd7PS1146B	Section B, Rotunda, Fountain Area, Subdivision (7)	1.46–1.56	Base sherd	13.196
14TRN 24	RFASd7PS2146B	Section B, Rotunda, Fountain Area, Subdivision (7)	1.46–1.56	Body sherd	11.382
14TRN 25	RFASd8PS1134	Section B, Rotunda, Fountain Area, Subdivision (8)	1.34–1.57	Rim sherd	9.882
14TRN 26	RFASd8PS2134	Section B, Rotunda, Fountain Area, Subdivision (8)	1.34–1.57	Body sherd	11.387
14TRN 27	RFASd8PS1145	Section B, Rotunda, Fountain Area, Subdivision (8)	1.45	Body sherd	12.156
14TRN 28	RFASd8PS2145	Section B, Rotunda, Fountain Area, Subdivision (8)	1.45	Body sherd	10.611
14TRN 29	CSNWSd4PS1085A	Crawl Space North West Subdivision (4)	0.85–1.5	Body sherd	9.918
14TRN 30	CSNWd4PS2085A[2]	Crawl Space North West Subdivision (4)	0.85–1.5	Body sherd	11.901
14TRN 31	CSNESd1PS1129	Crawl Space North East Subdivision (1)	1.29–1.53	Body sherd	11.340
14TRN 32	CSNESd1PS2129	Crawl Space North East Subdivision (1)	1.29–1.53	Body sherd	13.236
14TRN 33	CSNWSd4PS1085B	Crawl Space North West Subdivision (4)	0.85–1.5	Body sherd[3]	10.434
14TRN 34	CSNWSd4PS2085B	Crawl Space North West Subdivision (4)	0.85–1.5	Body sherd	13.182
14TRN 35	CSNWSd4PS1136	Section A, Crawl Space North West Subdivision (4)	1.36–1.55	Body sherd	9.635
14TRN 36	CSNWSd4PS2136	Section A, Crawl Space North West Subdivision (4)	1.36–1.55	Body sherd	9.181

[1] Sample code on bag was G43Sd21PS2108.
[2] Sample code on bag was CSNWSd4PS2085A.
[3] Sample was a rim sherd.

Preparation of TMS Derivatives

A 200 μL aliquot of the total lipid extract solution was placed in a screw-top vial and dried under nitrogen. Trimethylsilyl (TMS) derivatives were prepared by treating the lipid with 70 μL of N,O-bis(trimethylsilyl)trifluoro-acetamide (BSTFA) containing 1% trimethylchlorosilane, by volume (70°C; 30 min). The sample was then dried under nitrogen, and the TMS derivatives were redissolved in 100 μL of hexane.

Solvents and chemicals were checked for purity by running a sample blank. Traces of fatty acid contamination were subtracted from sample chromatograms. Relative percentage compositions were calculated by dividing the integrated peak area of each fatty acid by the total area of fatty acids present in the sample. In order to identify the residue on the basis of fatty acid composition, relative percentage composition was determined first with respect to all fatty acids present in the sample (including very long chain fatty acids) and second with respect to the ten fatty acids utilized in the development of the identification criteria (C12:0, C14:0, C15:0, C16:0, C16:1, C17:0, C18:0, C18:1ω9, C18:1ω11 and C18:2) (not shown). The second step is necessary for the application of the identification criteria presented in table 5.2. It must be understood that the identifications given do not necessarily mean that those particular foods were actually prepared, because different foods of similar fatty acid composition and lipid content would produce similar residues (see table 5.3). It is possible only to say that the material of origin for the residue was similar in composition to the food(s) indicated. High temperature gas chromatography and high temperature gas chromatography with mass spectrometry are used to further clarify the identifications.

Table 5.2. Criteria for the Identification of Archaeological Residues Based on the Decomposition Patterns of Experimental Cooking Residues Prepared in Pottery Vessels

Identification	Medium Chain	C18:0	C18:1 Isomers
Large herbivore	≤15%	≥27.5%	≤15%
Large herbivore with plant or bone marrow	low	≥25%	$15\% \leq X \leq 25\%$
Plant with large herbivore	≥15%	≥25%	no data
Beaver	low	Low	≥25%
Fish or corn	low	≤25%	$15\% \leq X \leq 27.5\%$
Fish or corn with plant	≥15%	≤25%	$15\% \leq X \leq 27.5\%$
Plant (except corn)	≥10%	≤27.5%	≤5%

Table 5.3. Known Food Sources for Different Types of Decomposed Residues

Decomposed Residue Identification	Plant Foods Known to Produce Similar Residues	Animal Foods Known to Produce Similar Residues
Large herbivore	Tropical seed oils, including sotol seeds, cocoa butter	Bison, deer, moose, fall–early winter fatty elk meat, javelina meat
Large herbivore with plant or bone marrow		
Low fat content plant (plant greens, roots, berries)	Jicama tuber, buffalo gourd, yopan leaves, biscuit root, millet	Cooked camel's milk
Medium-low fat content plant	Prickly pear, Spanish dagger	None
Medium fat content (fish or corn)	Corn, mesquite beans, cholla	Freshwater and marine fish, Rabdotus snail, terrapin, late winter fat-depleted elk
Moderate-high fat content (beaver)	Texas ebony	Beaver and probably raccoon or any other fat medium-sized mammals
High fat content	High-fat nuts and seeds, including acorn and pecan	Rendered animal fat (other than large herbivore), including bear fat
Very high fat content	Very high fat nuts and seeds, including pine nuts	Freshly rendered animal fat (other than large herbivore)

Gas Chromatography Analysis Parameters

GC analysis was performed on a Varian 3800 gas chromatograph fitted with a flame ionization detector connected to a personal computer. Samples were separated using a VF-23 fused silica capillary column (30 m × 0.25 mm I.D.; Varian). An autosampler injected the sample using a split/splitless injection system; hydrogen was used as the carrier gas with a column flow of 1.0 mL/min. Column temperature was increased from 80°C to 140°C at a rate of 20°C per minute then increased to 185°C at a rate of 4°C per minute. After a four-minute hold, the temperature was increased to 250°C at 10°C per minute and held for two minutes. Chromatogram peaks were integrated using Varian MS Workstation software and identified through comparisons with external qualitative standards (NuCheck Prep).

High Temperature Gas Chromatography and Gas Chromatography with Mass Spectrometry

Both HT-GC and HT-GC/MS analyses were performed on a Varian 3800 gas chromatograph fitted with a flame ionization detector and a Varian 4000 mass spectrometer connected to a personal computer. For HT-GC analysis, samples were injected onto a DB-1HT fused silica capillary column (15 m × 0.32 mm I.D.; Agilent J&W) connected to the flame ionization detector, using hydrogen as the carrier gas. Column temperature was held at 50°C for one minute, then increased to 350°C at a rate of 15°C per minute and held for twenty-six minutes. For HT-GC/MS analysis, samples were injected onto a DB-5HT fused silica capillary column (30 m × 0.25 mm ID; Agilent J&W) connected to the ion trap mass spectrometer in an external ionization configuration using helium as the carrier gas. After a one-minute hold at 50°C, column temperature was increased to 180°C at a rate of 40°C per minute then ramped up to 230°C at a rate of 5°C per minute and finally increased to 350°C at a rate of 15°C per minute and held for 27.75 minutes. The Varian 4000 mass spectrometer was operated in electron-impact ionization mode scanning from m/z 50–700. Chromatogram peaks and MS spectra were processed using Varian MS Workstation software and identified through comparisons with external qualitative standards (Sigma Aldrich; NuCheck Prep), reference samples and the National Institute of Standards and Technology database.

Residue Identification

Over the last four decades, different instrumental techniques have been used to obtain information about archaeological lipid residues. The most commonly employed involve component separation with gas chromatography: gas chromatography with a flame ionization detector (GC), gas chromatography with mass spectrometry (GC/MS) and, recently, gas chromatography-combustion-isotope ratio analysis (GC-C-IRMS).

Samples were removed from the artefacts and the fatty acid extracts were analysed using gas chromatography. Fatty acids are the major constituents of fats and oils (lipids) and occur in nature as triglycerides in different relative amounts and combinations in various plants and animals, making them ideal for linking archaeological residue to the foods that produced them. Polyunsaturated fatty acids, which are found widely in fish and plants, decompose more readily than saturated fatty acids or monounsaturated fatty acids, sterols or waxes (Solomons 1980; Frankel 1991).

Since employed by Condamin et al. (1976), gas chromatography has been used extensively to analyse the fatty acid component of absorbed archaeological residues. The technique for identifying archaeological pottery residues on the basis of fatty acid composition was developed by Malainey (1997; Malainey et al. 1999a, 1999b, 1999c, 2001a). Instead of relying on the fatty acid ratios observed in fresh animals and plants (Marchbanks 1989; Skibo 1992; Loy 1994), an approach similar to Patrick et al. (1985), which simulated the effects of long-term decomposition on seal meat, was followed.

Table 5.4. Summary of Average Fatty Acid Compositions of Modern Food Groups Generated by Hierarchical Cluster Analysis

Cluster	A					B						C			
Sub-cluster	I	II	III	IV	V	VI	VII	VIII	IX	X	XI	XII	XIII	XIV	XV
Type	Mammal Fat and Marrow	Large Herbivore Meat	Fish	Fish	Berries and Nuts	Mixed	Seeds and Berries	Roots	Seeds	Mixed	Greens	Berries	Roots	Greens	Roots
C16:0	19.90	19.39	16.07	14.10	3.75	12.06	7.48	19.98	7.52	10.33	18.71	3.47	22.68	24.19	18.71
C18:0	7.06	20.35	3.87	2.78	1.47	2.36	2.58	2.59	3.55	2.43	2.48	1.34	3.15	3.66	5.94
C18:1	56.77	35.79	18.28	31.96	51.14	35.29	29.12	6.55	10.02	15.62	5.03	14.95	12.12	4.05	3.34
C18:2	7.01	8.93	2.91	4.04	41.44	35.83	54.69	48.74	64.14	39.24	18.82	29.08	26.24	16.15	15.61
C18:3	0.68	2.61	4.39	3.83	1.05	3.66	1.51	7.24	5.49	19.77	35.08	39.75	9.64	17.88	3.42
VLCS	0.16	0.32	0.23	0.15	0.76	4.46	2.98	8.50	5.19	3.73	6.77	9.10	15.32	18.68	43.36
VLCU	0.77	4.29	39.92	24.11	0.25	2.70	1.00	2.23	0.99	2.65	1.13	0.95	2.06	0.72	1.10

VLCS = very long chain (C20, C22 and C24) saturated fatty acids

VLCU = very long chain (C20, C22 and C24) unsaturated fatty acids

First the fatty acid compositions of over 130 food plants and animals native to North America were determined (Malainey 1997; Malainey et al. 1999a, table 5.4). Then the effects of decomposition due to cooking and degradation processes that act over long periods of time were explored (Malainey 1997; Malainey et al. 1999b; Quigg et al. 2000, 2001). This work enabled the development of criteria for the characterization of archaeological lipid residues (table 5.2). The results of further research (Malainey et al. 2000a, 2000b, 2000c, 2001a) has enabled Malainey (2007) to refine the identification criteria and determine which plant and animal foods produce similar residues (table 5.3).

Evershed (1993, 2000; Evershed et al. 1990, 1991, 1997a, 2001) and others have had great success in identifying biomarkers using high temperature gas chromatography (HT-GC) and gas chromatography with mass spectrometry (HT-GC/MS). Biomarkers for the conifer products (Shackley 1982; Heron and Pollard 1988), birch (Sauter et al. 1987), brassica family leafy vegetables (Evershed et al. 1991; Charters et al. 1997) and beeswax (Heron et al. 1994; Evershed et al. 1997b) are well established. The potential use of a variety of other compounds, or distributions of compounds, to serve as possible biomarkers for other products have also been proposed (Dudd and Evershed 1998; Eerkens 2002; Regert 2007; Reber et al. 2004). The compilation edited by Barnard and Eerkens (2007) includes examples of the use of both biomarkers and criteria based on fatty acid composition to identify lipid residues. Our methods, described below, are based on similar techniques.

RESULTS OF ARCHAEOLOGICAL DATA ANALYSIS

The full lipid compositions of twenty-three residues are presented in table 5.5. The heading "Area" represents the area under the chromatographic peak of a given fatty acid, as calculated by the Varian MS Workstation software minus the solvent blank. The heading "Rel%" represents the relative percentage of the fatty acid with respect to the total fatty acids in the sample. Hydroxide or peroxide degradation products can interfere with the integration of the $C22:0$ and $C22:1$ peaks; these fatty acids were excluded from the analysis. Overall, lipid recoveries from many Red House pottery samples were poor. Ideally, residues should have total area counts of 200,000 or more; many of the residues extracted from Red House pottery had total area counts of about 100,000. Low lipid recoveries increases the uncertainty associated with the identifications; results of the HT-GC and HT-GC/MS analyses of thirteen residues with insufficient fatty acids to attempt identification are presented in table 5.6.

Residues were analysed for the presence of lipid biomarkers and triacylglycerols (TAGs) using HT-GC and HT-GC/MS. The data obtained is useful for distinguishing plant residues, animal residues and plant/animal combinations.

Table 5.5. Lipid Compositions and Identifications of Residues from Red House Pottery

Fatty Acid	14TRN 6		14TRN 7		14TRN 10		14TRN 11		14TRN 15	
	Area	Rel%	Area	Rel%	Area	Rel%	Area	Rel%	Area	Rel%
C12:0	2282	1.55	1372	1.17	862	0.72	1540	1.38	0	0.00
C14:0	3909	2.65	2305	1.97	2593	2.16	3178	2.84	617	0.58
C15:0	1364	0.93	665	0.57	1733	1.45	1388	1.24	594	0.55
C16:0	60145	40.85	55991	47.92	49483	41.31	47601	42.56	46211	43.12
C16:1	0	0.00	0	0.00	0	0.00	0	0.00	0	0.00
C17:0	1781	1.21	1777	1.52	1312	1.10	1933	1.73	1636	1.53
C17:1	0	0.00	0	0.00	0	0.00	0	0.00	0	0.00
C18:0	30463	20.69	30566	26.16	28610	23.89	24036	21.49	27646	25.80
C18:1s	35244	23.94	18441	15.78	28452	23.75	20848	18.64	22657	21.14
C18:2	2392	1.62	818	0.70	795	0.66	2091	1.87	906	0.85
C18:3ω3	0	0.00	0	0.00	0	0.00	0	0.00	0	0.00
C20:0	4315	2.93	4285	3.67	4040	3.37	4480	4.01	3542	3.30
C20:1	4303	2.92	611	0.52	918	0.77	2630	2.35	2726	2.54
C24:0	1042	0.71	0	0.00	976	0.81	2108	1.88	639	0.60
Total	147240	100.00	116831	100.00	119774	100.00	111833	100.00	107174	100.00
Biomarkers	Possibly cholesterol; dehydroabietic acid		Possibly dehydroabietic acid		Possibly cholesterol; Possibly β-sitosterol dehydroabietic acid		Probably cholesterol; dehydroabietic acid		Possibly β-sitosterol; possibly dehydroabietic acid	
Triacylglcerols	Possible C48 and C50 TAGs and possible traces of others; plant and animal combination		Possible C48 and C50 TAGs and possible traces of others; plant and animal combination		Possible C48, C50 and C52 TAGs and possible traces of C54; animal and plant combination, dominated by animal products		C50 TAG, possible C48 TAG and possible traces of others; animal and plant products, dominated by animal		C50 TAG, possible C48 TAG and possible traces of others; animal and plant products, dominated by animal	
Identification	Medium fat content (fish) and plant		Elevated C18:0 and medium fat content; similar to large herbivore and plant or bone marrow		Medium fat content (fish), plant probably present		Medium fat content (fish) and plant		Elevated C18:0 and medium fat content; similar to large herbivore and plant or bone marrow	

Table 5.5 continues

Fatty Acid	14TRN 16		14TRN 17		14TRN 18		14TRN 19		14TRN 20	
	Area	Rel%	Area	Rel%	Area	Rel%	Area	Rel%	Area	Rel%
C12:0	0	0.00	0	0.00	0	0.00	0	0.00	922	0.61
C14:0	1321	1.23	815	0.60	609	0.63	1252	1.32	2232	1.48
C15:0	971	0.91	827	0.61	584	0.60	512	0.54	872	0.58
C16:0	49484	46.16	54617	40.38	39030	40.29	41786	44.07	57888	38.28
C16:1	0	0.00	0	0.00	0	0.00	529	0.56	0	0.00
C17:0	2028	1.89	2170	1.60	1682	1.74	1464	1.54	1924	1.27
C17:1	0	0.00	0	0.00	0	0.00	0	0.00	0	0.00
C18:0	29934	27.93	30579	22.61	26796	27.66	21401	22.57	30244	20.00
C18:1s	14852	13.86	32333	23.90	21282	21.97	18702	19.73	42368	28.02
C18:2	1290	1.20	1897	1.40	1368	1.41	1428	1.51	2817	1.86
C18:3ω3	0	0.00	0	0.00	0	0.00	0	0.00	0	0.00
C20:0	5012	4.68	5229	3.87	3216	3.32	4222	4.45	4214	2.79
C20:1	1745	1.63	5724	4.23	2312	2.39	2997	3.16	6494	4.29
C24:0	555	0.52	1077	0.80	0	0.00	517	0.55	1229	0.81
Total	107192	100.00	135268	100.00	96879	100.00	94810	100.00	151204	100.00
Biomarkers	β-sitosterol; probably stigmasterol; probably dehydroabietic acid		Possibly β-sitosterol; probably dehydroabietic acid		Possibly cholesterol, β-sitosterol and stigmasterol; probably dehydroabietic acid		Possibly β-sitosterol; dehydroabietic acid		Possibly cholesterol; probably dehydroabietic acid	
Triacylglcerols	Possible C48 and C50 TAGs and possible traces of others; plant and animal combination		C48 and C50 TAGs and possible traces of others; plant and animal combination		C48 TAG, possible C50 and C52 TAGs and possible trace of C54 TAG; plant and animal products, dominated by plant		Possible C48 and C50 TAGs and possible traces of others; plant and animal combination		Possible C48 and C50 TAGs and possible traces of others; plant and animal combination	
Identification	High 18:0 level food; plant products occur, animal products probably present		Medium fat content (fish) and plant		High 18:0 level food and medium fat content; similar to large herbivore and plant or bone marrow		Medium fat content (fish) and plant		Moderate-high fat content and plant	

Table 5.5 continues

Table 5-5. Lipid Compositions and Identifications of Residues from Red House Pottery (*continued*)

Fatty Acid	14TRN 21		14TRN 22		14TRN 24		14TRN 25		14TRN 26	
	Area	Rel%	Area	Rel%	Area	Rel%	Area	Rel%	Area	Rel%
C12:0	0	0.00	0	0.00	983	0.75	2450	1.32	1575	0.93
C14:0	1368	1.18	2888	2.45	3138	2.41	4826	2.61	4370	2.59
C15:0	923	0.80	2039	1.73	1754	1.35	2016	1.09	1885	1.12
C16:0	50712	43.70	55160	46.79	58648	45.01	73627	39.75	72698	43.00
C16:1	0	0.00	0	0.00	0	0.00	0	0.00	571	0.34
C17:0	1760	1.52	2101	1.78	1966	1.51	2183	1.18	2125	1.26
C17:1	0	0.00	0	0.00	0	0.00	0	0.00	0	0.00
C18:0	32710	28.18	31814	26.99	36617	28.10	35774	19.31	35321	20.89
C18:1s	15906	13.71	13778	11.69	16209	12.44	50449	27.23	32223	19.06
C18:2	1990	1.71	2482	2.11	2279	1.75	2019	1.09	1815	1.07
C18:3ω3	0	0.00	0	0.00	0	0.00	0	0.00	0	0.00
C20:0	4235	3.65	4322	3.67	2604	2.00	4883	2.64	4792	2.83
C20:1	5193	4.47	2703	2.29	5043	3.87	5518	2.98	10502	6.21
C24:0	1262	1.09	598	0.51	1047	0.80	1501	0.81	1175	0.70
Total	116059	100.00	117885	100.00	130288	100.00	185246	100.00	169052	100.00
Biomarkers	Possibly β-sitosterol; dehydroabietic acid		Probably cholesterol; dehydroabietic acid		Possibly β-sitosterol; probably dehydroabietic acid		Possibly cholesterol and β-sitosterol; dehydroabietic acid		Probably cholesterol; dehydroabietic acid	
Triacylglcerols	C48 and C50 TAGs and possible traces of others; plant and animal combination		Possible C48 and C50 TAGs and possible traces of others; plant and animal combination		Possible C48 and C50 TAGs and possible traces of others; plant and animal combination		C48, possible C50 TAGs and possible traces of others; plant and animal products dominated by plant		Possible C48 and C50 TAGs and possible traces of others; plant and animal combination	

Table 5.5 continues

Fatty Acid	14TRN 27		14TRN 28		14TRN 29 Dilluted		14TRN 31		14TRN 32	
	Area	Rel%	Area	Rel%	Area	Rel%	Area	Rel%	Area	Rel%
C12:0	896	0.53	0	0.00	1111	0.11	875	0.60	775	0.62
C14:0	3568	2.10	1832	1.37	23158	2.24	2257	1.56	2337	1.87
C15:0	1457	0.86	990	0.74	33045	3.20	1200	0.83	837	0.67
C16:0	70363	41.40	46714	34.93	267266	25.91	69521	47.92	51433	41.17
C16:1	0	0.00	0	0.00	1115	0.11	0	0.00	0	0.00
C17:0	2267	1.33	1734	1.30	69896	6.77	2344	1.62	1664	1.33
C17:1	0	0.00	0	0.00	1580	0.15	0	0.00	0	0.00
C18:0	39313	23.13	22919	17.14	504883	48.94	36024	24.83	30032	24.04
C18:1s	40114	23.60	53601	40.08	23402	2.27	27481	18.94	34142	27.33
C18:2	2127	1.25	991	0.74	0	0.00	821	0.57	1270	1.02
C18:3ω3	0	0.00	0	0.00	0	0.00	0	0.00	0	0.00
C20:0	5182	3.05	2933	2.19	105344	10.21	4550	3.14	2446	1.96
C20:1	3899	2.29	2017	1.51	0	0.00	0	0.00	0	0.00
C24:0	758	0.45	0	0.00	876	0.08	0	0.00	0	0.00
Total	169944	100.00	133731	100.00	1031676	100.00	145073	100.00	124936	100.00
Biomarkers	Possibly cholesterol and β-sitosterol; dehydroabietic acid		Possibly β-sitosterol; probably dehydroabietic acid		Cholesterol; possibly β-sitosterol and possibly dehydroabietic acid		Dehydroabietic acid		Possibly stigmasterol; dehydroabietic acid	
Triacylglcerols	Possible C48 and C52 TAGs and possible traces of others; animal and plant combination, possibly dominated by animal products		Possible C48 and C50 TAGs and possible traces of others; plant and animal combination		C48: C50: C52: C54 TAG Peak Ratio 9.3: 7.3: 3.3: 1; plant and animal products dominated by plant		C48, possible C50 TAGs and possible traces of others; plant and animal products dominated by plant		C50 TAG, possibly C48 and possible traces of others; animal and plant combination dominated by animal	

Table 5-5 continues

Table 5.5. Lipid Compositions and Identifications of Residues from Red House Pottery (*continued*)

Fatty Acid	14TRN 34		14TRN 35		14TRN 36	
	Area	Rel%	Area	Rel%	Area	Rel%
C12:0	1001	0.53	0	0.00	0	0.00
C14:0	5622	2.99	2307	1.96	2696	2.55
C15:0	1933	1.03	760	0.65	1525	1.44
C16:0	86537	46.06	54953	46.68	38701	36.60
C16:1	0	0.00	0	0.00	0	0.00
C17:0	3296	1.75	1816	1.54	1502	1.42
C17:1	0	0.00	0	0.00	0	0.00
C18:0	43367	23.08	24067	20.44	21447	20.28
C18:1s	38180	20.32	25110	21.33	33448	31.63
C18:2	901	0.48	5258	4.47	1884	1.78
C18:3ω3	0	0.00	0	0.00	0	0.00
C20:0	5972	3.18	3445	2.93	2328	2.20
C20:1	543	0.29	0	0.00	2208	2.09
C24:0	518	0.28	0	0.00	0	0.00
Total	187870	100.00	117716	100.00	105739	100.00
Biomarkers	Probably β-sitosterol, stigmasterol and dehydroabietic acid		Possibly β-sitosterol and stigmasterol; dehydroabietic acid; possibly Azelaic acid		Dehydroabietic acid	
Triacylglcerols	Possible C48 and C50 TAGs and possible traces of others; plant and animal combination		Possible C48 and C50 TAGs and possible traces of others; plant and animal combination		Possible C48 TAG and possible traces of others; plant products dominant	
Identification	Medium fat content (fish), plant probably present		Medium fat content (fish) with traces of plant seeds		Moderate-high fat content; possibly dominated by plant	

Table 5.6. Biomarker and TAG Distributions of Lipid Residues with Insufficient Fatty Acids

Lab No.	Biomarkers Detected	Occurrence of Triacylglycerols (TAGs)	Identification
14TRN 1	Probably dehydroabietic acid	Possible C48 and C50 TAGs and possible traces of others; plant and animal combination	Plant and animal products; conifer products probably present
14TRN 2	Possibly β-sitosterol; dehydroabietic acid	Possible C48 TAG and possible traces of others; plant products dominant	Plant products; conifer products present
14TRN 3	Possibly cholesterol; possibly dehydroabietic acid	Probable C48 TAG and possible traces of others; plant products dominant	Plant and animal products; conifer products may be present
14TRN 4	Possibly cholesterol; dehydroabietic acid	Possible C48 and C50 TAGs and possible traces of others; plant and animal combination	Plant and animal products; conifer products present
14TRN 5	Probably dehydroabietic acid	Possible C48 and C50 TAGs and possible traces of others; plant and animal combination	Plant and animal products; conifer products probably present
14TRN 8	Dehydroabietic acid	Possible C48 and C50 TAGs and possible traces of others; plant and animal combination	Plant and animal products; conifer products present
14TRN 9	Possibly β-sitosterol; probably dehydroabietic acid	Possible C48 and C50 TAGs and possible traces of others; plant and animal combination	Plant and animal products; conifer products probably present
14TRN 12	Dehydroabietic acid	C48, possible C50 TAGs and possible traces of others; plant and animal products dominated by plant	Plant and animal products, dominated by plant, conifer products present
14TRN 13	Possibly β-sitosterol; probably dehydroabietic acid	C50, possible C48 TAGs and possible traces of others; animal and plant products dominated by animal	Plant and animal products; conifer products probably present, possibly dominated by animal
14TRN 14	Probably cholesterol, β-sitosterol and dehydroabietic acid; possibly stigmasterol	Possible C48 TAG and possible traces of others; plant products dominant	Plant and animal products, dominated by plant; conifer products present
14TRN 23	Probably dehydroabietic acid	Possible C48 and C50 TAGs and possible traces of others; plant and animal combination	Plant and animal products; conifer products probably present
14TRN 30	Probably dehydroabietic acid	C48 TAG and possible traces of others; plant products dominant	Plant products; conifer products probably present
14TRN 33	Possibly stigmasterol; probably dehydroabietic acid	Possible C48 and C50 TAGs and possible traces of others; plant and animal combination	Plant and animal products; conifer products probably present

The sterol cholesterol is associated with animal products; β-sitosterol, stigmasterol and campesterol are associated with plant products. The presence and abundance of TAGs varies with the material of origin. When present, amounts of TAGs tend to decrease with increasing numbers of carbon atoms in plant residues (Malainey et al. 2010, 2014, in press). The peak arising from the C48 TAG is largest, and peak size (and area) progressively decreases, with the C54 TAG peak being the smallest. A line drawn to connect the tops of the C48, C50, C52 and C54 TAG peaks slopes down to the right. In animal residues, amounts of TAGs tend to increase with carbon numbers, with the C52 or C54 TAG peaks being the largest (Malainey et al. 2010, 2014). A line drawn to connect the tops of the C48, C50, C52 and C54 TAG peaks either resembles a hill or the line slopes up to the right. A parabola-like pattern, such as the shape of a "normal distribution", can also occur in the residues of oil seeds that contain high levels of C18:1 isomers (Malainey et al. 2010, 2014, in press).

Medium Fat Content and Low Fat Content Plant Residues

Ten residues extracted from Red House pottery appear to result from the preparation of medium fat content plant and/or animal foods; plant material is present or possibly present in all of these residues. These residues are characterized as medium fat content because their levels of C18:1 isomers range between 18.64% and 23.94%. Examples of plant foods known to produce medium fat content residues include mesquite, corn and cholla. Freshwater and marine fish, terrapin, *Rabdotus* snail, marine mollusc and late winter, fat-depleted elk are examples of animal foods known to produce medium fat content residues, and based on the faunal remains recovered from the site, fish and molluscs are the probable source of these residues. Given the variability in the fatty acid compositions of the residues, it is likely that the residues from more than one fish and/or mollusc species occur. Remains of members of the *Chondrichthyes* (shark) class, *Ariidae* (catfish) and *Dasyatidae* (stingray) families were recovered and must be considered the possible sources of some of these residues (Reid 2015). Reid (2015) reported that over twenty-four types of molluscs were recovered from the site. Of these, the mangrove oyster (*Crassostrea rhizophorae*), lucine (*Codakia* sp.) and Caribbean crown conch (*Melongena melongena*) are most common and the probable sources. All of these residues have C18:0 levels that exceed 20% of the relative fatty acid composition, which also indicates the presence of animal products. Maize phytoliths were recovered from the site; maize is a medium fat content plant and it could be present in certain samples.

Five of these residues – 14TRN 6, 14TRN 11, 14TRN 17, 14TRN 19 and 14TRN 26 – are identified as medium fat content (probably fish or molluscs) and plant. The presence of low fat content plant products (greens, roots and berries) is strongly indicated by the elevated levels of medium chain saturated (C12:0, C14: C15:0) and very long chain (C20:0 and C20:1) fatty acids in the residues; the latter are fatty acids that commonly occur in low fat content plants from warmer environments. The sum of these fatty acids in the residues exceeds 10% of the relative fatty acid composition. The animal sterol cholesterol is probably or possibly present in residues 14TRN 6, 14TRN 11 and 14TRN 26. The plant sterol β-sitosterol may occur in residues 14TRN 17 and 14TRN 19. Dehydroabietic acid occurs or may occur in all of these residues; this biomarker indicates the presence of conifer products, which may have been introduced from firewood, resins, pine nuts or other conifer products. The triacylglycerol (TAG) distributions detected in residues 14TRN 6, 14TRN 17, 14TRN 19 and 14TRN 26 are consistent with a combination of plant and animal products. The prominent C50 TAG in residue 14TRN 11 indicated that animal products dominate the residue but that plant products also occur.

Low fat content plant material is probably present in three other medium fat content residues, 14TRN 10, 14TRN 27 and 14TRN 34. The presence of plant material is suggested by the somewhat elevated levels of medium chain saturated and very long chain fatty acids in the residues. The sums of these fatty acids form between 8.30% and 9.29% of their relative fatty acid compositions. Both the animal sterol cholesterol and the plant sterol β-sitosterol may occur in residues 14TRN 10 and 14TRN 27. The plant sterols β-sitosterol and stigmasterol are probably present in residue 14TRN 34. The biomarker for conifer products, dehydroabietic acid, occurs or probably occurs in all residues. While the TAG distributions of all three residues suggest the presence of both plant and animal products, animal products appear to dominate residues 14TRN 10 and 14TRN 27.

On the basis of their relative fatty acid compositions, two residues, 14TRN 31 and 14TRN 35, are identified as medium fat content (probably fish or molluscs) with traces of plant. The presence of plant in these residues is suggested by the slightly elevated levels of medium chain saturated and very long chain fatty acids, about 6%. No sterols were detected in residue 14TRN 31. The plant sterols β-sitosterol and stigmasterol may occur in residue 14TRN 35; azelaic acid may occur. Azelaic acid is a short chain dicarboxylic acid associated with the oxidation of unsaturated fatty acids (Regert et al. 1998). Unsaturated fatty acids are most abundant in seed oils, so it is possible that residue 14TRN 35 in part reflects the processing of plant seeds. The biomarker for conifer products, dehydroabietic acid, occurs or may occur in both residues. The TAG distributions detected in these residues suggest the presence of both plant and animal products; however, plant products dominate residue 14TRN 31.

Residues with High Levels of C18:0

The levels of the fatty acid C18:0 in eight residues, 14TRN 7, 14TRN 15, 14TRN 16, 14TRN 18, 14TRN 21, 14TRN 22, 14TRN 24 and 14TRN 29, exceed 25%. In North American sites, similarly high levels of C18:0 are typically associated with the preparation of large herbivores, such as bison, deer, moose, fat elk meat or other bovines or cervids (table 5.2). However, javelina meat, tropical oil seeds and cocoa butter also produce residues high in C18:0 and must be considered as potential sources where available (table 5.3). On the basis of the faunal recoveries, red brocket deer (*Mazama americana trinitatis*) and collared peccary/wild pig (*Tayassu tajacu*) are potential sources of residues with high levels of C18:0 that are of animal origin (Reid 2015).

The level of C18:0 in residue 14TRN 29 was unique in that it was very high, 48.94%, and the level of C18:1 isomers was very low, only 2.27%. Residues of similar composition are known to result from the preparation of very lean large herbivore meat but other high C18:0 plant foods could produce similar residues. Medium chain saturated and very long chain fatty acids form 15.85% of the residue composition, which indicates that low fat content plants are present. The presence of the animal sterol cholesterol was confirmed; the plant sterol β-sitosterol and the conifer biomarker dehydroabietic acid may occur. The ratio of C48, C50, C52 and C54 TAG peaks is 9.3: 7.3: 3.3: 1, which suggests residue 14TRN 29 represents a plant and animal combination dominated by plant. It is also important to note that the amount of the total lipid extract in the residue 14TRN 29 FAMES analysed needed to be one-fifth that of the other Red House pottery residues so that it would not overload the column. Even so, the total area count of the fatty acid peaks in residue 14TRN 29 was about ten times greater than other residues from the site. This seems to indicate that the function of the vessel from which residue 14TRN 29 was extracted may have been different from other Red House vessels examined.

The fatty acid compositions of three residues, 14TRN 16, 14TRN 21 and 14TRN 24, are practically identical. The levels of C18:0 in these residues fall between 27.93% and 28.18%, and C18:1 isomer levels range from 12.44% to 13.86%. The levels of medium chain saturated and very long chain fatty acids are just over 11% in residue 14TRN 21 and 14TRN 24, which indicates that low fat content plants are present. The level is just under 9% in residue 14TRN 16, suggesting that some low fat content plant products are probably present. The presence of plant products is supported by the confirmed presence of the plant sterol β-sitosterol in residue 14TRN 16 and its possible presence in residues 14TRN 21 and 14TRN 24. The plant sterol stigmasterol probably occurs in residue 14TRN 16. The biomarker for conifer products, dehydroabietic acid, occurs or probably occurs in all residues. The distributions of TAGs in all three residues suggest they represent plant and animal combinations.

The levels of the fatty acid C18:0 in residues 14TRN 15 and 14TRN 18 are similar to those described above, ranging from 25.80% to 27.66%; however, the levels of C18:1 isomers is much higher, over 21%. The fatty acid composition of residue 14TRN 7 is also quite similar, but the level of C18:1 isomers is 15.78%. Foods known to produce residues with similar compositions are bone marrow and combinations of large herbivore products and medium fat content plant material, such as corn (table 5.2; Malainey et al. 1999b). As noted above, large herbivore products, javalina meat, tropical seed oils and cocoa butter are known to produce residues with high levels of C18:0. A combination of any of these products with a medium fat content plant material would produce residues of similar composition. The animal sterol cholesterol and the plant sterols β-sitosterol and stigmasterol may occur in the residue 14TRN 18. The plant sterol β-sitosterol may occur in residue 14TRN 15. No sterols were detected in residue 14TRN 7. The biomarker for conifer products, dehydroabietic acid, probably or possibly occurs in all residues. The distributions of TAGs in all residues suggests that both plant and animal products are present; however, plant products dominate residue 14TRN 18 and animal products dominate residue 14TRN 15.

The fatty acid composition of residue 14TRN 22 is quite similar to those described above, but the level of C18:1 isomers is lower, only 11.69%, and the level of medium chain saturated and very long chain fatty acids is higher, 10.65%. It is possible that the same foods that produced residue 14TRN 7 were prepared in this vessel, but low fat content plants, such as greens, roots and berries, were also present. The animal sterol cholesterol probably occurs; the conifer biomarker dehydroabietic acid is present. The distribution of TAGs in the residue suggests that plant and animal products are present.

High Fat Residues: Residues with High Levels of C18:1 Isomers

Residue 14TRN 28 was unique in that the level of C18:1 isomers was high, exceeding 40%; these fatty acids are the major constituents of pure fats and oils. Foods known to produce residues with similarly high levels of C18:1 isomers include nut and seed oils and the rendered fat of animals, other than large herbivores. Historic or ethnographic accounts may provide information as to whether fat rendering was a traditional practice and, if so, which types of animal fat were selected for this purpose. The level of C18:0 was fairly low, just over 17%; the level of medium chain saturated and very long chain fatty acids was less than 6%. The plant sterol β-sitosterol may occur; the conifer biomarker dehydroabietic acid probably occurs. The distribution of TAGs in this residue suggests that both plant and animal products are present.

Residues with Moderate-High Levels of C18:1 Isomers

The levels of C18:1 isomers in two residues, 14TRN 20 and 14TRN 36, are moderately high, 28.02% and 31.63%, respectively. Foods known to produce similar moderate-high fat content residues include plant seeds, such as Texas ebony, and the fatty meat of medium-sized mammals, such as beaver. The remains of agouti (*Dasyprocta leporina*), lappe (*Cuniculus paca*) and manicou (*Didelphis marsupialis insularis*) were recovered from the site (Reid 2015). If the fatty acid compositions of these mammals are similar to those of North American rodents and marsupials, they would be potential animal sources for residues with moderate-high levels of C18:1 isomers. Without knowing the fatty acid composition of the nine-banded armadillo/tatu (*Dasypus novemcinctus*) or green iguana (*Iguana iguana*) meat, it is impossible to comment on these animals as possible residue sources. The levels of C18:0 in both residues were about 20%. Medium chain saturated and very long chain fatty acids exceed 10% of the relative fatty acid composition of residue 14TRN 20, indicating the presence of low fat content plants. The level in residue 14TRN 36 is 8.28%, suggesting that plant material is probably present. The animal sterol cholesterol may occur in residue 14TRN 20; no sterols were detected in residue 14TRN 36. Dehydroabietic acid, the biomarker for conifers, occurs or probably occurs in both residues. Based on the TAG distributions, residue 14TRN 20 represents a combination of plant and animal products and residue 14TRN 36 appears to be dominated by plant material.

Residues Bordering Medium and Moderate-High Fat Content

The levels of C18:1 isomers in two residues, 14TRN 25 and 14TRN 32, were 27.23% and 27.33%, respectively, which places them on the border between medium and moderate-high fat content foods. As indicated earlier, examples of plant foods known to produce medium fat content residues include mesquite, corn and cholla. Freshwater and marine fish, terrapin, *Rabdotus* snail, marine molluscs and late winter, fat-depleted elk are examples of animal foods known to produce medium fat content residues. As indicated earlier, faunal recoveries indicate fish, such as members of the *Chondrichthyes* (shark) class, *Ariidae* (catfish) and *Dasyatidae* (stingray) families and molluscs, such as the mangrove oyster (*Crassostrea rhizophorae*), lucine (*Codakia* sp.) and Caribbean crown conch (*Melongena melongena*), should be considered possible sources for medium fat content residues. Foods known to produce moderate-high fat content residues and potential candidates from the Red House faunal assemblage are outlined above. The level of C18:0 in residue 14TRN 32 is 24.04%, which indicates animal products are probably present. The level of this fatty acid is 19.31% in residue

14TRN 25. Medium chain saturated and very long chain fatty acids form 11.44% of the relative fatty acid composition of residue 14TRN 25, indicating the presence of low fat content plants. These fatty acids form only 5.12% of residue 14TRN 32. Plant and animal products likely occur in both residues. The animal sterol cholesterol and the plant sterol β-sitosterol may occur in residue 14TRN 25; the plant sterol stigmasterol may occur in residue 14TRN 32. On the basis of the distribution of TAGs, both residues represent plant and animal combinations but residue 14TRN 25 is dominated by plant products and residue 14TRN 32 is dominated by animal products.

Residues with Insufficient Fatty Acids for Identification

Residues recovered from thirteen samples yielded insufficient fatty acids to attempt identification. These residues are characterized on the basis of the presence of lipid biomarkers and triacylglycerol distributions obtained using HT-GC and HT-GC/MS (table 5.6). Ten residues – 14TRN 1, 14TRN 3, 14TRN 4, 14TRN 5, 14TRN 8, 14TRN 9, 14TRN 13, 14TRN 14, 14TRN 23 and 14TRN 33 – appear to represent plant and animal combinations with conifer products present or probably present. Animal products may dominate residue 14TRN 13, and plant products dominate the three remaining residues. Based on the TAG distribution, residue 14TRN 12 appears to be a plant and animal combination dominated by plant products. Plant products occur in residues 14TRN 2 and 14TRN 30; there is no evidence of animal products. Conifer products occur or probably occur in these residues as well.

DISCUSSION

There were pronounced differences in the lipid recoveries from sherds associated with the various areas of the Red House site. Lipid recoveries were particularly low for potsherds submitted from section A of the Red House site; insufficient fatty acids were recovered from ten of the eighteen sherds from this area to attempt identification. Insufficient fatty acids were recovered from five of the six sherds from section A, G43; two of the four sherds from section A, G38, and three of the eight sherds from section A, north parliament. By comparison, only one of the ten potsherd residues from section B, rotunda, fountain area, and two of the six pottery residues from crawl space, northwest subdivision, samples had insufficient fatty acids for identification. Both residues from the crawl space, northeast subdivision, potsherds were identifiable on the basis of fatty acid composition.

Most of the residues from Red House site pottery appear to represent combinations of plant and animal material. The only residue from section A, G43 with sufficient fatty acids was identified as medium fat content (fish) and plant. This was the most common residue identification at the site. One residue identified as a medium fat content (fish) with plant material probably present and another identified as high C18:0 and medium fat content, similar to large herbivore and plant or bone marrow, were extracted from section A, G38 sherds. Two residues from section A, north parliament chamber, were identified as medium fat content (fish) and plant and two residues were identified as high C18:0 and medium fat content, similar to large herbivore and plant or bone marrow.

The lipid compositions of residues from section B of the Red House site were much more diverse. Residues extracted from section B, rotunda, fountain area, included three identified as medium fat content (fish) with, or probably with, plant; two residues identified as high C18:0; one residue identified as high C18:0 and medium fat content together with low fat content plant; one residue identified as high fat, one residue identified as moderate-high fat content and plant and one residue that fell on the border between medium and moderate-high fat content. Lipid residues extracted from crawl space, northwest subdivision, pottery included one identified as high C18:0, one identified as medium fat content (fish) probably with plant, one identified as medium fat content with traces of plant seeds and one identified as moderate-high fat content. One residue from crawl space, northeast subdivision, pottery was identified as medium fat content food with traces of plant, and the other was on the border between medium and moderate high fat content. The ubiquitous presence or possible presence of dehydroabietic acid, the biomarker for conifer products, suggests that either conifer wood was commonly used as firewood or conifer resins were routinely applied to pottery vessels as a sealant.

Lipid residue analysis is unique in that it provides insights into site activities, pottery vessel function and food preparation patterns. The paucity of absorbed lipid residues from sherds recovered from section A is of particular interest, especially when compared to sherds submitted from other parts of the site (section B, crawl space, northeast subdivision, and crawl space, northwest subdivision). Less than one-half of the sherds from section A retained sufficient fatty acids for identification; most notably, 83.3% of the sherds from section A, G43 had insufficient lipids for analysis. In the absence of evidence of differential preservation, poor lipid recoveries suggests that the majority of vessels in this area were not used for cooking. Perhaps they were employed for the storage of dry goods or for the processing of non-food materials. It is possible that the sherds submitted from section A, G43 were from new or special purpose vessels that were rarely used. Conversely, the majority (83.3%) of sherds from section B, rotunda, fountain area, crawl space, northwest subdivision, and crawl space, northeast subdivision, were probably from cooking vessels. In terms of food preparation across the site, many (41%) of the sherds had residues consistent with the preparation of fish or molluscs, alone or with plants. Another 33% of the sherds were from vessels used to prepare high $C18:0$ level foods, such as large red brocket deer and collared peccary/wild pig, alone or with plants. Lipid residues from the remaining 26% of the sherds suggest seed processing, fat rendering or the preparation of other food combinations. Even more insights could be gained if the pottery was reconstructed, at least partially, so that the vessel forms and capacities could be established.

In his study of Caribbean pottery residues, VanderVeen (2006) examined lipid residues extracted from pottery from the Dominican Republic dating to the time of European contact. Although the Taino and Red House assemblages differ in many respects, the occurrence of plant greens, fish, molluscs, seeds and other animals in the vessel residues from the Dominican Republic reported by VanderVeen (2006) is broadly similar to those from pre-contact vessels from Trinidad. It is interesting to note that VanderVeen (2006) also detected evidence of ruminants in several Taino vessels. He (2006, 140) attributed its presence to the use of cattle (either escaped or taken from European ranches) or, less likely, trade with people living on the mainland coasts, although "spoiling meat would not make for a pleasant trip". Given the presence of native species, such as large red brocket deer and collared peccary, and proximity to the South American coast, the occurrence of large herbivores in pre-contact Indigenous pottery from Trinidad is easier to explain.

CONCLUSION

It is difficult to explain the marked differences between lipid residues discerned in section A versus section B. The difficulty stems from the fact that the Red House site, as a result of repeated cycles of construction and backfilling since the construction of the original building in 1844, is heavily disturbed. During excavations, pre-colonial material culture (mostly pottery) and faunal materials were often found commingled with European material culture in several archaeological strata. Despite this, it is likely that many of the lipid residues from the thirty-six ceramic samples were derived from several of the faunal and plant material recovered from the site, namely terrestrial animals, molluscs, a variety of fishes, maize and palms. Conceivably, these foods were prepared, cooked and/or consumed in the ceramic vessels, represented by the thirty-six pre-colonial pottery samples. The analysis of lipid residues absorbed into the walls of pottery can be used to establish the former contents of vessels and, by extension, the subsistence patterns and food preparation techniques of the Red House pre-colonial community. This study is the first of its kind for Trinidad and Tobago and therefore represents an important milestone in archaeological research in the twin island republic.

REFERENCES

Barnard, H., and J.W. Eerkens, eds. 2007. *Theory and Practice of Archaeological Residue Analysis*. BAR International Series 1650. Oxford: British Archaeological Reports.

Boomert, A. 2000. *Trinidad, Tobago, and the Lower Interaction Sphrere: An Archaeological/ Ethnohistorical Study*. Alkmaar, the Netherlands: Cairi.

Charters, S., R.P. Evershed, A. Quye, P.W. Blinkhorn and V. Denham. 1997. "Simulation Experiments for Determining the Use of Ancient Pottery Vessels: The Behaviour of Epiticular Leaf Wax during Boiling of a Leafy Vegetable". *Journal of Archaeological Science* 24:1–7.

Condamin, J., F. Formenti, M.O. Metais, M. Michel and P. Blond. 1976. "The Application of Gas Chromatography to the Tracing of Oil in Ancient Amphorae". *Archaeometry* 18 (2): 195–201.

Dudd, S.N., and R.P. Evershed. 1998. "Direct Demonstration of Milk as an Element of Archaeological Economies". *Science* 282:1478–81.

Eerkens, J.W. 2002. "The Preservation and Identification of Pinon Resins by GC-MS in Pottery from the Western Great Basin". *Archaeometry* 44 (1): 95–105.

Evershed, R.P. 1993. "Biomolecular Archaeology and Lipids". *World Archaeology* 25 (1): 74–93.

———. 2000. "Biomolecular Analysis by Organic Mass Spectrometry". In *Modern Analytical Methods in Art and Archaeology*, edited by E. Ciliberto and G. Spoto, 177–239. Vol. 155, *Chemical Analysis*. New York: John Wiley.

Evershed, R.P., C. Heron and L.J. Goad. 1991. "Epicuticular Wax Components Preserved in Potsherds as Chemical Indicators of Leafy Vegetables in Ancient Diets". *Antiquity* 65:540–44.

Evershed, R.P., H.R. Mottram, S.N. Dudd, S. Charters, A.W. Stott, G.J. Lawrence, A.M. Gibson, A. Conner, P.W. Blinkhorn and V. Reeves. 1997a. "New Criteria for the Identification of Animal Fats in Archaeological Pottery". *Naturwissenschaften* 84:402–6.

Evershed, R.P., S.J. Vaugh, S.N. Dudd and J.S. Soles. 1997b. "Fuel for Thought? Beeswax in Lamps and Conical Cups from Late Minoan Crete". *Antiquity* 71:979–85.

Evershed, R.P., S.N. Dudd, M.J. Lockheart and S. Jim. 2001. "Lipids in Archaeology". In *Handbook of Archaeological Sciences*, edited by D.R. Brothwell and A.M. Pollard, 331–49. New York: John Wiley.

Evershed, R.P., C. Heron and L.J. Goad. 1990. "Analysis of Organic Residues of Archaeological Origin by High Temperature Gas Chromatography and Gas Chromatography-Mass Spectroscopy". *Analyst* 115:1339–42.

Folch, J., M. Lees and G.H. Sloane-Stanley. 1957. "A Simple Method for the Isolation and Purification of Lipid Extracts from Brain Tissue". *Journal of Biological Chemistry* 191:833.

Frankel, E.N. 1991. "Recent Advances in Lipid Oxidation". *Journal of the Science of Food and Agriculture* 54:465–511.

Heron, C., and A.M. Pollard. 1988. "The Analysis of Natural Resinous Materials from Roman Amphoras". In *Science and Archaeology, Glasgow 1987. Proceedings of a Conference on the Application of Scientific Techniques to Archaeology, Glasgow, 1987*, edited by E.A. Slater and J.O. Tate, 429–47. BAR British Series 196 (ii). Oxford: British Archaeological Reports.

Heron, C., N. Nemcek, K.M. Bonfield, J. Dixon and B.S. Ottaway. 1994. "The Chemistry of Neolithic Beeswax". *Naturwissenschaften* 81:266–69.

Loy, T. 1994. "Residue Analysis of Artifacts and Burned Rock from the Mustang Branch and Barton Sites (41HY209 and 41HY202)". In *Archaic and Late Prehistoric Human Ecology in the Middle Onion Creek Valley, Hays County, Texas*. Vol. 2: *Topical Studies*, edited by R.A. Ricklis and M.B. Collins, 607–27. Studies in Archaeology 19. Austin: Texas Archaeological Research Laboratory, University of Texas at Austin.

Malainey, M.E. 1997. "The Reconstruction and Testing of Subsistence and Settlement Strategies for the Plains, Parkland and Southern Boreal Forest". PhD dissertation, University of Manitoba.

———. 2007. "Fatty Acid Analysis of Archaeological Residues: Procedures and Possibilities". In *Theory and Practice of Archaeological Residue Analysis*, edited by H.B. and J.W. Eerkens, 77–89. BAR International Series 1650. Oxford: British Archaeological Reports.

Malainey, M.E., M. Álvarez, I. Briz i Godino, D. Zurro, E. Verdún i Castelló and T. Figol. 2014. "The Use of Shells as Tools by Hunter-Gatherers in the Beagle Channel (Tierra del Fuego, South America): An Ethnoarchaeological Experiment". *Archaeological and Anthropological Sciences*. DOI: 10.1007/s12520-014-0188-1.

Malainey, M.E., P.J. Innes and T.J. Figol. 2010. "Taking a Second Look: Results of the Re-analysis of Archaeological Lipid Residues from North America and Beyond". Paper presented at the 75th Annual Meeting of the Society for American Archaeology, St Louis, MO, April 2010.

———. In press. "Taking a Second Look: A Functional Analysis of Burned Rock Features from Eight Sites in Texas and Arizona". Chapter prepared for a volume edited by H. Hoekman-Sites and M. Raviele to be published by the University of Colorado Press.

Malainey, M.E., K.L. Malisza, R. Przybylski and G. Monks. 2001a. "The Key to Identifying Archaeological Fatty Acid Residues". Paper presented at the 34th Annual Meeting of the Canadian Archaeological Association, Banff, Alberta, May.

Malainey, M.E., R. Przybylski and B.L. Sherriff. 1999a. "The Fatty Acid Composition of Native Food Plants and Animals of Western Canada". *Journal of Archaeological Science* 26:83–94.

———. 1999b. "The Effects of Thermal and Oxidative Decomposition on the Fatty Acid Composition of Food Plants and Animals of Western Canada: Implications for the Identification of Archaeological Vessel Residues". *Journal of Archaeological Science* 26:95–103.

———. 1999c. "Identifying the Former Contents of Late Precontact Period Pottery Vessels from Western Canada Using Gas Chromatography". *Journal of Archaeological Science* 26 (4): 425–38.

———. 2001b. "One Person's Food: How and Why Fish Avoidance May Affect the Settlement and Subsistence Patterns of Hunter-Gatherers". *American Antiquity* 66 (1): 141–61.

Malainey, M.E., R. Przybylski and G. Monks. 2000a. "The Identification of Archaeological Residues Using Gas Chromatography and Applications to Archaeological Problems in Canada, United States and Africa". Paper presented at the 11th Annual Workshops in Archaeometry, State University of New York at Buffalo, February.

———. 2000b. "Refining and Testing the Criteria for Identifying Archaeological Lipid

Residues Using Gas Chromatography". Paper presented at the 33rd Annual Meeting of the Canadian Archaeological Association, Ottawa, May.

———. 2000c. "Developing a General Method for Identifying Archaeological Lipid Residues on the Basis of Fatty Acid Composition". Paper presented at the Joint Midwest Archaeological and Plains Anthropological Conference, Minneapolis, MN, November.

Marchbanks, M.L. 1989. "Lipid Analysis in Archaeology: An Initial Study of Ceramics and Subsistence at the George C. Davis Site". MA thesis, University of Texas at Austin.

Patrick, M., A.J. de Konig and A.B. Smith. 1985. "Gas Liquid Chromatographic Analysis of Fatty Acids in Food Residues from Ceramics Found in the Southwestern Cape, South Africa". *Archaeometry* 27 (2): 231–36.

Piperno, D. 2014. "Report on Phytolith and Starch Grain Analysis of Selected Grinding Stones from Redhouse Site, Trinidad". Dolores R. Piperno, Senior Scientist, Smithsonian Institution. Submitted to Dr Basil A. Reid, lead archaeologist, Red House Restoration Archaeological Excavations, Office of the Parliament of the Republic of Trinidad and Tobago.

Quigg, J.M., C. Lintz, S. Smith and S. Wilcox. 2000. "The Lino Site: A Stratified Late Archaic Campsite in a Terrace of the San Idelfonzo Creek, Webb County, Southern Texas". Technical Report No. 23765, Texas Department of Transportation, Environmental Affairs Division, Archaeological Studies Program Report 20. Austin: TRC Mariah Associates.

Quigg, J.M., M.E. Malainey, R. Przybylski and G. Monks. 2001. "No Bones About It: Using Lipid Analysis of Burned Rock and Groundstone Residues to Examine Late Archaic Subsistence Practices in South Texas". *Plains Anthropologist* 46 (177): 283–303.

Reber, E.A., S.N. Dudd, N.J. van der Merwe and R.P. Evershed. 2004. "Direct Detection of Maize in Pottery Residue via Compound Specific Stable Carbon Isotope Analysis". *Antiquity* 78:682–91.

Regert, M. 2007. "Elucidating Pottery Function Using a Multi-Step Analytical Methodology Combining Infrared Spectroscopy, Chromatographic Procedures and Mass Spectrometry". In *Theory and Practice of Archaeological Residue Analysis*, edited by H. Barnard and J.W. Eerkens, 61–76. BAR International Series 1650. Oxford: British Archaeological Reports.

Regert, M., H.A. Bland, S.N. Dudd, P.F. van Bergen and R.P. Evershed. 1998. "Free and Bound Fatty Acid Oxidation Products in Archaeological Ceramic Vessels". *Philosophical Transactions of the Royal Society of London, B* 265 (1409): 2027–32.

Reid, B.A. 2015. *Red House Restoration Archaeology Project Report, Phase 1, for the Period July 1, 2013–January 31, 2015*. Port of Spain: Office of the Parliament of the Republic of Trinidad and Tobago.

Rottländer, R.C.A. 1990. "Lipid Analysis in the Identification of Vessel Contents". *MASCA Research Papers in Science and Archaeology* 7:37–40.

Sajo, Alexandra. 2014. "Palo Seco (Trinidad)". In *Encyclopedia of Caribbean Archaeology*, edited by Basil A. Reid and R. Grant Gilmore III, 273–74. Gainesville: University Press of Florida.

Sauter, F., E.W.H. Hayek, W. Moche and U. Jordis. 1987. "Betulin aus archäologischem Schwelteer". *Zeitschrift für Naturforschung* 42c (11–12): 1151–52.

Shackley, M. 1982. "Gas Chromatographic Identification of a Resinous Deposit from a 6th Century Storage Jar and Its Possible Identification". *Journal of Archaeological Science* 9:305–6.

Skibo, J.M. 1992. *Pottery Function: A Use-Alteration Perspective*. New York: Plenum Press.

Solomons, T.W.G. 1980. *Organic Chemistry*. Toronto: John Wiley.

VanderVeen, J.M. 2006. "Subsistence Patterns as Markers of Cultural Exchange: European and Taino Interactions in the Dominican Republic". PhD dissertation, Indiana University.

CHAPTER 6

Initial Interpretations of the Red House Faunal Assemblage

ZARA ALI, BRENT WILSON, MIKE RUTHERFORD, LANYA FANOVICH,
JOHN KRIGBAUM AND LAURA VAN VOORHIS

THE FAUNAL ASSEMBLAGE SUGGESTS THAT THE INDIGENOUS OCCUPANTS of the Red House site had a well-founded terrestrial and maritime economy. Subsistence modes and methods of food processing at Saladoid and post-Saladoid sites are very similar. Across Trinidad the assemblages are "relatively uniform" (Boomert 2016, 26), and those discussed here (molluscs, mammals, birds, reptiles and fish) are typical of such habitation sites. The catchment areas for Saladoid and post-Saladoid sites fall within a radius of 1 to 3 kilometres from the settlement and may extend to 5 kilometres "in the case of specific procurement activities" (Boomert 2016, 32). Saladoid sites in Trinidad and Tobago are regularly found near (within 500 metres) a potable freshwater source, such as the St Ann's River before its diversion in 1787 (Reid 2015, 11), "and contour elevations of less than 100 m" (Boomert 2016, 26), such as the Northern Basin. These features, along with the productive hunting grounds provided by the Northern Range, made the Red House site a good location for indigenous settlement.

Excavation units were located both inside the Red House building and around its perimeter (Reid 2015). The building is divided into three sections: section A, the northern third, north of the rotunda; section B, also called "rotunda", the middle part of the building with all adjoining rooms; section C, the southern third, south of the rotunda; and the peripheral units are named BAR units. The analysed sample of invertebrates used herein came from all of the defined areas, while the vertebrates were derived from sections A, B and C. Forty faunal samples comprised of molluscan and vertebrate samples were radiocarbon dated.

Faunal remains from various pre-Columbian sites in Trinidad and Tobago, ranging in age from the Ortoiroid period (6000–200 BCE) to the Mayoid period (ca. 1450–1800) were documented throughout the last century by Bullbrook (1917–1963), Harris (1973) and Boomert (2000, 2016), among others. The faunal assemblage from the Red House site, however, has only been briefly mentioned in the final report of the archaeological activities of the site by Reid (2015) as well as in a preliminary checklist of molluscan findings by Mohammed and Fanovich (2016). Therefore, as described in the title, this chapter is the first discussion of a more detailed analysis of this assemblage.

This chapter is divided into three parts: the first part covers the invertebrates and includes a measure of diversity using the Shannon Function (H) and a measure of dominance with the Berger-Parker Index. The second part considers an overview of the preliminary work done on the vertebrate group, including isotopic analysis of associated fauna. Herewith, our study aims to identify the animals present, to determine if there was a preference for a particular type of animal/s or procurement area/s and identify the origins of ten mammalian specimens. The third section highlights some of the artefacts made from faunal remains.

INVERTEBRATES

Materials and Method

A total of 72,907 complete valves (of gastropods and bivalves) were catalogued from sections A, B, C and the BAR units. That quantity makes the molluscan assemblage the second most abundant of all finds, following pre-Columbian ceramics. Of that total, 56.89% (n = 41,477) comprise the analysed sample used in this chapter. This large-scale sampling facilitated an examination of the spatial distribution, diversity and dominance of molluscs across the entire site. In 2013 and 2014, sixteen samples of Caribbean mangrove oysters (*Crassostrea rhizophorae*), acquired from sections A, B and C, were submitted to BETA Analytic, Incorporated (Miami, Florida) for radiocarbon dating.

The primary excavation method utilized pickaxes and shovels, which could account for some degree of destruction and loss of invertebrate remains. The fill was dry sieved using standing sieves with quarter-inch mesh, following which a proportion of molluscs were sampled for scientific tests, while the remainder was washed and air-dried. Whole valves and fragments were separated by species or other applicable taxa, which were then catalogued – the last step in the on-site processing of the molluscs. Standard methods of quantification, such as the number of individual specimens (NISP) and minimum number of individuals (MNI), were used. The available dry mass weights were inadequate for interpretation. While most molluscs were found in relatively good condition, the periostraca of several shells were either mostly or completely worn, making identification difficult.

Comparative collections of molluscs from the University of the West Indies Zoology Museum (UWIZM), St Augustine, and the *Peterson Field Guide to Shells* (Abbott and Morris 1995) were used to aid identification. The diversity of the molluscs was examined using the Shannon-Weiner function, the dominant species were determined through use of the Berger-Parker Index and Principal Components Analysis was applied to the sample to establish the best discriminators per section. These analyses are explained in the following section.

Results

A total of 41,477 mollusc shells and shell fragments were recovered from 223 samples from the Red House site (= 186 per sample), with 50 distinct taxa recognized. Of these, 12 taxa (24% of those identified: *Anadara* spp., *Codakia* spp., *Conus* spp., *Cymatium* sp., *Cypraea* sp., *Donax* spp., *Lucina* spp., *Neritina* spp., *Tagelus* sp., *Tellina* sp., *Thais* sp., *Tivela* sp.) were left in open nomenclature. Only 425 mollusc remains (1.02%) could not be identified to genus level, indicating the high quality of the dataset. Mangrove oysters (32.18% of total recovery, MNI = 13,347.5) dominated the molluscan finds, with lesser numbers of the marine clam lucines (*Codakia* spp.) (12.85% of total recovery, MNI = 5,329.5) and Caribbean crown conch, *Melongena melongena* (6.0% of total recovery, MNI = 2,489). The majority of species were rare, with 15 taxa (30% of those recovered) represented by singletons.

In sum, 14,563 mollusc specimens (35% of total recovery) came from ninety-six samples in section A, while thirty nine samples from section B yielded 2,470 specimens (6% of recovery). Section C yielded 22,634 specimens (54.6%) from seventy-one samples, and the peripheral BAR units yielded 1,806 specimens (4.3%) from seventeen samples. Analysis of variance (ANOVA) indicated that the mean recovery per sample differed between the sections ($F_{3,219}$ = 3.61, p = 0.014), being highest in section C (= 319 specimens per sample), and of intermediate values in section A (= 152 specimens per sample) and around the periphery (= 106 specimens per sample). Mean recovery was lowest from section B (= 63 specimens per sample). Thus, the intensity of disposal of mollusc fragments varied around the Red House site, being highest south of the rotunda and lowest in the mid-section.

Of the 223 samples analysed, only seventy-six (34%) yielded ≥100 mollusc shells. Of the ninety-six samples from section A, thirty-three (34.4%) yielded ≥100 specimens, while seven out of thirty-nine samples from section B (21.2%) yielded ≥100 specimens. In section C samples, thirty-three of the seventy-one samples (46.5%) yielded ≥100 specimens, while of the seventeen peripheral samples, three (17.6%) yielded ≥100 specimens, confirming that the intensity of disposal varied across the site, with the highest degree of disposal in section C and intermediate intensity in section A. In contrast to these two sections, disposal was lowest in section B.

The diversity of the mollusc assemblages, measured using the Shannon

Table 6.1. Percentile Representations of Principal Components Analysis of Molluscs

Taxon	Section A	Section B	Section C
Codakia spp.	11.7	33.8	34.0
Crassostrea rhizophorae	80.8	59.2	58.5
Turbinella angulata	0.01	0.0	0.02

Function (H), ranged between 0.032 and 1.59, both maximum and minimum values being within section C, crawl space southwest, subdivision 2, 61–102 cm and section C, crawl space southeast, subdivision 1, 64 to 150 cm, respectively. The mean H did not differ significantly between sections A (= 0.58), B (= 0.66) and C (= 0.74; $F_{2,70}$ = 1.39, p = 0.25). However, the mean evenness varied significantly between the sections, with higher values at section B (= 0.66) than at section A (= 0.35) or section C (= 0.39). Dominance measured using the Berger-Parker index max (p_i) ranged between 0.35 and 0.99 (i.e., the percentage of each sample represented by the dominant species ranged between 35 and 99%). The mean dominance differed between the sections ($F_{2,70}$ = 3.303, p = 0.042), being highest in section A (= 0.81) and lowest in section C (= 0.69). This shows that a more varied mollusc assemblage was dumped in section C rather than in section A.

Principal components analysis indicates that the best taxa for discriminating between the sections are lucines, oysters and the West Indian chank shell (*Turbinella angulata*). As shown in table 6.1, the percentage of the total assemblage that was lucines was higher in samples from sections B and C than from section A. In contrast, the percentage of the assemblage that was oysters was higher in section A than in sections B and C. For all seventy-six samples with ≥100 identified specimens, the percentage abundances of lucines and oysters were significantly inversely correlated (r = −0.93, p < 0.00001. Chank shells, though rare (only 0.02% of total mollusc recovery), were significant in not being recovered from section B. These data indicate that significantly different assemblages of molluscs were being dumped in sections A and C, with section B molluscs being most similar to those in section C.

Discussion

The abundance of molluscs at the site is likely because of its proximity to the riparian and estuarine collection areas, so the pre-Columbian inhabitants could have expended little energy in transport costs. The three most populous molluscs, which are all edible, presented from most to least frequent, were the swamp dwelling Caribbean mangrove oyster (*Crassostrea rhizophorae*), shallow water lucines (*Codakia* spp.) and the large marine gastropod, Caribbean crown conch (*Melongena melongena*). Mangrove oysters can be plucked by hand from the

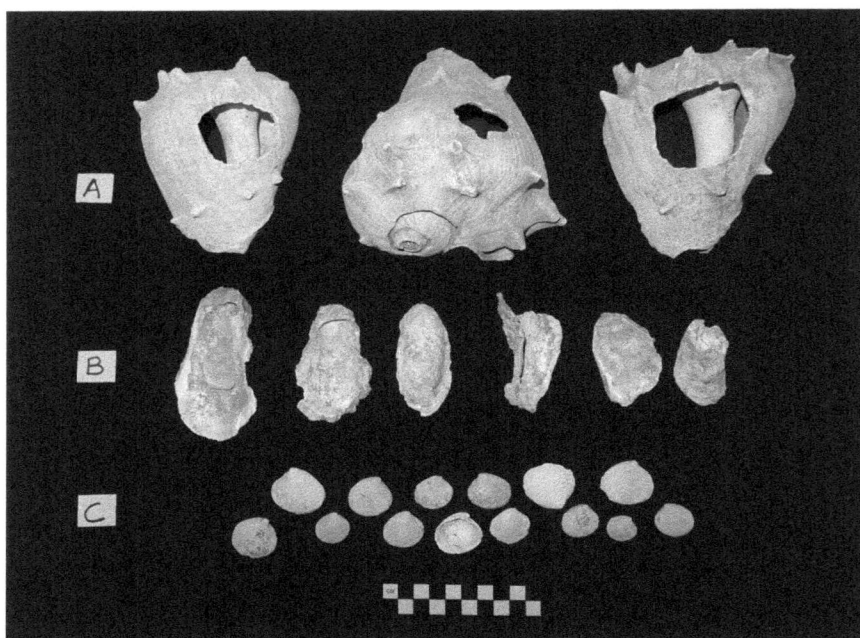

Figure 6.1.
Specimens of the three most populous molluscs: row A: Caribbean crown conch (*Melongena melongena*); row B: mangrove oysters (*Crassostrea rhizophorae*); row C: Lucines (*Codakia* spp.).

roots and low branches of the red mangrove (*Rhizophora mangle*), especially in low tide, and lucines also could have been easily gathered in their nearshore habitat. Crown conchs, collected from the inshore, may have been used as a food source, as raw materials for tools (though none were identified) or as bait (Claassen 1998, 10) for reef and pelagic fish. Signs of processing on several specimens from BAR 4 (figure 6.1, row A) correlate with the Lucayan Taino method of meat extraction from queen conchs by boring "a round hole in the top using the spire of another conch shell" (Keegan and Carlson 2008, 64), hereby creating a kill hole. This gives the harvester maximum access to the meat because it causes "the animal to release its hold on the shell" (Wing and Reitz 1999, 127).

The selected sieve size worked well for the overall intention of the Red House excavations and for the recovery of molluscs, particularly for the yielded species. Thus, for molluscs, the method of recovery did not create a bias in the excavated assemblage toward larger specimens, as it might have in the vertebrate assemblage.

The majority of human skeletons were found in association with molluscs and animal bones. Several human burials were found lying upon and within "shell-beds" dominated by oysters (Reid 2015, 41). Examples of this were found in section A, G43, subdivision 1, at a depth of 1.33 m (skeleton 3) and section A, G43, subdivision 2, at 1.08 m (skeleton 1). Additionally, the notion of using molluscs as grave goods is supported by radiocarbon results of Caribbean mangrove oysters from the two previously mentioned levels (1.33 m and 1.08 m), which are contemporaneous with those of the respective Saladoid skeletons (340–575

CE and 475–640 CE) from the same stratigraphic levels. Section C, crawl space southwest, had the highest number of molluscs of any excavation unit, including the most Caribbean mangrove oysters, but no faunal remains were carbon dated from here. However, all 6 molluscan radiocarbon dates from section C come from crawl space southeast, subdivisions 1, 2 and 3. The sample from subdivision 1, 0.46 m–0.59 m produced a post-Saladoid date of 1250–1320 CE, while the other 5 samples generated essentially colonial and postcolonial dates ranging between 1460 CE and post-1950. The only other material radiocarbon dated from section C was a charcoal sample, which also came from subdivision 3, 0.89 m–1.30 m, but it had a colonial age range (1680–post-1950 CE). Despite section B being the last part of the building to be constructed, all the molluscs tested from here dated 365–665 CE, and section A results were also principally Saladoid and post-Saladoid (225–720 CE).

Two main patterns emerged from the statistical analyses of the molluscan assemblage. First, the intensity of the disposal of molluscs varied across the site, with highest levels of variability within section C; and second, the variety of molluscs disposed was also greatest within section C. Analysis of variance showed that mean recovery from sections A, B, C and the BAR units were as follows: section A (= 152 specimens per sample), section B (= 63), section C (= 319) and BAR units (= 106 specimens per sample). This means that the intensity of disposal of molluscs varied across the Red House site, with the greatest variance being south of the rotunda and the lowest in the midsection.

The ten most populous taxa of molluscs (table 6.2) account for 99.36% (n = 41,213) of the total analysed sample, while the remaining 40 taxa contribute the other 0.64% (n = 264) of the sample – an average of a mere 6.60 specimens per taxon. Uncommon species such as "chipchip" (*Donax* spp., MNI = 2), thick lucines (*Phacoides pectinatus*, MNI = 3.5) and the West Indian top shell (*Cittarium pica*, MNI = 2) may be accidental collections resulting from shellfishing for other species in the intertidal zone. However, they are all common food resources at other local, contemporaneous sites (Boomert 2000). Land snails such as *Megalobulimus oblongus* (n = 28) and *Plekocheilus glaber* (n = 18) in the sample may have been commensals that foraged and scavenged in the ample organic refuse across the site (Wing and Reitz 1999, 115).

Crabs are very poorly represented by 4 chelae (0.14% of non-molluscan NISP), which could be explained by Watters and Rouse, who state that "Saladoid Indians who lived on the South American coast and in the adjacent part of the Lesser Antilles obtained their protein primarily from fish, shellfish, birds and land animals, without making much use of crabs" (1989, 136). The proximity of the site to the swamp and coast suggests that crab remains could likely be the blue land crab (*Cardisoma guanhumi*) or the mangrove crab (*Ucides cordatus*) (R.S. Mohammed, pers. comm., 2016).

Table 6.2. Ten Most Abundant Molluscan Taxa from the Red House Site

Species	Habitat	NISP	MNI	14C Results
Caribbean mangrove oyster (*Crassostrea rhizophorae*)	Intertidal (mangrove)	26,695	13,347.5	Sec A (225–720 CE) Sec B (365–665 CE) Sec C (1250–post-1950 CE)
Lucines (*Codakia* spp.)	Marine (shallow water)	10,659	5,329.5	N/A
Caribbean crown conchs (*Melongena melongena*)	Intertidal (mangrove)	2,489	2,489	N/A
Ark clam (*Anadara* spp.)	Marine (shallow water)	546	273	N/A
Unidentified gastropods (*Gastropoda*)	N/A	374	374	N/A
Virgin nerite (*Neritina virginea*)	Marine/Brackish/Freshwater	185	185	N/A
Cross-barred venus clam (*Chione cancellata*)	Marine (shallow water)	138	69	N/A
Rock shells (*Thais* spp.)	Intertidal (rocky shore)	53	53	N/A
Giant ramshorn snail (*Marisa cornuarietis*)	Freshwater	48	48	N/A
Gaudy asaphis (*Asaphis deflorata*)	Marine (shallow water)	26	13	N/A
Totals		41,213	22,181	

VERTEBRATES

Materials and Method

The collection methods for the vertebrate assemblages were similar to those for the molluscs. The analysed vertebrate sample came from catalogued specimens from sections A, B and C of the Red House basement. No materials from the BAR units were included. The total vertebrate NISP was 30,417. Of that figure, 8.79% (n = 2,675) were positively identified and therefore used for discussion here, while bearing in mind the "disadvantages of the NISP . . . as the sole index of species abundance" (Klein and Cruz-Uribe 1984, 25). The remaining 27,742 specimens comprise bones too fragmented to be adequately identified as well as specimens from the excluded BAR units. The overall fragmentary nature of the bones is understandable, undeniably due in part to the taphonomic changes influenced by the various episodes of destruction and construction of the Red House. The comparative collections at the UWIZM, St Augustine, and *Human and Nonhuman Bone Identification: A Concise Field Guide* (France 2011) were primarily used to identify the vertebrate remains.

Twenty-four animal bone and tooth samples, all from sections A and B, were sent to BETA Analytic Incorporated in Miami, Florida, for radiocarbon dating. None of these samples were of animals introduced during the colonial period (post-1498). Nine samples of dog teeth and one peccary tooth, as mentioned above, were sent for isotopic analyses at the University of Florida, Gainesville.

Results

Among the eighteen taxa identified, the majority were mammals (eleven species), fish were the second most numerous (five families, one superorder), with reptiles and birds categorized as one species and class, respectively (table 6.3). All non-molluscan taxa identified are edible and are known to have been

Table 6.3. Quantities and Radiocarbon Results of the Vertebrate Assemblage from Sections A, B and C of the Red House Site

Species	Habitat	NISP	% of Total NISP	14C Results
Mammals				
Agouti (*Dasyprocta leporina*)	Mixed forest types	438	16.37	255–680 CE
Collared peccary (*Tayassu tajacu*)	Mixed forest types	263	9.83	250–535 CE
Red brocket deer (*Mazama americana trinitatis*)	Mixed forest types	259	9.68	230–650 CE
Nine banded armadillo (*Dasypus novemcinctus*)	Mixed forest types	191	7.14	255–1215 CE
Black-eared opossum (*Didelphis marsupialis insularis*)	Mixed forest types	150	5.60	400–545 CE
Lowland paca (*Cuniculus paca*)	Mixed forest types	88	3.28	220–545 CE
Dog (Canis familiaris)	Domestic	65	2.42	130–390 CE
Red howler monkey (*Alouatta macconnelli*)	Mixed forest types	2	0.07	N/A
Mammals – Colonial Introductions				
Cow (*Bos primigenius*)	Domestic	85	3.17	N/A
Domestic pig (*Sus scrofa domesticus*)	Domestic	54	2.01	N/A
Horse (*Equus ferus caballus*)	Domestic	3	0.11	N/A
Fish				
Catfish (*Ariidae*)	Marine, Brackish, Freshwater	637	23.81	N/A
Sharks (*Selachimorpha*)	Marine	80	2.99	N/A
Tunas and mackerels (*Scombridae*)	Marine	68	2.54	N/A
Groupers (*Serranidae*)	Marine	12	0.44	N/A
Barracudas (*Sphyraenidae*)	Marine	6	0.22	N/A
Stingrays (*Dasyatidae*)	Marine	2	0.07	N/A
Others				
Birds (*Aves; Ardeidae*)	Various	175	6.54	N/A
Green iguana (*Iguana iguana*)	Mixed forest types	93	3.47	420–570 CE

consumed by indigenous populations at other Saladoid and post-Saladoid sites in Trinidad. Additionally, the ranges of radiocarbon results for human burials (125–1395 CE) and vertebrate remains (130–1215 CE) correlate, implying a definite interaction between the indigenes and the fauna that inhabited the surrounding environment. According to Peres (2010, 23), "Microscopic analysis of residues on ceramic sherds and stone tools" can be indirect sources of information about animal consumption. Lipid residue analysis of pre-Columbian pottery samples revealed that the residues on them match materials that could have come from the larger mammals identified in the faunal assemblage (see chapter 5, this volume).

Section A of the building contained the highest number of vertebrate faunal remains (1,309 = 48.93%) and the highest number of human burials (49 = 81.66%) (Reid 2015, 228–29). Section B produced the lowest number of vertebrate remains (386 = 14.42%) and the second highest number of human burials (11 = 18.33%). The southern "third" of the building, or section C, had the second highest number of faunal specimens (1,034 = 38.65%) and no human burials. However, given that the archaeological remains at the Red House are so commingled because of several episodes of site disturbance, it is nearly impossible to establish any clear patterns of association in the archaeological record.

Miscellaneous Fauna

The animals are presented below in decreasing order of their relative abundance in the total vertebrate NISP. The indigenes were not adversely affected by seasonality in this tropical island, because the native terrestrial and marine vertebrates were, and still are, available throughout the year. No hearth features were uncovered, which could be a result of site disturbance. However, a few fragments of burnt bone (long bones, ribs) and ones with cut marks were found. While these may be evidence of cooking and butchering, respectively, more detailed investigations of food preparation at this site were not done at the time of writing this chapter.

Mammals

Mammalian teeth and bones comprised 59.73% (n = 1,598) of the entire vertebrate faunal assemblage. A breakdown of this percentage shows that mammals native to Trinidad account for 54.42% (n = 1,456, of which dogs are 4.06%, n = 65), while those introduced by Europeans comprise 5.30% (n = 142). From these percentages, it is evident that the indigenous inhabitants utilized hunting as their primary means of subsistence. Hunting would likely have taken place in the forests of the Northern Range, which is a habitat for all of the seven native species identified.

Stahl states that "large mammals are rare, elusive and susceptible to over-predation" (1995, 168), and this may account for the two largest mammals, peccaries and deer, being the second and third most populous animals in the sample. On the other hand, the larger animals are more heavily butchered than smaller animals (Stahl 1995, 169), which increases their relative portion of the NISP and aids in transporting them from the kill site to the settlement site, preparing them to be cooked and handling them during cooking. However, teeth account for over 50% of peccary and deer remains.

Dogs

Dog (*Canis familiaris*) remains account for 2.42% (n = 65) of the total vertebrate assemblage. 87.69% (n = 57) of these elements were teeth. Dogs were domesticated by the indigenous peoples who moved into the Caribbean from South America, and Boomert explains that while "little is known about the specific hunting strategies employed, it is certain that from Saladoid times onwards, the dog invariably accompanied the indigenous hunters" (Boomert 2016, 33). Dog burials have been found at Saladoid sites, such as at La Sorcé in Puerto Rico (Saunders 2005, 159), and they have also been interred with humans, but only in Early Ceramic Age sites in the Caribbean (Hoogland and Hofman 2013). While no dog burials were found at the Red House (Reid 2015, 51), the existence of these remains, and their radiocarbon results of 130–390 CE, suggest that dogs were present at the site during Saladoid occupation in the Early Ceramic Age (500 BCE–650/800 CE). Comparable radiocarbon dates for hunted food animals suggest that during the Saladoid time the dogs may indeed have been used by people as companions during hunting expeditions. Dogs were also brought to the Caribbean by the European colonizers (Wing 1991, 136), but the pre-colonial radiocarbon dates from the Red House site rule out their association with Europeans.

Native Mammals

The mammals found naturally in the Northern Range or along the St Ann's River in pre-colonial times include the peccary or "quenk" (*Tayassu tajacu*), red brocket deer (*Mazama americana trinitatis*), black-eared opossum or "manicou" (*Didelphis marsupialis insularis*), lowland paca or "lappe" (*Cuniculus paca*), agouti (*Dasyprocta leporina*), nine-banded armadillo or "tatu" (*Dasypus novemcinctus*) and red howler monkey (*Alouatta macconnelli*). The abundance of ground-dwelling, small to medium-sized mammals suggests that hunting took place primarily in swidden plots and areas with primary and secondary forest. All of these mammals are well known from other Saladoid settlement sites in Trinidad such as Palo Seco, Blanchisseuse and Manzanilla 1 (Delsol and Grouard 2016) and were procured and processed for food purposes.

Teeth and tusks amounted to 50.19% (n = 132) and 25.47% (n = 67) of the peccary specimens. Two specimens were radiocarbon dated to between 250 and 680 CE. Teeth also made up the largest portion (62.16%, n = 161) of the deer biofacts, with fragments of jaws and antlers (figure 6.2, row A) comprising the remaining percentage. Peccaries and deer are two high utility animals, which would have made them valuable captures. The solitary, nocturnal lowland pacas would also have contributed a fair amount of meat to the diet. 40.09% (n = 36) of the NISP of pacas were teeth. Their radiocarbon dates were 220–545 CE,

Figure 6.2. Mammalian specimens: row A: red brocket deer (*Mazama americana trinitatis*); row B: black-eared opossum (*Didelphis marsupialis insularis*); row C: lowland paca (*Cuniculus paca*); row D: agouti (*Dasyprocta leporina*); row E: nine-banded armadillo (*Dasypus novemcinctus*) scutes and ulna.

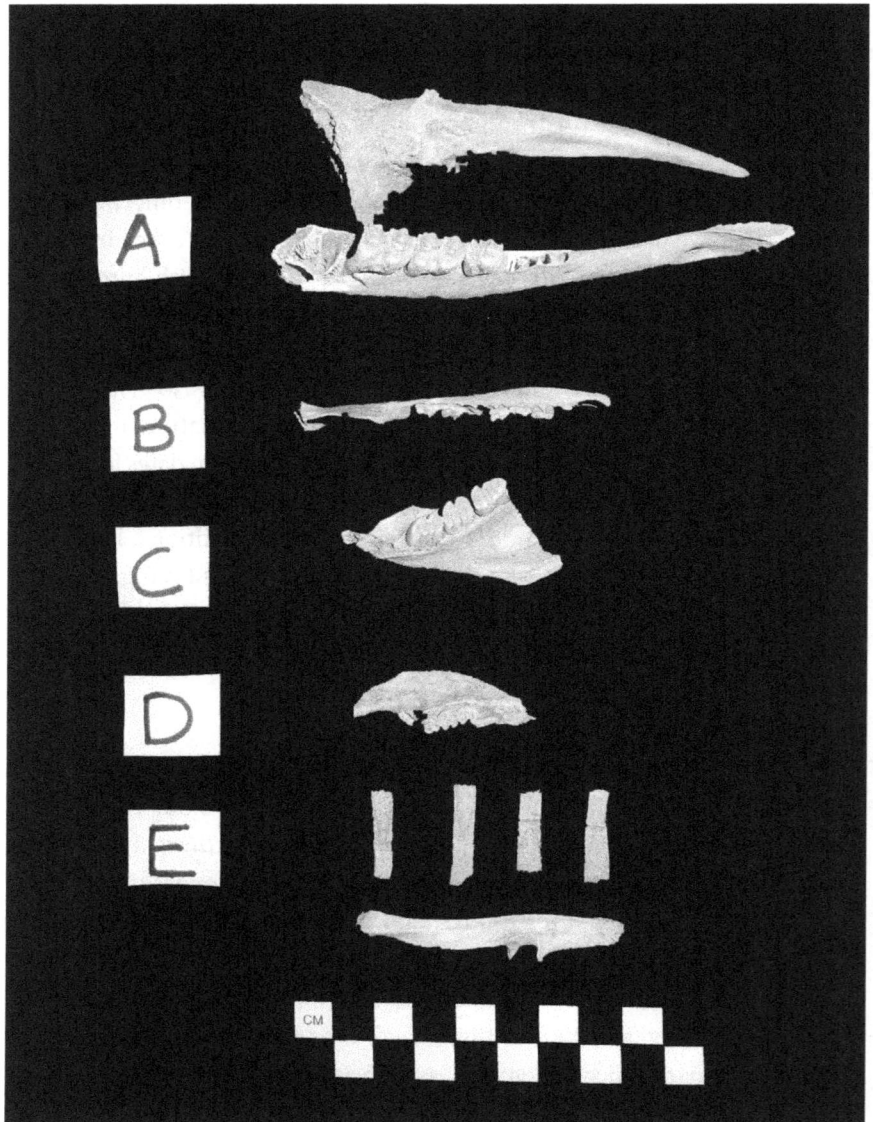

thus making the pacas, deer and peccaries contemporary with the Saladoid occupation of the site.

Of the opossum remains, 71.33% were teeth, and the result of the one sample dated was 400–545 CE. Agoutis, a popular Amerindian food source, account for 16.37% of the total vertebrate sample, giving it the second highest NISP. Of the agouti specimens, teeth accounted for 71% (n = 311). The four radiocarbon dates for these diurnal rodents ranged between 255 and 680 CE. The nine-banded armadillo (*Dasypus novemcinctus*) was identified primarily by its dermal scutes and distinctive long bones. There were thirty-one teeth present, which accounted for 16.23% of all armadillo specimens. Radiocarbon dates ranged between 255 and 535 CE for three samples, placing them within the Saladoid period. A fourth sample gave a post-Saladoid age of 1035–1215 CE from section B, north rotunda, room G44, subdivision 1. This is the most recent radiocarbon date in the vertebrate assemblage, but it still falls within the pre-colonial period. The presence of two red howler monkey (*Alouatta macconnelli*) jaw fragments is insufficient evidence to draw conclusions regarding the reason for their presence at the site. According to LeFebvre and deFrance (2018), during the pre-Columbian period the terrestrial fauna of Trinidad and Tobago included taxa such as monkeys (e.g., *Alouatta seniculus, Cebus albifrons*), although there is no evidence suggesting these primate taxa were domesticated. It is interesting to note, however, that the remains of a juvenile capuchin monkey (*Cebus* sp.) found at the Wanápa site on Bonaire were undoubtedly those of a pet that died in captivity (Newsom and Wing 2004, 72).

Colonial Introductions: Horses, Cows and Domesticated Pigs

Cows (*Bos primigenius*), horses (*Equus ferus caballus*) and domestic pigs (*Sus scrofa domesticus*) were introduced into the Western Hemisphere by Christopher Columbus in 1493 (Crosby 1972, 75) as beasts of burden and food sources. In 1569 Juan Trejo Ponce de León received a charter from the Spanish crown which required that he take, among other things for the purpose of settlement, "one hundred horses, three hundred mares, five hundred cows, one thousand sheep, and two hundred pigs and goats" (Padrón 2012, 39) to Trinidad. For centuries thereafter horses remained an important means of transport in Trinidad. Furthermore, forty-five horseshoes and a horse's toothbrush (Reid 2015, 119) supplement the equine assemblage of three teeth. Before the Red House was built, "the site was unoccupied and one of its possible uses was a grazing area for free range livestock belonging to townsfolk" (Reid 2015, 120), some of which could have been pigs and cows. Of the fifty-four pig remains, teeth made up 66.66% (n = 36). Teeth also made up the majority of the cow remains, accounting for 96.47% (n = 82) of the specimens.

Fish

Seasonal fishing of groundfish such as mackerels and bonitos (Scombridae), groupers (Serranidae), catfish (Ariidae) and barracudas (Sphyraenidae) is most productive between January and July in Trinidad's waters (Mohammed et al. 2011, 318). Little is known of the fishing techniques used by Saladoid and post-Saladoid peoples; however, archaeological records demonstrate hook and line, bow and arrow, seines and spears as likely methods (Boomert 2000, 335). Fish remains make up 30.07% of the total vertebrate NISP, which is subdivided into five families and one superorder: Ariidae (catfish) at 23.81%; Scombridae (tunas, mackerels) at 2.54%; Serranidae (groupers) at 0.44%; Sphyraenidae (barracudas) at 0.22%; Dasyatidae (stingrays) at 0.07%, and Selachimorpha (sharks) amounted to 2.99%. Traces of fish residues were found on some of the pottery sherds that underwent lipid residue analysis (chapter 5, this volume), suggesting fish were possibly cooked or stored in those vessels. No fish samples were radiocarbon dated.

Catfish specimens represented the highest percentage (23.81%, n = 637) of any member of the vertebrate assemblage. Catfish are easily caught using a variety of fishing methods, including seining as well as hook and line, as they inhabit inshore-estuarine environments such as the St Ann's River and the Caroni Swamp along the coast. Demersal species such as groupers as well as pelagic barracudas and mackerels are likely to be fished using hook-and-line or spears, depending on their depths. The diagnostic features for these fish were primarily their teeth and jaws, while sharks and stingrays were identified by their vertebrae and spines, respectively. Sharks' flesh was possibly consumed, and their "teeth, skin, and vertebrae were used as tools, weapons and decoration" (Keegan and Carlson 2008, 23), whereas stingray spines could have been used as the tips of spears and arrows (Boomert 2000, 335). However, with only two spines present, we can only speculate about their significance in the Red House assemblage.

Birds

On Saladoid sites in Trinidad, birds were not caught often (Boomert 2016, 33). The NISP of avian remains is 6.54% (n = 175) of all vertebrates, and the majority (85.14%) of these were long bone fragments. Most of the avian remains could only be identified to the rank of class, barring the employment of genetic identification methods; however, beak fragments exhibiting features likely belonging to the heron and egret family Ardeidae, common visitors to the surrounding swamp habitats, were found. Birds are known to be an important part of Saladoid and post-Saladoid mythology and religious beliefs, evidenced by the avian zoomorphic adornos found at the Red House site. To indigenous peoples of the Caribbean, birds were often appreciated more for their plumage than as a food source (Saunders 2005, 3), but as of now their significance at the Red House site is unclear.

Reptiles

Green iguanas (*Iguana iguana*) are native to the Caribbean and are not uncommon on Saladoid and post-Saladoid sites in Trinidad. There were ninety-three iguana specimens recorded, and 89.24% (n = 83) of these were teeth. Using the jaw bone fragments (n = 10) to determine an MNI was unsuccessful, due to their degree of fragmentation. Tortoises (Testudinidae) are said to be a favourite hunting choice among terrestrial reptiles for the Saladoids and post-Saladoid groups in Trinidad (Boomert 2000, 343). Despite the quality habitat of the Northern Range located well within the catchment area and the proximity of the site to the sea, no tortoise or freshwater or marine turtle remains were found. However, the shell gorget (figure 6.6, row B) fashioned after a turtle's carapace implies that the indigenes were at least acquainted with these reptiles, or were in contact with other Amerindians that were familiar with them.

Isotopic Analysis (Mammals)

Isotopic ratios of carbon ($\delta^{13}C_{en}$), oxygen ($\delta^{18}O_{en}$) and strontium ($^{87}Sr/^{86}Sr$) from tooth enamel are a novel approach to assess diet and local versus non-local status (e.g., Laffoon et al. 2012, 2013b), and faunal remains are increasingly being analysed using these methods to assess the degree to which particular nonnative taxa may have been purposefully managed (e.g., Giovas et al. 2016; Laffoon et al. 2013a, 2016). This is particularly interesting with respect to commensal mammals, such as dogs, that are frequently associated with humans, and as mentioned above, are valuable companions when hunting. Teeth "capture" isotopic signals into tooth enamel during enamel mineralization when a tooth is developing. Carbon isotopes within tooth enamel represent an average "total" diet, whereas oxygen isotopes reflect overall patterns of body water, which is affected by myriad factors, including natural patterns of precipitation, evaporation and other sources of water made available. Strontium ratios ($^{87}Sr/^{86}Sr$) are principally incorporated into tooth enamel by plants consumed, which in turn largely reflects bioavailable sources of strontium across the landscape, which varies by geological formation. Sr ratios are quite variable, given the geologically diverse nature of Trinidad.

Isotopic analysis was conducted at the University of Florida Bone Chemistry Lab (BCL) following standardized protocols (see chapter 3, this volume). Select faunal teeth of nine dogs and one peccary were sampled and each sample was assigned a unique BCL number. Each tooth was initially cleaned by hand to remove any surface debris, and tooth enamel was subsequently sectioned with a Dedeco cutting disc and a Brassler dental drill. Tooth enamel chunks were cleaned of debris and adhering dentine under a dissecting microscope with a Brassler dental drill and carbide bit (1 mm).

For light isotope analysis of carbon ($\delta^{13}C$) and oxygen ($\delta^{18}O$), a small portion of the sampled tooth chunk was reduced to powder with an acid-cleaned agate mortar and pestle set. Sampled powder was weighed (ca. 20 mg) and loaded into a microcentrifuge tube and chemically pretreated with 2.5% sodium hypochlorite (dilute bleach) for eight hours and rinsed to neutral pH, and then 0.2 M acetic acid was added for eight hours to remove potential secondary carbonates. Samples were then rinsed to neutral pH, placed in a freezer and then lyophilized (freeze-dried), weighed and loaded for mass spectrometry using a Kiel carbonate prep device connected to a Finnigan MAT 252.

A bulk sample of tooth enamel (ca. 40–50 mg) was retained for heavy isotope analysis of strontium (Sr) and lead (Pb) isotope ratios following "clean lab" procedures and ion chromatography. Pb and Sr ratios were measured on a Nu Plasma multiple-collector inductively coupled plasma-mass spectrometer (MC-ICP-MS) and are reported relative to analyses of known standards (NBS 981 for Pb and NBS 987 for Sr).

Results

The context and isotopic results for carbon, oxygen and strontium are presented in table 6.4 for the Red House site dogs (n = 9) and peccary (n = 1) sampled. Three of the dog samples may be considered "modern" due to the anthropogenic Pb ratios measured in their tooth enamel. These three dogs were unlikely contemporary with either Saladoid or post-Saladoid contexts at the Red House Site (see chapter 3, this volume).

A comparison of $^{87}Sr/^{86}Sr$ values for the Red House site sampled fauna can be made with published Sr ratios for faunal tooth enamel sampled from other localities, based on the published work of Laffoon and colleagues (2013a, 2016). Figure 6.3 presents the Red House site peccary and Red House Site prehistoric dogs compared with published $^{87}Sr/^{86}Sr$ ratios from prehistoric dogs from Anse à la Gourde and Morel, two sites on Grande-Terre, Guadeloupe (Laffoon et al. 2013a) and mainland South American margay sampled from Dos Mosquises Island, Venezuela (Laffoon et al. 2016). The $^{87}Sr/^{86}Sr$ ratios of the Red House dogs range from 0.7088 to 0.7107 with an average of 0.7101 (close in comparison to the human $^{87}Sr/^{86}Sr$ average of 0.7107, presented in chapter 3, this volume). Importantly, all faunal Sr ratios including the high Sr value for the peccary, are consistent with expected variability of bioavailable strontium, particularly

Table 6.4. Isotopic Ratios for Red House Fauna Tooth Enamel Apatite Samples

Taxon	Provenience	Depth	Tooth[2]	BCL #	$\delta^{13}C_{en}$ (‰ vs VPDB)	$\delta^{18}O_{en}$ (‰ vs VPDB)	$^{87}Sr/^{86}Sr$
Tayassu tajacu	A-NPC-2	0.24-0.40	I2	3405	−13.9	−0.3	0.7132
Canis familiaris	A-NWCS-1	0.22–1.50	M1	3402	−10.8	−3.2	0.7101
Canis familiaris	B-R-G35-2	1.36–1.57	C	3403	−10.1	−1.9	0.7101
Canis familiaris	B-G26-NW Rotunda-2	1.04–1.54	C	3404	−10.1	−3.5	0.7101
Canis familiaris	Rotunda Fountain-5	1.09	M1	3406	−11.3	−3.0	0.7097
Canis familiaris	BM #1 Ext	1.87–1.98	PM4	3410	−10.6	−3.6	0.7107
Canis familiaris	BAR #5	0.37	PM4	3411	−4.8	−3.4	0.7101
Canis familiaris[1]	A-NECS-5	0.00–0.52	PM4	3407	−8.2	−4.6	*0.7089*
Canis familiaris	A-NPC-NCS (East)-G57	0.00–0.19	C	3408	−8.2	−4.1	*0.7092*
Canis familiaris	A-NPC-6	0.27	PM4	3409	−8.4	−4.8	*0.7088*

[1]"Modern" dog isotope data are italicized (see chapter 3 for discussion).
[2]C = canine, I2 = second incisor, M1 = first molar, PM4 = premolar.

for the metamorphic region in the northern part of Trinidad. Thus, both the peccary and all prehistoric dogs from the Red House site are consistent with "local" Trinidad origin. However, when employing a broader, regional comparison of Sr values, a general trend of similar and lower (less radiogenic) $^{87}Sr/^{86}Sr$ values in the Lesser Antilles is also noted. For example, the prehistoric dogs from Guadeloupe exhibit lower Sr ratios, compared to the prehistoric peccary or the South American margay, reported by Laffoon and colleagues (2016), which reflects the expected broad range of bioavailable strontium characteristic of the mainland.

The light isotope results of $\delta^{13}C_{en}$ and $\delta^{18}O_{en}$ for the dogs and the peccary (n = 1) are also presented in table 6.4. Not considering the three "modern" dogs, the prehistoric average (n = 6) for Red House site dogs is $\delta^{13}C_{en}$ is −9.6 ± 2.41‰. A cluster of five of these dog samples is quite similar to the human average $\delta^{13}C_{en}$ of −10.2‰ (see chapter 3, this volume) (figure 6.4). More specifically, this $\delta^{13}C_{en}$ average for these five dogs falls directly in between the average $\delta^{13}C_{en}$ for the human Saladoid sample of −12.0 ± 1.09‰ and the average of the human post-Saladoid sample of −9.7 ± 0.97‰. This indicates that these dogs were consuming locally and contemporaneously with dietary patterns similar to those of the humans, including C_3-based and maritime dependence. This also supports previous remarks that the dogs, if not domesticated, were at the very least accompanying Saladoid and perhaps post-Saladoid individuals. Interestingly, the elevated $\delta^{18}O$

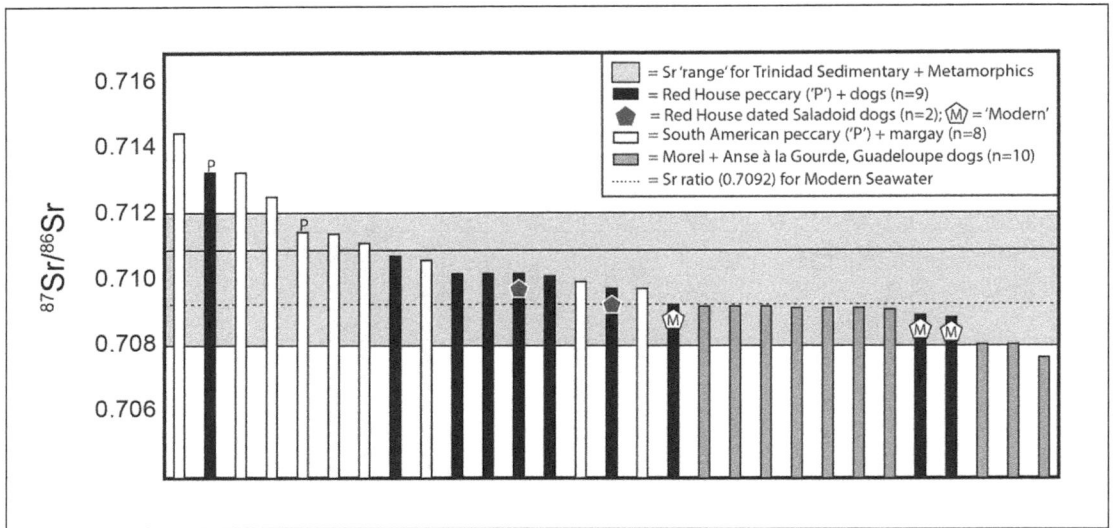

Figure 6.3. Strontium ($^{87}Sr/^{86}Sr$) ratios for sampled Red House site fauna (black bars). Shaded zone indicates broad range (±2σ) of sampled metamorphic (0.7079 to 0.7108) and sedimentary (0.7090 to 0.7118) contexts on Trinidad (Laffoon et al. 2012). Comparative data include (1) South American margay "cat" (*Leopardus wiedii*) from Dos Mosquises Island, Venezuela (Laffoon et al. 2016), which illustrates Sr range of bioavailable strontium for northern "mainland" contexts (white bars); and (2) prehistoric dogs from Guadeloupe (Laffoon et al. 2013a), which illustrates less radiogenic Sr ratios characteristic of the Lesser Antilles (grey bars).

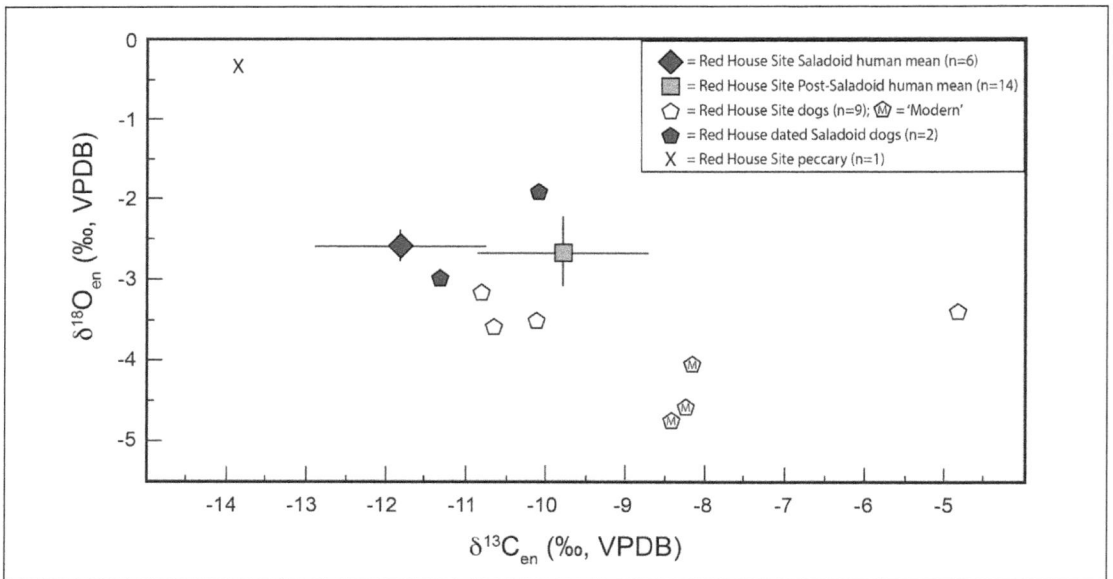

Figure 6.4. Bivariate plot of $\delta^{13}C_{en}$ and $\delta^{18}O_{en}$ from tooth enamel sampled from Red House site fauna. Red House human Saladoid and post-Saladoid mean values include 1σ error bars. The "outlier" peccary is from a forested environment, with values that are enriched in ^{18}O and depleted in ^{13}C. Note three "modern" dogs as determined by Pb ratios (see chapter 3, this volume) are depleted in ^{18}O, and "outlier" prehistoric dog is enriched in ^{13}C ($\delta^{13}C = -4.8‰$), which suggests a C_4-based maize diet.

values for the dogs are broadly comparable to the $\delta^{18}O$ values observed for the Red House site human sample (chapter 3). The peccary, in contrast, has a $\delta^{18}O$ value (−0.3‰) that is more positive (^{18}O-enriched) than that observed among the humans and dogs. This indicates that the peccary inhabited a forested area, which is consistent with its dwelling habits and habitats frequented by local hunters. This conclusion is also consistent with the peccary's $^{87}Sr/^{86}Sr$ ratio, which is the highest among the fauna sampled for the Red House site, not to mention all of the humans sampled. Curiously, this radiogenic Sr ratio is consistent with the metamorphic rocks found on the South American mainland (present-day Venezuela), as well as the metamorphic sequence of rocks observed along the Northern Range of Trinidad, however, its Pb ratios suggest the peccary is "local" to Trinidad (see chapter 3).

ARTEFACTS

Some of the more well-made bone and shell tools and personal adornments are listed here according to the sections in which they were unearthed. Bone tools included spatulas and awls (figure 6.5), and jewellery comprised mostly pendants.

There were several blank bone beads, two bone pendants (figure 6.6: row A), as well as an awl and other tools from section A. Section B contained the most outstanding shell and bone artefacts, including the aforementioned shell gorget in the shape of a turtle carapace (figure 6.6: row B, right), and an unusual, fish-shaped pendant possibly made from bone with an engraved eye and mouth on

Figure 6.5.
Bone tools (*left*: spatula; *right*: two awls) from section A, crawl space northwest, subdivision 1, 0.22 m–1.46 m.

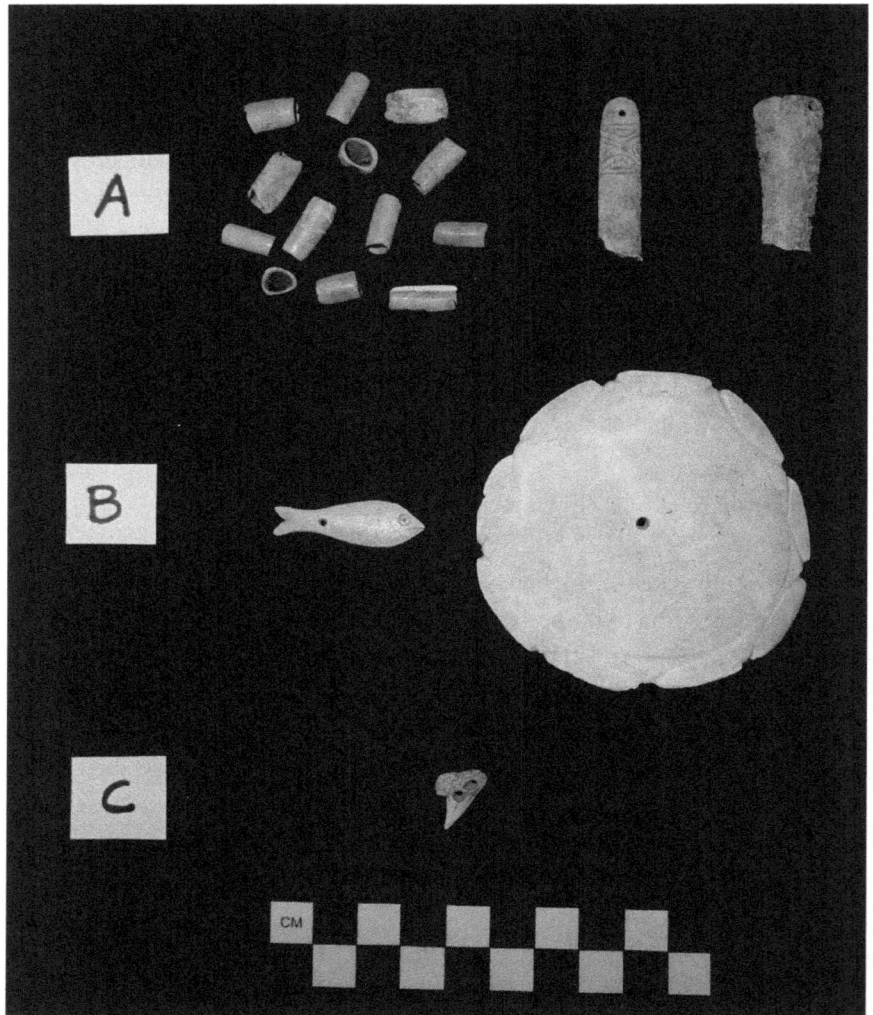

Figure 6.6. Bone and shell ornaments. Rows A, B and C comprise items from the homonymous sections of the Red House. Row A: blank bone beads, bone pendant with incised design, long bone pendant; row B: fish-shaped pendant, shell gorget; row C: shark tooth pendant.

each side (figure 6.6: row B, left). A shark tooth pendant (figure 6.6: row C), an awl, and a possible bone fishhook were excavated in section C. Although there are fish remains on site, the lack of fishing accessories such as fishhooks could be explained by Newsom and Wing, who state that "fishhooks are rare on West Indian sites, perhaps because they were made of material that does not preserve well" (Newsom and Wing 2004, 52). Bone artefacts were dispersed across the entire basement, with the greatest accumulation in section A, followed by section C, then B. While this artefact distribution coincides with that of the vertebrate assemblage, the high degree of site disturbance precludes a feasible argument for the cause of this association.

CONCLUSION

The animals identified indicate that there was a preference for molluscs from the intertidal zone and shallow marine waters during the Saladoid and post-Saladoid occupations of the Red House site. The analysis of variance across the site showed that section C contained more molluscs than the other parts (sections A, B and BAR units) of the site. Section C also had the greatest diversity of molluscan species. Additionally, the section A mollusc samples contained more of the dominant species (oysters, lucines, Caribbean crown conchs) than samples from other areas. The indigenes fished in pelagic waters, but more often exploited the closer, more accessible freshwater/brackish habitats favoured by catfish. Their terrestrial food choices were dominated by forest mammals, which was typical of pre-colonial indigenous groups in Trinidad. The isotopic faunal data support this conclusion with evidence of native dogs with broadly similar dietary patterns as those of the humans sampled from the Red House site. The bone and shell artefacts highlighted here show that animals were sought for purposes beyond subsistence.

This preliminary examination of the excavated faunas from the Red House site lays a foundation for further zooarchaeological studies of the analysed sample and other parts of the faunal assemblage that were not considered here. This will hopefully create a deeper understanding of the foodways of the indigenous occupants of both the Red House site and other sites with both indigenous and colonial influences.

ACKNOWLEDGEMENTS

Gratitude is extended to all the Excavation and Finds Processing staff, particularly those who helped with gathering primary data for both the invertebrates and vertebrates. Such essential contributions were made by Shawntelle-Ann Syriac-Lynch, Kerry-Ann Khell and Krystal Singh for the invertebrates and Kristianne Bhagan-Rambaran and Stephanie Logie for the vertebrates. We also would like to thank Dr Ashley Sharpe for her identification of the collared peccary incisor sampled for isotopic analysis and for her assistance with column chemistry. Drs George Kamenov and Jason Curtis (University of Florida) are gratefully acknowledged for their assistance in securing the strontium ratios and carbon and oxygen isotope data, respectively.

REFERENCES

Abbott, R.T., and P.A. Morris. 1995. *A Field Guide to Shells – Atlantic and Gulf Coasts and the West Indies.* Peterson Field Guide Series, edited by R.T. Peterson. 4th ed. New York: Houghton Mifflin.

Boomert, A. 2000. *Trinidad, Tobago and the Lower Orinoco Interaction Sphere: An Archaeological/Ethnohistorical Study*. Alkmaar, the Netherlands: Cairi.

———. 2016. *The Indigenous Peoples of Trinidad and Tobago: From the First Settlers Until Today*. Leiden: Sidestone Press.

Bullbrook, J.A. 1917–1963. *The Bullbrook Papers*. Special Collection, West Indiana, Alma Jordan Library, University of the West Indies, St Augustine.

Claassen, C. 1998. *Shells*. Cambridge: Cambridge University Press.

Crosby, A.W. 1972. *The Columbian Exchange: Biological and Cultural Consequences of 1492*. Westport: Greenwood Press.

Delsol, N., and S. Grouard. 2016. "Comments on Amerindian Hunting Practices in Trinidad (West Indies): Tetrapods from the Manzanilla Site (Late Ceramic Age AD 300–900)". *Journal of Island and Coastal Archaeology* 11:385–410.

France, D L. 2011. *Human and Nonhuman Bone Identification: A Concise Field Guide*. Boca Raton: CRC Press.

Giovas, C.M., G.D. Kamenov, S.M. Fitzpatrick and J. Krigbaum. 2016. "Sr and Pb Isotopic Investigation of Mammal Introductions: Pre-Columbian Zoogeographic Records from the Lesser Antilles, West Indies". *Journal of Archaeological Science* 69:39–53.

Harris, P.O'B. 1973. "Summary of Trinidad Archaeology". In *Proceedings of the Fifth International Congress for the Study of Pre-Columbian Cultures of the Lesser Antilles*, 110–16.

Hoogland, M.L.P., and C.L. Hofman. 2013. "From Corpse Taphonomy to Mortuary Behavior in the Caribbean: A Case Study from the Lesser Antilles". In *The Oxford Handbook of Caribbean Archaeology*, edited by W.F. Keegan, C.L. Hofman and R. Rodríguez Ramos, 452–69. New York: Oxford University Press.

Keegan, W.F., and L.A. Carlson. 2008. *Talking Taíno: Essays on Caribbean Natural History from a Native Perspective*. Tuscaloosa: University of Alabama Press.

Klein, R.G., and K. Cruz-Uribe. 1984. *The Analysis of Animal Bones from Archaeological Sites*. Chicago: University of Chicago Press.

LeFebvre, Michelle J., and Susan D. deFrance. 2018. "Animal Management and Domestication in the Realm of Ceramic Age Farming". In *The Archaeology of Caribbean and Circum-Caribbean Farmers (6000 BC–AD 1500)*, edited by B.A. Reid, 149–70. London: Routledge.

Laffoon, J.E., G.R. Davies, M.L.P. Hoogland and C.L. Hofman. 2012. "Spatial Variation of Biologically Available Strontium Isotopes ($^{87}Sr/^{86}Sr$) in an Archipelagic Setting: A Case Study from the Caribbean". *Journal of Archaeological Science* 39:2371–84.

Laffoon, J.E., E. Plomp, G.R. Davies, M.L.P. Hoogland and C.L. Hofman. 2013a. "The Movement and Exchange of Dogs in the Prehistoric Caribbean: An Isotopic Investigation". *International Journal of Osteoarchaeology* 25:454–65.

Laffoon, J.E., T.F. Sonnemann, M.M. Antczak and A. Antczak. 2016. "Sourcing Nonnative Mammal Remains from Dos Mosquises Island, Venezuela: New Multiple Isotope Evidence". *Archaeological and Anthropological Sciences*. DOI 10.1007/s12520-016-0453-6.

Laffoon, J.E., R. Valcarcel Rojas and C.L. Hofman. 2013b. "Oxygen and Carbon Isotope Analysis of Human Dental Enamel from the Caribbean: Implications for Investigating Individual Origins". *Archaeometry* 55:742–65.

Mohammed, E., L. Ferreira, S. Soomai, L. Martin and C.C.A. Shing. 2011. "Coastal Fisheries of Trinidad and Tobago". In *Coastal Fisheries of Latin America and the Caribbean: FAO Fisheries and Aquaculture Technical Paper 544*, edited by S. Salas, R. Chuenpagdee, A. Charles and J.C. Seijo, 315–56. Rome: Food and Agriculture Organisation of the United Nations.

Mohammed, R.S., and L. Fanovich. 2016. "Mollusc Shell Findings from the Red House Excavation, Trinidad". In *Living World, Journal of the Trinidad and Tobago Field Naturalist's Club*, 33–37.

Newsom, L.A., and E.S. Wing. 2004. *On Land and Sea: Native American Uses of Biological Resources in the West Indies*. Tuscaloosa: University of Alabama Press.

Padrón, F.M. 2012. *Spanish Trinidad*. Kingston: Ian Randle.

Peres, T.M. 2010. "Methodological Issues in Zooarchaeology". In *Integrating Zooarchaeology and Paleoethnobotany: A Consideration of Issues, Methods and Cases*, edited by A.M. VanDerwarker and T.M. Peres, 15–36. New York: Springer.

Reid, B.A. 2015. *Red House Restoration Archaeology Project Report, Phase 1, for the Period July 1, 2013–January 31, 2015*. Port of Spain: Office of the Parliament of the Republic of Trinidad and Tobago.

Saunders, N.J. 2005. *The Peoples of the Caribbean: An Encyclopedia of Archaeology and Traditional Culture*. Santa Barbara: ABC-CLIO.

Stahl, P.W. 1995. "Differential Preservation Histories Affecting the Mammalian Zooarchaeological Record from the Forested Neotropical Lowlands". In *Archaeology in the Lowland American Tropics: Current Analytical Methods and Recent Applications*, edited by P.W. Stahl, 154–80. Cambridge: Cambridge University Press.

Watters, D.R., and I. Rouse. 1989. "Environmental Diversity and Maritime Adaptations in the Caribbean Area". In *Early Ceramic Population Lifeways and Adaptive Strategies in the Caribbean*, edited by P.E. Siegel, 129–44. BAR International Series 506. Oxford: British Archaeological Reports.

Wing, E.S. 1991. "Economy and Subsistence I: Faunal Remains". In *Prehistoric Barbados*, edited by P. Drewett, 134–52. London: Institute of Archaeology, University College London.

Wing, E.S., and E.J. Reitz. 1999. *Zooarchaeology*. New York: Cambridge University Press.

CHAPTER 7

Petrographic and Chemical Analyses of Pre-colonial Ceramics from the Red House Site

PATRICK DEGRYSE, CORINNE L. HOFMAN,
BASIL A. REID, BERT NEYT AND KRYSTAL SINGH

SIXTEEN CERAMIC SAMPLES FROM THE RED HOUSE SITE in Trinidad were petrographically and chemically analysed at Leuven University (Belgium) from 2013 to 2015. Funded by Humanities in the European Research Area (HERA grant number 1133 and the European Research Council (ERC Synergy grant number 319209), and coordinated by Professor Corinne Hofman, the analysis was part of the CARIB and NEXUS1492 projects done in collaboration between Leiden University and KU Leuven. The Red House samples were among a total of one hundred ceramic samples from fifteen other Trinidadian sites that were subjected to petrographic and geochemical analyses. These sites included Sanders Bay, Savaneta, San Pedro, Tacarigua, Whitelands, Blanchisseuse, Guayaguayare, Rest House, Atagual, Cedros, Palo Seco, Erin, Quinam, Bontour and St Joseph. One of the primary purposes of this exercise was to determine whether any of the Red House ceramic samples belonged to the Arauquinoid and Mayoid cultural periods, given the pre-colonial chronology of the site. The other important objective of this study was to ascertain whether the pottery of the Red House was made from local or non-local raw materials, and this was based on the premise that presence of non-local ceramic fabric may be indicative of either intra-island trade or trade relations between the Red House natives and their counterparts outside of Trinidad.

THE RED HOUSE SITE AND CONVENTIONAL MODELS FOR TRINIDAD'S PRE-COLONIAL HISTORY

The pre-colonial chronology of the Red House site spans from 125 to 1395 CE. According to conventional pre-colonial models for Trinidad, the Saladoid,

Arauquinoid and Mayoid series are located within this timeline, and are usually ascribed with the following chronologies: Saladoid (500 BCE–600/650 CE), Arauquinoid (650–1300 CE) and Mayoid (1300–1800 CE) (Boomert 2000, 2014; Reid 2010).

Saladoid Cultural Period

As indicated in both the introduction and chapter 1 of this volume, the pre-colonial pottery recovered from the Red House site appears to be distinctly Saladoid. While most of the Saladoid potsherds found at the site are undecorated, the presence of decorated and complex modelled sherds provide the diagnostic evidence attesting to their Saladoid cultural origin (Reid 2015). Although the Red House pre-colonial ceramics are distinctly Saladoid, certain defining characteristics of the assemblage suggest that they can properly be defined as Saladoid (Palo Seco). Palo Seco pottery vessels come in a variety of shapes and sizes. The common forms are bowls with a wide range of rims, from thick to elaborate compound rims. In the south and central parts of Trinidad, Palo Seco ceramics are tempered with fine crushed shell and/or medium to coarse grog (Boomert 2000; Sajo 2014). However, in north Trinidad it is tempered with fine to medium-coarse sand temper containing quartz and mica particles combined with grog (Boomert 2000; Sajo 2014).

Arauquinoid Cultural Period

Evidence for the existence of another mainland ceramic series, Arauquinoid, in Trinidad is presented by Harris in his modification of Rouse's sequential cultural framework for the island (Harris 1978). The Arauquinoid series is known as Guayabitoid in Trinidad and in the northeastern part of Venezuela, mainly because only some traits of this series diffused to Trinidad during this period (Dorst 2000, 35). According to Harris (1978), the collapse of Barrancoid communities in the Middle Orinoco on the South American mainland (around 650 CE) facilitated Arauquinoid expansion from the Orinoco delta to the Caribbean's most southerly island. The Guayabitoid series can be divided into four complexes: St Catherine's, Bontour, St Joseph and Marac. An increasing population density throughout Trinidad is suggested by a large increase of the number of sites during the Arauquinoid period (Boomert 2014). An important characteristic of Arauquinoid ceramic temper is the presence of *cauixi*, or sponge spicules (Boomert 2000). Cauixi relate to the following species: *Drulia* sp., *Trochospongilla* sp., *Stratospongilla* sp.

Mayoid Cultural Period

The Mayoid series was the final Amerindian ceramic tradition of Trinidad before European contact. It emerged in 1300 CE, about two centuries before Columbus encountered the island on his third journey to the West Indies in 1498. Mayoid pottery may have been manufactured until the mid-eighteenth century. The strong resemblance between Mayoid cooking jars and the "buck-pots" (pepper pots) of the Arawak (Lokono) in the Guianas suggests strong cultural affinities between the two groups. This connection is further bolstered by the rare occurrence of a typically Koriabo-Cayo necked vessel in Mayoid archaeological sites. Mayoid ceramics of Trinidad were apparently manufactured by both the Nepoio and Arawak (Lokono) Amerindians (Boomert 2014).

Mayoid pottery is invariably tempered with *caraipé,* the ash of the quartz-rich bark of small trees belonging to the *Licania* genus (Boomert 2016). *Licania* trees were once indigenous to Trinidad's Northern Basin, as specimens of this genus have been collected in the O'Meara and Aripo savannahs in 1861 and 1913, respectively (Boomert 2016). As earlier indicated, the pre-colonial timeline of the Red House terminated in 1395 CE, that is, during the very early stages of the Mayoid series. It is therefore doubtful whether this cultural period was a major factor at the site. As a cautionary measure, however, the Red House ceramic samples were tested for the presence of caraipé.

Geological and Soils Profile of Port of Spain and Its Environs

As earlier indicated, the Red House is located in Port of Spain. Given that ceramic samples from the Red House were petrographically and chemically analysed, a brief discussion of the geological and soils profile of Port of Spain and its environs would be useful.

Port of Spain stretches from the foothills of the Northern Range to the shores of the Gulf of Paria. The capital city is located on the western edge of the North Basin of Trinidad, an area characterized by a broad synclinal trough, a half-graben situated between 0 and 60 metres above the mean sea level and bounded by the El Pilar fault and the Central Range. The central and northern portions of the Gulf of Paria form the western extension of this depression (Boomert 2000, 26; Andel and Sachs 1964).

The Northern Basin is composed of Jurassic and Cretaceous rock overlaid by thick Pleistocene and more recent sediments, including those deposited by Trinidad's largest river, the Caroni. The Northern Range of Trinidad which is an eastern extension of the Coastal Range of the Andes is the oldest geological formation of Trinidad and Tobago (Kenny 2000, 16) and consists primarily of metasedimentary rocks made up of metamorphosed phyllites, quartzites and recrystallized limestone (see chapter 3, this volume). Limestone, in particular, is found in many locations including Laventille, Diego Martin, and Maraval. Present also in the valleys and flood plains of the rivers flowing through the Northern Range are colluvial and alluvial parent material deposits (Agard et al. 2004).

Most soils of the Northern Range are not suitable for agriculture (Boomert 2000, 26). For instance, the soils on the terraces that are well drained may provide some agricultural potential but are limited due to the incidence of low fertility and a lack of moisture, while the poorly drained terrace soils are all together of little agricultural potential (Agard et al. 2004). The valley bottoms however, are characterized by alluvial soils on the flood plains which have high agricultural capabilities (Boomert, 2000, 26; Agard et al. 2004).

METHODOLOGY

Sixteen ceramic samples from the Red House site in Trinidad were subjected to petrographic analysis and chemical analysis. For the petrographic analysis, thin sections were made of all samples, and these were described using a petrographic microscope. Bulk chemical analysis was done by ICP-OES (Inductively Coupled Plasma Optical Emission Spectrometry), giving results for the following main elements (as oxides): Na_2O, MgO, Al_2O_3, SiO_2, P_2O_5, K_2O, CaO, MnO, TiO_2 and Fe_2O_3, and the following trace elements: Sc, V, Cr, Ni, Cu, Zn, Sr, Y, Zr, Ba, La and Pb.

RESULTS

Petrographic analysis divides the assemblage in two main groups and two outliers. The first main group (n = 9) (figure 7.1) contains a variety of grog fragments. The second main group (n = 5) (figure 7.2) contains metamorphic rock fragments, both quartzite and micaschist. Two samples of this group contain abundant quartzite (2013-CSpSW,Sd3-0/1.08 and 2013-CSpNW,Sd2-0.71/1.5), while the other three contain abundant micaschist. One outlier contains crushed shell fragments (figure 7.3), and the other outlier contains mainly plagioclase inclusions (figure 7.4).

DISCUSSION

Petrography and Chemistry

All samples from the grog group contain grog in different shapes and sizes, made in at least three different ways. One subgroup has grog that contains

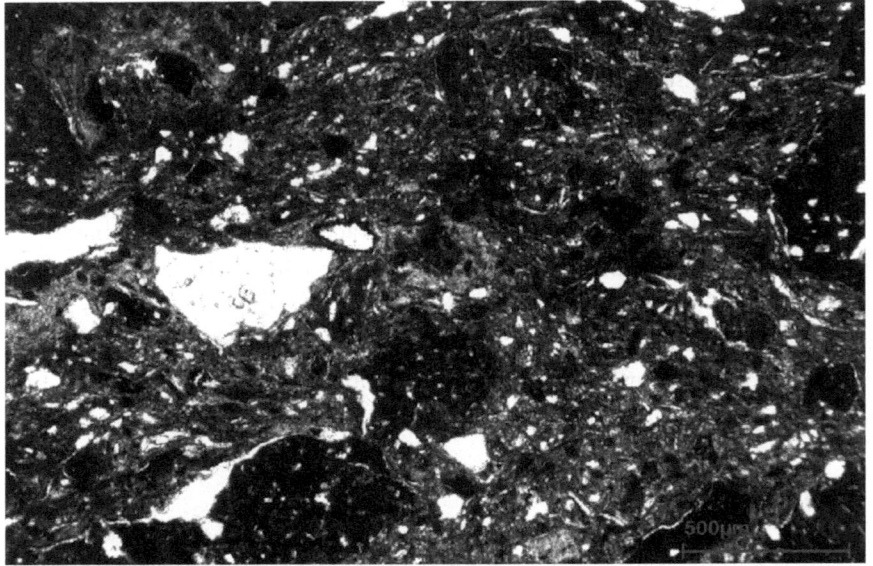

Figure 7.1. Sample CB15BN027 (2013-CSpNE,Sd3-0.87/1.37), under parallel polaroids. This fabric is characterized by the presence of various grog and clay fragments in a heterogeneous clay matrix. It is likely that raw material for this fabric was soil rather than material from a clay deposit. This fabric contains Fe-oxides in variable amounts. Other inclusions attested are minor amounts of small to medium-sized quartz next to rare quartzite and limestone.

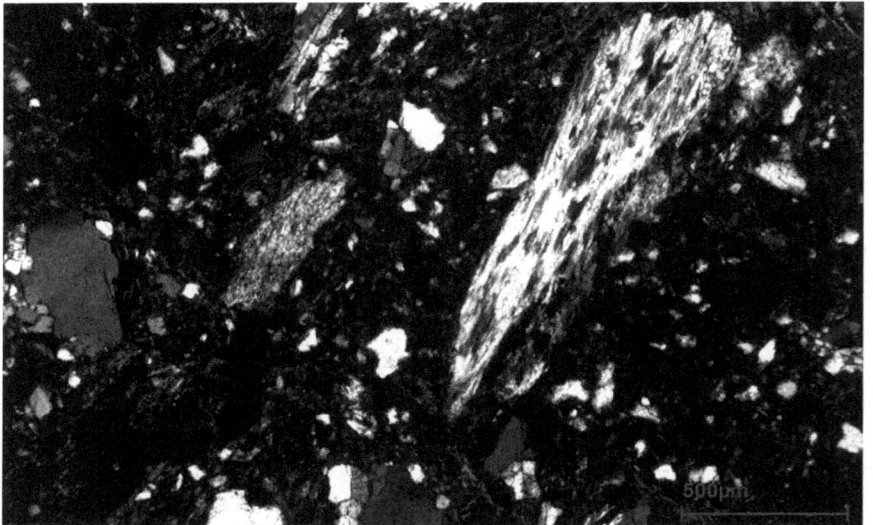

Figure 7.2. Sample CB15BN023 (2013-CSpNW,Sd2-0.71/1.5), under crossed polaroids. This fabric is characterized by the presence of large micaschist and quartzite inclusions in variable quantities. The size of these inclusions goes up to 3 mm, and their mode is substantially larger than for other inclusions. These metamorphic inclusions were most likely added as a temper to the clay paste. Substantial amounts of the metamorphic temper has a subrounded appearance. Other inclusions are mainly quartz, which shows a bimodal distribution. The sample shows a moderate to high optical activity of the clay matrix, so low firing temperatures were applied.

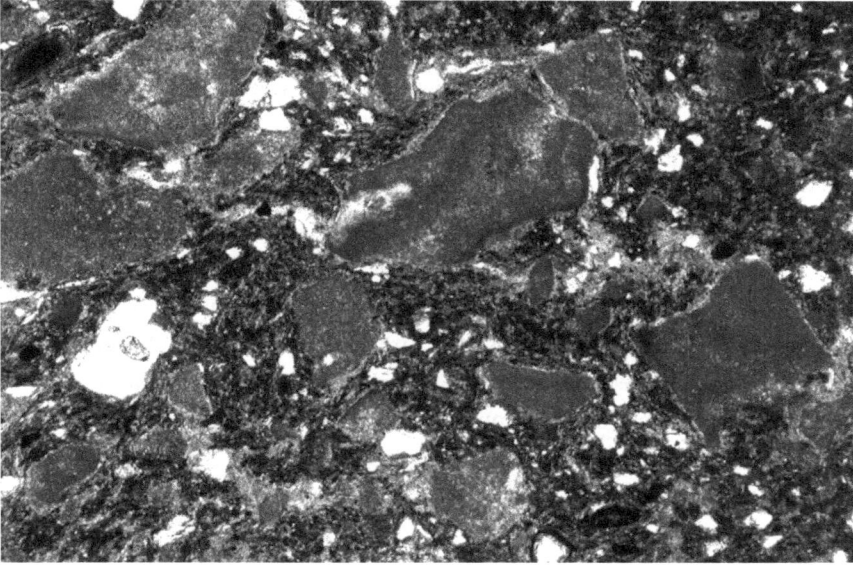

Figure 7.3. Sample CB15BN013 (2013-CEP14-0.48/1.41), under parallel polaroids. This fabric is characterized by the addition of shell temper. Shell fragments up to 2.2 mm are present, and other inclusions are mainly small subangular quartz grains with a mode of 50 μm. This sample was fired in oxidizing atmosphere, at a low firing temperature.

Figure 7.4. Sample CB15BN015 (2013-CEP15-0.53/1.975), under crossed polaroids. This fabric is characterized by the presence of plagioclase and quartz inclusions in a densely packed matrix. Total percentage of inclusions is 25–30%. Sorting is poor. Quartz inclusions are up to 2.2 mm and plagioclase inclusions are up to 2.8 mm, but their modes are rather low (0.2–0.5 mm). They were most likely added as temper. Firing conditions were oxidizing and firing temperatures was low, as testified by the high to medium optical activity of the clay matrix. Porosity is average.

quartz and mica, the second subgroup contains red oxidized grog fragments, and the third subgroup contains opaque grog fragments. To what extent these differences are intentional is unclear. They are not seen in the chemical analysis.

The metamorphic group can be divided into two subgroups: one group with abundant quartzite, and one group with abundant micaschist. These subgroups can be distinguished chemically, as the quartzite group has higher Cr values than the rest of the samples. However, the group with the abundant micaschist is chemically similar to the samples of the grog group. This could be an indication that the clay used for their production is similar. The size, shape, abundance and distribution of the metamorphic rock fragments suggests their intentional use as temper. The two petrographic outliers can easily be distinguished chemically from the other samples.

Provenance

For the grog group, it is difficult to determine the geological provenance based on petrography alone. The metamorphic group however is easily linked to the quartz-mica schist formations present in the Northern Range of Trinidad. Hence these samples are most likely locally produced. Comparing the chemistry of the Red House ceramics from the two main petrographic groups with the chemistry of a range of clay raw materials from Trinidad, collected by a team from Leiden University and analysed using XRF by the Department of Earth Sciences at VU Amsterdam under the direction of Professor Dr Gareth Davies, suggests an affiliation of the ceramics with the northern clay samples taken from Trinidad and less with clay samples from the central and southern parts of the island (figures 7.5 and 7.6). This coincides with the observed use of metamorphic rock from the Northern Range of the island as temper for some of the samples, and suggests local provenance of the raw material for the ceramics from the two main petrographic groups.

It is unknown yet where the plagioclase-rich sample originates from. There may be a link to the volcanic islands to the north of Trinidad (Grenada, St Vincent). Figure 7.4 illustrates similarities of the plagioclase sample from the Red House site with ceramics from St Vincent, suggesting a connection.

HYPOTHESIS TESTING

The following five hypotheses and responses thereto were used as an important frame of reference for interpreting the data.

Hypothesis: Saladoid (Palo Seco) potsherds are usually moderately thick, coarse and soft, grit-tempered pottery. How many Red House samples fit these criteria?

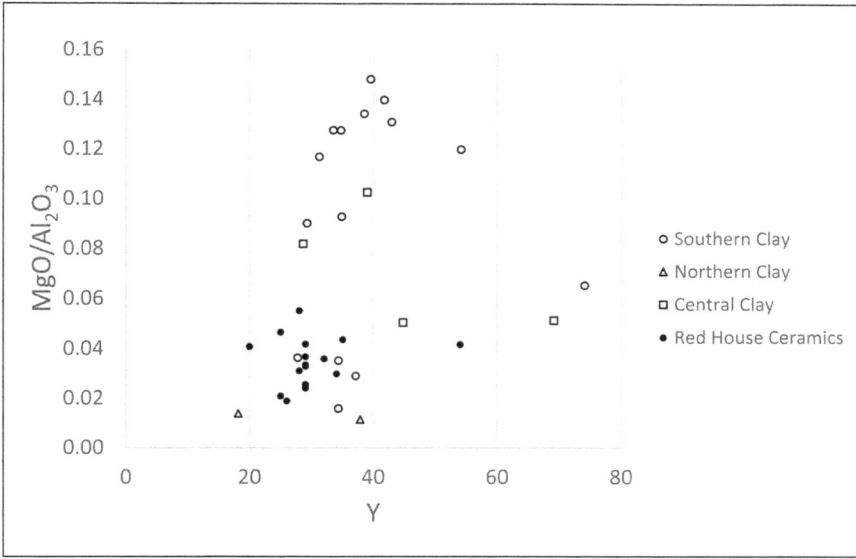

Figure 7.5
Red House ceramics
(grog and metamor-
phic group) com-
pared to Trinidad
clay samples.

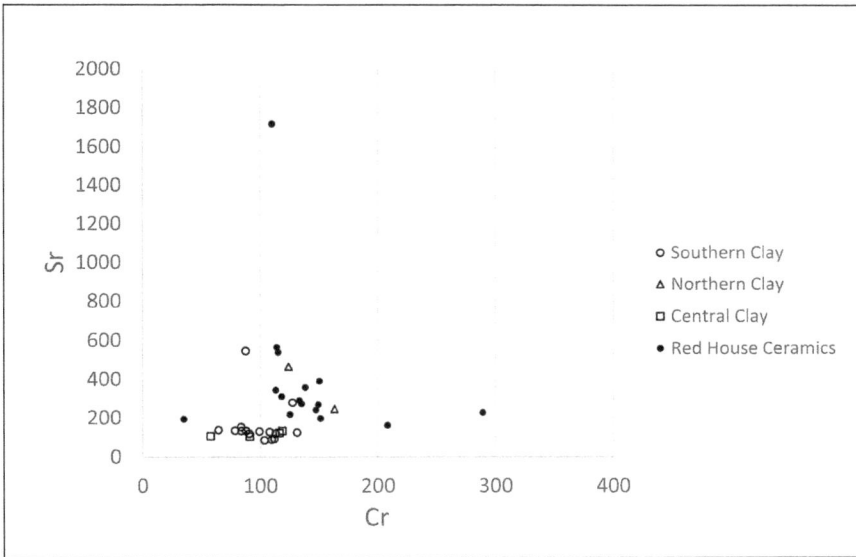

Figure 7.6
Red House ceramics
(grog and metamor-
phic group) com-
pared to Trinidad
clay samples.

Response(s): There are fifteen Red House samples that have been tempered with medium to coarse diverse grog fragments, medium to coarse metamorphic rock temper or coarse crushed shell. Only the sample with the plagioclase inclusions is a finer fabric. If the definition of grit in this context means "fragments of sand-size", then these fifteen samples fit this criterion.

Hypothesis: In the south and central parts of Trinidad, Palo Seco ceramics are tempered with fine crushed shell and/or medium to coarse grog. However, in north Trinidad it is tempered with fine to medium-coarse sand temper containing quartz and mica particles combined with grog. If temper characteristic of

Figure 7.7.
Comparison of samples with similar petrography from southern Trinidad sites (Palo Seco, Erin, Quinam and Cedros) and the Red House site.

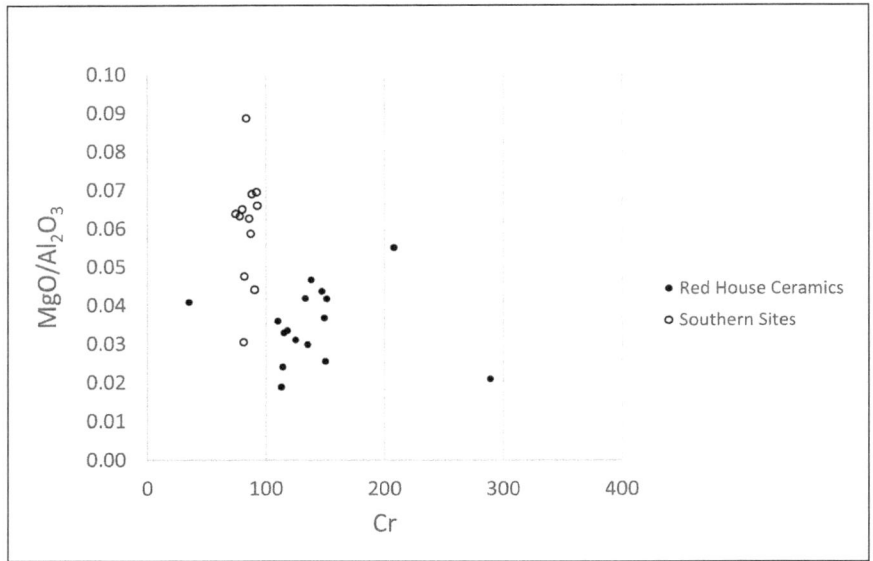

Palo Seco ceramics of south and central Trinidad are found at the Red House site (in north Trinidad), could this be indicative of intra-island trade?

Response(s): No samples with fine crushed shell were found, but one sample with coarse crushed shell was observed. Most samples were tempered with grog or sand-sized metamorphic rock fragments. The petrographic group with the grog fragments is petrographically similar to ceramics from southern sites. However, chemical analysis reveals a division between the Red House samples and the ceramics from the southern sites (data from XRF database produced by VU Amsterdam) (figure 7.7). Furthermore, clays from northern locations show more chemical similarities with the Red House ceramics than clays from southern locations (figures 7.5 and 7.6). This is a good indication that the Red House ceramics do not originate from the same sources as the southern samples. Hence, on basis of these data, intra-island trade is not likely for these samples.

Hypothesis: Although radiocarbon dates of the Palo Seco assemblage range from the time of Christ to 650 CE, from 350 CE onwards, the Palo Seco style reflects an increasing Barrancoid influence. The sample will include examples of known Barrancoid-influenced Palo Seco potsherds such as D-shaped handles, complex modelled adornos, nubbins and the like. Do the fabric analysis results of these Barrancoid-influenced Palo Seco ceramics reveal a distinctive archaeological pattern with respect to the Red House samples?

Response(s): The two Red House adornos belong to the metamorphic group, together with the sherd with incised lines and punctures, and a body sherd and a rim sherd from the crawl space. Conversely, the Red House handle belongs to the grog group.

Hypothesis: Arauquinoid pottery is usually very light, porous and soft paste tempered with freshwater sponge spicules (cauxi). Cauxi is the Brazilian Portuguese name for the silica bodies of aquatic sponge spicules that are commonly used as temper for pre-Columbian pottery in much but certainly not all of the basin. Is cauxi present in any of the Red House samples? If so, which ones?

Response(s): None of the Red House sherds contains freshwater sponge spicules. However, three samples from the Erin and Quinam excavations, also studied petrographically, reflected the use of these sponge spicules as temper.

Hypothesis: The Mayoid series represented the final Amerindian ceramic tradition of Trinidad before European contact. The exclusive use of *caraipé* (burnt tree bark) as a tempering material was one of Mayoid pottery's defining characteristics. Is caraipé present in any of the samples? If so, which ones?

Response(s): None of the sherds from Red House contain caraipé. However, one sample in the dataset of Mayoid ceramics from the St Joseph site in Trinidad, did show the presence of caraipé as a temper.

CONCLUSIONS

While the results of these analyses indicate that fifteen of the ceramic samples belong to the Saladoid (Palo Seco) complex, no verifiable evidence for either Guayabitoid or Mayoid ceramics was discerned. The fabric of most of the ceramic samples point to local clay sourcing with the Northern Range being the primary source of such raw materials. There is tantalizing evidence, however, that there might have been some trade with St Vincent based on the fabric analysis of the ceramic samples.

The study also suggests that the Saladoid population of Trinidad was not completely replaced by the Arauquinoid newcomers and that the Red House might have been inhabited by a locally based indigenous community that produced pottery from local clays for over an extended period. This view is supported by Boomert (2014), who argues that the Saladoid population of Trinidad was not completely replaced by the Arauquinoid newcomers. On the contrary, "a steady cultural transition that primarily involved a locally based population characterized Trinidad throughout the Ceramic Age" (Boomert 2014, 338; Boomert et al. 2013, 140).

REFERENCES

Agard, J.M., Alkins-Koo, A. Cropper, F. Homer and S. Maharaj. 2004. *Report of an Assessment of the Northern Range of Trinidad, Trinidad and Tobago*. Port of Spain: Environmental Management Authority.

Andel, V., and P.L. Sachs. 1964. "Sedimentation in the Gulf of Paria during the Holocene Transgression: A Subsurface Reflection Study". *Journal of Marine Research* 22 (1): 30–50.

Boomert, A. 2000. *Trinidad, Tobago, and the Lower Interaction Sphrere: An Archaeological/Ethnohistorical Study*. Alkmaar, the Netherlands: Cairi.

———. 2014. "Trinidad and Tobago". In Reid and Gilmore 2014, 335–38.

———. 2016. *The Indigenous Peoples of Trinidad and Tobago: From First Settlers until Today*. Leiden: Sidestone Press.

Boomert, A., B. Faber-Morse and I. Rouse. 2013. *The Yale University Excavations in Trinidad of 1946 and 1953*. New Haven: Yale University Press.

Dorst, Marc. 2000. "Manzanilla I: An Archaeological Survey of a Pre-Columbian Site in Trinidad". MA thesis, University of Leiden.

Harris, P. O'B. 1978. "A Revised Chronological Framework for Ceramic Trinidad and Tobago". In *Proceedings of the VII International Congress for Caribbean Archaeology, Caracas 1977*, 47–63.

Kenny, J.S. 2000. *Views from the Ridge: Exploring the Natural History of Trinidad and Tobago*. Port of Spain: Prospect Press.

———. 2010. *Archaeology, GIS and Cultural Resource Management in Trinidad*. Saarbrücken, Germany: Lambert Academic.

———. 2015. *Red House Restoration Archaeology Report, Phase 1, for the Period July 1, 2013–January 31, 2015*. Port of Spain: Office of the Parliament of the Republic of Trinidad and Tobago.

Reid, B.A., and R.G. Gilmore III, eds. 2014. *Encyclopedia of Caribbean Archaeology*. Gainesville: University Press of Florida.

Sajo, A. 2014. "Palo Seco (Trinidad)". In Reid and Gilmore 2014, 273–74.

Part 2

THE COLONIAL PERIOD

CHAPTER 8

The Colonial History of Port of Spain and the Red House

From the Late Fifteenth Century to 1907

LOVELL FRANCIS

EVERY SOCIETY HAS ITS IMPORTANT AND SYMBOLIC STRUCTURES. The Americans have their White House, the Russians celebrate their Kremlin and the Greeks their very ancient Acropolis. In Trinidad and Tobago the building that has undoubtedly been most representative of the culture and identity of the nation is the Red House. So baptized for its unusually earthy colour, this structure has become a cultural emblem of its own. In fact, so central has it been to issues of officialdom, authority and power, the provision of legal documents both significant and minor, and many other matters of governance locally that it is still possible to hear contemporary Trinidadians and Tobagonians suggest that they have to visit this building to access some governmental service or another that have long been removed from its hallowed halls. The history of Trinidad's Red House is arguably as colourful as the shade that adorns its walls, and this is a story that should be examined and remembered by every Trinidadian and Tobagonian. This chapter places scholarly spotlight on the growth and development of the city of Port of Spain, which the physical edifice of the Red House once thoroughly dominated.[1]

FROM ST JOSEPH TO PORT OF SPAIN (1498–1797)

The original name of the island of Trinidad, Iere, has not been lost to antiquity (Winer 2008, 45). Instead, the fact that this word is remembered points to the existence of a thriving Amerindian civilization on the island long before it became the destination of Spanish treasure seekers at the end of the fifteenth century. However, the change in name to Trinidad, and the clearly Castilian origin of the name of what remains today its capital city, help to establish the significance of the arrival of the Spaniards. Interestingly, Puerto de España, or

Port of Spain, which was established in 1560 (La Borde 1876, 135), was not the first capital of the island. That instead was the former Amerindian village of Goanagoanare, which was renamed San José de Oruna or St Joseph (Padron 2013, 74) and which is far more to the east and the interior of the island. This might appear to be little more than a quaint historical curiosity; however, the choice of this capital was a strategic decision that says quite a lot about the relationship of the Spaniards and Amerindians and the early history of Port of Spain and Spanish Trinidad.

Logic suggests that the Spaniards who accidently arrived in the Caribbean as seekers of gold and silver would have seen the clear benefits of establishing a main coastal settlement in a safe harbour like Port of Spain. However, the move into the interior of Trinidad was encouraged by important safety considerations. Port of Spain was not an empty space when Christopher Columbus arrived here. Instead, according to the French writer Alexandre de Humboldt, the island of Trinidad was actually populated by seven different native ethnic groups. These were the Araucas, Chaimes, Tamanaques, Chaguanes, Salines, Quaquas and the Caraïbes, the last of which was further subdivided into the Nepoïos, Yaïos, Carinepagatos and Cumanagatos. These people did not stand by idly while the invading Spaniards tried to take their lands and homes.

There were no mythical peaceful Arawaks and warlike Caribs in Trinidad.[2] Instead there were people who were willing to fight to protect their homes and families, despite the great cruelty often displayed by the Spaniards.[3] The Amerindians of the Port of Spain area proved (at least initially) to be more than a military match for these European invaders (Padron 2013, 54). Their acts of self-defence meant that they would be condemned into slavery for supposedly being savage by the Spaniards (54). However, this was because in Trinidad they faced groups of natives who were brave and committed to protecting their homeland (50–54). The Amerindians proved to be well led, quite organized and competent fighters, who despite some early disagreement on how to act against the brazen Spanish, still managed to launch a series of early and well thought out military strikes that slowed the progress of the Spanish invasion, and thus struck great fear into them (50–54).

This situation, however, requires further explanation. There were bad relations in Trinidad between the Amerindians and the Spaniards long before Spain decided to formally take control of Trinidad in the 1580s. Much of this stemmed from mass kidnappings conducted by the Spaniards. None other than Diego Columbus, the son of Christopher had suggested to King Ferdinand that

> there were many Indians in the island of Trinidad who were doing nothing useful and whose souls were going to perdition for lack of instruction in the faith. But Ferdinand refused for the time being, to allow them to be kidnapped. His argument can be antic-

ipated; he had heard that there was gold in Trinidad, and moreover if the Trinidad Indians were stirred up they might interfere with the pearl fishing. (Simpson 1950, 25)

Ferdinand later relented when it was noted that Trinidad had no gold and in 1515 a Spaniard named Joan Bono captured and sold into slavery 185 natives from Trinidad; he repeated the act in 1516 (Padron 2013, 28). These kidnappings made the natives of Trinidad wary and distrustful of the Spaniards and likely to meet their encroachments with armed responses. For example, they greeted the arrival of Trinidad's first governor, Antonio de Sedeño, with pitched battles and the use of deadly poison arrows. Additionally, it was noted that the natives who lived in coastal areas like Port of Spain deliberately did not practise agriculture close to the coast. They preferred to bring provisions from afar in a strategy that was used to deny the Spaniards food and resources close to their ships (49).

However, Sedeño's 1533 move to create what appeared to be a permanent Spanish settlement in Port of Spain encouraged an escalation in the warfare between the natives and the invaders. The Amerindians, who were previously divided on how to act against the Spaniards, quickly united. A number of local chiefs including Guyna, Pamacoa, Diamaná, Utuyaney, Amanatey and Paraguany mustered their warriors, and in a lightning attack that lasted only half an hour they overwhelmed the Spaniards, wounding twenty five while killing two men and five horses (Padron 2013, 49). Sedeño was forced to flee Trinidad. Thus the hatred bred by the cruelties of the Spaniards led to fierce Amerindian resistance, which made the island virtually inhospitable to further Spanish encroachments. It was not until the 1580s that the Spanish again seriously ventured into Trinidad.

Aside from staunch native resistance in Port of Spain, the choice of St Joseph placed added protection against another danger to the Spaniards that is often forgotten. This was the fact that the early Spanish settlers lived in constant fear of invasion and death by their fellow countrymen. It is sometimes an ignored historical truth that while the Spanish American empire eventually became very bureaucratic,[4] in its earliest period it was an adhocracy. This meant that many of the early conquistadors were literally free agents who were independent of the authority of the Spanish monarchy. The early power of the Spanish Crown to control their actions was very limited.[5] Hence the New World, in the age of men like Cortés and Pizarro, was really a massive land grab.

Consequently, there were a number of individual Spanish claimants to the island of Trinidad in the sixteenth century. Interestingly, these included Juan Trejo Ponce de Léon, the son of the adventurer made famous by his search for the mythical fountain of youth in Florida. As mandated by the 1569 charter awarded to him, he is recorded as bringing into Trinidad in a four-year period not only the second group of enslaved Africans on the island[6] (the first was brought by Antonio Sedeño numbering one hundred fifty enslaved), but also a significant amount of livestock, which included one hundred horses, three hundred mares, five hundred cows, one thousand sheep and two hundred pigs and goats (Padron 2013, 63) – ensuring that the diet of the early Spanish settlers would be supplemented with protein of European origin to go along with the fish, game and provisions abundantly available locally. However, the rivalry between different groups of Spaniards over Trinidad often led to warfare, which helped to ensure that a major settlement on an open coastline was not safe for whichever group of claimants happened to be interested in the island.

Despite the dangers involved, however, both Trinidad – and particularly Port of Spain – retained strategic and economic significance in the development of the Spanish American empire. This was so chiefly because up until 1600 it was still believed to be the gateway to a hard-to-find but unimaginable wealth. The acceptance of the existence of El Dorado, a supposed city of gold to be found in the northern part of the South American continent, was the greatest, if not the only justification for a permanent Spanish settlement in Trinidad.[7] In fact, a number of Trinidad's early governors, including Antonio Sedeño,[8] Juan Ponce de Leon and Antonio de Berrio (La Borde 1876, 132), were little more than conquistadors, who only accepted the responsibility as an excuse to go into the South American mainland to locate a city that only existed in their collective imaginations.

In fact, prior to the Cedula of Population of 1783, the slow-in-coming realization that El Dorado did not exist was the single most important event in the "development" of Trinidad under Spanish control. The eventual understanding that the city of gold did not exist encouraged the beginning of a period within which Trinidad would be relegated to backwater status within the massive Spanish American Empire. Trinidad became the forgotten island (La Borde 1876, 132). Spain no longer cared about it, and consequently until 1783 Spanish Trinidad remained poor, underdeveloped and underpopulated. Furthermore, the few Spanish settlers who remained on the island were forced to make a meagre living by cultivating various crops and by trading with whichever ships happened to periodically call on the island. Accordingly, the nineteenth-century local historian E.L. Joseph (1838, 153) summed up the unflattering situation on the island in the late eighteenth century thus: "The prosperity of the colony had by this time sunk to its lowest ebb, and indolence and apathy had seized its inhabitants to a degree that is almost incredible. They were, what in ordinary language is called 'poverty struck' – ever complaining, and even begging of the general government for that relief which their own exertion ought to have procured them."

In fact, the generally neglectful nature of Spanish colonialism in Trinidad meant that successive Spanish governors who came to the island refused to take up lodgings in the fairly dilapidated and crumbling capital town of St

Joseph. They opted instead to set up residence at the underdeveloped but far more convenient Port of Spain. In 1757 the latter town became the new centre of power on the island because the then new governor, Don Pedro de la Moneda, could not (or refused to) locate suitable accommodations at the old capital (La Borde 1883, 127). This set up a relatively lengthy legislative struggle between successive Spanish governors and the local municipal body, the *cabildo*. The cabildo ignored the governors and continually refused to relocate to Port of Spain. In fact, it did not have its first sitting there until more than two decades later, on 1 August 1783. However, by that time St Joseph had been reduced to political and socio-economic obsolescence and Port of Spain had emerged as a developing and soon to be booming port town.

The next phase in the development of the town of Port of Spain was directly related to a major shift in the perception of the economic potential of Trinidad in the Spanish American empire. A coming together of forces in the late eighteenth century, including the weakening economic state of Spain, the success of the British and French West Indian sugar economies and a keen desire to produce greater wealth out of Spanish America, encouraged the monarchy in Spain to see Trinidad in a much altered economic light. The island, like the rest of the empire, was needed to become a wealth producer to uphold the weak Spanish economy. This resulted in profound changes locally.

Empires never waste high-quality administrative talent on unimportant or provincial colonies. Thus, if Trinidad needed to become wealthy, Spain had to provide a governor with the talent to make that happen. Primary school children in Trinidad and Tobago still learn the mantra that Don José María Chacón was the last and the best of all of the Spanish governors in Trinidad. This is a fair statement. However, one must remember that he was working for a European colonizing power and that he arrived because Spain wanted to benefit from any progress made in Trinidad. This was made evident on one hand by the royal warrant issued to Chacón before his coming to Trinidad, which assured his salary at three thousand ducats a year;[9] it was also made clear by the issuance of the Cedula of Population of 1783.[10] The articles of this important document ensured that Trinidad would become a relatively rich colony within a relatively short period.

The aforementioned document encouraged the arrival of French immigrants who were versed in sugar-cane cultivation and sugar production. They came with enslaved Africans, and the stage was then set at the end of the eighteenth century for the late but successful arrival of the sugar industry in Trinidad. This new and immediate prosperity also allowed the industrious Chacón[11] to expand and modernize the colony's capital town of Port of Spain. In fact, it can be argued that the current shape and size of the city owes as much to this individual as to any Spanish, English or Trinidadian technocrat who came before or after him. The island of Trinidad by the 1780s was still tremendously underpopulated,[12] but its capital city was undergoing a substantial facelift. On 18 January 1787 the governor informed the cabildo that Port of Spain was going to be expanded (La Borde 1883, 220). He proceeded to employ a chief engineer named Don José del Pozo, who utilized both the forced labour of some 630 enslaved Africans, as well as the efforts of another 405 freed people (220) to bring this sizeable task to fruition.

Port of Spain during the era of the late Spanish governors was a relatively small town of eleven streets built along a classic Spanish mode. Its causeways were organized in a grid running north to south and east to west. According to E.L. Joseph, these causeways were of equal length and breadth and were lined with buildings and houses made of wood, with roofs that were thatched or composed of shingles; the verandas of these structures often protruded into the streets (Joseph 1838, 176). The town was also bordered by marshlike and swampy areas to the north and south (like today's Sea Lots), which hindered development and posed health risks, particularly for dangerous outbreaks of cholera.

The town's upgrade under Chacón was extensive. It included a ditch a mile and a half long which crossed the town and is today known as the Dry River. It completely diverted the course of the St Ann's River (La Borde 1883, 221), and the creation of this structure allowed for the draining of some marshy areas and also for Port of Spain to be extended eastwards. The work on the town also included a seven hundred–foot pier at the Plaza del Marina (later Marine Square, Independence Square and today the Brian Lara Promenade, close to Frederick Street), the construction of two new batteries for the defence of the town and the building of a number of structures for public services that included a hospital at what is now Charlotte Street (221). In all of this it remains important to note that during this era the Plaza del Marina bordered the sea coast (figure 8.1), which means that all of the lands which today constitutes the south of Port of Spain – and that are really lands reclaimed from the sea – did not exist as it does today._

Chacón altered Port of Spain and created the framework for the development of a larger and healthier city. Later, even the island's British conquerors who commissioned surveys of Trinidad soon after its conquest, and many of whom found very little worthy of praise in Spain's former dominion over Trinidad,[13] were moved to admire the beauty of the Spanish town they had conquered. A good example of that esteem is found in the following description:

> Puerto D'Éspana or Port of Spain, the capital of Trinidad, embossed in an amphitheatre of hills, is one of the finest towns in the West Indies. The numerous buildings are of an imposing appearance and constructed of a massive stone cut. No houses are allowed to be erected of wood, or independent of a prescribed form: the streets are wide and, long (shaded with trees), and laid in parallel lines from the land to the

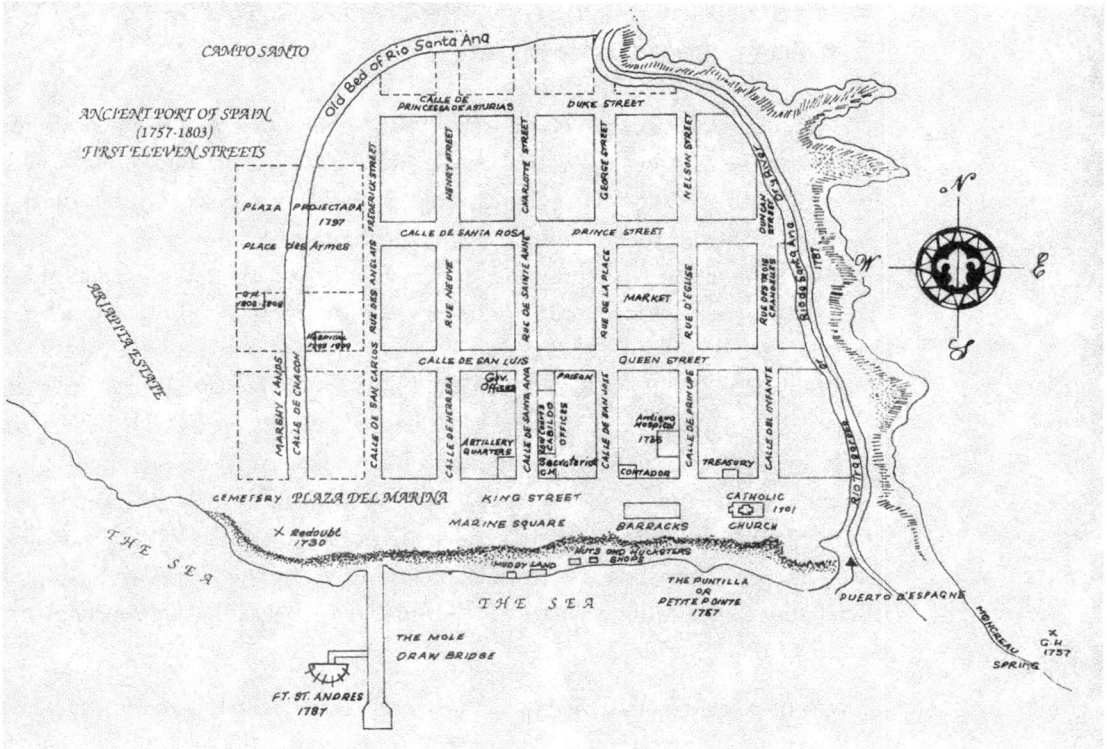

Figure 8.1. Map of Port of Spain (1757–1803) showing the alterations made by Chacón. Map Collection, West Indiana Section, Alma Jordan Library, University of the West Indies, St Augustine. Reproduced courtesy of Paria Publishing Ltd.

sea, intersected but not intercepted by cross streets, thus catching every breeze that blows. (Martin 1839, 23)

Some of the changes noted in the aforementioned quotation – such as the use of stone as the main building tool – were encouraged by subsequent events (which will be discussed), but it must be noted and reinforced that the foundation for the development of an enlarged and more contemporary Port of Spain took place under the tenure of Trinidad's last Spanish governor.

By 1797 three hundred years of disorganized Spanish tenure in Trinidad had seemingly been righted. This island, which initially had significance only as a launching pad for the futile search for El Dorado and which later became a backward and forgotten place, had via the arrival of sugar and the labour of captured Africans been transformed into an economically viable colony. It also had an improved capital that was indicative of its rising wealth and stature. It was difficult to dispute the fact that Don José María Chacón had successfully fulfilled the mandate presented to him by the Spanish monarchy. In the end, however, Spain was neither to bask in the new wealth of this island nor the splendour of the extended and improved Port of Spain for very long.

THE COMING OF THE BRITISH AND CONSTRUCTION OF
THE FIRST RED HOUSE (1797–1897)

Trinidad, which since 1498 had been a Spanish territory in both the nominal and then the real sense, was captured by the British in 1797. Lured by the new wealth of this late-blooming sugar colony, they came to Port of Spain first as capitalists and then a few years later as conquerors. However, the almost bloodless takeover (Abercrombie 1807, 11–12) of the capital, and because of it the island, created some lasting problems particularly in the political and legal realms. Many of Spain's laws and customs were retained after the fact. This engineered a complex situation within which English governance centred in Port of Spain was forced to coexist with Spanish laws, customs and habits (1–10), and owing to the arrival of the immigrants in the wake of the Cedula of 1783, French norms and values. This created close to a century of cultural conflict in Trinidad that affected even the question of religion, which is illustrated by this far from harmless 1840 communication sent by the Anglican bishop of Barbados to the Anglican clergy in Trinidad, which was then in conflict with the Catholic Church:

> As the ministers of national church within this island, it belongs to your office, my reverend brethren, not to interfere with any other branch of the [C]atholic [C]hurch, nor with any other religious persuasion, but yet ever to regard yourselves as the pastors of all within its limits, bound to instruct, advise, and administer spiritually unto all, of whatever denomination they may be. You shall with God's help feed your own flock faithfully; and refuse none who shall take refuge within the national fold. (Church Pastoral Aid Society 1840, 23)

Despite this complicated situation, Britain henceforth dominated colonial Trinidad. Its early tenure was marked by the stark barbarism of the Picton regime, as detailed by Colonel William Fullerton (Fullerton 1804), and by a calamity the likes of which the capital had never before experienced. During the dry season, fires are a constant risk in Trinidad and Tobago, so much so that it is still illegal to set them publicly during this period. Port of Spain by the early 1800s, because it was largely built of wood, constituted a tremendous fire risk. This was not missed by nineteenth-century callers on the island. For example, one tourist in 1803 wrote the following after visiting the town:

> Puerto De Espana, or Port of Spain is situated about thirty miles from the *Bocas del Drago,* on the north east side of the gulf of Paria, having a jetty quay of masonry, with a battery *en babette*, built by the Spaniards, almost even with the water's edge, for the defence of the town on the west side. The town is laid out regularly enough but the houses are shabby, yet admirably well adapted to roast human beings alive; environed with lofty mountains in a semicircular manner as if the founders intended it for an oven. (McCullum 1805, 22)

This writer was one Pierre F. McCullum, and his sarcasm proved prophetic, because on the night of 24 April 1808 an initially small domestic fire broke out in Port of Spain that almost succeeded in razing the entire town from roughly modern day Abercromby to Charlotte Street and everything in between (figure 8.2). The following constitutes a brief description of that event:

> At Trinidad between ten and eleven o'clock on the night of the 24th of April, a fire broke out in the house of Dr Schaw in Frederick street, the combustible materials of the doctor's shop burnt with the greatest fury, the flame spread among the surrounding houses which were all wood, and involved the whole town in destruction; twelve squares were entirely consumed and nine partially. Four hundred and thirty five principal houses with the fronts to the street, besides back stores and out houses, which were estimated at four times that number, were destroyed. The government house, the customs-house, the hospitals, the Protestant church, the gaol, the town hall, a part of the public archives and the treasurer's office all fell a sacrifice to the flames. (Southey 1827, 410)

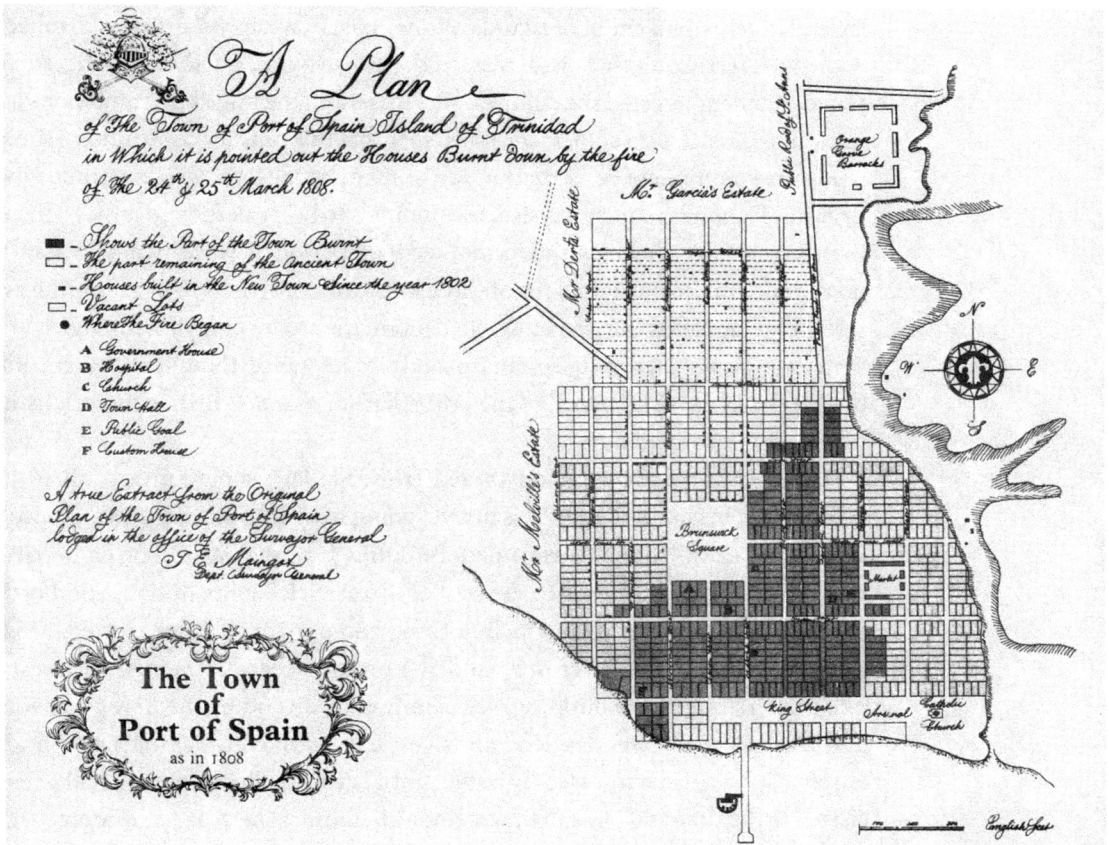

Figure 8.2. Map showing the areas of Port of Spain devastated by the 1808 fire. Map Collection, West Indiana Section, Alma Jordan Library, University of the West Indies, St Augustine. Reproduced courtesy of Paria Publishing Ltd.

The loss of life was minimal, given the scale of this catastrophe, because three quarters of the town was destroyed (Joseph 1838, 176). However, it prompted some profound changes that affected further urban development in Trinidad. For example, Governor Hislop banned the construction of buildings out of wood in Port of Spain, and thereafter stone from the hills of Laventille became the accepted norm in the town. The capital of Trinidad therefore solidly reemerged out of the ashes of 1808 fire. Thus, the actions of Chacón and the Great Fire of Port of Spain – one a deliberate process and the other clearly a disaster – set the stage for the emergence of a new, stronger and thus safer and modern capital. It was no surprise therefore that by the 1840s Trinidad required a new, larger and more striking government building, a fact that offers a segue into the beginning of understanding the emergence of a structure like the Red House as both an English architectural type and the "living" embodiment of the British Empire's control of Trinidad.

The culture of British colonialist imperialism was central to the construction of a structure like the Red House. Trinidad became British at the start of the British century, the 1800s constituting the true zenith of the empire. By the 1840s this relatively small chain of islands off the coast of western Europe controlled enormous territories that criss-crossed the entire globe. Furthermore, its supposed grandeur affected the culture of the times and the minds and ambitions of its technocrats. It is no coincidence therefore that this century constituted a time of massive monument construction across many of the territories controlled by Britain. If empires require physical testimonials to bespeak their greatness, then these Western European islanders marked their period of world ascendance and dominance in the most obvious of ways. Thus the construction of a building as relatively colossal as the Red House to contain the seat of government in British Trinidad was not an unusual or an isolated circumstance; though utilitarian, its boldness was part and parcel of the pride that surrounded British imperialism in its most decorated days.

The construction of what constituted Trinidad's largest monument to British colonialism began in 1844. It was not yet going to be known as the Red House. Instead it was called the Government Building. It was to be built on eight parcels of formerly private land to the west of Brunswick Square (today Woodford Square) in Port of Spain on which nothing had previously been erected. This site was boxed in by Abercromby and St Vincent Streets to the east and west. The cornerstone of the building was ceremoniously laid by the new governor of the island, Sir Henry Macleod on 15 February with considerable pomp and fanfare. It was also witnessed by a substantial crowd of localsm who had been alerted to the time and place of the ceremony in the local newspapers.[14] Moreover, according to contemporary news reports on the following day, this mildly theatrical laying was well received by a very captive audience, which observed as

His Excellency then took the trowel, and having spread the mortar, the stone was lowered to its place after which his Excellency addressed the crowd as follows – "I believe it is quite unnecessary for me to mention my earnest wishes for the welfare of Trinidad; and I lay this Stone with the prayer that the Officers who may preside in the respective Buildings, may perform the duties entrusted to them, with firmness and integrity and for the advancement of the Colony." Three cheers were given by the assembled crowd for Queen Victoria, and one more cheer for His Excellency Sir Henry Macleod. (*Gazette*, 16 February 1844)

The plan for the Government Building was designed by an English artist named Richard Bridgens, who was neither an engineer nor an architect, but the initial contract for its erection was awarded to Messrs Pierre and De La Sauvagère (*Gazette*, 16 February 1844). This was not going to be a simple task because the proposed building was both massive and complex, and meant to house the public offices of the government, the chamber of the local legislative council, the Hall of Justice and the public offices of the judiciary.

Moreover, these two contractors were hired solely to build the walls and the part of the structure to be utilized as the courthouse. However, it was noted that they were asked to progress with the construction of the latter at the expense of the former and as quickly as possible (*Gazette*, 16 February 1844). Early construction was made more difficult by the fact that the building as envisioned was going to be built over what was then called Prince Street (now Sackville Street), one of the horizontal thoroughfares that makes up the latticework that is Port of Spain. To deal with this problem, it was decided to construct the Government Building with two large arches so that pedestrians and what then constituted vehicular traffic (carriages) could still flow freely on that causeway (figures 8.3 and 8.4).

It was a known fact from the very onset that the Government Building was going to be a very expensive venture. Preliminary work to prepare the site for construction which began in 1843 cost some £5,662.16 (*Trinidad Blue Book* 1844). In 1844 a further £8,510 was expended on the building itself (*Trinidad Blue Book* 1844). However, by 1847 the first phase of the structure remained unfinished, but a massive £14,124.35 had already been spent (*Trinidad Blue Book* 1844). It was not until 1848 under the tenure of Governor Lord Harris that at least the part that was set aside for the courthouse was completed. It was duly opened by him in 1848 and according to the following in the *Port of Spain Gazette* ("The New Public Buildings", 22 February 1848), the feedback on it was rather mixed:

That section of the new Public Building intended as a Court House, will we understand be ready for occupancy on Monday next, and the approaching Criminal sections (commencing on Tuesday the fourteenth March) will be held in the new Building. The exertions made recently to complete the necessary accommodations have been very considerable. Although from the Imperative necessity which existed for

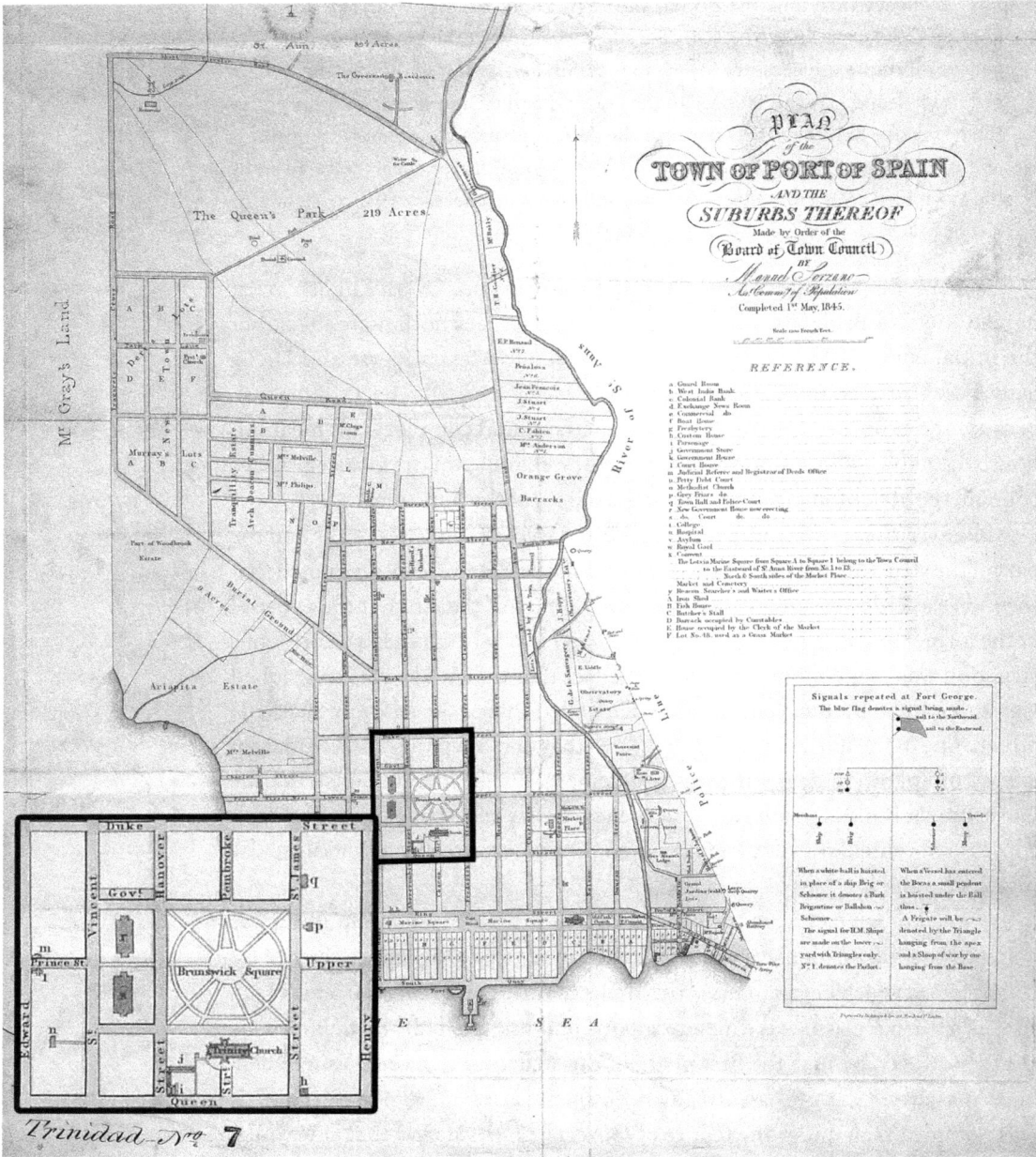

Figure 8.3. Map of Port of Spain ca. 1845, highlighting the original Government Building, comprised of two independent structures connected by a colonnade. Map Collection, West Indiana Section, Alma Jordan Library, University of the West Indies, St Augustine.

Figure 8.4. The first government buildings. Note the roadway to the right of the carriage and the colonnade connecting the north and south buildings. Map Collection, West Indiana Section, Alma Jordan Library, University of the West Indies, St Augustine.

economising the expenditure for this purpose, the fittings up and accommodations for the Public are not exactly in keeping with the rich style of the building and some of the Furniture of the old Court House looks shabby and out of place, still as a whole the coup d'oeil of the new "Palais de Justice" will be very imposing and equal, if not superior, to anything of the kind in the West Indies.

Little substantial work was done on the Government Building after that for more than fifty years. It can be argued that as the fortunes of the Trinidadian sugar industry, the island's economic mainstay, dipped in the middle decades of the nineteenth century, there was less funding available to complete the building. In the end, it took a major universal event in the annals of British colonialism for the unfinished Government Building to be hastily but adequately completed.

In 1897 the monarch of the British Empire, Queen Victoria, recorded her sixtieth year as the reigning sovereign of Britain and its territories around the world. The British government considered this to be a momentous occasion to be officially celebrated throughout the empire, as is illustrated by this correspondence from the secretary of state to the governor of Trinidad:

If it were possible to inaugurate any joint or uniform celebration throughout the Colonies, it would doubtless greatly add to the interest that must in any circumstances attach to the commemoration of this unique and auspicious event. But, apart from other considerations it appears to me that the great variations of climate and season that are to be found throughout Her Majesty's Colonial Empire at any given period of the year, would alone render such action impracticable; and I prefer therefore to leave it to local initiative in each case to make whatever arrangements may be suggested by local circumstances . . . to celebrate the event in a manner befitting the occasion. ("Alterations to Government Buildings")

This event shook the colonial government in Trinidad out of its malaise where the unfinished Government Building was concerned. Consequently, in 1896 hasty moves were being made to ensure that it would be completed and the building opened in time for Queen Victoria's Jubilee celebrations. To this end, the governor of the island, F. Napier Broome, brought a motion to the legislative council in 1896 to ensure that the project would not suffer from a lack of funding. In these circumstances cost overruns seemed irrelevant, and the governor duly suggested: "As it appears very expedient that the works now in progress at the Government building should proceed without intermission, and as the vote of £5,000 on account for 1896 is nearly exhausted, the Governor has the honour to request the Honourable Legislative Council to authorise a further expenditure of £3,000 on these works during the current year, the estimates for 1897 being relieved of this sum" ("Alterations to Government Buildings").[15] The funding was of course approved (*Trinidad Blue Book* 1897), and the building was completed in time for the celebrations (figure 8.5). Thus, along with the ornate gift sent to the Queen from Trinidad,[16] the island was itself gifted in 1897 with a brand new and much improved Government Building. As it was hastily painted red, it was henceforth known officially and unofficially as the Red House. It was a magnificent structure that symbolically and concretely projected the strength of British colonialism in Trinidad. However, though generally very impressed with the size and beauty of the structure, some Trinidadians still found reasons to criticize something about it. This is shown by the following scathing critique, "The Red House Railings", of the railings which surrounded the building (*Gazette,* 12 June 1897):

Everyone acquainted with what was going on at the time, had reasonable ground for believing, from the elaborate designs submitted and the voluminous correspondence which took place in connection with it, that there would have been a railing worthy of the building which it was intended to surround, and one which would have borne favourable comparison with the Brunswick Square railings. But the mountain has brought forth a most ridiculous little mouse, and a railing is being installed upon the diminutive dwarf walls which any gentleman with an aesthetic turn of mind would scorn the idea of having around his grounds. . . . Where is the symmetry between the massive gates of the building and these insignificant little rails?

Figure 8.5. Postcard ca.1901 following renovations for Queen Victoria's jubilee. Note the title in the upper right: the name has been changed to "Red House". Map Collection, West Indiana Section, Alma Jordan Library, University of the West Indies, St Augustine.

Nevertheless, though it took over half a century, the first Red House was finally completed, in 1897, and it remained a proud symbol of governance and government in Trinidad. This was until just a few years later in 1903, when another fire, this time of a more deliberate nature, managed to burn down what was then the most impressive architectural structure in Port of Spain.

THE BURNING OF THE FIRST RED HOUSE AND THE COMING OF THE SECOND

Buildings have symbolic meanings that exceed their particular and peculiar functions. Government structures are certainly not exempt from this reality. It is therefore not surprising that the Red House during its history has been the focal point of many political and socio-economic rumblings in Trinidad. The most recent and one of the most tragic (and misguided) of these occurred in 1990, in the midst of the attempted Muslimeen coup on July 27. Hence, given the significance of this structure to officialdom, it was not at all amazing that it became a symbolic target against which disgruntled citizens often vented their frustrations.

It can be argued that the pattern for this historical behaviour was firmly established by the events of 1903 in Port of Spain, which the first Red House structure did not survive. The so-called Water Riots of that year have gone down as one of the major examples of local resistance to the arbitrariness of British colonialism in Trinidad. However, its start was somewhat unspectacular. It began as a move by a citizens group called the Rate Payers Association to prevent the passage of an ordinance intended to raise the cost of pipe-borne water in the city (figure 8.6). Interestingly, the Commission of Enquiry, subsequently convened to investigate the riots and the destruction of the Red House, provides a good description of the building as it existed in 1903. According to this commission's document:

> The principal Government offices in Port of Spain were comprised in a single block of buildings generally known as the Red House. This block had been formed by connecting a northern and southern building originally separate, so as to leave a central court or quadrangle. The Red House was a two-storey building and the Council Chamber occupied the whole width of the upper storey of the northern block having on either side of it a verandah (or as it is locally termed "gallery"), overlooking St Vincent Street and Abercrombie Street on the west and east sides respectively, with Knox Street on the north and Hart Street on the south side. In the southern block were situated the Law Courts, the offices of the Registrar-General, and several other public offices. The whole building was surrounded by a small compound separated from the neighbouring

Figure 8.6. Image depicting the crowd gathered on 14 March 1903 to debate the Waterworks Ordinance (UK National Archives). Map Collection, West Indiana Section, Alma Jordan Library, University of the West Indies, St Augustine.

streets by a low ornamental wall and railing. . . . There was also a passage running through the ground floor of the building underneath the Council Chamber from the north to south, to which access could be gained either from Knox Street, or from the central quadrangle (*Report of the Commission of Enquiry 1903*, 4).

The *Gazette* of 23 March states that what started off as an organized protest meeting at Brunswick Square by the Rate Payers' Association against the reading of the Water Works Ordinance, and the decision to bar the public from entering the Red House, quickly escalated into a movement against the government. There, altercations with the police officers on duty helped to create a riot. According to the newspaper, the start of the disturbance went as follows:

> It appears that for some offence a woman on the lawn to the east of the Red House was arrested by a constable; who was immediately struck by a couple of stones flung by two small boys. Thereupon the officer released the woman; and was at once attacked by her too. Several members of the crowd closed on her and the boys and dragged them back; but most unfortunately the evil was done. In a moment the stone throwing was wildly taken up by the crowd; and the stones were pelted in a terrific shower in the Council Chamber through the glass doors. People and police alike on the Eastern gallery fled inside and the Council came to a standstill. ("The Red House Stoned", *Gazette*, 25 March 1903)

Events intensified, the *Gazette* reported, and the crowd on the western side began to stone the Red House. The building was then stormed, and the officers present proved unable to contain the onrush (figure 8.7). In the midst of this general melee the building was set ablaze (figure 8.8). According to the commission's report:

> It was hoped that the arrival of the sailors from H.M.S. "Pallas" (a British naval ship moored in Trinidad) and the volunteers from the St James's Barracks would render it possible to restore order without the use of firearms. But at about half-past two o'clock it was discovered that the building had been set on fire and the flames were making rapid progress . . . the perpetrators of which have not been identified. Fire was first set in the Registrar-General Office, close to the quadrangle apparently in two or perhaps three places . . . the furniture of the public offices and the papers which they contained constituted an abundance of inflammable material. (*Report of the Commission of Enquiry 1903*, 9)

Then, according to the *Gazette*, the police opened fire on the crowd, killing and wounding some forty-two individuals ("The Killing and Wounded", 25 March 1903), the names of whom were inscribed in the same issue of the *Gazette*. The fire, however, could not be contained, which meant that the Red House could not be saved. In a matter of a few hours only its outer walls remained standing and the rest of the building had been burnt flat ("The Burning Buildings", *Gazette*, 25 March 1903). Ironically, a structure which had taken some fifty-four years

Figure 8.7. Water riots. Crowd on the eastern side of the Red House toward Abercromby Street. Map Collection, West Indiana Section, Alma Jordan Library, University of the West Indies, St Augustine.

Figure 8.8. Image of the Red House on fire, view from Knox Street. Map Collection, West Indiana Section, Alma Jordan Library, University of the West Indies, St Augustine.

Figure 8.9. Ruins of the Red House after the 1903 fire, view from Hart Street. Map Collection, West Indiana Section, Alma Jordan Library, University of the West Indies, St Augustine.

to complete had been destroyed in almost no time at all (figure 8.9). No lives were lost in the actual Red House fire, but the death toll after this ordeal greatly outnumbered that recorded in the Port of Spain fire of 1808.

This however was not to be the end of this building. A decision was taken to rebuild the Red House and at the same site. This of course entailed another sizeable economic undertaking. In the period 1903–1904, £2,058 16s 10d was spent on this project (*Trinidad Blue Book 1903–05*, 37–38). During the following year the figure utilized was a relatively massive £18,146 14s 5½d (*Trinidad Blue Book 1904–05*, 46–56). In 1906–1907, however the work on the structure was completed at a cost of £5,418 0s 3½d (*Trinidad Blue Book 1906–07*, 23–24), with a separate and comparatively small sum of £57 10s and 3d being expended for making alterations to the Prisoners Waiting Room in the court (39–40). Thus, on 4 February the second building to be known as the Red House was opened by Sir Henry Moore Jackson, the governor of Trinidad and Tobago (which had been joined with the larger island as a unitary state in 1897). As reported by the *Gazette* on 5 February 1907, the governor's welcoming address suggested that these fine building are infinitely more suitable to the steadily growing importance of the Colony, as well as to the Council and of the Public, than those which they replace, and had their construction been undertaken merely as an improvement which the growth of the Colony demanded, and our resources justified then my task today would be easier than it is. But honourable gentlemen it is I fear, inevitable that, in entering into possession of our new abode, our thoughts should travel back to the old one, and to the events that deprived us of it.

Remarkably this speech, made in the largest symbol of British colonialism, included the admission that part of the fault for the loss of the former building lay on the colonial government.

The second and current Red House has had a much longer and successful tenure than the first. The Urban Development Corporation of Trinidad and Tobago (UDeCOTT) has been given the responsibility of restoring the Red House, including retrofitting the interiors for adaptive reuse by Trinidad and Tobago's parliament. Although currently under renovation, it is still an imposing edifice in the heart of the capital city, Port of Spain. Many of the functions that were once associated with this building have subsequently been removed to their own premises, but up until its recent closure the building still served as the seat of the Parliament of Trinidad and Tobago. One can conclude that it has provided very good returns on the sums invested in its reconstruction.

CONCLUSION

The stories of both Port of Spain and the Red House have not been incident free since the very vivid periods documented in this chapter. Both have subsequently faced trauma inspired by socio-economic and political situations and carry the scars to illustrate that fact. The city has expanded to become a sizeable urban sprawl that extends both east and west, and other buildings have arisen that eventually surpassed the longstanding seat of government in magnitude and grandeur. The Red House, long before its recent closure, no longer claimed the title of the most impressive structure in the city. Interestingly, however, after the ongoing renovation it might emerge anew to once again capture the local imagination. That remains a distinct possibility. However, if it fails to do so that will remain a moot point. Its place in the annals of the history of Trinidad and Tobago will always be unchallenged and unquestioned. Regardless of how many times it is built or rebuilt, the Red House will always be the Red House. It is part of the lore of Trinidad and Tobago.

NOTES

1. For a more detailed discussion of social life in nineteenth-century Port of Spain, Trinidad, readers are advised to review the following: Brereton 1981; Dickman 1992; Ottley 1962; Trotman 1986.

2. Self-serving assessments like these were ironically often contradicted by the reports of other Western Europeans. For example, according to the English Trinidad was inhabited by "Caribs" who were light coloured, well formed, industrious and mild and who lived harmoniously until early Spanish encroachments (Martin 1839, 23).

3. Bartolomé de las Casas, for example, recounts a grisly tale of the massacre of a friendly group of natives by the early Spaniards in Trinidad (1991, 58).

4. Spain's bureaucracy in the Americas was immense and detailed. See, for example, Jara and Tepaske (1990).

5. For example, Vasco Núñez de Balboa, widely considered the first European to view the Pacific Ocean from the so-called New World was a desperado and a cutthroat who repudiated centralized Spanish control and took over the mission to traverse the Central American isthmus by murder and other forms of coercion.

6. The original number he introduced was five hundred, of which one third were supposed to be women.

7. This myth allegedly owned its beginning to an encounter between one of Francisco Pizarro's lieutenants, Sebastian de Belacazár, and an Amerindian named Muequetá, who was an emissary of the great chief Bogotá. Muequeta's story of a golden city caught the attention of Belalcazár and spread like wildfire through Spanish America.

8. Sedeño received the first charter to govern Trinidad.

9. Royal Provision appointing Don José María Chacón, governor of the island of Trinidad (in the Libro de Toma y Razón of the Royal Accounts of the Department of the Windward Island of Trinidad, 1783–1789). Previously, governors had usually lived in poverty in Trinidad.

10. The correct name of the document that has traditionally been called the Cedula of Population of Trinidad is *Real Cédula De S.M. Que Contiene el Reglamento Para la Poblacion y Comercio de la Isla De la Trinidad de Barlovento*.

11. Unlike some of his predecessors, within the first few years of his arrival he completed a number of statistical reviews of Trinidad.

12. In 1786, there were about nine thousand people in Trinidad. This included free persons, enslaved Africans and natives.

13. Some English writers spoke of a benighted Spanish system in Trinidad that continued after the conquest.

14. For example, an advertisement was placed in the *Gazette* advising would-be attendees of the time and place of the laying of the building's cornerstone

15. An elaborate description of the gift can be found in "Centenary Celebrations: Minute (No. 19-1897)".

16. Despite extensive searches employed to unearth why the building was painted in this particular colour, the evidence (or lack thereof) suggests that it was more a matter of expediency than one of concerted judgement or policy.

REFERENCES

Abercrombie, Sir Ralph. 1807. *A Political Account of the Island of Trinidad from Its Conquest by Sir Ralph Abercrombie to the Present Time in the Form of a Letter to His Grace the Duke of Portland*. London: C. and W. Galabin.

"Alterations to Government Buildings: Minute (No. 64) from the Governor asking authority for a further expenditure of £3000 during the current year". 1896. Council Paper No. 149 of 1896. Port of Spain, Government Printing Office.

Bartolomé de las Casas, Fray. 1991. *The Diario of Christopher Columbus First Voyage to America 1492–1493*. Translated by Oliver Dunn and James E. Kelley Jr. Norman: University of Oklahoma Press.

Brereton, B. 1981. *A History of Modern Trinidad 1783–1962*. London: Heinemann.

"Centenary Celebrations: Minute (No. 19-1897) by His Excellency the acting Governor laying correspondence with the Secretary of State in connection with the Trinidad Centenary Celebrations". 1897. Council Paper No. 47 of 1897. Port of Spain: Government Printing Office.

Church Pastoral Aid Society. 1840. *Church of England Magazine* 9 (July–December). London: Joseph Rogerson.

Dickman, E. 1992. "An Urban History of Port of Spain, Trinidad and Tobago". Master's thesis, McGill University.

"Her Majesty's the Queen's Reign: Acting Governor's Minute (No. 14-1897) Local Celebration of the 60th year of Her Majesty's Accession to the Throne". 1897. Council Paper No. 37 of 1897. Port of Spain: Government Printing Office.

Jara, Álvaro, and John Jay Tepaske, eds. 1990. *The Royal Treasuries of Spanish Empire in America*. Vol. 4, *Eighteenth Century Ecuador*. Durham, NC: Duke University Press.

Joseph, E.L. 1838. *History of Trinidad*. London: A.K. Newman and Company.

Fullerton, Colonel William. 1804. *A Statement, Letters and Documents Respecting the Affairs of Trinidad Including a Reply to Colonel Picton's Address to the Council of that Island Submitted to the Consideration of the Lords of His Majesty's Most Honourable Privy Council*. London, Promenade.

La Borde, P.G. 1876. *The History of the Island of Trinidad Under the Spanish Government: First Part 1498–1622: Discovery, Conquest and Colonization*. Translated by James Alva Bain. Paris: Maisonneuve et Cie.

———. 1883. *The History of the Island of Trinidad Under the Spanish Government: Second Part 1622–1797:* Translated by James Alva Bain. Paris: Maisonneuve et Cie.

Martin, R.M. 1839. *Statistics of the Colonies of the British Empire in the West Indies, South America, North America, Asia, Austral-Asia and Europe*. London: W.H. Allen.

McCullum, P.F. 1805. *Travels in Trinidad during the Months of February, March and April, 1803: In a Series of Letters Addressed to a Member of the Imperial Parliament of Great Britain*. London: Longman, Hurst and Rees.

Ottley, C.R. 1962. *The Story of Port of Spain: Capital of Trinidad, West Indies: From Earliest Times to the Present Day*. Glasgow: Robert MacLehose, University Press.

Padron, F.M. 2013. *Spanish Trinidad*. Edited and translated by Armando Garcia de la Torre. Kingston: Ian Randle.

Return of All Public Works, Civil Roads, Canals, Bridges and Buildings Being Undertaken

During the Year 1897. *Trinidad Blue Book 1897.* Section J33–34. Port of Spain: Government Printing Office, 1897.

Return of All Public Works, Civil Roads, Canals, Bridges and Buildings Being Undertaken During the Year 1844. *Trinidad Blue Book 1844.* Section J40–41. CO. Port of Spain: Government Printing Office, 1844.

Return of All Public Works, Civil Roads, Canals, Bridges and Buildings Being Undertaken During the Year 1845. *Trinidad Blue Book 1845.* Section J36–37. CO 300/56. Port of Spain: Government Printing Office, 1845.

Return of All Public Works, Civil Roads, Canals, Bridges and Buildings Being Undertaken During the Year 1847. *Trinidad Blue Book 1847.* Section J50–51. CO 300/58. Port of Spain: Government Printing Office,1847.

Return of All Public Works, Civil Roads, Canals, Bridges and Buildings Being Undertaken During the Year 1897. *Trinidad Blue Book 1897.* Section J33–34. CO. Port of Spain: Government Printing Office, 1897.

Return of All Public Works, Civil Roads, Canals, Bridges and Buildings Being Undertaken During the Year 1903–04. *Trinidad Blue Book 1903–05.* J37–38. CO. Port of Spain: Government Printing Office, 1905.

Return of All Public Works, Civil Roads, Canals, Bridges and Buildings Being Undertaken During the Year 1904–05. *Trinidad Blue Book 1904–05.* Section J56–46. CO. Port of Spain: Government Printing Office, 1905.

Return of All Public Works, Civil Roads, Canals, Bridges and Buildings Being Undertaken During the Year 1906–07. *Trinidad Blue Book 1906–07.* Section J39–40. CO. Port of Spain: Government Printing Office, 1907.

Simpson, L.B. 1950. *The Encomienda in New Spain: The Beginning of Spanish Mexico.* Berkeley: University of California Press.

Southey, Captain Thomas. 1827. *Chronological History of the West Indies in Three Volumes.* Vol. 3. London: Longman.

Trotman, D.V. 1986. *Crime in Trinidad: Conflict and Control in Plantation Society 1838–1900.* Knoxville: University of Tennessee Press.

Winer, L. 2008. *Dictionary of the English/Creole of Trinidad and Tobago.* Montreal: McGill-Queen's University Press.

1903. *Report of the Commission of Enquiry into the Recent Disturbances at Port of Spain, Trinidad.* July.

CHAPTER 9

An Archaeological Review of the Colonial Red House Site, 1844–1907

MAKINI EMMANUEL, GEORGIA L. FOX AND GIFFORD WATERS

THIS CHAPTER REVIEWS PRIMARY COLONIAL FINDS RECOVERED FROM the Red House.[1] The finds include ceramics, buttons, glass, marbles, clay tobacco pipes and bowls, coins, metals, horseshoes, pen nibs, inkwells and faunal remains. The majority of these finds relate chronologically to the nineteenth and twentieth centuries. In a nutshell, these discoveries mirror the life and times of the Red House as a grandiose British colonial space; a work facility for a succession of British governors and their staff; a venue for meetings between governors and members of the legislative council; and the scene of social gatherings involving invited dignitaries and members of the local elite. The presence of faunal remains may also be indicative of the site being used as a grazing area for free-range livestock belonging to townsfolk prior to the construction of the original government building in 1844.

The Red House colonial findings constitute important elements of Port of Spain's and Trinidad and Tobago's rich historical legacy. Although Trinidad and Tobago has had a diverse colonial past, very few archaeological studies of this period have been undertaken (Agorsah and Samaroo 2014; Clement 1997; Lopinot and Venter 2014). This chapter is therefore noteworthy in that it provides an archaeological synopsis of an era in Trinidad and Tobago's history that has received insufficient scholarly attention over the years.

THE RED HOUSE BUILDINGS

Built in 1907, the Red House has been the seat of Trinidad and Tobago's parliament for over one hundred years. This structure, is the second to be built on the site; the foundation stone for the first was laid by then governor of Trinidad, Sir Henry McLeod on 15 February 1844. In celebration of the Diamond Jubilee of Queen Victoria in 1897, the buildings comprising the Red House were given a coat of red paint, and the public promptly referred to them as the "Red House"

(Mavrogordata 2010, 268). The buildings preceding the current Red House (figure 9.1) were destroyed by fire during the Water Riots on 23 March 1903, when sixteen people were killed and more than forty people were injured. Construction of the current Red House commenced the following year at the same location and was opened to the public on 4 February 1907, by the governor, Sir Henry Moore Jackson (see chapter 8, this volume).

Figure 9.1.
Image of the Red House following the 1903 fire.

The original buildings comprising two main blocks, north and south, were to be connected by a double archway, similar to the present-day Red House but on a smaller scale (Mavrogordata 2010, 267) (see figure 8.5, chapter 8). The double archway was a feature required by the City Council to keep Prince Street open, because the building was built over the street. It was stipulated that the passageway remain open to the public for pedestrians and wheeled traffic to pass through freely (Mavrogordata 2010, 267).

This roadway passed through where the present-day rotunda at the Red House is situated. To the northern side of Prince Street, the Government Office building served as the office of the registrar. To the southern side was the chamber of the legislative council and the courthouse. The council chamber was formally inaugurated in 1848 with much ceremony by Lord Harris, after an impressive ceremony in Trinity Cathedral. The plans proposed by the director of public works, J.E. Tanner, showed that two new buildings of two stories each were to be erected at the southern corners of the northern building. In addition, two similar structures were to be constructed on other side of the carriageway, abutting the courthouse or southern building. One of these became the Office of the Registrar, and the urgent need for a proper record office having arisen, the other became the Record Office (Mavrogordata 2010, 268). According to the *Port of Spain Gazette* of 1892: "Nothing further had been done to complete the buildings since their erection some fifty years ago. The only attempt to relieve the monotony of the whole is to be seen in the arching of the courtyard which is a perfect skeleton and, like the ruins of Pompeii, is more suggestive of what the buildings must have been than of what they are intended to be." Official records do not confirm the presence of specifically assigned sleeping quarters in the building, but this possibility should not be ruled out given the very lengthy nature of frequent debates in the old legislature and the concomitant need to rest on occasion (Lovell Francis, pers. comm., 29 June 2015).

As earlier indicated, the Red House was on either side of Prince Street. Prince Street traversed through Brunswick Square, and the square served as an open green space in the blossoming urban town of nineteenth-century Port of Spain. It could be viewed as an outdoor extension of the household spaces of the urban blacks, who might have found respite in this public park from their cramped barrack-type houses. The square also served as an informal commercial space, where vendors traded livestock and draught animals.

COLONIAL FINDS

Ceramics

The original buildings would have been frequented by elite members of the colonial society. As a result, it is likely that the buildings would have been stocked with a variety of earthenwares suitable to the tastes of the hegemonic class. It is also possible that there might have been a preference for cheaper, more durable wares over finer, more expensive wares. The Red House colonial ceramic assemblage comprises porous, semi-vitreous and vitreous ceramics, with the exception of architectural elements and clay tobacco pipes.

Ceramic vessel forms reveal such distinctly British cultural practices as tea drinking rituals. The teawares are particularly symbolic of the class of the officials who occupied the Red House. Other artefacts hint at status, and the artefacts associated with coffee and tea service and consumption were used to underscore the cultural and social mores of the British. The afternoon tea tradition, started in 1841, had evolved into an elaborate social affair, and by the 1860s tea was being served between lunch (one o'clock) and dinner (seven o'clock). By the early nineteenth century, tea drinking had achieved a position of prominence in the daily lives of the English (Fromer 2008), and the presence of numerous teaware sherds alludes to a cultural practice imported into Trinidad from England. Since officials spent long hours in the government building, indulging in tea drinking would have been a welcome respite from work, a ritualized time for taking "a break, a challenge to the crawling hours" (Shand in Mintz 1985, 142).

Another vessel form that was recovered from the site was the tureen, a type of hollowware. This vessel would have served as the centrepiece of formal dining rituals in the European tradition. Because dining was an important activity in French and British societies, this practice would have been perpetuated by expatriates and their creole offspring. The recovery of a significant volume of tableware fragments at the Red House site is therefore not surprising (see Borchardt et al. 2002), given the variety of social gatherings that frequently occurred at the Red House during the colonial period.

The ceramic ware types and decorative styles represented in the archaeological record indicate that Trinidad-based colonial officials were influenced by what was popular in Britain during the nineteenth century. Approximately 41,000 plain fragments of refined earthenware, identifiable as pearlware, creamware and whiteware, have been catalogued, the majority of them identified as pearlware (figures 9.2 and 9.3) (for the defining characteristics of pearlware, see Stelle 1989). In addition to earthenwares, several stoneware bottles were discovered in the northwestern basement of the Red House (figure 9.4), indicating that this space might have been used for storage.

Other types of decorated refined earthenwares that were also found include transfer print wares, sponged ware, annular ware (banded), annular ware (mocha), annular ware (marbleized) and shell-edged and other hand-painted wares. Most surface treatments were popular from the end of the eighteenth century to the close of the nineteenth century, and similar types of ceramics have

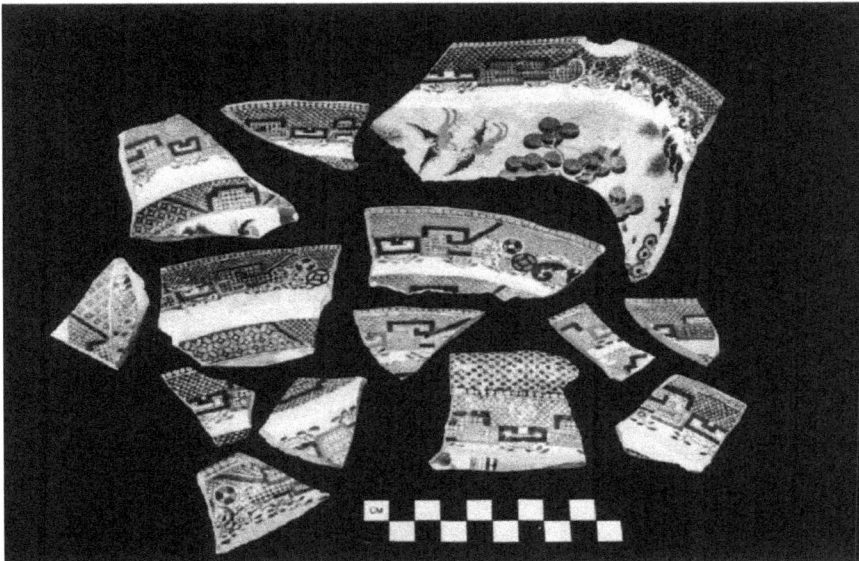

Figure 9.2.
Fragments of a pearlware, transfer printed serving dish.

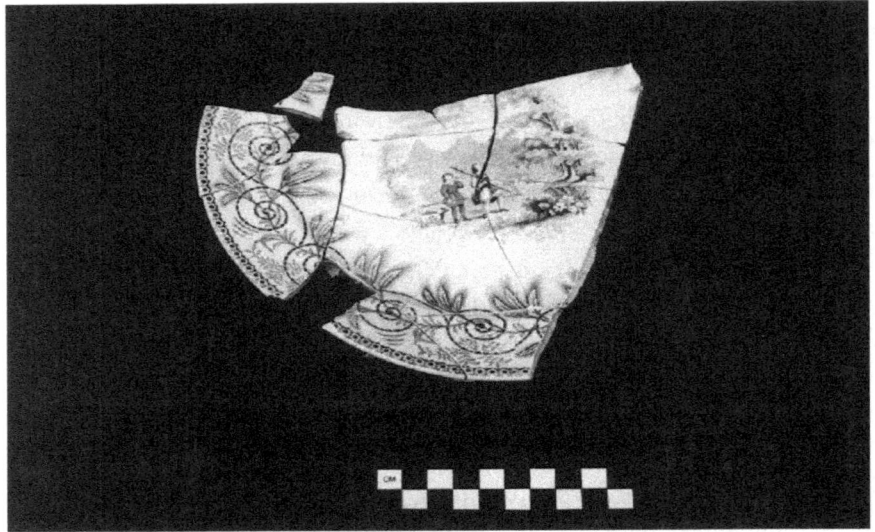

Figure 9.3.
A pearlware, transfer printed plate with a hunting scene.

Figure 9.4.
Stoneware bottles discovered by field assistants in the northwestern basement of the Red House.

been found at most British colonial sites in the Americas and elsewhere for this time period. The people who occupied these sites would have purchased ceramic items reflecting cultural identities rooted in England (White and Beaudry 2009).

Majolica is a ceramic type consisting of a coarse earthenware paste and examples of it produced by the Spanish, French and British have been unearthed at the site. Majolica produced in France is called *faience*, and eighteen sherds of faience (inclusive of faience Rouen polychrome) were identified. One of the vessel forms associated with majolica, tin-enamelled ointment pots, at the Red House is represented by fragments. Originally containing ointments used to cure ailments or provide first-aid treatments for the Red House's colonial occupants, the provenance of these artefacts is yet to be established, especially since there is an absence of manufacturers' marks. It seems unlikely that the ointment vessels were produced in Britain, because majolica manufactured in Britain was usually lead glazed and the ones found at the Red House are not. Their presence at the site is indicative of trade contacts between Trinidad and other colonies and European countries during the British colonial period. The *Trinidad Blue Book* of 1876 indicates that majolica was imported from Venezuela. Majolica is one of the least expensive ceramic wares shipped to the colony and therefore should not be mistakenly viewed as reflecting negatively on the social status of the colonial occupants of the Red House.

Another vessel form identified among the ceramic artefacts is the chamber pot. Chamber pots were used before 1907. The second Red House was constructed in 1907 and had plumbed toilet facilities. The chamber pots were probably installed in the commodes of executive offices in the original government buildings and used by the governor, the officials of the legislative council and the ancillary staff.

Janitorial staff of the Red House consisted of free blacks, yet few artefacts testify to their presence on the site. Eight coarse earthenware fragments with a polished surface identified as African Caribbean ware are but a meager representation of the people who laboured on the site. There are two factors that can explain the dearth of African Trinidadian material culture at the site. The first is the possibility that because the entire site has not been completely investigated, African Trinidadian material culture has not yet been unearthed. Second, since the Red House was not a domestic space and was situated in an urban area, it is possible that things produced by blacks would not feature prominently. The Red House was located in the heart of the city, close to many shops, so it would have been easier to purchase and stock the Red House with British and other European imports instead of having the servants bring in home-produced wares. Because Brunswick Square was used as an informal market space (and possibly recreational space) by the Blacks, excavation activity there may reveal a higher incidence of implements associated with Trinidadians of African descent. A total of eight coarse earthenware fragments with a polished surface have been identified as African Caribbean ware from the site.

Buttons

A total of thirty-six buttons were found and catalogued. The buttons are characterized by a variety of shapes, sizes, special designs, manufacturing types and materials, some of which can provide date ranges, as well as insights into the cultural profiles of persons wearing them (Marcel 1994). Clothing is one of humanity's basic needs and represents an expression of the wearer's social and cultural tastes and societal position.

The body is the common locale for individuation, and therefore accoutrements used for dress and aesthetics are touchpoint[s] for multiple aspects of the archaeological pasts (Rivers 1999). In other words, analysing an individual's clothing allows us to interpret the wearer's identity, occupation, ethnicity and social class. Unfortunately, because no clothing was recovered from the Red House site, the following comments on the cultural context of buttons from the site are tentative.

Small China and Mother-of-Pearl Buttons

Two of the buttons include a mother-of-pearl shank button and a four-holed, sewn-through porcelain button. There is a suggestion that mother-of-pearl buttons tend to be discovered more frequently in archaeological contexts (Lindbergh 1999). However, only one mother-of-pearl button was found at the Red House. However, the possibility exists that more will be recovered during phase 2 of the Red House Project.

According to Lindbergh (1999), mother-of-pearl shank buttons date from the early eighteenth century. However, they were produced in greater numbers with the use of machines from the mid-nineteenth century onwards. The porcelain button, which is also identified as "small china", has a diameter of 11.4 millimetres and is unglazed. Based on its size, the button was probably used as a fastener for a shirt. "Small chinas" were produced by both the English and French (the French referred to them as *bapterosses*). A general timeline for the porcelain button is 1830 to 1930.

The mother-of-pearl and small china can be broadly classified as generic buttons. They would have been attached to undergarments and shirts, possibly worn by any member of the colonial society. This includes ordinary visitors who used the public thoroughfare traversing the Red House compound from Woodford Square (formerly Brunswick Square).

Military Buttons

Military buttons retrieved during excavation can furnish useful information about the history of the site. Military uniform buttons were recovered from Room G21 in the southwest rotunda, crawl space southeast and the northeast rotunda. The button recovered from room G 21 has diagnostic features of a Fourteenth Regiment button. According to Pitts (1948), foot soldiers of the Fourteenth Regiment had occupied Trinidad during the British colonial period. Because the Red House served as the governor's office, legislative council and courthouse, it stands to reason that military personnel was assigned to the Red House on rotating guard duty.

Glass

Glass artefacts found at the Red House were voluminous, comprising the largest assemblage recovered from the site. To date, 55,285 glass artefacts have been catalogued. Glass artefacts comprise whole glass bottles (figure 9.5), fragments of glass vessels, fragments of drinking vessels, non-identifiable glass fragments and large quantities of window glass. The glass shards should be interpreted as vestiges of a historic-period site where colonials were engaged in social gatherings involving the use of wines and other alcoholic beverages imported from France, Portugal and even Germany. The bulk of glass vessels indicates that considerable sums of money were spent importing glass vessels of wine, beer and champagne during the nineteenth and early twentieth centuries.

Forty-eight intact glass bottles were found. These were catalogued according to the following designations: medicinal/druggist (figure 9.6), liquor and spirits, food, wine, beer, soda and unidentifiable. Several bottles display manufacturers' marks, indicating their provenance. Bottles in the assemblage originated in Denmark, France, Britain, Holland and Germany. In addition to glass bottles, one undamaged glass ink well was unearthed.

Figure 9.5.
Various beer, brandy and wine bottles found in the basement of the Red House site.

Figure 9.6.
A collection of medicinal/druggist bottles at various stages of devitrification. The four bottles on the right are phials.

Marbles

A total of six marbles were recovered. Although the Red House primarily served an administrative role, the presence of marbles indicates public access and use by children, since the playing of marbles has long been associated with them.

Clay Tobacco Pipes

Ceramic clay tobacco pipes salvaged from the Red House site are highly fragmented. They were found throughout the site, with the highest concentration recovered from crawl space southwest. Sixty-one complete pipe bowls and 103 pipe bowl fragments have been catalogued so far. Also retrieved from the site were thirty-four whole clay pipe stems, of which two were glazed, as well as 770 clay stem fragments, of which nine were glazed.

The resistant nature of high-fired clay tobacco pipes often results in their ability to survive harsh depositional environments, thus contributing to their abundance in the archaeological record (Gojak and Stuart 1999). Tobacco pipes and bowls entered the archaeological record as discards after their owners disposed of them when they became damaged. Clay pipes were relatively cheap and easily replaced when broken. Their short life spans, and the fact that they were easily replaceable, account for the relatively large volume of pipe fragments in the Red House archaeological record. Tobacco clay pipes were introduced in England in the sixteenth century and were available throughout Britain until the twentieth century. Makers' mark information on several stem and bowl fragments provide the location of places where these pipes were manufactured, and the word "GLASGOW" is featured prominently. The names "W. White" and "McDougall" are among the impressed makers' marks on a large amount of recovered clay pipe stems, representing the Scottish Glasgow firms of William White and Sons and the D. McDougall Company, both leading firms in the export market, with the McDougall firm being the largest of the Glasgow pipe manufacturers (Fox 1999, 149, 184).

The majority of clay tobacco pipes recovered from the site, however, were plain and devoid of any decorative motifs. The more ornate pipe bowls include the "Bird Claw", Coiled Rope" and "Negro Head" motifs (figure 9.7).

Smoking in the nineteenth and twentieth centuries was a pastime that involved both elites and ordinary people. Among the upper classes, smoking was associated with leisure and contemplation in contrast to the working class, where smoking was associated with work and raucous entertainment (Gojak and Stuart 1999). Some of the pipes and bowls might have been discarded by the occupants of the Red House, but the frequency of clay tobacco pipes can also be attributed to the utilization of the Red House as a public space by both wheeled and pedestrian traffic.

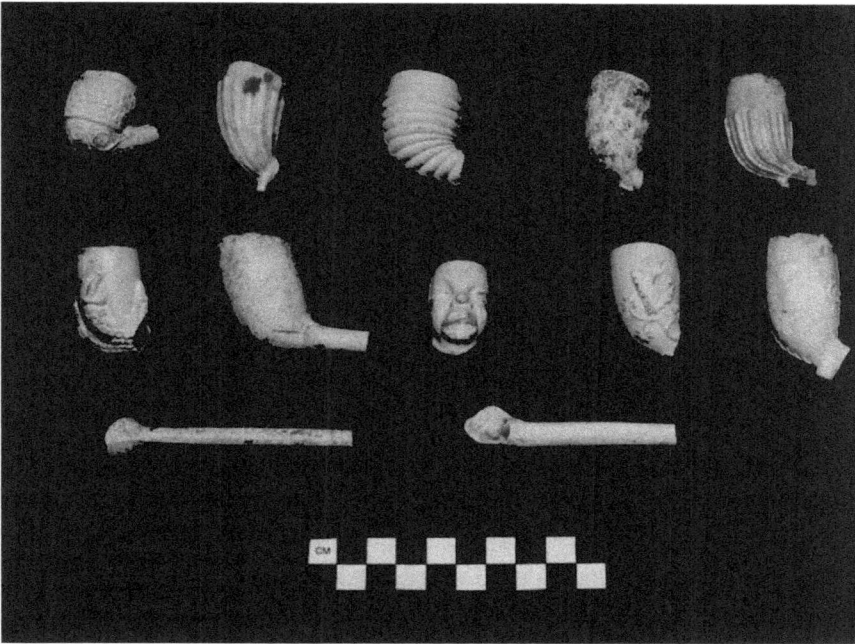

Figure 9.7. Ornate pipe bowls that have been found at SGE-51. Third in the second row is the Negro Head pipe, a style of English Figural pipes produced between ca. 1860 and 1920. The pipe bowl on the extreme left of the second row is part of a Claw pipe ca. 1830–1920. The third row depicts two pipe stems.

Coins

Twenty-one coins were recovered from the Red House site. Coins are both archaeological artefacts and historical documents (Blackburn 2011). The designs on a coin should be regarded as complementing the inscriptions and as conveying a message. Whereas it is important to distinguish between the date of production of a coin and the date of its loss (Blackburn 2011), the latter is problematic for recovered coins due to the heavily disturbed nature of the site. However, coins can contribute to archaeological research at a very basic level, as they can provide *terminus ante* and *post quem* dating with much greater accuracy and certainty than any other object.

Coins were found commingled with an array of unrelated finds, but several can provide insights into the chronological trajectory of occupations of the Red House site from the mid-nineteenth century to Trinidad's postcolonial era. One of the earliest datable coins in the assemblage is a British one-cent coin minted in 1853, exactly ten years after the original Red House buildings were built. The most recent coins consist of three Trinidad and Tobago ten-cent pieces minted in 2007. Both the earliest and most recent coins were retrieved from excavation units (BAR 4 and BAR 6).

The 1853 British one-cent coin was found commingled with shards of wine-bottle glass, corroded nails and colonial ceramic sherds, and was probably an unintentional loss like the other coins. Diagnostic features identified on both the obverse and reverse surfaces of the coins were noted during cataloguing. The relatively small size of the coin discoveries, coupled with their diverse chronologies, indicate that these coins were the result of accidental losses at different points in time during the Red House's history.

Special Coins

Perhaps the most significant coin discovery at the Red House site is a Liberty Head 1851 US$1 gold coin (figure 9.8). Prior to the 1850s, gold was considered a precious and genuinely rare metal (Green 1999). From the period 1800–1850, the total world gold production was around 1,200 metric tons. However, during the period 1851–1900 a substantial increase to 10,400 metric tons was recorded worldwide. This was probably due to an upsurge in gold discoveries in the United States, Australia and South Africa (Green 1999).

The 1851 US$1 gold coin is comprised of 90% gold and 10% copper. The California Gold Rush of 1848–1850 helped to rebirth the manufacture of gold currency in the United States. However, there were gold discoveries in North Carolina and Georgia in the early 1800s – not on the same scale as the California Gold Rush, but enough to cause rushes to those places (Williams 2014). The US government then opened two mints, one in Charlotte, North Carolina, and the other in Dahlonega, Georgia. Before then, the mint in Philadelphia, Pennsylvania, was the country's only such facility – established in 1792 when the city was the national capital (Williams 2014) – and it appears that this gold coin from the Red House site was minted in Philadelphia. According to http://www.coinvalues.com/liberty-head-gold-coin/1851:

> [The] 1851 gold $1 coins are relatively common as a date type, thanks to a large load of pieces that were struck at the Philadelphia mint. However, the branch-mint pieces – most especially the Charlotte (C) and Dahlonega (D) mint coins – are quite scarce and are much more expensive than the other two varieties. Liberty Head gold dollars, designed by James B. Longacre, are the smallest coin that the U.S. Mint has ever produced. In fact, they measure just 13 millimeters in diameter – compare that to a modern U.S. dime, which has a diameter of 17.9 millimeters! What's more, a $1 gold coin weighs in at a mere 1.672 grams – less than a penny, which has just 1/100th the face value. While these tiny dollar coins may actually be worth more than their weight in gold (the bullion value for these coins is quite small, and these coins are valued higher due to their numismatic worth), they can be had more cheaply than some of the larger gold coins of a newer vintage. Here's a breakdown of 1850 $1 gold coins and their values:

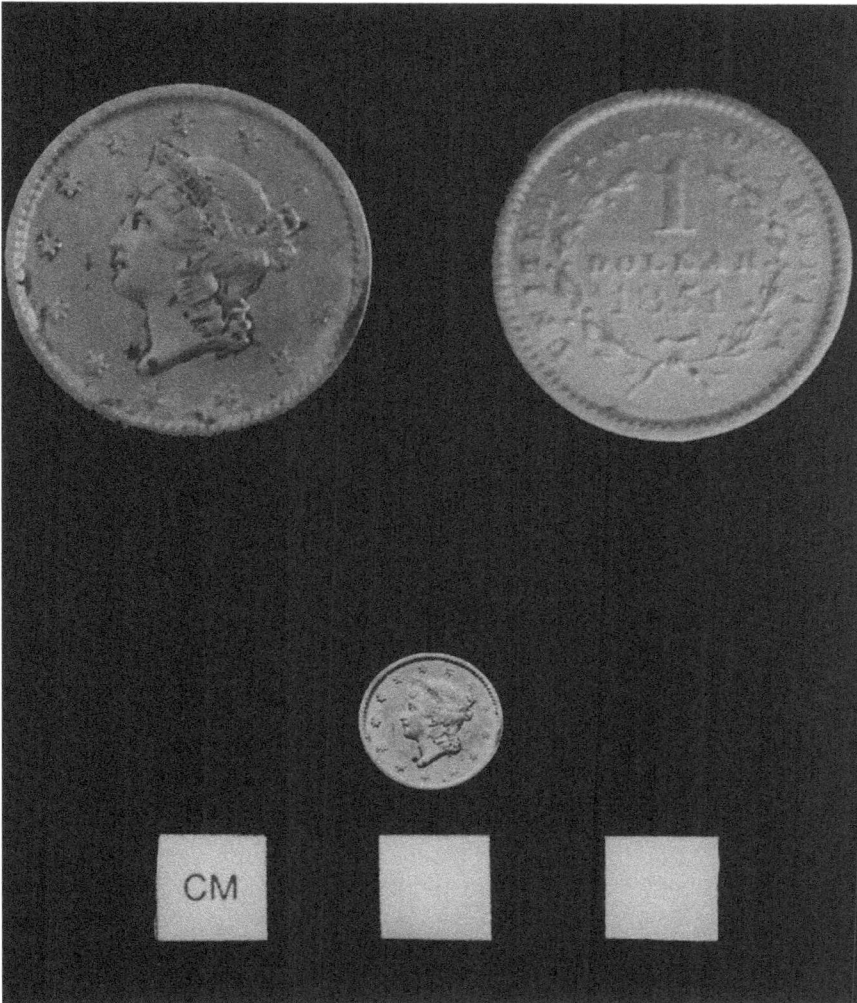

Figure 9.8.
The US$1 gold coin.

1851 – 3,317,671 minted – $250
1851 – C, 41,267 – $1,150
1851 – D, 9,882 – $1,350
1851 – O, 290,000 – $270

The presence of the gold coin at the Red House suggests trade relations between the United States and the British Caribbean in the mid-1800s. The coin might have even been used for local transactions. Given its value, this US$1 gold coin was most certainly an accidental loss.

Another special coin, a Wren Farthing, was minted in 1946. The obverse side depicts an embossed image of the head of King George VI, accompanied by the text "GEORGIVS VI D: G: BR: OMN: REX F: D: IND IMP". On the reverse side of the coin is an image of a wren with the production date positioned above the head of the bird. The coin is made of copper or bronze and has a diameter of approximately 20 millimetres. It has a medium dark green patina, but it bears no evidence of physical deterioration.

A French Guiana two-sous coin found at the site was probably directly related to the French presence in Trinidad during the late eighteenth century. During this period (ca. 1789), the French government issued a series of two-sous coins for its colonies. The coin was very thin, with a diameter of approximately 21.75 millimetres. The obverse has the words "COLONIE DE CAYENNE", whereas the reverse has the words "LOUIS XVI. R.DE FR.ET DE NAV", along with the French Empire logo and crown. This coin provides evidence of the cosmopolitan demography of Port of Spain during the late eighteenth century, which witnessed a marked increase in French colonials on the island. The 1783 *Cedula of Population,* which offered attractive incentives to foreign migrants who were willing to establish plantations in the colony, was particularly appealing to free coloured planters from the French West Indian colonies who flocked to Trinidad in relatively large numbers (Brereton 1981, 13–14).

A silver sixpence coin with the image of Queen Victoria on the obverse side was also recovered from the site. Queen Victoria, originally named Princess Alexandrina Victoria of Kent, was born on 24 May 1819. She reigned as the British monarch from 1837 to 1901, the longest in the history of the British monarchy. The expansion of the empire, British industry, trade and population engendered a need for vast quantities of coins. As a result of the long duration of Victoria's reign, the coinage issued in her name was one of the most prolific in British history, rivalled only by that of Elizabeth II (de Wardt Lane 2010; Snodgrass 2003). The sovereign and its half and multiple equivalents struck under Queen Victoria are the oldest remaining British coins with legal tender status, although they are obviously no longer used for general circulation. The Victorian coin found at the Red House site appears to be inscribed with the year 1888. This is a fairly modern issue but one of the hardest to find. The reason for its shortage cannot be ascertained, but it was a scarce coin issue (see http://www.cointrust .co.uk/Victoria-Old-Head-Silver-Sixpence-1893-1901-p/1168b.htm).

Metals

This assemblage is comprised of all ferrous and non-ferrous metals. Coins and metal buttons were excluded from this assemblage for cataloguing/diagnostic reasons. The metal assemblage is relatively large. To date 13,247 metal artefacts have been catalogued, nails accounting for the majority of them (82%). A total of 2,073 (16%) of the processed metal artefacts are unidentifiable due to corrosion (Mircea et al. 2012).

Horseshoes

A total of forty-five horseshoes, all covered with thick corrosive encrustations, were found. Embossed coating formations are also visible, which indicates that the horseshoes were subjected to incineration, possibly as a direct result of the fire that occurred after the 1903 water riots.

Pen Nibs and Inkwells

Three pen nibs were obtained from the site. These artefacts have a thin grey-green patina. The pen nibs appear to be the type used in "dipping pens", prevalent throughout the nineteenth century, or "nib pens". Partially damaged glass and stoneware ink wells were also found (figure 9.9). Stoneware ink bottles from Doulton-Lambeth were specifically found in crawl space southwest SD3 (please review Hume 2001, 112–15, for a discussion of stoneware). The inkwells were in all likelihood used in tandem with dipping pens for record keeping and note taking, activities that were in line with the administrative and legislative functions of the colonial-period Red House. One stoneware ink bottle contained red ink, significant because red ink was traditionally reserved for use by the highest officials. In British African colonies, for example, only colonial secretaries were allowed to use red ink (Gann and Duignan 1978, 47).

Figure 9.9. All the vessels in this photograph, except the fourth from left, were used as ink wells. Fourth from left is a brown salt-glazed stoneware bottle which contained red ink at the time of discovery.

SPECIAL FINDS: NEWSPAPERS ON CONCRETE SLABS

During 19–20 February 2014, Amcoweld workers removed slabs of concrete (terrazzo) flooring from section A, room G 52 C of the Red House (figure 9.10). It was observed that sheets of newspaper had fused to the base of the concrete slabs. A total of ninety-five pieces were recovered. Some newspaper prints were legible, whereas others were too faded and damaged to read. The legible prints revealed that the newspaper pages were from the *Port-of-Spain Gazette*, the first official newspaper of Trinidad. It was first published on 21 September 1825 and last in June 1956. The date *May 6, 1919*, discernible on two slabs, suggests that additional renovations were undertaken on the building following the rebuilding of the second Red House in 1907.

LAVENTILLE SITE VISIT

Soil from the Eastern Quarry site in Laventille[2] was used to backfill the original Red House building in 1844 as well as the second Red House building in 1907. As such, there was much uncertainty concerning the origin of several colonial finds found at the Red House site at the very outset of the archaeology project. To ascertain where the majority of colonial finds originated, the Red House crew undertook archaeological surveys of the Eastern Quarry in Laventille on 22 October 2014 and 22 January 2015. Based on site reconnaissance and shovel test pits, the surveys produced very negligible amounts of artefacts or biofacts (figure 9.11). This indicates that the Red House, not Laventille, was the primary point of abandonment/discard for the bulk of colonial-period material culture and biofacts found at the former.

Figure 9.10.
An example of a concrete (terrazzo) slab with newsprint from section A, room G 52 C of the Red House.

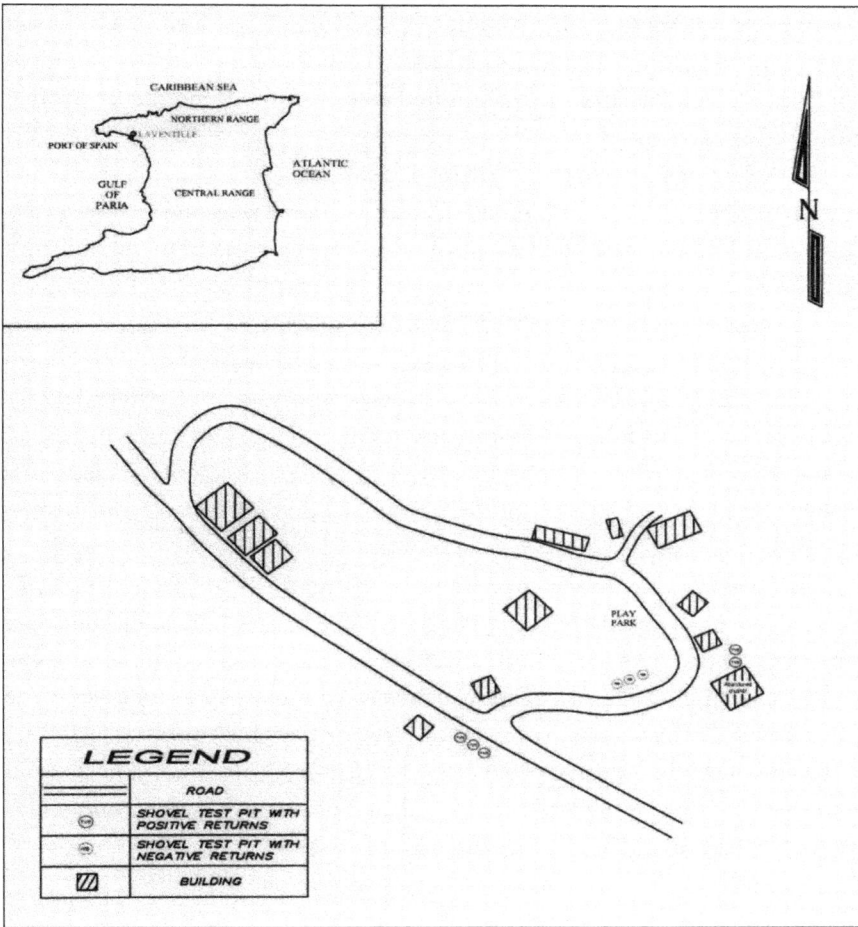

Figure 9.11.
Archaeological survey of the Eastern Quarry site (Laventille).

THE 1903 WATER RIOTS

The First Red House was gutted by fire in March 1903 as a result of the water riots in Port of Spain (see chapter 8, this volume; Williams 1962, 181–87). Samples of burnt paper were found at 1.05 metres from topsoil within the Red House's basement in section B, room G 24, southwest rotunda, and yielded radiocarbon ages of 1890–1905 CE. Within the margin of error usually associated with Carbon-14 chronology, the ages correlate well with the fire that followed on the heels of the 1903 water riots.

FAUNAL REMAINS

New types of mammals were introduced to Trinidad with the appearance of Europeans. Several conquistadores were given charters to import Old World animals into the island to be used as food and beasts of burden. According to

Lovell Francis (chapter 8, this volume), Ponce de Leon was awarded a charter in 1569, allowing him to bring domesticated animals to Trinidad: "one hundred horses, three hundred mares, five hundred cows, one thousand sheep, and two hundred pigs and goats".

The skeletal remains of the following fauna were unearthed: pig (*Sus scrofa domesticus*), horse (*Equus ferus caballus*) and cow (*Bos primigenius* or *Bos taurus*). During the initial period of Spanish colonization of the island in the sixteenth century, horses were among the first animals to be introduced. A rudimentary Spanish settlement in Mucurapo, located near present-day Port of Spain, was described as follows: "It was a fortified camp and consisted of thirty-one houses with kitchens, stables, smithy and storehouses" (Besson 2012). After the original government buildings were constructed two centuries later, horses (and mules) continued to be an important feature of Trinidad's colonial society. This is supported by the discovery of forty-five corroded horseshoes and a worn horse's toothbrush.

Pigs were initially imported to Trinidad to augment the protein requirements of the early Spanish colonials (see chapter 8, this volume). Fifty-four pig remains, comprised of loose teeth and a jaw fragment, were been found at the Red House. Eighty-five cow remains, consisting mostly of loose teeth, were also recovered. The pig and cow remains indicate that these animals were part of the diet of colonial-period occupants and visitors. Prior to the construction of the Red House, the site was unoccupied, and one of its possible uses was for grazing by free range livestock belonging to townsfolk.

CONCLUSION

The Red House colonial site adds another important chapter to our understanding of not only specific local developments in Port of Spain but also the broader span of the Caribbean's diverse colonial past. As a grandiose colonial space, the archaeology of the Red House reveals both the mundane aspects of daily life and the symbolic representations of British imperial power and control. The site is also unique for being the first urban colonial site in Trinidad and Tobago to be subjected to scholarly investigations. Future archaeological investigations of the Red House and its general locale may yield further information about the colonial period. Several areas of research are promising, including aspects of consumer choice, diet, health and disease, and the agency of local actors in response to colonial dominance. The Water Riots and other local conflicts offer the opportunity to explore the archaeology of resistance at the Red House and in colonial Trinidad for the period. Other promising areas for study are gender roles and group affiliations of Red House inhabitants and the role archaeology plays in revealing aspects of their daily lives, as well as the existing social boundaries and creolization. The archaeology of the Red House, as the focus of British colonial rule, may offer some surprising results upon further archaeological analyses. What appears to be the bastion of British culture and society in the periphery may have been something else altogether – a hybrid of local and European practices and traditions that in some ways became a society of its own making. While reflecting an emulation of certain tastes and trends, the idea of the transplanted middle- and upper-class British mental templates as a response to living abroad may not have always been the case, as Caribbean historical archaeology has shown time and again throughout the region. In this vein, the Red House provides the opportunity to study the mechanisms of culture change on Trinidad. It is hoped that further archaeological research will be conducted at the Red House as well as at other historical sites on Trinidad. The prehistory of Trinidad and Tobago offer some of the best of Caribbean archaeology, and for the historic period these islands hold great promise for future endeavors when and where they become available.

NOTES

1. When compared to the pre-colonial period, interpreting the colonial archaeology of the Red House site was slightly more problematic. Pre-colonial material culture and biological remains, although often commingled with colonial materials throughout much of the site, benefited from the following: (1) the presence of an identifiable Amerindian cultural horizon in the Red House basement, (2) multiple radiocarbon dates and (3) a battery of forensic, DNA, isotopic, starch grain, phytolith, lipid and ceramic analyses.

    Despite this, our interpretations of colonial finds were aided considerably by a relatively rich array of documentary/archival sources concerning both the Red House and Port of Spain. Further, the archaeology crew was able to obtain data on similar colonial finds found elsewhere in the world. This body of information was used to cross-reference and interpret several of the colonial finds recovered from the site.

2. The quarry site is located about 1 kilometre east of Port of Spain.

REFERENCES

Agorsah, E.K., and B. Samaroo. 2014. "Hondo River Settlement (Trinidad)". In *Encylopedia of Caribbean Archaeology*, edited by B.A. Reid and R.G. Gilmore III, 186–88. Gainesville: University Press of Florida.

Besson, G.A. 2012. "The Caribbean History Archives: The Caribs Fear the Horses". http://caribbeanhistoryarchives.blogspot.com/2012/01/caribs-fear-horses.html. Accessed 1 July 2015.

Blackburn, M. 2011. "Coinage in Its Archaeological Context". In *The Oxford Handbook of Anglo-Saxon Archaeology*, edited by D.A. Hinton, S. Crawford and H. Hamerow. http://www.oxfordhandbooks.com/view/10.1093/oxfordhb/9780199212149.001.0001 /oxfordhb-9780199212149-e-30.

Borchardt, S., M. Crowell, E. Donald and B. Farner. 2002. "Gunston Hall Plantation: Room Use Study". http://www.gunstonhall.org/mansion/room_use_study/methodology.html.

Brereton, B. 1981. *A History of Modern Trinidad, 1783–1962*. London: Heinemann.

Clement, C.O. 1997. "Settlement Patterning on the British Caribbean Island of Tobago". *Historical Archaeology* 31 (2): 93–106.

Coin UK Trust. 2015. http://www.cointrust.co.uk/Victoria-Old-Head-Silver-Sixpence -1893-1901-p/1168b.htm. Accessed 11 July 2015.

CoinsValues.com. 2015. http://www.coinvalues.com/liberty-head-gold-coin/1851. Accessed 11 July 2015.

deWardt, R. 2010. "Encyclopedia of Small Silver Coins: Brother Can You Spare a Dime". http://www.dewardt.net/brother.html.

Fox, G. 1999. *The Archaeology of the Clay Tobacco Pipe. XV. The Kaolin Clay Tobacco Pipe Collection from Port Royal, Jamaica*, edited by Peter Davey. Oxford: BA International Series 809.

Fromer, J.E. 2008. *A Necessary Luxury: Tea in Victorian England*. Athens: Ohio University Press.

Gann, L., and P. Duignan. 1978. The Rulers of British Africa, 1870–1914. Stanford, CA: Stanford University Press.

Gojak, D., and I. Stuart. 1999. "The Potential for the Archaeological Study of Clay Tobacco Pipes from Australian Sites". *Australasian Historical Archaeology* 17:38–49.

Green, T. 1999. *Central Bank Gold Reserves: An Historical Perspective since 1845*. Research Study no. 23. London: World Gold Council.

Hume, I.N. 2001. *A Guide to Artifacts of Colonial America*. Philadelphia: University of Pennsylvania Press.

Lindbergh, J. 1999. "Buttoning Down Archaeology". *Australasian Historical Archaeology* 12:50–57.

Lopinot, N.H., and M.L. Venter. 2014. "La Reconnaissance Site (Trinidad)". In *Encyclopedia of Caribbean Archaeology*, edited by B.A. Reid and R.G. Gilmore III, 219–21. Gainesville: University Press of Florida.

Marcel, S.E. 1994. "Buttoning Down the Past: A Look at Buttons as Indicators of Chronology and Material Culture". University of Tennessee Honors Thesis Projects.

Mavrogordata, O. 2010. "The Red House". In *The Book of Trinidad*, edited by G. Besson and B. Brereton, 267–68. Port of Spain: Paria.

Mintz, S.W. 1985. *Sweetness and Power: The Place of Sugar in Modern History*. New York: Penguin.

Mircea, O., I. Sandu, V. Vasilache and I. Sabdu. 2012. "A Study of the Deterioration and Degradation of Metallic Archaeological Artifacts". *International Journal of Conservation Science* 3 (3). http://ijcs.uaic.ro/pub/IJCS-12-18-Mircea.pdf.

Pitts, H.C. 1948. "100 Years Together: A Brief History of Trinidad from 1797–1897". Port of Spain, Trinidad.

Rivers, S. 1999. "An Analysis of the Buttons from Three Historic Homes in Western Kentucky". *Ohio Valley Historical Archaeology* 14:29–35. http://infosys.murraystate.edu/KWesler/Symposium%20OVHA%20Volume%2014/V14_p029-035.pdf.

Snodgrass, M.E. 2003. *Coins and Currency: An Historical Encyclopedia*. Jefferson, NC: McFarland.

Stelle, L. 1989. "An Archaeological Guide to Historic Artifacts of Central Illinois". 1 January. http://virtual.parkland.edu/lstelle1/len/archguide/documents/arcguide.htm. Accessed 17 September 2013.

White, C., and M. Beaudry. 2009. *International Handbook of Historical Archaeology*. New York: Springer.

Williams, A.R. 2014. "Who Buried the $10 Million in Coins Found by a California Couple—and Why?" *National Geographic*, 27 February. https://news.nationalgeographic.com/news/2014/02/140226-gold-coins-hoard-california-discovery-numismatics/.

Williams, E. 1962. *History of the People of Trinidad and Tobago*. London: Andre Deutsch.

PART 3.

HERITAGE MANAGEMENT

CHAPTER 10

Developing a GIS Archaeological Information System for the Red House

MICHAEL SUTHERLAND, AMIT SEERAM, SARAH HOSEIN
AND BASIL A. REID

ARCHAEOLOGICAL DATA RECOVERED FROM THE RED HOUSE SITE are quite diverse, ranging from pre-colonial pottery, stone artefacts, biological remains (including human skeletons, human bone fragments and molluscs) to European material culture such as glazed ceramics, glass bottles, metals, pipe stem and bowl fragments, roofing tiles and buttons (see chapters 1, 4, 5, 6, 7 and 9, this volume). Radiocarbon dates, together with the timeline of various European ceramics, suggest a multi-period site spanning from 125 CE to the nineteenth century. The range of the archaeological assemblage suggests that the Red House is an important multi-component, multi-period site (Reid 2015). The site is clearly one of the most significant archaeological discoveries in Trinidad and Tobago and the wider Caribbean (Reid 2015). Archaeological remains may be seen as finite and non-renewable resources that are in many cases highly fragile and vulnerable to damage and destruction. They may contain irreplaceable information about our past and therefore may increase our potential for further knowledge in the future (Ramlal and Reid 2008, 86).

It is against this background that an archaeological information system (AIS) of the site, based on geographical information systems (GIS) was developed by Dr Michael Sutherland and his team. The AIS will not only facilitate easy access of information but will provide a digital database amenable to continuous updating as new information on the Red House comes to light. Thematic and positional archaeological data, primary and secondary topographical and global positioning system (GPS) data, together with data from the digitization of floor plans, were all processed in an ArcGIS environment to produce vector and raster outputs in an archaeologically relevant GIS, capable of being queried and visualized in multiple dimensions. This project was guided by cultural resource management (CRM), which can be defined succinctly as the management and preservation of cultural resources, such as cultural landscapes, archaeological sites, historical records, historic buildings and industrial heritage and artefacts. The twinning of GIS and CRM is clearly premised on the growing recognition throughout the Caribbean that GIS is a powerful tool for the management of heritage sites (Reid 2008b, 5).

GIS AND AIS

The use of maps in archaeology is intuitive and has a long tradition. Maps, according to González-Tennant (2009), are among an archaeologist's "most fundamental" tools. Mapping and spatial analyses are fundamental to GIS, so it is not hard to envisage archaeology benefiting from this form of geoinformatics. Of benefit to archaeology is the fact that GIS permits maps to be perceived as "interactive visualizations" instead of "two dimensional static objects" (Stine 2000). This interactive visualization in multiple dimensions, along with GIS capability to do spatio-temporal scenario analysis/predictive modelling and support spatial patterns analysis (among other things), adds to the traditional confirmatory analytical techniques to give archaeologists other valuable dimension of analyses (Christopherson et al. 1996; Stine 2000; Neubauer 2004).

From its early beginnings in the United States and Canada, CRM has driven the use of, and research into, archaeological GIS (Judge and Sebastian 1988). From these eminently practical origins, GIS have migrated to academia, where researchers are applying them for purposes other than the management of cultural resources (van Leusen 1995). In the Caribbean, the twinning of GIS and CRM to produce AIS is clearly premised on the growing recognition throughout the Caribbean that GIS is a powerful tool for the management of heritage sites. A primary example is Kevin Farmer's (2008) discussion of a project to develop a "Sites and Monuments Inventory System" at the Barbados Museum and Historical Society through a grant from UNESCO – a project driven by the need to properly document sites that are being threatened by rapid urbanization in the small Caribbean nation. Yet another example is the design and development of an archaeological information system (AIS) for the Archaeology Centre at the University of the West Indies, St Augustine, using Arc View GIS and Microsoft Access software (Ramlal and Reid 2008). Considered as far superior to conventional paper-based methods, a GIS-AIS not only provides a means for accessing information but also a digital database that may be maintained and updated with new information as it becomes available.

According to van Leusen (1995, 27), a GIS-AIS can be used in two distinct ways. The first is the use of GIS as a data management and presentation toolbox, which provides archaeological resource managers with a quick method of collecting, combining and presenting that data relevant to their work. Alternatively, GIS can be used as a research instrument for the development of new and better ways of mapping and evaluating the archaeological record, reconstruction of (paleo-) environmental variables and data about (post-) depositional processes, cartographic reconstructions of the past and/or present state of the archaeological heritage can be made (van Leusen 1995, 27).

Of course, the stage of GIS development determines what could be accomplished, and how it could be accomplished. Petrie et al. (1995) produced an edited bibliography that cited sources going back to the 1980s and 1990s that either implicitly or explicitly associate archaeology with GIS. The capabilities of contemporary GIS, having developed with that of information and communication technology (ICT) represent significant evolutionary steps beyond what was available in the 1980s and 1990s. Contemporary GIS offers a rich toolbox of functions beneficial to archaeology, including sophisticated thematic and spatial analyses along with visualizations in two and three dimensions (four dimensions, when considering time series or other temporal data).

However, like all GIS operations, converting source material into spatial and attribute data for the sake of cultural resource management (CRM) can be very time consuming. Although GIS can be used to quickly make maps and tables, archaeologists, historians and cultural resource managers should be prepared to invest considerable time in designing systems, acquiring data and converting material from manuscript and print sources (including paper maps) into digital forms (Reid 2008a). Despite this, GIS enables us to generate permanent records of sites, combine and jointly analyse diverse sources, understand how cultural heritage relates spatially to surrounding natural and human environment, communicate knowledge and network databases, test proposed development models and conservation strategies, and facilitate monitoring and management of cultural resources.

DEVELOPMENT OF THE RED HOUSE AIS

The AIS described in this chapter is effectively a 3D geodatabase managed within ArcGIS (ArcMap and ArcScene). Sections below comprise the methodology utilized in developing the AIS. Development of the AIS was accomplished through consultation with the intended primary user, as well as through the collection and processing of primary and secondary thematic and positional data. This was achieved in a number of stages: user needs analysis, collection of secondary data, topographical surveys, preliminary data processing in AutoCAD and data processing in ArcGIS (ArcMap and ArcScene). The steps taken to develop the AIS served the objectives of modelling the relative positions of archaeological artefacts found at the Red House (in 2D and 3D), and permitting the execution of appropriate thematic and spatial queries relevant to the found artefacts and remains.

User Needs Analysis

As it ought to be with the development of any system, it is imperative that the developer obtain the system needs of the potential users. In the case of the AIS, the developer needed to understand the physical site environment from an archaeological point of view and, from the users' points of view, understand the entities (i.e., inspection units, crawl spaces, sections, artefacts and remains) that are to be represented in the AIS along with their attributes, how the entities are to be represented and how the system will be used by archaeologists in terms of the types of necessary enquiries to be made of the system and the types of outputs and visualizations desired. This information was obtained through discussions with the chief archaeologist responsible for the Red House site and with those giving assistance to the archaeological work being done. One very specific requirement was that the AIS be capable of visualizations in 2D and 3D. The first output from the user needs analysis was an Excel file (figure 10.1) containing definitions of entities and their attributes.

Collection of Secondary Data

Developing the AIS would have been a tremendous undertaking if all necessary data were collected from scratch. Therefore, secondary data played a very important role. These data included floor plans in PDF format, a topographic map in AutoCAD format that was derived from a previous exercise and handwritten archaeological field notes of previously found artefacts and remains. These data were used to support digitization of the Red House shape and archaeologically important components, in topographical data integration exercises, and to create initial spatial objects in the AIS, respectively (figure 10.2).

Figure 10.1. Sample of AIS entities and attributes.

ENTITY	SPATIAL OBJECT TYPE	ATTRIBUTES	DATA TYPE	VALUE
Inspection Unit	Polygon	CEP_BM_Number	Text	CEP#; BM#
		Location	Number	eastings; northing; depth
		Depth	Number	#.#
		Crawl Space	Text	relative description
		Section	Text	A; B; C
Crawl Space	Polygon	Location	Number	subdivision #; eastings; northing; depth
		Description	Text	relative description
		Depth	Number	#.#
Section	Polygon	Location	Number	eastings; northing; depth
		Description	Text	A; B; C
		Depth	Number	#.#
Human Skeleton	Point	Location	Number	eastings; northing; depth
		Inspection Unit	Text	CEP#; BM#
		Crawl Space	Text	subdivision #; eastings; northing; depth
		Section	Text	A; B; C
		Chronology	Text	Saladoid (Palo Seco) (AD 0- AD 650); Arauquinoid (AD750/800 - AD 1300); Mayoid (AD 1300 - AD 1750; Spanish Colonial Period (1498 - 1797); English Colonial Period (1797-1962)
		Orientation	Text	North - South; East-West; Other
		Position	Text	Supine; Flexed; Crouched; Prone; Other
		Biological_Sex	Text	Male; Female
		Age_Range	Number	child; juvenile; adult
		Condition	Text	Articulated; Disarticulated
		Carbon_14_Chronology	Text	relative description
		Isotopic Analysis	Number	predominantly terrestrial; predominantly marine; mixed
Human Bone Fragments	Point	Location	Number	eastings; northing; depth
		Inspection Unit	Text	CEP#; BM#

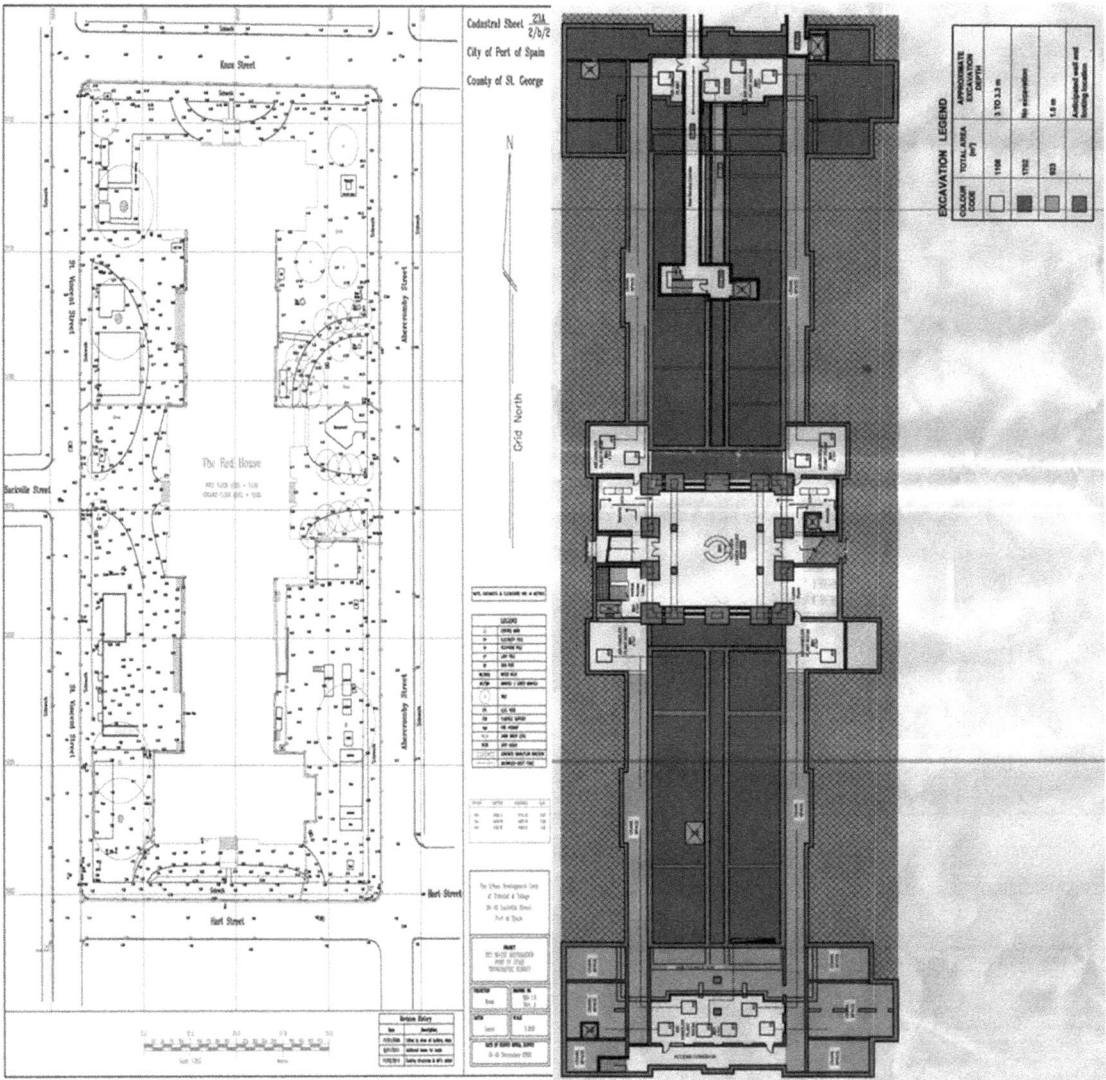

Figure 10.2.
Red House topo-
graphic map (*left*)
and floor plan.

Primary Topographical Survey Data Collection

Over periods of four days, on-site topographical surveys were done in relation to the main archaeological areas (i.e., inspection units, crawl spaces and areas identified as sections A, B and C). This was necessary to spatially model the physical layout of the archaeological site. Topological surveys were also done with regard to the Red House compound external to the building itself. Primary controls were established using GPS, facilitating the necessary 2D point positions used to establish a control network within the Red House compound. This was also compulsory for connecting the survey data to previous surveys using common survey brass points located outside the archaeological site. Vertical and

Figure 10.3.
Primary topographic
survey at the Red
House.

horizontal traverses were also carried out and spatially connected to a Lands and Surveys primary survey trigonometric station located on the Red House compound. These exercises made it possible to obtain the horizontal (x, y) and vertical (z) positions of inspection units, crawl spaces and sections where artefacts and remains were, and expected to be, found. The horizontal and vertical positions (x, y, z) collected were then ready to be processed in AutoCAD and ArcGIS (figure 10.3).

Data Processing in AutoCAD and ArcGIS

Primary and secondary data were processed in AutoCAD and ArcGIS software environments where appropriate to eventually produce a 3D geodatabase that, when accessed through ArcGIS (ArcMap and ArcScene), represent the

AIS. AutoCAD was used to georeference the topographic drawing of the Red House (using data from the primary topographic survey) and to create some 3D features. AutoCAD outputs were imported into ArcGIS (ArcMap), as was the graphic representation of the Red House floor plan with defined crawl spaces, sections and inspection units. The georeferenced floor plan, together with primary topographic data, was used to digitize crawl spaces, sections and inspection units in both two and three dimensions. Handwritten archaeological notes were used to populate the entity databases in ArcMap with both positional and thematic attributes. Hyperlinks were also created in ArcGIS (ArcMap), linking digitized inspection units and artefacts to pictures taken of them. This added another layer of information that may be retrieved. Appropriate symbols were also chosen for each entity type to assist with visual analyses and assessments.

The Archaeological Information System (Functions)

Fully developed, the Red House AIS consists of a 3D geodatabase that is manipulated in ArcMap and ArcScene environments to obtain desired results. ArcMap is used to add and modify entities, and for 2D visualization (figure 10.4). Figure 10.4 also shows thematic information retrieved from an associated attribute table. ArcScene is used to visualize the geodatabase in 3D (figures 10.5 and 10.6). Both ArcMap and ArcScene are used to facilitate thematic and spatial queries.

As with any system associated with databases, a measure of the quality of the AIS is its ability to return useful results to queries. Apart from information gained from viewing attribute tables, the AIS uses the power of GIS to respond to a variety of thematic queries. In other words, the system can accurately

Figure 10.4.
2D representation of the Red House with entities identified in blue.

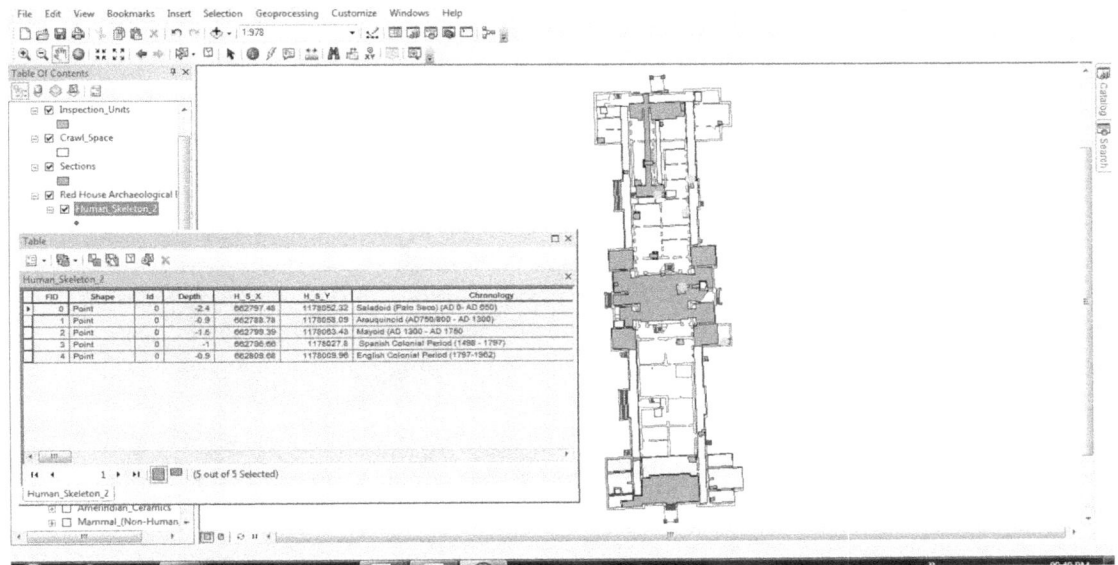

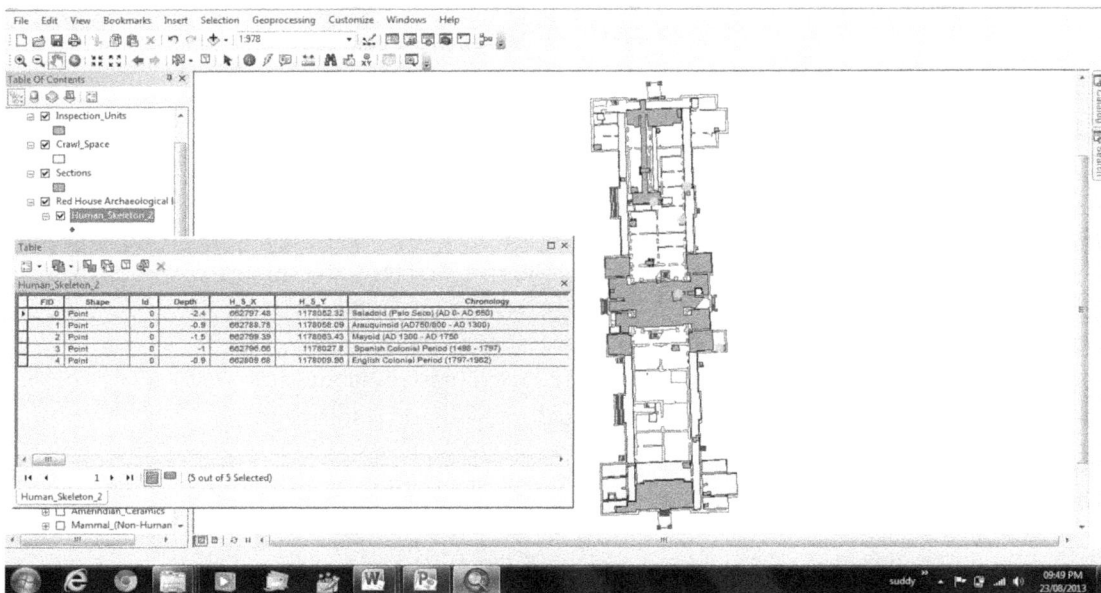

Figure 10.5. 3D representation of the Red House – view from above.

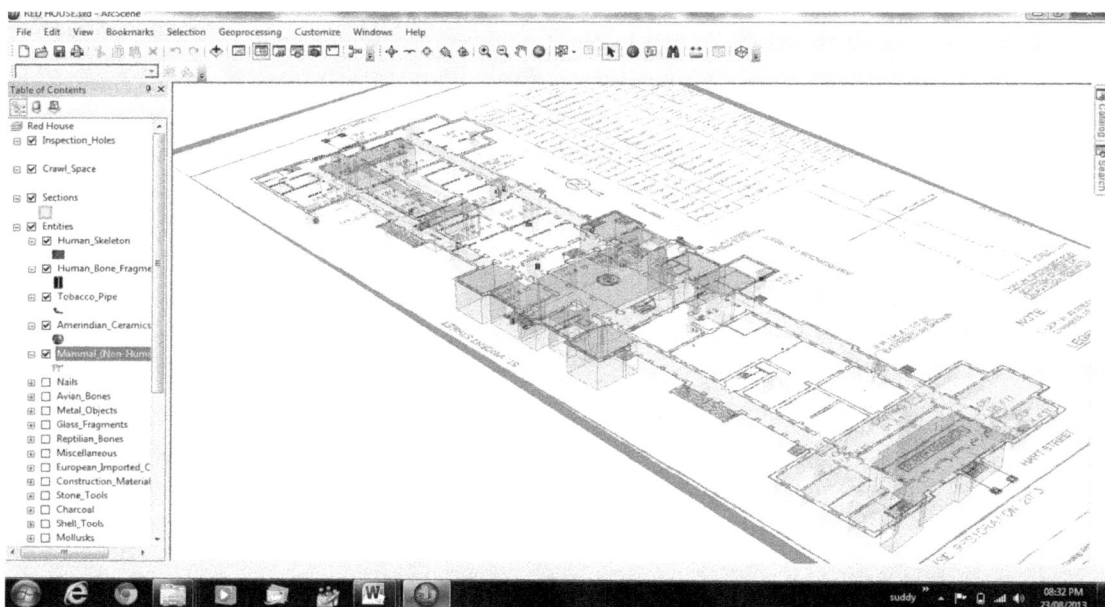

Figure 10.6. 3D representation of the Red House – view from below.

respond to queries about entities based on their non-positional qualities. For example, the system could be queried to identify entities that are all of the same type (or types, if multiple entities are queried) or share some quality (e.g., chronology). The power of a GIS can also be used to query entities based on the vertical and horizontal positions of entities, which in archaeology may be important to determine time periods. For example, the system could be queried to identify entities that are at defined depths, or within depth ranges at particular locations; defined depths, or within depth ranges across the site of interest; particular locations (e.g., within an inspection unit or crawl space); defined proximities to other entities.

The Red House AIS also makes use of hyperlinks within the GIS environment to retrieve pictures, documents and websites associated with found archaeological artefacts or remains. The added dimensions of information possible with this function are important to archaeologists using the AIS, who wish to obtain more relevant information not stored directly in the database. Figure 10.7 shows an example of a hyperlinked picture retrieved in association with a particular inspection unit. Figure 10.8 shows an example of multiple entities identified through a defined query and, as well, multiple associated pictures retrieved through hyperlinks. Overall, the AIS uses visual, thematic and spatial analyses to support investigations of artefacts found at the Red House site.

Figure 10.7. Photograph accessed through a hyperlink associated with an inspection unit.

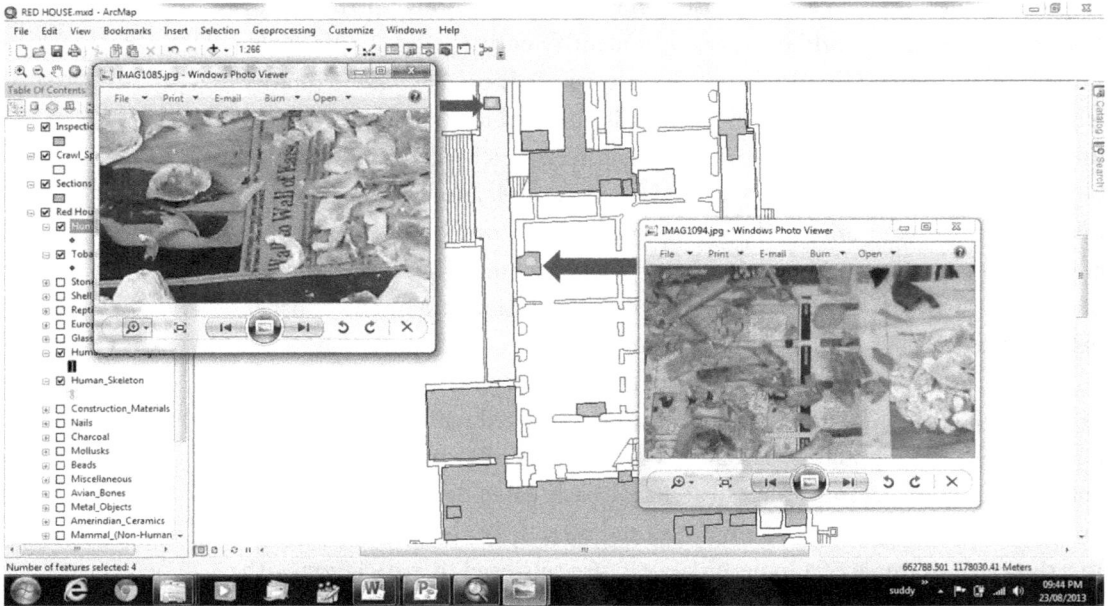

Figure 10.8. Sample query result – artefacts found at specified depth range.

DISCUSSION AND CONCLUSION

While it is possible to have a perfectly adequate non-GIS database that records site location and other information in a spreadsheet or paper card index relating to the Red House site, such a database may pose significant challenges when spatial information becomes a key part of the record. The creation of a Red House GIS-AIS was specifically designed to manage, visualize, interrogate and analyse a 3D spatial and temporal data generated during the project. Data related to the archaeological finds, such as spatial context and other thematic attributes of artefacts, were entered into Microsoft Excel spreadsheets. These spreadsheets were then joined to relevant attribute tables in ArcGIS, thereby linking empirical archaeological data to constructed spatial objects. ArcMap was used to generate two-dimensional (2D) images while ArcScene was used to produce 3D representations of the archaeological data. These spatial databases are far superior, as they are able to record morphology and topology in formats that can be queried in ways that attribute-only data cannot.

From the perspective of cultural resource management, the advantages of having such an integrated system that permits the flexible interrogation of sites within their broader spatial context are enormous. The Red House GIS-AIS provides a suitable environment for the easy retrieval and mapping of spatial data. It also provides a sound strategy for the capture, storage, management, analysis and dissemination of archaeological data.

Wescott and Brandon (2000, back cover) are of the view that GIS is "the most powerful technological tool to be applied to archaeology since the invention of radiocarbon dating" but it has also been described as a technology without intellectual vigour, overly dependent on simple presuppositions about the importance of spatial patterns in a dehumanized artificial space (cf. Pickles 1999, 50–52). Although there are elements of truth in both of these perspectives, one of the greatest strengths of the use of GIS in archaeology is its diversity (Conolly and Lake 2006, 10). In some cases, simply organizing our data more efficiently is enough to prompt new ideas about the past. In other cases, it is necessary to construct new methods within the framework of conventional GIS (Conolly and Lake 2006). It is envisaged that the Red House GIS-AIS will be fully utilized by scholars, professionals and government officials in order to learn more about the rich archaeological legacy of the site.

REFERENCES

Christopherson, G.L., D.P. Guertin and K.A. Borstad. 1996. "GIS and Archaeology: Using ARC/INFO to Increase our Understanding of Ancient Jordan". *Proceedings of the Sixteenth Annual ESRI User Conference*, Palm Springs, CA: Environmental Systems Research Institute.

Conolly, J., and M. Lake. 2006. *Geographical Information Systems in Archaeology.* Cambridge: Cambridge University Press.

Farmer, K. 2008. "Forward Planning: The Utilization of GIS in the Management of Archaeological Resources in Barbados". In Reid 2008a, 74–85.

González-Tennant, E. 2009. "Using Geodatabases to Generate 'Living Documents' for Archaeology: A Case Study from the Otago Goldfields, New Zealand". *Historical Archaeology*, 43 (3): 20–37.

Judge, W.J., and L. Sebastian. 1988. "Quantifying the Present and Predicting the Past: Theory, Method, and Application of Archaeological Predictive Modelling". Denver: US Department of the Interior, Bureau of Land Management.

Neubauer, W. 2004. "GIS in Archaeology—the Interface between Prospection and Excavation". *Archaeological Prospection*, 11 (3): 159–66.

Petrie, L., I. Johnson, B. Cullen and K. Kvamme. 1995. *GIS in Archaeology: An Annotated Bibliography.* Sydney: Sydney University Archaeological Methods, Series 1.

Pickles, J. 1999. "Arguments, Debates and Dialogues: The GIS Social-Theory Debate and the Concern for A". In *Geographical Information Systems*, edited by P.A. Longley, M.F. Goodchild, J.D. Maguire and D.W. Rhind. Vol. 1, *Principles and Technical Issues*, 49–60. New York: John Wiley.

Ramlal, B., and B.A. Reid. 2008. "Developing an Archaeological Information System for Trinidad and Tobago". In Reid 2008a, 86–96.

Reid, B.A. 2008a. *Archaeology and Geoinformatics.* Tuscaloosa: University of Alabama Press.

———. 2008b. "Introduction". In Reid 2008a, 1–9.

———. 2015. *Red House Restoration Archaeology Report, Phase 1, for the Period July 1, 2013– January 31, 2015.* Port of Spain: Office of the Parliament of the Republic of Trinidad and Tobago.

Stine, R. 2000. "Finding the Forge: Geographic Visualization in Archaeology". *Historical Archaeology* 34 (4): 61–73.

van Leusen, P.M. 1995. "GIS and Archaeological Resource Management: A European Agenda". In *Archaeology and Geographical Information Systems: A European Perspective,* edited by G. Lock and and Z. Stančič, 27–41. London: Taylor and Francis.

Westcott, K.L., and R.J. Brandon, eds. 2000. *Practical Application of GIS for Archaeologists: A Predictive Model.* London: Taylor and Francis.

CHAPTER 11

The Red House Restoration Archaeological Project

An Example of Archaeological and Values-Based Heritage Management

BASIL A. REID, NEIL JAGGASSAR AND PETER E. SIEGEL

THIS CHAPTER EXPLORES THE RED HOUSE RESTORATION ARCHAEOLOGICAL Project within the context of archaeological and values-based heritage management. Built in 1907, the Red House has been the seat of Trinidad and Tobago parliament for over one hundred years. This is the second structure to be built on the site; the foundation stone for the first was laid by the then-governor of Trinidad Sir Henry McLeod, on 15 February 1844.

The Urban Development Corporation of Trinidad and Tobago (UDeCOTT) was tasked to restore the Red House, including retrofitting the interiors for adaptive reuse by Trinidad and Tobago's parliament. UDeCOTT became involved in the Red House Project in 2003, when it took over from the National Insurance Property Development Company Limited. This was during the third term of the Honourable Patrick Manning as prime minister and when Calder Hart was the chairman of UDeCOTT. When the Partnership Government came into power in 2010, UDeCOTT continued to manage the project, but the designs were changed and the government agreed to a revised project in 2011. Physical work on the Red House commenced in 2012 (Neil Jaggassar, pers. comm., 2016).

In March and April 2013, human skeletal remains, molluscs, and pre-colonial and colonial cultural materials were unearthed in the basement of the Red House during restoration works. The Office of the Parliament of the Republic of Trinidad and Tobago retained Dr Basil Reid and his crew to undertake a detailed archaeological study of the Red House site (between 1 July 2013 and 31 January 2015). A comprehensive research agenda was initiated, involving both local and international scholars.

Some of the most significant archaeological findings in Trinidad and Tobago were recovered. Due to the discovery of several Amerindian burials, the First

Peoples of the twin island republic revere the Red House as a sacred site. As a result of its rich history, relative longevity, and imposing edifice in the heart of Port of Spain, nationals of the twin island republic generally consider the Red House to be both iconic and an integral part of the city's historical landscape. The project therefore had to satisfy the often-competing interests of diverse stakeholders: the government, academic community, First Peoples and the general public. We discuss the holistic approach taken in managing what was arguably a landmark archaeological project in Trinidad and Tobago. Given their importance to this chapter, the concepts of (a) archaeological heritage management and (b) values-based heritage management are discussed below.

ARCHAEOLOGICAL HERITAGE MANAGEMENT

The International Committee on Archaeological Heritage Management (ICAHM) defines archaeological heritage as "all vestiges of human existence and consists of places relating to all manifestations of human activity, abandoned structures, and remains of all kinds . . . together with all the portable cultural material associated with them" (ICAHM 1990: Article 1). The scientific, cultural and humanistic importance of archaeological resources is based on the contextual associations of artefacts and ecofacts with each other and to features of the landscape in which they are situated. Modern development projects, forces of nature and, indeed, archaeological excavations themselves are all destructive agents of the archaeological record.

The ICAHM charter includes a logical series of recommendations that all nations should follow in regard to archaeological heritage management (ICAHM 1990):

1. Develop integrated policies "relating to land use, development, and planning";
2. Enact legislation requiring appropriate archaeological investigations conducted in advance of proposed development projects;
3. Perform archaeological surveys and maintain site inventories to be used in developing integrated cultural resource management plans;
4. Conduct archaeological studies and excavations, appropriate to the specific threats to an archaeological resource;
5. Produce a report detailing the goals, methods, results, and implications of the archaeological study;
6. Maintain and conserve archaeological sites and properly curate associated documents and archaeological collections;
7. Present results of archaeological studies to the public, as appropriate;
8. Ensure that archaeological investigations are carried out by individuals with proper qualifications;

9. Promote international cooperation, thereby maintaining and furthering best practices in archaeological heritage management.

Archaeological Heritage Management in the Caribbean

There is considerable variability across Caribbean islands regarding the recognition and implementation of the ICAHM charter. Many islands do not explicitly reference the charter but have legislation that, if implemented, would serve the same purpose. Unfortunately, most islands do not comply with their own heritage legislation, especially in the face of development projects (Siegel 2014). The following review briefly examines heritage management practices in a sample of Caribbean island nations and territories, including Trinidad and Tobago, to assess variation in policy and implementation across the region (Hofman and Haviser 2015; Siegel 2011a, 2011b, 2014; Siegel and Righter 2011; Siegel et al. 2013).

In Barbados, if listed heritage resources are within the area of potential effects of a development project, then the Town and Country Planning Act of 1985 requires developers to address those resources. The Barbados Museum and Historical Society maintains "the list of archaeological sites . . . [which] in the past has been shared with the Town Planning Department" (Farmer 2011, 116). There is no legal mechanism requiring archaeological surveys in advance of development projects in areas where no sites have been previously documented. As observed by Farmer (119), "The development of land is carried out with little attention given to the archaeology that may be found there due to an absence of a law requiring archaeological assessment."

The Antiquities, Monuments and Museums Act of 1998 of the Bahamas provides for "the preservation, conservation, restoration, documentation, study and presentation of sites" (Pateman 2011, 4). Through this act, heritage management has been centralized into a single agency, resulting in better regulatory oversight. However, managers of multimillion-dollar development projects have been able to avoid the requirements of conducting archaeological investigations and at best pay a paltry fine "for the purposeful destruction of heritage resources" (8).

In Jamaica, heritage resources protection falls within the purview of the Jamaica National Heritage Trust, which was formed in 1985 as a statutory agency. The trust is mandated "to promote the preservation of national monuments and anything designated as protected national heritage for the benefit of the island" (http://www.jnht.com/mission_function.php). The act has been implemented slowly, and in some cases it has been misinterpreted.

The islands of Basse-Terre, Grande-Terre, Île des Saintes, Marie-Galante, La Désirade, Martinique, St Martin and St Barthélemy make up the French West Indies. These islands have been integrated into France as overseas departments since 1946, and as such French heritage legislation, called the Code du Patrimoine, applies to the French West Indies (Bérard and Stouvenot 2011).

Heritage management in the Dutch Caribbean is more difficult to describe than other islands or island groups because of the changing governance structure across those islands. The Netherlands Antilles was dissolved on 10 October 2010, and the political statuses of the constituent islands changed. Bonaire, St Eustatius and Saba became municipalities of the Netherlands, while Aruba, Curaçao and St Maarten became autonomous entities (Haviser and Gilmore 2011). The National Archaeological Anthropological Museum is a government foundation that oversees heritage management primarily on Curaçao. Curaçao is considered to have "the most effective heritage management programme" in the Dutch Caribbean (Haviser and Gilmore 2011, 137). In 2007 the Netherlands Antilles ratified the Malta Convention affirming support for the consideration and protection of heritage resources. Unfortunately, implementation of the Malta Convention is rarely carried out in the Dutch Caribbean.

In 2000 the state secretary of culture in the Dominican Republic mandated coordination "across state institutions that deal with cultural issues" by establishing the Ministry of Culture and enactment of Law 41-00 (Prieto Vicioso 2011, 37). The legislation promoted a strategy to "protect the tangible and intangible patrimony of the Nation" (Prieto Vicioso 2011, 37). However, the problem with Dominican heritage protection is the nonexistent or uneven enforcement of relevant legislation and inadequate support for the relevant agencies to "carry out their mandates" (Prieto Vicioso 2011, 45).

In Trinidad and Tobago, heritage protection falls within the purview of the National Trust of Trinidad and Tobago; the Archaeological Committee of Trinidad and Tobago; the Advisory Committee on Historic Wrecks; the Archaeology Centre of the Department of History at the University of the West Indies; and the World Heritage Convention (Reid and Lewis 2011, 126–30). Heritage resources managers face challenges, including lack of enforcement: "Mandates requiring archaeological investigations in advance of development are ignored." Poor inter-agency coordination is a problem, and there is no centralized plan for regulatory oversight. As a result, consideration of heritage resources on Trinidad and Tobago is less than adequate (Reid and Lewis 2011, 130–31).

VALUES-BASED HERITAGE MANAGEMENT

Values-based heritage management, by definition, is "the coordinated and structured operation of a heritage site with the primary purpose of protecting the significance of the place as defined by designation criteria, government authorities or other owners, experts of various stripes, and other citizens with legitimate interests in the place" (Mason et al. 2003, 1). This is in contrast to traditional-based heritage management, which typically involves decisions and significance assessment mandated by experts and researchers without input from local communities.

One of the first attempts in the area of value and significance assessment in the cultural heritage field was embarked on by the Getty Conservation Institute in the late 1990s. Randall Mason, Setha M. Low, Susana Mourato and Massimiliano Mazzanti, Theresa Satterfield and David Throsby published their work on the values of cultural heritage in the 2002 volume, *Assessing the Values of Cultural Heritage*, which was edited by Marta de la Torre. This and similar studies have over the years offered rich insights into ongoing investigations of the more holistic approach of values-based heritage management.

Value can be defined as "simply a set of positive characteristics or qualities perceived in cultural objects or sites by certain individuals or groups" (de la Torre and Throsby 2002, 4). De la Torre (2013) equates value with usefulness if the place can be used for productive purposes, such as the education of citizens, or with significance, if the place symbolizes something larger and more important than merely the ruins. It is clear that the term "value" could easily be and is often replaced by the term "significance" (Australia ICOMOS 2000). The expression *cultural significance* was defined under the Burra Charter article 12 as "aesthetic, historic, scientific, social or spiritual value for past, present and future generations" (Australia ICOMOS 2000, 2). Heritage sites have multiple values (Mason 2002), depending on the range of stakeholders (Doumas 2013; de la Torre 2013). There are many types, such as cultural value, aesthetic value, religious value and social value (Ababneh 2016).

Values-Based Heritage Management in the Caribbean

Values-based heritage management does not appear to be prominently highlighted in the heritage legislation and management practices of many Caribbean territories. However, the concept of value (or significance) is reflected in the selection of World Heritage sites in the Caribbean.[1] To date, over twenty-one sites in the Caribbean (cultural, natural and mixed) have been designated World Heritage sites.[2] So far, no site in Trinidad and Tobago has been given World Heritage status; although the Banwari Trace archaeological site, the La Brea Pitch Lake and the Tobago Main Ridge Forest Reserve are on the tentative list for consideration as World Heritage sites (Susan Shurland, secretary general, Trinidad and Tobago National Commission for UNESCO, pers. comm. 2016).

SOME GENERAL COMMENTS ON THE RED HOUSE SITE WITH RESPECT TO ARCHAEOLOGICAL HERITAGE MANAGEMENT AND VALUES-BASED HERITAGE MANAGEMENT

The Red House site is enigmatic. It is not a World Heritage site. It is not even gazetted and protected under the Trinidad and Tobago National Trust Act (1991).[3] The management of archaeological activity at the Red House site did not fall under the auspices of the National Trust of Trinidad and Tobago (the country's primary heritage agency) but instead was both administratively spearheaded and funded by the Office of the Parliament of the Republic of Trinidad and Tobago.

Perhaps the decision to undertake the archaeological project was a function of where the discoveries were made. They were made in the basement of a government building that has been the seat of Trinidad and Tobago parliament for over one hundred years, a building with considerable iconic and historical importance to the people of Trinidad and Tobago. Further, the presence of Amerindian burials (confirmed by radiocarbon dates) made the Red House site sacred to the First Peoples of Trinidad and Tobago. The initial discoveries at the Red House also generated intense media attention both locally and regionally. Given these circumstances, the then Government of Trinidad and Tobago took the decision to launch, facilitate and fund archaeological activity at the Red House. This approach was deemed necessary to recover finds of local, regional and international significance, and by so doing set the example for the rest of the twin island republic and the Caribbean region.

THE HISTORY OF THE RED HOUSE RESTORATION ARCHAEOLOGICAL PROJECT

In March 2013, possible human bones were discovered in the basement of the Red House in Port of Spain, Trinidad. Results of bioarchaeological analysis and radiocarbon dating confirmed that the finds were indeed human bones, dating to about 430 CE. From 1 July 2013 to 31 January 2015, the Office of the Parliament and the UDeCOTT, supporting and working in conjunction with lead archaeologist Dr Basil Reid, successfully completed one of the largest archaeological projects in the anglophone Caribbean. The government, through its funding and appointment of a committee to oversee the discovery of the bones and historical cultural materials, ensured the inclusion of the main stakeholders, particularly the Carib and First Peoples' communities, and this enriched the quality and purpose of the project.

Since 1997 there have been several unsuccessful attempts to restore the Red House, the traditional home of Trinidad and Tobago's parliament. Over time the client, project manager, and design strategy and methodology have changed, and in 2011 the cabinet agreed to a revised project for the restoration of the Red House based on the 2000 project. UDeCOTT, which had been associated with restoration attempts from 2003, was retained as the project manager, and the Office of the Parliament replaced the Office of the Prime Minister as the client. The designs and methodology were altered and now involved the excavation of several small test pits throughout the length and breadth of the Red House along the building's foundation for structural inspection works.

Preliminary Actions

Excavations for the project were undertaken by the contractor Amcoweld Engineering Services Limited, a company hired by UDeCOTT. Subsequent to the initial discovery on 26 March 2013, followed by other discoveries, the Office of the Parliament convened a meeting at the Red House site on 7 April 2013. Among those present were archaeologist, the late Peter Harris; the late Louis B. Homer, representing the Ministry of National Diversity and Social Integration; anthropologist Dr Kumar Mahabir; Ricardo Bharath, chief of the Santa Rosa Carib community; ethnographer Patricia Elie; Rhoda Bharath, lecturer at the University of the West Indies; Rudylynn De Four Roberts, parliamentary consultant; and Neil Jaggassar, project administrator.

Figure 11.1. Meeting held on 19 April 2013 on the third floor, Office of the Parliament. *From right to left*: Jacqui Sampson-Meiguel (back to camera), clerk of the House, Office of the Parliament; Rudylynn De Four Roberts, parliament's consultant architect; Peter Harris, archaeologist (deceased); Neil Jaggassar, project administrator, Office of the Parliament; Mike TamWarao Elder (San Fernando); Franklin Richard, Carieta (Great Hawk) Second Elder, South Western Peninsula Council of Elders of the Warao People; Rabina Shar, informal leader of the People of Warao Descent and spokesperson and general secretary. Courtesy of the Office of the Parliament of the Republic of Trinidad and Tobago.

Two days later the Office of the Parliament facilitated the examination of selected discoveries by forensic pathologist Dr Valery Alexandov at the Forensic Sciences Centre of Trinidad and Tobago, who confirmed that human bones and human skeletal parts were among the remains. Based on these preliminary assessments, an archaeological excavation team was immediately assembled by the Office of the Parliament to carefully retrieve all human skeletal remains and artefacts. This team was headed by Peter Harris and included nine field assistants.

Following more discoveries of a similar nature, the clerk of the house, Office of the Parliament, held a meeting on 19 April 2013 with UDeCOTT's site construction staff, a representative of the National Trust of Trinidad and Tobago, values-based heritage management consultants, the archaeologist (the late Peter Harris), a legal officer, and three groups representing the Trinidad and Tobago Amerindian and First Peoples' communities (figure 11.1). It was agreed that the Office of the Parliament would make arrangements for further testing of the bones, as requested by the on-site archaeologist.

Expert Testing

The Office of the Parliament arranged for samples of the historical cultural material that was discovered to be analysed for DNA at D. Andrew Merriwether's Ancient DNA and Forensic Lab at Binghamton University, New York, and at Beta Analytic, Inc., in Miami, Florida, for $N15/N14$ isotope ratios and $C14$ (radiocarbon dating) testing. The Office of the Parliament also contracted Ecotex Environmental Services Limited to analyse soil samples from the Red House compound, the Port of Spain Foreshore, and the hill contiguous to the old Government Lime Kiln in Laventille. Soil sampling at Laventille was considered important, as soil from the Eastern Quarry site in Laventille was used to backfill the original Red House building in 1844 as well as the second Red House building in 1906/7 (Reid 2015).

Recommendation for Appointment of the Committee

On 6 May 2013 representatives of the Office of the Parliament, the National Trust of Trinidad and Tobago, archaeological specialists and consultants, and a representative of UDeCOTT met under the chairmanship of the senate president, the Hononorable Timothy Hamel-Smith, to consider issues relative to the discovery. The meeting discussed the international standards and protocols that should be followed for the handling of such historical cultural finds, public relations issues, security matters and the implications of the discovery on the project work schedule.

The Office of the Parliament knew that the Republic of Trinidad and Tobago is a signatory to the United Nations Declaration on the Rights of Indigenous Peoples. It was therefore agreed that if the cultural material discovered under the Red House was not handled with respect and due dignity, the entire values-based heritage management could be enveloped in adverse and undesirable controversy.

After receiving the radiocarbon results, the Speaker of the House and president of the senate sent a note to the cabinet recommending the establishment of a Red House historical cultural heritage team to manage all aspects of the archaeological findings and to ensure conformity with best practices and international protocols. The cabinet agreed, and a committee comprising the following officers was appointed:

- Speaker of the House of Representatives (chair)
- President of the senate (vice-chair)
- Clerk of the House
- Permanent secretary, Ministry of National Diversity and Social Integration
- Project administrator, Red House Restoration Unit, Office of the Parliament
- Legal officer, Office of the Parliament
- Chair, Archaeological Sub-Committee of the National Trust of Trinidad and Tobago
- Librarian, Office of the Parliament
  Director, Corporate Communications, Office of the Parliament
- Representative of values-based heritage management manager, UDeCOTT

Committee Meetings and Recommendations

This committee met on three occasions from the date of its appointment on 20 June 2013 to the termination of phase 1 of the archaeological project on 31 January 2015. On each occasion that the committee met, representatives from the Santa Rosa Carib community, Partners for First Peoples' Development, People of Warao Descent and Western Peninsula Council of Elders of the Warao People were present. At their request, the First People's communities were allowed to hold religious ceremonies on the grounds of the Red House. The cabinet-appointed team agreed in principle that all skeletal remains of the First Peoples' ancestors recovered from the site should be reinterred in a suitable spot on the grounds of the Red House, with an appropriate insignia indicating the significance of the area. Further, the cabinet-appointed team gave the assurance that they would continue to work closely with the First Peoples and the lead archaeologist and his team with a view to ensuring the respectful treatment and analysis of human remains recovered from the site.

The Launch of the Red House Restoration Archaeological Project

Subsequent to the untimely demise of Peter Harris in May 2013, the Office of the Parliament secured the services of Dr Basil Reid, senior lecturer in archaeology at the University of the West Indies, St Augustine, as the lead archaeologist in June of that year. The Office of the Parliament organized meetings with the lead archaeologist, UDeCOTT, the historical architects and the engineers, CEP Limited. Dr Reid outlined a plan of action that was divided into (a) the archaeological retrieval phase, (b) the finds processing phase and (c) the cataloguing phase. He supplied the Office of the Parliament with a budget and advised the Office of the Parliament of the composition of the team that would be working with him during the archaeological retrieval phase.

In order to concentrate fully on this project, Dr Reid applied for no-pay leave from the UWI. This was granted, and he assembled a group of workers including university students, some of whom had previously worked on archaeological sites. He conducted a one-day seminar at UWI for the persons who had applied to work. As the project unfolded, Dr Reid formed a network of specialists in various disciplines to provide assistance when needed. These specialists, both foreign and locally based, included:

Dr Lars Fehren-Schmitz (Assistant Professor in Anthropology, University of California, Santa Cruz)

Dr R. Grant Gilmore III (Associate Professor of Archaeology and Addlestone Chair in Historic Preservation, College of Charleston, South Carolina)

Cecil Hodge (Land Surveyor)

John Krigburm (Associate Professor of Anthropology, University of Florida)

Dr Mary E. Malainey (Professor of Anthropology and chair, Brandon University, Canada)

Dr Andrew A. Merriwether (Associate Professor of Anthropology, Binghamton University, New York)

Patrisha L. Meyers (Graduate Student, University of Central Florida, Orlando)

Dr Dolores Piperno (Smithsonian Tropical Research Institute, Panama City)

Dr John J. Schultz (Associate Chair, Department of Anthropology, University of Central Florida, Orlando)

Dr Michael Sutherland (Lecturer in Land Management, Department of Geomatics Engineering and Land Management Faculty of Engineering, the University of the West Indies)

Professor Brent Wilson (Professor of Paleontology And Geology, the University of the West Indies, St Augustine)

Request for and Disbursement of Funds

In separate notes sent to the cabinet by the Speaker of the House of Representatives, the Office of the Parliament requested the allocation of funds to support the project. Whenever necessary, arrangements were made with the comptroller of accounts for overseas payments by wire transfer for services rendered by foreign-based professionals. Local professionals were paid by cheque, while arrangements were made with the comptroller of accounts for payment to the archaeological workers to be made in cash fortnightly. The Office of the Parliament provided funds received from the cabinet to defer the cost of goods and services for the project. In total, the Office of the Parliament expended approximately TTD$11,000,000 (US$1,630,222) for phase 1 of the Red House Archaeological Project.

The Development of the Archaeological Information System

Dr Michael Sutherland designed and developed the Red House geographic information system (GIS) and archaeological information system (AIS). This was the first such system developed in the field of archaeology for the Port of Spain area and represented an important milestone in automated data capture in Trinidad and Tobago (see chapter 10, this volume).

Role of UDeCOTT

As project manager, UDeCOTT provided a variety of services, including consultancy, engagement of security, maintenance and construction companies for the protection of the site, maintenance of the grounds, and construction and remedial works to be done on the Red House building. Following the engagement of Dr Basil Reid as lead archaeologist, UDeCOTT advised that he and his staff should have easily recognizable identification badges which must be worn at all times, especially to gain entry to the compound. UDeCOTT also advised that members of the archaeology crew must wear personal protective equipment when on the Red House grounds and while working in the pits and crawl spaces. The project manager also arranged for a training session on health and safety issues with Zaheer Mohammed, safety officer of the on-site Amcoweld Engineering Services Limited.

In addition to the excavation of inspection pits, the work involved the excavation of approximately 4,000 cubic metres of soil from within the building (figures 11.2 and 11.3). This soil was from inspection pits and crawl spaces on the eastern and western length of the building and rotunda area. The concrete floors, and in some places the wooden flooring, had to be removed. This was

Figure 11.2.
From front to back:
Adrian Maraj,
Dion Carrington
and Caleb Lewis
engaged in
excavation.

done by Amcoweld under a small works contract negotiated with UDeCOTT. Safety bridges with hand rails were also installed by Amcoweld to provide the archaeological staff with safe and easy access across the already excavated crawl spaces.

During the Archaeological Restoration Project from 1 July 2013 to 31 January 2015, UDeCOTT coordinated a programme of weekly progress meetings. These meetings were usually held on Thursdays and helped to build good working relationships between all on-site personnel. Attending these meetings were the lead archaeologist or his representative, the engineers, the parliamentary consultant architect and engineer, the project administrator, representatives of Amcoweld Engineering Services Limited and UDeCOTT. At the first of these

Figure 11.3.
Kevin Ali (*left*),
Aaron Maxwell
(*centre*) and Keith
Guevara (*right*)
engaged in sieving.

weekly meetings, Atiba De Souza of UDeCOTT advised that in accordance with
law, in particular the Workmen's Compensation Act Ch. 88:05, all personnel on
the site must have insurance coverage, including those engaged in archaeological
work. As a consequence, workmen's compensation insurance was secured by the
Office of the Parliament with Colonial Fire and General Insurance Company
Limited through Brokers Risk Management Limited.

The first phase of the Red House Restoration Archaeological Project cul-
minated with the lead archaeologist negotiating an arrangement with Dr John
J. Schultz of the Department of Anthropology, University of Central Florida,
which resulted in the Office of the Parliament entering into an agreement for
Dr Schultz and his graduate student Patrisha L. Meyers to visit Trinidad to
conduct an osteological analysis of the human skeletons recovered during the
Red House Archaeological Project. Patrisha Meyers arrived in Trinidad on 14
December 2014, while Dr Schultz arrived on 2 January 2015. He returned on 13
January 2015 and Ms Meyers's visit was extended to 28 January 2015.

Dr Schultz's and Ms Meyers's arrivals coincided with ongoing finds processing
and cataloguing phase of the project. They were able to reconstruct and analyse
several skeletons. During their stay, several aspects of their work were captured
on film by the parliament's Corporate Communications and Productions Unit,
which will eventually be shown on the Parliament Channel in Trinidad and
Tobago. Dr Shultz and Ms Meyers produced an extensive and detailed report
on their findings, which is available in the parliament's library. This report is
an asset to anyone interested in the Red House Restoration Archaeological
Project. In addition to the payment of fees and stipends, their accommodation
was provided by the Office of the Parliament.

Tours

During phase 1 of the Red House project, tours of the site were organized for the following: the former Speaker of the House, Honourable Wade Mark and his retinue, and the former president of the senate, Honourable Timothy Hamel Smith. Tours were also organized for history/archaeology undergraduate students from the University of the West Indies, St Augustine, and teachers and students from Pleasantville Secondary School in San Fernando (Trinidad and Tobago).

PUBLICIZING THE RED HOUSE RESTORATION
ARCHAEOLOGICAL PROJECT

Phase 1 of the Red House Restoration Archaeological Project officially ended on 31 January 2015. However, before and since that time, there have been some important developments relating to sensitizing the general public to the project. In August 2015 a 465-page report detailing the research data generated by phase 1 of the project was submitted to the Office of the Parliament by Dr Basil Reid. The report was a record of archaeological findings relating to both the pre-colonial and colonial periods. Appended to this document were other reports written by project specialists. Copies of the report have been distributed to all members of parliament in Trinidad and Tobago; to the National Library of Trinidad and Tobago; to the Heritage Library and the National Archives in Trinidad and Tobago; to the Alma Jordan Library of the University of the West Indies, St Augustine; and to project scholars and key scholars in the twin island republic and beyond who have shown an interest in the project. An electronic copy of the report is also available on UWISpace at the Alma Jordan Library at the UWI, St Augustine, thereby making the report accessible to library users on all four campuses of the University of the West Indies.

In order to sensitize the public to the value of the Red House, two articles on the project were published in the *Trinidad Express*: one on 18 May 2015 and the other on 16 and 17 February 2016. The articles, published under the heading "UWI Research in Action", were authored by Dr Basil Reid and members of his archaeological crew. The publication of these was facilitated by both of the Office of the Campus Principal and Marketing and Communications at the University of the West Indies, St Augustine. On 5 May 2016, Professor Bridget Brereton wrote an article on the project in the *Trinidad Express* entitled "An Amerindian Settlement in the City".

Scholarly Works

The Red House project has also spawned a number of scholarly works. In 2016, Patrisha L. Meyers, the forensic anthropologist graduate student from the University of Central Florida who worked at the site in January 2015, completed and successfully defended her master's thesis entitled "Bioarchaeological Investigations of a Unique Pre-Columbian Caribbean Population: Demography and Paleopathology at the Red House Archaeological Site, Port of Spain (Trinidad)". Makini Emmanuel, who was a finds processing manager at the Red House site, is currently working on her MA in heritage studies at the University of the West Indies (Department of History and Archaeology), Mona, Jamaica. The topic of her thesis is "Colonial Bottles from the Red House Site, Port of Spain (Trinidad)".

In September 2015, a poster on the Archaeology of the Red House site was featured at the UWI-NGC Research Expo on the St Augustine campus. On 13 November 2015, Dr Reid gave a PowerPoint presentation entitled "The Precolonial Archaeology of the Red House Site (Port of Spain, Trinidad)" at the University of the West Indies, St Augustine, and in April 2016, a poster entitled "Life in the Caribbean: An Overview of Skeletal Pathology from the Red House Archaeological Site, Port of Spain, Trinidad" by Patrisha Meyers was presented at the 2016 Paleopathology Association (PPA) Conference in Atlanta, Georgia. Additionally, in October 2016 a paper entitled "The Precolonial Red House Site in Port of Spain (Trinidad and Tobago)", co-authored by Dr Reid, Patrisha Meyers and John Schultz, was submitted to Professor Theodore Lewis, chair of the Ministry of Education Textbook Project on the History of Trinidad and Tobago. This submission will be part of a collection of essays that are expected to be published by the Government of Trinidad and Tobago. Copies of the book will be made available to members of the public, including schoolchildren.

Proposed Museum

There are plans by the Government of Trinidad and Tobago to establish a museum at the Red House site after all of the renovation works have been completed. The museum will showcase a selection of artefacts and biofacts recovered from the site relating to both the pre-colonial and colonial periods. However, in deference to the wishes of the First Peoples of Trinidad and Tobago, the human remains of their ancestors will not be displayed; instead, these remains will be reinterred on the grounds of the Red House.

DISCUSSION AND CONCLUSION

The values associated with the Red House are multifaceted. The Red House site holds political significance, as the building was the seat of Trinidad and Tobago's parliament for one hundred years. The site also has much historical significance. During the colonial period, it was both the venue for meetings between British governors and members of the legislative council and the scene of social gatherings involving invited dignitaries and members of the local elite. In 1897, as Trinidad was preparing to celebrate the Diamond Jubilee of Queen Victoria, the buildings were given a coat of red paint, and the public promptly referred to them thereafter as the Red House. It was also the scene of the water riots of 1903, which led to the building being gutted by fire and subsequently rebuilt in 1907. In addition, in July 1990 the Red House was the site of the Jamaat al Muslimeen coup attempt, during which the prime minister and other members of the government were held hostage for six days and twenty-four people were killed. Prior to 2000/2001 the Red House was utilized by members of the public for civil marriage ceremonies as well as for the registration of births, deaths and land titles. Generations of schoolchildren in Trinidad and Tobago grew up hearing about the importance of the Red House from their parents, teachers and other caregivers.

The Red House site also bears both cultural and archaeological significance. It represents one of the most important archaeological discoveries in Trinidad and Tobago. Based on radiocarbon dates, it is clear that from 125 to 1395 CE the site was continuously inhabited by a pre-colonial Amerindian community. It was also occupied during the colonial period from 1843–1844 to the present. The Red House is considered architecturally significant because of its Beaux-Arts style. The building itself has symbolic significance, given its relative longevity as an icon in the heart of Port of Spain. And due to the discovery of several Amerindian human burials, the First Peoples of the twin island republic revere the Red House as a sacred site, so in this regard the Red House has religious significance. The project therefore had to satisfy the often-competing interests of its diverse stakeholders, namely, the government, the academic community, the First Peoples and the general public.

There are a number of challenges that many territories in the Caribbean continue to face concerning archaeological heritage management. Against this background, the Red House Restoration Archaeological Project is indeed encouraging and can be considered a quintessential example of both archaeological and values-based heritage management in Trinidad and Tobago and the wider Caribbean. The project is a stellar example of efforts taken to mitigate adverse effects to a significant heritage resource in Trinidad and Tobago. Excavations and analyses, public outreach, and community engagement in the form of tours, newspaper articles, and scholarly works have all helped to make the project a major success. The Government of the Republic of Trinidad and Tobago, through the Office of the Parliament, has facilitated, organized and funded a worthwhile endeavour. The research data generated by this project will remain an integral part of the rich historical and archaeological legacy of the twin island republic for several generations to come.

NOTES

1. According to UNESCO (http://whc.unesco.org/en/guidelines [as of 2015]; accessed 24 November 2016), World Heritage status may be ascribed if the property is of outstanding universal value, i.e., if it meets one or more of the following criteria:
   a. Represents a masterpiece of human creative genius;
   b. Exhibits an important interchange of human values, over a span of time or within a cultural area of the world, on developments in architecture or technology, monumental arts, town-planning or landscape design;
   c. Bears a unique or at least exceptional testimony to a cultural tradition or to a civilization which is living or which has disappeared;
   d. Is an outstanding example of a type of building, architectural or technological ensemble or landscape which illustrates a significant stage(s) in human history;
   e. Is an outstanding example of a traditional human settlement, land use, or sea use which is representative of a culture (or cultures), or human interaction with the environment especially when it has become vulnerable under the impact of irreversible change;
   f. Is directly or tangibly associated with events or living traditions, with ideas, or with beliefs, with artistic and literary works of outstanding universal significance;
   g. Contains superlative natural phenomena or areas of exceptional natural beauty and aesthetic importance;
   h. Is an outstanding example that represents major stages of earth's history, including the record of life, significant ongoing geological processes in the development of landforms, or significant geomorphic or physiographic features;
   i. Is an outstanding example that represents significant ongoing ecological and biological processes in the evolution and development of terrestrial, freshwater, coastal and marine ecosystems, and communities of plants and animals;
   j. Contains the most important and significant natural habitats for in-situ conservation of biological diversity, including those containing threatened species of Outstanding Universal Value from the point of view of science or conservation;
   k. Must also meet the conditions of integrity and/or authenticity and must have an adequate protection and management system to ensure its safeguarding.
2. Among the World Heritage sites in the sites are Barbados's Historic Bridgetown and its Garrison (Cultural, 2011); Cuba's Old Havana and its Fortification System

(Cultural, 1982) and Trinidad and the Valley de los Ingenios (Cultural, 1988), San Pedro de la Roca Castle, Santiago de Cuba (Cultural, 1997), Desembarco del Granma National Park (Natural, 1999), Viñales Valley (Cultural, 1999) and the Archaeological Landscape of the First Coffee Plantations in the South-East of Cuba (Cultural, 2000); Curacao's Historic Area of Willemstad, Inner City and Harbour (Cultural, 1997); St Lucia's Pitons Management Area (Natural, 2004); Suriname's Central Suriname Nature Reserve (Natural, 2000) and the Historic Inner City of Paramaribo (Cultural, 2002); Puerto Rico's La Fortaleza and San Juan National Historic Site (Cultural, 1983); Belize's Barrier Reef Reserve System (Natural, 1996); and Jamaica's Blue and John Crow Mountains (Natural, 2015).

3.   To date, thirteen sites have been gazetted and protected under the Trinidad and Tobago National Trust Act (1991). They are Queen's Royal College, Hayes Court, Roomor/Ambard's House, Mille Fleur, Archbishop's Palace, Whitehall, Stollmeyer's Castle, Fort King George (Tobago), Banwari Trace Archaeological Site, Tranquillity Methodist Church, Old Mayaro Post Office, Royal Victoria Institute and Fort Picton.

REFERENCES

Ababneh, A. 2016. "Management and Interpretation: Challenges to Heritage Site-Based Values, Reflections from the Heritage Site of Umm Qais, Jordan". *Journal of the World Archaeological Congress* 12 (1): 38–72.

Australia ICOMOS. 2000. "The Burra Charter: The Australia ICOMOS Charter for Places of Cultural Significance 1999, with Associated Guidelines and Code on the Ethics of Coexistence". http://australia.icomos.org/wp-content/uploads/The-Burra-Charter -2013-Adopted-31.10.2013.pdf.

Bérard, B., and C. Stouvenot. 2011. "French West Indies". In Siegel and Righter 2011, 80–89.

de la Torre, M. 2013. "Values and Heritage Conservation". *Heritage and Society* 6 (2): 155–66.

de la Torre, M., and D. Throsby. 2002. *Assessing the Values of Cultural Heritage: Research Report*. Los Angeles: Getty Conservation Institute.

Doumas, C.G. 2013. "Managing the Archaeological Heritage: The Case of Akrotiri, Thera (Santorini)". *Conservation and Management of Archaeological Sites* 15 (1): 109–20.

Farmer, K. 2011. "Barbados". In Siegel and Righter 2011, 112–24.

Haviser, J.B., and R.G. Gilmore III. 2011. "Netherlands Antilles". In Siegel and Righter 2011, 134–42.

Hofman, C.L., and J.B. Haviser, eds. 2015. *Managing Our Past into the Future: Archaeological Heritage Management in the Dutch Caribbean*. Leiden: Sidestone Press.

International Committee on Archaeological Heritage Management. 1990. *ICOMOS Charter for the Protection and Management of the Archaeological Heritage*. Paris: International Council on Monuments and Sites. http://icahm.icomos.org/documents/charter.htm l#anchor201504. Accessed 19 April 2018.

Mason, R. 2002. "Assessing Values in Conservation Planning: Methodological Issues and Choices". In *Assessing the Values of Cultural Heritage Research Report*, edited by M. de la Torre, 5–30. Los Angeles: Getty Conservation Institute. http://www.getty.edu /conservation/publications_resources/pdf_publications/pdf/assessing.pdf.

Mason, R., M. Maclean and M. de La Torre. 2003. *Hadrian's Wall World Heritage Site: A Case Study*. Los Angeles: Getty Conservation Institute.

Pateman, M.P. 2011. "The Bahamas". In Siegel and Righter 2011, 1–8.

Prieto Vicioso, E. 2011. "Dominican Republic". In Siegel and Righter 2011, 35–45.

Reid, B.A. 2015. *Red House Restoration Archaeology Report, Phase 1, for the Period July 1, 2013–January 31, 2015*. Port of Spain: Office of the Parliament of the Republic of Trinidad and Tobago.

Reid, B.A., and V. Lewis. 2011. "Trinidad and Tobago". In Siegel and Righter 2011, 125–33.

Siegel, P.E. 2011a. "Intersecting Values in Caribbean Heritage Preservation". In Siegel and Righter 2011, vii–xi.

———. 2011b. "Protecting Heritage in the Caribbean". In Siegel and Righter 2011, 152–62.

———. 2011c. "Puerto Rico". In Siegel and Righter 2011, 46–57.

———. 2014. "Archaeological Heritage Management". In Siegel and Righter 2011, 47–51.

Siegel, P.E., and E. Righter, eds. 2011. *Protecting Heritage in the Caribbean*. Tuscaloosa: University of Alabama Press.

Siegel, P.E., C.L. Hofman, B. Bérard, R. Murphy, J.U. Hung, R.V. Rojas and C. White. 2013. "Confronting Caribbean Heritage in an Archipelago of Diversity: Politics, Stakeholders, Climate Change, Natural Disasters, Tourism, and Development". *Journal of Field Archaeology* 38:376–90.

Glossary of Terms

acid. A solution with a pH less than 7 (neutral); a solution in which the hydronium ion concentration is higher than the hydroxide ion concentration; a substance that readily donates protons to form hydronium ions.

adorno. A relief ornament applied to a ceramic piece.

aliquot. A fractional portion of a larger amount of material.

amide. An organic compound that contains a carbonyl group attached to a nitrogen atom.

anhydrous. Without water; containing no water.

anion. An atom that carries a negative charge because the number of electrons is greater than the number of protons.

antemortem. Trauma occurring during life that is generally identified by signs of healing.

anthropogenic. Anthropogenic isotopic values, such as Pb, result from modern human activities (e.g., the nuclear processing of fuels) such that the inherent isotopic signature of the sample is contaminated.

ArcGIS. A GIS, created by Environmental Systems Research Institute, containing a suite of programs designed to manage and analyse geospatial data.

archaeological heritage management. According to the International Committee on Archaeological Heritage Management (ICAHM), "'archaeological heritage' . . . comprises all vestiges of human existence and consists of places relating to all manifestations of human activity, abandoned structures, and remains of all kinds . . . together with all the portable cultural material associated with them" (ICAHM 1990: Article 1). "Protection and proper management [of archaeological heritage] is . . . essential to enable . . . scholars to study and interpret it . . . on behalf of . . . present and future generations" (ICAHM 1990: introduction).

archaeometry. The application of scientific methods and technology to archaeological study. It can also be defined as the *"use of scientific techniques to determine the ages of archaeological specimens as well as their places and circumstances of origin"*.

ArcMap. The main program in the ArcGIS suite of programs, used to create, edit, map and analyse geospatial data.

ArcScene. An ArcGIS program used to visualize geospatial data in 2D and 3D.

atom. A particle consisting of a nucleus containing protons and neutrons surrounded by electrons, except for hydrogen, which consists of only one electron and one proton; the smallest portion of an element that retains its fundamental properties.

autosampler. A device that automatically loads the next sample into an instrument when analysis of the previous sample is complete.

archaeology. The systematic study of past human life and culture through the recovery and examination of remaining material evidence, such as graves, buildings, tools and pottery.

AutoCad. A commercial computer aided design (CAD) and drafting software application. Developed and marketed by Autodesk, AutoCAD was first released in December 1982 as a desktop app running on microcomputers with internal graphics controllers.

BCE. The abbreviation for Before the Common Era or Before the Current Era, BCE is the alternative name for the calendar era also known as Before Christ, or BC. Since BC is of a Christian nature, the more inclusive BCE has become the preferred label in secular writing. Both BCE and BC label years before the first year in the Gregorian Calendar. For example, an artefact dated to 3017 years before writing of this description (in year 2017) belongs to year 1000 BCE, or 1000 BC.

Beaux-Arts style. Developed in the last decades of the nineteenth century. The name is taken from the École des Beaux Arts in Paris which was put under direct state control by Napoleon III. Beaux-Arts buildings are massive, usually constructed with stone, with a symmetrical *façade* or front, and flat or low-pitched roofs. The façade of Beaux-Arts buildings typically features adornment reminiscent of Greek and Roman Architecture, such as *balustrades*, or vertical posts, on *balconies* (a porch that protrudes from a building), held up by large decorative pillars called *columns*, arched windows and grand arched entryways topped with triangular gables called *pediments*. Building details and decorations are elaborate and include 3-dimensional carved panels called *bas-relief* and rounded convex surfaces called *cartouches*. These are typically surrounded by *garlands* or vines, decorative *swags* (garlands raised up in the middle) and *medallions* or medal-like ornamentation. Interiors typically have grand stairways and polished marble floors. Arched doorways lead to large rooms and decorations inside the buildings are as ornate as those on the exterior.

Government buildings built in the Beaux-Arts style typically have high, vaulted ceilings and central domes.

beta (β)-sitosterol. A sterol found in plant tissue; a structural lipid present in cell membranes.

biological affinity. A term used to describe the ancestral group to which the individual was most likely associated.

biological profile. A profile or description of an individual made from their skeletal remains, which includes the attribution of sex, estimation of age, stature (height), attribution of ancestry and any identifying previous injuries or diseases affecting the skeleton.

biomarker. A molecule associated with a narrow range of substances, or the presence and distribution of certain types of lipid, that enables a residue to be identified with a high degree of precision.

bivalve. Molluscs of the class Bivalvia, such as oysters and clams, that have a shell made of two valves or parts and an umbo at the top of each valve.

bricolage. *Bricolage* is the construction or creation of a work from a diverse range of things that happen to be available, or a work created by mixed media. The term *bricolage* has also been used in many fields, including anthropology, philosophy, critical theory, education, computer software and business.

bricoleur. A person who engages in *bricolage*.

carapace. The hard anterior or top shell of crustaceans and turtles.

carbohydrate. An organic compound produced by plants that can be broken down into monosaccharides; a group of compounds that includes sugars, starches and cellulose.

carboxylic acid. An organic compound with a carboxyl group at the end of a carbon chain, named by replacing the -e of the corresponding alkane with -oic acid.

CE. The abbreviation for Common Era or Current Era, CE is the alternative name for the calendar era also known as Anno Domini, or AD (Medieval Latin for "in the year of the Lord"). Since AD is of a Christian nature, the more inclusive CE has become the preferred label in secular writing. Both CE and AD label years in the Gregorian calendar. For example, this description was written in year 2017, or 2017 CE.

chelae. The claw or pincer appendage of crabs and other crustaceans.

chloritic schist. Is usually metamorphosed from basalt in a low-grade metamorphic condition. Since basalt contains no quartz, chlorite schist does not contain quartz either.

cholesterol. The major sterol in animal tissue; a structural lipid present in cell membranes.

chromatography. The name given to techniques used to separate a sample mixture, carried by a mobile phase, into its constituent compounds through their differential interactions with a stationary phase.

commensals. Organisms that participate in commensalism (interaction between two species in which one benefits and the other neither benefits nor loses).

compound. A pure substance made up of more than one element in fixed proportions; a substance made up of identical molecules.

cranial modification. Modification of an individual's head which occurs as a result of intentional binding of the soft bones of an infant's skull with boards or cords, or the unintentional modification which occurs as a result of the repeated positioning of an infant's skull in such a way that the bones are modified.

culturally modified biological traits. Biological traits that are modified or change through cultural behaviors such as artificial cranial modification and extreme dental wear.

cyclical time. Cyclical time, characteristic of many non-Western societies, emphasizes repetition and is very much influenced by the cycles apparent in the natural world. In all likelihood, the Amerindians of Trinidad and Tobago had a predominantly cyclical time conception. Based on South American/Antillean cosmology, their time conception was heavily focused on birth, death, burial rites, interment, rebirth, renewal, propagation and ancestor veneration. For more contemporary groups, such as the Luo people of western Kenya, time, or history, is also cyclical, comprising a host of temporal measures involving life, generational and ritual cycles.

delta value. Stable isotope compositions that denote the portion of an element that is present in the analysed sample are expressed in terms of delta values (δ) relative to the isotopic ratio of the standard.

demersal. The part of the marine environment near to or directly above the sea floor.

dental wear. Wear caused to the teeth as a result of diet consisting of coarse food, or abrasive substances introduced to the food during processing, as well as the use of teeth as tools.

DNA. DNA is deoxyribonucleic acid and is a molecule in the human body that stores genetic information. DNA can be used to identify relatedness between different individuals and populations, and ancient DNA can often be obtained from well-preserved tissue, including bone/teeth.

dominance. A calculation of the most abundant species using the Berger-

Parker Index. In the case of linear distributions, the fraction of total sampled individuals that is contributed by the most abundant species, known as the Berger-Parker Index.

electron. A negatively charged subatomic particle that occurs at discrete energy levels around the nucleus of an atom (in the extranuclear space); a subatomic particle with a mass approximately 1,836 times smaller than a proton.

electron impact. In mass spectrometry, a hard ionization technique that involves the destabilization and fragmentation of sample molecules; the most common method of producing ions for mass analysis.

element. A pure substance consisting entirely of atoms with the same number of protons; substances that appear in the Periodic Table of Elements.

elite exchange. Elite exchange can be defined as gift-giving among elite groups with the purpose of building alliances locally and regionally.

ester. An organic compound containing a carbonyl group linked to an alkyl group through an oxygen atom; organic compounds synthesized from a carboxylic acid and an alcohol in the presence of water.

ethnography. A method used by researchers in many social science fields whereby participant observation of a people, an ethnic group or settlement patterns permits the collection of (mostly empirical) data that are used to interpret various aspects of social, economic and material culture.

ethnohistory. The study of (often non-Western) cultures of the recent past using documentary sources such as the accounts of oral histories and other archival materials, often supplemented with archaeological data.

excavation. The exposure, recording, recovery, processing and analysis of buried cultural material using specialized techniques, skills and careful preparation.

fatty acid. A carboxylic acid with hydrocarbon chains ranging from four to thirty-six carbon atoms in length; saturated fatty acids consist of carbon atoms connected through single bonds; unsaturated fatty acids contain at least one double bond between carbon atoms. The shorthand convention for designating fatty acids, Cx:ywz, contains three components. The "Cx" refers to a fatty acid with a carbon chain length of x number of atoms. The "y" represents the number of double bonds or points of unsaturation. The "wz" indicates the location of the most distal double bond on the carbon chain, that is, closest to the methyl end.

fatty acid methyl esters (FAMES). Derivatives of fatty acids suitable for analysis using gas chromatography, prepared by treating the total lipid extract with methanol in either an acidic or alkali environment in order to release fatty acids attached to the glycerol backbone and replace the hydrogen (H-) of the carboxyl group with a methyl (CH_3-) group.

flame ionization detector (FID). In gas chromatography, a device that measures the time required for a separated component to pass through a column (retention time) and its concentration in the mobile phase.

forensic anthropology. The study of human osteology in medicolegal context with a focus on the identification of biological traits (the biological profile), which can help law enforcement with the identification of human skeletal remains.

gas chromatography (GC). A method of separating individual sample components from a mixture on the basis of volatility and affinity; an analytical technique that involves the vaporization of a liquid sample through progressive heating and transport of vaporized components by a gaseous mobile phase through a fused silica column coated on the interior with a liquid stationary phase.

gas chromatography-mass spectrometry (GC-MS). An analytical technique that enables the mass analysis and identification of components separated from a sample by gas chromatography; an analytical technique that combines gas chromatography with mass spectrometry.

gas chromatography-combustion-isotope ratio mass spectrometry (GC-C-IRMS). An analytical technique used to measure the ratio between two stable isotopes of an element in components separated from a sample by gas chromatography; an analytical technique that combines gas chromatography with isotope ratio mass spectrometry.

gastropod. Molluscs of the class Gastropoda, such as snails, which have a coiled dorsal shell, radula and muscular foot.

geodatabase. A method in ArcGIS to store various geospatial information in one large file (e.g., multiple layers of points, polygons, etc.).

geographic information system (GIS). GIS is a system designed to capture, store, manipulate, analyse, manage and present spatial or geographic data.

global positioning system (GPS). A global navigation satellite system, owned by the Government of the United States of America and operated by the United States Air Force, GPS provides 3D geolocation and time information to GPS receivers.

gorget. An engraved pendant, made of shell, worn around the neck or chest.

half-graben. A geological structure bounded by a fault along one side of its boundaries, unlike a full graben where a depressed block of land is bordered by parallel faults.

haplogroup. When studying genetic relationships with living humans or archaeological skeletons, scientists can identify closely related groups through inherited genetic markers that indicate similar geographic ancestry. The haplogroup is a group of linked alleles in an individual's genome. If two people share a haplogroup, then that they share a common ancestor in the deep past and they also share similar geographic ancestry.

hearth. An archaeological feature/structure representing a fireplace.

historical archaeology. The study of the material remains of past societies that also left behind some other form of historical evidence. Generally covering the period from about 1500 to the Second World War, historical archaeology embraces the interests of a diverse group of scholars representing the disciplines of anthropology, history, geography and folklore. In the New World, historical archaeologists work on a broad range of sites preserved on land and underwater. These sites document early European settlement and its effects on Indigenous peoples, as well the subsequent spread of the frontier and later urbanization and industrialization. By examining the physical and documentary record of these sites, historical archaeologists attempt to discover the fabric of common everyday life in the past and seek to understand the broader historical development of their own and other societies.

history (revisionist definition). Traditional accounts have all too often portrayed prehistoric societies as "cold" and virtually unchanging for centuries or millennia. However, since the 1980s and 1990s, this Eurocentric concept of history has come under heavy academic scrutiny. History is increasingly being defined as embracing all human actions, whether these were recorded orally or in writing or reflected exclusively in the archaeological record.

hydroxide. Compound containing the oxygen-hydrogen (-OH) functional group.

hyperlink. In the context of ArcGIS, a reference link to data not normally included in a map's attribute table (e.g., images; documents etc.).

indigene (pl., indigenes). Indigenous or native person.

intertidal. The area of coastline exposed at low tide and submerged at high tide.

ion. An atom that carries a positive or negative charge because the number of electrons does not match the number of protons.

ion trap. A very compact type of mass analyser that uses constant and oscillating electric fields to control the movement of sample ions; a device that can either sort sample ions according to mass or selectively accumulate a limited number of ions with a desired mass.

ionization. The process of creating ions from electrically neutral atoms or molecules, usually by the removal of electrons.

isomers. Compounds with the same molecular formula that differ with respect to how the atoms are joined. Structural isomers differ with respect to the order in which atoms are joined; stereoisomers differ with respect to the arrangement of atoms in space, but the order in which the atoms are attached is identical.

isotopes. Isotopes are atoms of the same element that have different numbers of neutrons but the same numbers of protons and electrons.

lapidary. A lapidary is an artisan who practices the craft of working, forming and finishing stones, minerals, gemstones and other suitably durable materials (amber, shell, jet, pearl, copal, coral, horn and bone, glass and other synthetics) into functional, decorative or wearable items. Lapidary trade relates to the trading of those items. Indigenous groups such as the Saladoid practised lapidary work and trade.

lead isotopes. Lead (Pb) is composed of four naturally occurring isotopes (^{208}Pb, ^{207}Pb, ^{206}Pb and ^{204}Pb). The abundance of the four Pb isotopes vary in nature due to geological factors such as U, Th, Pb concentrations and age of the bedrock. Traces of Pb, accumulated in human and animal bones and teeth, can be used as "geochemical fingerprints" to discover where an individual has been. Pb replaces some of the calcium in the bone and tooth enamel. This means that by analysing Pb in bones and teeth, we can assess where an individual grew up and lived during his or her childhood and adult years.

linear time. Westerners think of the passage of the human experience along a straight, if branching, highway of time that is durational and irreversible. For example, in linear time, events that occurred on 12 December 1917 or 2 March 2001 can never be repeated and are therefore part of an irreversible time frame. Since the advent of the commoditized hourly clock system of European capitalism, Western linear time has been precisely measured and controlled through the use of watches, clocks and Greenwich Meridian time zones.

lipids. Lipids belong to a class of organic compounds that are fatty acids or their derivatives and are insoluble in water but soluble in organic solvents. They include many natural oils, waxes and steroids, fatty acids, triacylglycerols, terpenes, phospholipids, glycolipids and prostaglandins. Lipids are commonplace in nature and are present in nearly all foodstuffs. As they appear to get trapped in the ceramic matrix of unglazed pottery and remain there intact for centuries, they are potential targets for archaeological residue analysis.

mass spectrometer. An instrument used to produce molecular and elemental ions, sort them according to mass and detect their abundance to establish the composition of naturally occurring materials. There are many different mass spectrometers. An isotope ratio mass spectrometer (IRMS), for example, is used to measure light isotope ratios (e.g., carbon, nitrogen, oxygen) relative to a known standard. Another type of mass spectrometer is an inductively coupled plasma mass spectrometer (ICP-MS), which measures a variety of elemental ratios (e.g., lead and strontium) in ionized form.

metasandstone. A sandstone that has undergone metamorphism to some degree.

micro- (μ-). In the metric system, one thousandth of the base unit of measurement (i.e., metre, gram, litre); in sample analysis and instrumentation, a prefix commonly used for processes or instruments able to handle very small samples.

metric traits. Traits that can be measured and analysed from a statistical point of view.

midden. A refuse deposit left from past human activity, especially in relation to habitation areas. In the Caribbean, lengthy exploitation of a particular location's natural resources may result in significant deposition of refuse such as conch shells, fish and other remains together with fragments of pottery or artefacts of stone or bone. Archaeologists look for middens in their search for new habitation sites in order to better understand foodways and other aspects of past human history. A midden is also called "trash pit" or "trash pile".

millingstone. Any stone slab or basin that is used to process seeds, nuts and similar foods by rubbing, grinding or pounding them against this object with another stone.

MNI. Minimum number of individuals, determined by counts of skeletal parts unique to a species.

mole. The quantity of an element or compound with mass equal to its atomic or molecular weight in grams; 6.022×10^{23} atoms of an element or molecules of a compound.

molecule. A specific combination of elements bonded together to form a particular compound.

molluscs. Invertebrates of the phylum Mollusca, usually with a soft body encased by a calcareous shell.

monounsaturated. Fatty acids that contain one double bond between carbon atoms.

morphological. Based on morphology or shape.

NISP. Number of individual specimens; a count of bones from an identified taxon.

nonmetric traits. Traits that are not measured but which are observed and recorded based on shape or expression.

organic. In chemistry, compounds that contain carbon and are associated with living organisms.

osteology. The study of skeletal remains.

Other. A term used in anthropology in relation to subordinate groups in society such as minorities and women.

oxidation. The reaction between a substance and oxygen; a reaction that increases the oxygen content or decreases the hydrogen content of an organic molecule.

pathological conditions. Abnormal conditions, injuries or expression of disease, which are observable on the skeletal remains.

patrilocal residence. A pattern of residence where males reside in their natal group, while females tend to marry outside their natal group. Patrilocal residence or *patrilocality*, also known as *virilocal residence* or *virilocality*, are terms referring to the social system in which a married couple resides with or near the husband's parents. The concept of location may extend to a larger area such as a village, town or clan territory.

pelagic. The water column of the open ocean, away from the shore and above the bottom of the sea.

Partnership Government. Was a coalition of five political parties, United National Congress, Congress of the People, Movement for Social Justice, Tobago Organization of the People and National Joint Action Committee, with singular agenda to achieve a common goal.

perimortem. An injury which occurs at or around the time of death while the bone still exhibits "wet" or somewhat flexible characteristics. A perimortem injury to bone refers to an injury that most likely contributed to, or led to, death and is recognized as fresh fracture patterns with a lack of healing.

periostracum (pl. periostraca). The chitinous outermost layer of a bivalve's or gastropod's shell, often responsible for the patterns and other physical features of the mollusc.

peroxide. A compound containing two oxygen atoms bonded together in its molecule; a compound containing the O_2^- anion.

phyllite. A fine-grained metamorphic rock with a well-developed laminar structure, intermediate between slate and schist.

phytoliths. Phytoliths (from Greek, "plant stone") are rigid, microscopic structures made of silica, found in some plant tissues and persisting after the decay of the plant. These plants take up silica from the soil, whereupon it is deposited within different intracellular and extracellular structures of the plant. Phytoliths come in varying shapes and sizes. Although some use the term to refer to all mineral secretions by plants, it more commonly refers to siliceous plant remains.

polychrome. Painted or printed in several colours.

polyunsaturated. Fatty acids that contain multiple double bonds between carbon atoms.

postmortem. An injury that occurs after the time of death, after bone has dried out. Postmortem damage corresponds to bone fractures or erosion that occurred in the period after death and is recognized by distinctive dry-fracture patterns.

principal components analysis. An analytical technique used to highlight patterns in a data set.

protein. Giant molecules consisting of individual amino acids linked by peptide bonds. Fibrous proteins occur as long strands or sheets; globular proteins have precise three-dimensional arrangements.

radiocarbon dating. Radiocarbon dating (also referred to as *carbon dating* or *carbon-14 dating*) is a method of determining the age of an object containing organic material by using the properties of radiocarbon (^{14}C), a radioactive isotope of carbon. The method was invented by Willard Libby in the late 1940s and soon became a standard tool for archaeologists. Libby received the Nobel Prize for his work in 1960. The radiocarbon dating method is based on the fact that radiocarbon is constantly being created in the atmosphere by the inter-action of cosmic rays with atmospheric nitrogen. The resulting radiocarbon combines with atmospheric oxygen to form radioactive carbon dioxide, which is incorporated into plants by photosynthesis; animals then acquire ^{14}C by eating the plants. When the animal or plant dies, it stops exchanging carbon with its environment, and from that point onwards the amount of ^{14}C it contains begins to reduce as the ^{14}C undergoes radioactive decay. Measuring the amount of ^{14}C in a sample from a dead plant or animal, such as piece of wood or a fragment of bone, provides information that can be used to calculate when the animal or plant died. The older a sample is, the less ^{14}C there is to be detected and because the half-life of ^{14}C (the period of time after which half of a given sample will have decayed) is about 5,730 years. The age limit for reliable dates using radiocarbon dating is around 50,000 years ago but can be extended to 70,000 years ago with the use of accelerated mass spectrometry (AMS) C14 dating.

retention time. In gas chromatography, the time required for a separated com-ponent to emerge from the column.

scute. The bony plates forming the carapace of turtles or the dermal armour of armadillos.

serpentinite. Serpentinite is a rock composed of one or more serpentine group minerals. Minerals in this group are formed by serpentinization, a hydration and metamorphic transformation of ultramafic rock from the Earth's mantle. The mineral alteration is particularly important at the sea floor at tectonic plate boundaries.

shovel-shaped incisors. Incisors, which have a ridge running along the lin-gual (tongue) side edges of the tooth, giving the impression of a shoveled or indented shape. Shovel-shaped incisors are often indicative of Asian or Native American ancestry.

spatio-temporal data. Data representative of a phenomenon's state in space and time.

species diversity. A calculation of the number of species (species richness) and their relative abundance (species evenness), as depicted by the Shannon Function. Shannon Function, is the classical entropy measure denoted by symbol H-, is extensively used in ecological science as a measure of community and landscape diversity, or, in related forms, as an index of evenness and dominance.

spectrometer. An instrument used to monitor the wavelength and intensity of electromagnetic energy emitted or absorbed by a sample.

spectroscopy. The study of energy emitted or absorbed by matter; an analytical technique that involves monitoring the energy absorbed, emitted or the behavior of molecules in a higher energy or excited state.

stable isotope analysis. Stable isotope analysis of preserved bones and teeth in archaeology is a well-established method to reconstruct past individual diet. Stable isotope ratios of the light elements (e.g., carbon, nitrogen, oxygen) are expressed in delta (δ) notation in parts per mil (‰) and are reported relative to known standards. (Heavy isotope ratios – e.g., lead and strontium – are radiogenic and technically not "stable" isotopes.) Carbon ($\delta^{13}C$) and ($\delta^{15}N$) nitrogen stable isotope ratios of bone collagen can aid in understanding the role of dietary protein in the diet and can distinguish between C_3 and C_4 plants (two very different patterns of plant photosynthesis) and marine and terrestrial resources consumed. Crassulacean acid metabolism (CAM) plants are adapted to arid environments by minimizing photorespiration to conserve water and have intermediate $\delta^{13}C$ values (towards $\delta^{13}C$ values of C_4 plants). Nitrogen stable isotope ratios reflect dietary protein and tend to be quite high (>10‰) in populations dependent upon marine food resources. Carbon and oxygen isotope analysis of bone apatite/tooth enamel apatite can aid in understanding "total" diet, and these data collectively can reveal dietary differences in population sub-groups based on gender, social status and age. Oxygen isotope ratios ($\delta^{18}O$) are complex but reflect waters consumed that may reflect patterns of climate, precipitation and/or water storage. The difference between the $\delta^{13}C$ value of bone apatite and $\delta^{13}C$ of bone collagen (or $\Delta^{13}C_{ap-co}$) is also useful in paleodiet reconstruction. Because bone apatite reflects "total" diet and bone collagen reflects "protein" diet, the collagen-apatite spacing helps to clarify the character of the protein and energy portions of diet. Low spacing (~1–2‰) is typical of C_3-based diets and marine protein, while high spacing (>9‰) is typical of C_4-based diets and terrestrial protein, and intermediate spacing (~5–6‰) denotes a "monoisotopic diet" where protein and dietary carbohydrates are broadly similar in isotopic composition.

starch grain analysis. Starch analysis or starch grain analysis is a technique that is useful in archaeological research to determine plant taxa. In certain samples of food plants, spices, drugs and desiccated archaeological plant matter, the histological elements can survive and thus be identified, but in other samples, like carbonized (burnt) or older materials, this is extremely difficult. However, starch grains are much hardier. The technique relies on the fact that a researcher can analyse or microscopically observe starch grains found on artefacts or in soils. Starch grains, ubiquitous in plants, have individual characteristics and resistance to grinding and drying and even to light burning, so they are often preserved when other plant remains are lost – thus providing an additional tool to understand the past use of plants.

stationary phase. In chromatography, a phase consisting of a solid, gel or liquid over which or through a sample dissolved in a mobile phase passes to facilitate the separation of individual components.

sterols. Structural lipids containing the perhydrocyclopentanophenanthrene ring system; cholesterol is the major sterol in animal tissues; campesterol, stigmasterol and sitosterol are sterols found in plant tissue.

stigmasterol. A sterol found in plant tissue; a structural lipid present in cell membranes.

stratigraphy. The layering of deposits in an archaeological site. Stratigraphy is based on the principle of superposition that states that the layer on the bottom is the oldest; the layer on top is the youngest.

strontium isotopes. Strontium (Sr) is composed of four (^{84}Sr, ^{86}Sr, ^{87}Sr, ^{88}Sr) naturally occurring isotopes. The ratio of ^{87}Sr/^{86}Sr can be used as a "geochemical fingerprint" to decipher geographical location of an individual. Sr isotopes ultimately originate from the local bedrock and are introduced in the human or animal body via bioavailable Sr in the food chain. Sr replaces some of the calcium in bone and tooth enamel. This means that by analysing Sr in bones and teeth, we can use their Sr ratio to assess where that individual may have lived during their childhood and adult years.

swidden. Land cleared for agriculture by slashing and burning vegetation.

Taíno. The Taíno people were one of the indigenous peoples of the Caribbean at the time of Spanish contact. At the time of contact, they were the principal inhabitants of most of the Greater Antilles, the Bahamas and the Virgin Islands.

taxon (pl., taxa). An organism's formal name and situation within Linnaean classification (kingdom, phylum, class, order, family, genus, species), which categorizes living organisms with shared characteristics, descended from a common ancestor.

terpene. A lipid built up from two or more five-carbon isoprene units; the prefixes mono-, sesqui-, di- and tri- indicate compounds containing two, three, four and six isoprene units, respectively.

terpenoid. A terpene containing a hydroxyl group (-OH).

thematic data. In the context of a GIS, data consisting of discrete layers of spatial objects with similar characteristics.

time. The tendency by scholars to present the concepts of history and time as one and the same is reflective of the increasingly prevalent reconceptualization of history. All human actions produce time (or history), and every human act constitutes an event or part of a succession of events. (See *cyclical time*; *linear time*.)

topographical survey. Geospatial measurement and mapping of earth surface features, including contours, buildings, streets, foliage and so forth.

traverse. In the context of topographical surveys, a method for establishing survey control networks.

triacylglycerol. A glycerol molecule to which three fatty acids are bonded through ester linkages.

trigonometric station. A fixed surveying station, used in geodetic and other surveying methods.

values-based heritage management. The coordinated and structured operation of a heritage site with the primary purpose of protecting the significance of the place as defined by designation criteria, government authorities or other owners, experts of various stripes and other citizens with legitimate interests in the place. This is in contrast to traditional-based heritage management, which typically involves decisions and significance assessment mandated by experts and researchers without input from local communities.

volatility. A measure of how readily a liquid substance enters the gaseous phase or vaporizes through evaporation or boiling.

wax. A lipid consisting of a long chain alcohol connected to a long chain fatty acid through an ester.

Contributors

BASIL A. REID is Professor of Archaeology, Department of History, the University of the West Indies, St Augustine, Trinidad and Tobago. He was the lead archaeologist of the Red House Restoration Archaeological Project in the Office of the Parliament of the Republic of Trinidad and Tobago from 1 July 2013 to 31 January 2015.

ZARA ALI worked as a research assistant in the Archaeology Centre at the University of the West Indies, St Augustine, and a finds processing manager for the Red House Restoration Archaeological Project in the Office of the Parliament of the Republic of Trinidad and Tobago.

PATRICK DEGRYSE is Professor of Archaeometry, Department of Earth and Environmental Sciences, and Director, Centre for Archaeological Sciences, Katholieke Universiteit Leuven, Belgium.

LOUISE DEONANAN-DOVER worked on the finds processing team for the Red House Restoration Archaeological Project in the Office of the Parliament of the Republic of Trinidad and Tobago.

MAKINI EMMANUEL worked as a finds processing manager for the Red House Restoration Unit in the Office of the Parliament of the Republic of Trinidad and Tobago.

LANYA FANOVICH is a marine ecologist at the Environmental Research Institute Charlotteville. She worked as an assistant site manager for the Red House Restoration Unit in the Office of the Parliament of the Republic of Trinidad and Tobago.

LARS FEHREN-SCHMITZ is Associate Professor of Biological Anthropology, University of California Santa Cruz, and co-Director of UCSC Paleogenomics, United States.

TIMOTHY FIGOL is a research assistant at the Archaeological Lipid Residue Analysis Laboratory, Department of Anthropology, Brandon University, Manitoba, Canada.

GEORGIA L. FOX is Professor of Anthropology, Department of Anthropology, California State University, Chico, and Director, Museum Studies Program and the Valene L. Smith Museum of Anthropology, United States.

LOVELL FRANCIS is Minister of State, Ministry of Education, Government of the Republic of Trinidad and Tobago, and Member of Parliament for the constituency of Moruga-Tableland.

SADE GRANT worked as a site (excavation) manager of the Red House Restoration Archaeological Project in the Office of the Parliament of the Republic of Trinidad and Tobago.

CORINNE L. HOFMAN is Professor of Caribbean Archaeology, Faculty of Archaeology, Leiden University, the Netherlands.

SARAH HOSEIN is a PhD candidate in the Department of Geomatics Engineering and Land Management, Faculty of Engineering, the University of the West Indies, St Augustine, Trinidad and Tobago.

NEIL JAGGASSAR, now retired, was Clerk of the Senate/Deputy Head of the Office of the Parliament of the Republic of Trinidad and Tobago. He served as the project administrator for the Red House Restoration Project.

GEORGE D. KAMENOV is Associate in Geology, Department of Geological Sciences, University of Florida, Gainesville, United States.

JOHN KRIGBAUM is Associate Professor, Department of Anthropology, University of Florida, Gainesville, United States.

MARY MALAINEY is Professor of Anthropology, Department of Anthropology, Brandon University, Manitoba, Canada.

ANDREW MAURICE worked as a finds processor in the Red House Restoration Archaeological Project in the Office of the Parliament of the Republic of Trinidad and Tobago.

D. ANDREW MERRIWETHER is Professor of Anthropology and of Biology, Binghamton University (State University of New York), and Chair of the Department of Anthropology, United States.

PATRISHA L. MEYERS is Adjunct Professor of Anthropology, Seminole State College and Valencia College, Florida, United States.

BERT NEYT is Postdoctoral Fellow, Department of Earth and Environmental Sciences and the Centre for Archaeological Sciences, Katholieke Universiteit Leuven, Belgium.

SAMUEL REYES worked as site (excavation) manager of the Red House Archaeology Project in the Office of the Parliament of the Republic of Trinidad and Tobago.

MIKE G. RUTHERFORD is Curator, Zoology Museum, the University of the West Indies, St Augustine, Trinidad and Tobago.

JOHN J. SCHULTZ is Professor of Anthropology, University of Central Florida, and holds a secondary joint appointment in the National Center for Forensic Science, University of Central Florida, Orlando, United States.

AMIT SEERAM worked on surveying the physical locations of archaeological artefacts and, as well, on developing the archaeological information system (AIS).

MICHEL SHAMOON-POUR is Postdoctoral Fellow and visiting Assistant Professor of Molecular and Biomedical Anthropology, Binghamton University (State University of New York), United States.

PETER E. SIEGEL is Professor and Chair of Anthropology, Montclair State University, Montclair, New Jersey, United States.

KRYSTAL SINGH worked as a finds processor in the Red House Restoration Archaeological Project in the Office of the Parliament of the Republic of Trinidad and Tobago.

MICHAEL SUTHERLAND is Head, Department of Geomatics Engineering and Land Management, Faculty of Engineering, the University of the West Indies, St Augustine, Trinidad and Tobago.

J. MARLA TOYNE is Associate Professor in Anthropology, University of Central Florida, Orlando, United States.

LAURA VAN VOORHIS is a PhD candidate in the Department of Anthropology, University of Florida, Gainesville, United States.

GIFFORD WATERS is Collections Manager for Historical Archaeology, Florida Museum of Natural History, Gainesville, United States.

BRENT WILSON is Professor of Palaeontology and Geology, the University of the West Indies, St Augustine, Trinidad and Tobago.

9 789766 406721